Computational Synthesis and Creative Systems

Creativity has become the motto of the modern world: everyone, every institution, and every company is exhorted to create, to innovate, to think out of the box. This calls for the design of a new class of technology, aimed at assisting humans in tasks that are deemed creative.

Developing a machine capable of synthesizing completely novel instances from a certain domain of interest is a formidable challenge for computer science, with potentially ground-breaking applications in fields such as biotechnology, design, and art. Creativity and originality are major requirements, as is the ability to interact with humans in a virtuous loop of recommendation and feedback. The problem calls for an interdisciplinary perspective, combining fields such as machine learning, artificial intelligence, engineering, design, and experimental psychology. Related questions and challenges include the design of systems that effectively explore large instance spaces; evaluating automatic generation systems, notably in creative domains; designing systems that foster creativity in humans; formalizing (aspects of) the notions of creativity and originality; designing productive collaboration scenarios between humans and machines for creative tasks; and understanding the dynamics of creative collective systems.

This book series intends to publish monographs, textbooks and edited books with a strong technical content, and focuses on approaches to computational synthesis that contribute not only to specific problem areas, but more generally introduce new problems, new data, or new well-defined challenges to computer science.

More information about this series at http://www.springer.com/series/15219

Roberto Confalonieri • Alison Pease
Marco Schorlemmer • Tarek R. Besold
Oliver Kutz • Ewen Maclean
Maximos Kaliakatsos-Papakostas
Editors

Concept Invention

Foundations, Implementation, Social Aspects and Applications

 Springer

Editors
Roberto Confalonieri
Smart Data Factory
Free University of Bozen-Bolzano
Bolzano, Italy

Marco Schorlemmer
Artificial Intelligence Research Institute
Spanish National Research Council
Bellaterra, Barcelona, Spain

Oliver Kutz
KRDB Research Center
Free University of Bozen-Bolzano
Bolzano, Italy

Maximos Kaliakatsos-Papakostas
School of Music Studies
Aristotle University of Thessaloniki
Thessaloniki, Greece

Alison Pease
School of Computing
University of Dundee
Dundee, United Kingdom

Tarek R. Besold
TZI, Digital Media Lab
University of Bremen
Bremen, Germany

Ewen Maclean
School of Informatics
University of Edinburgh
Edinburgh, United Kingdom

ISSN 2509-6575   ISSN 2509-6583   (electronic)
Computational Synthesis and Creative Systems
ISBN 978-3-030-09743-1   ISBN 978-3-319-65602-1   (eBook)
https://doi.org/10.1007/978-3-319-65602-1

This Springer imprint is published by the registered company Springer Nature Switzerland AG
The registered company address is: Gewerbestrasse 11, 6330 Cham, Switzerland

Foreword

Almost two and a half decades have passed since the birth of the cognitive theory today known as 'conceptual blending' in 1993. In these 24 years, a lot has happened and much has been achieved concerning both theoretical development and empirical evaluation of conceptual blending. As of 2017, the core postulates of the theory are widely accepted, and its manifestations are studied across different disciplines from linguistics to cognitive psychology to computer science and artificial intelligence (and many more). But instead of focusing on a historical perspective on conceptual blending, we want to look at the *status quo* and into the future of the theory and its applications—and more specifically at its role and use in (computational cognitive models of) concept invention.

Roughly speaking, the word 'invention' usually describes a unique or previously unseen—i.e., novel—artifact, idea, or procedure, with examples ranging from musical compositions to technological devices to political theories. Concept invention, thus, is the mental process of creating novel concepts, which again can have many and highly diverse particular manifestations: mathematical theories, mythological creatures, or musical idioms, to name just a few. This capability to bring forth new concepts is often seen as a sign of creativity on the side of the producer, and has been investigated by psychologists, linguists, and cognitive scientists alike. Of course, these studies have also closely been followed by researchers in artificial intelligence, who in turn attempt to build computational models of this human mental faculty—first, to progress closer towards the (re)creation of cognition and intelligence with computational means, and second, to locate applications in support software for creative industries. Conceptual blending as a theoretical framework and as an empirically observable phenomenon is playing a key role in many of these efforts: it suggests a plausible mechanism combining previously independent concepts into—in the interesting cases—novel joint ones.

This also is the context in which the EU-FP7 Concept Invention Theory project (COINVENT), underlying the work reported in this book, is to be seen. Building upon previous efforts by some of the authors of different chapters, as well as by many other renowned researchers, COINVENT aimed to draw together several different lines of work in an attempt to provide conceptual blending-based concept invention with a solid theoretical grounding through a detailed formal model of the underlying processes, together with a worked-out implementation of a system performing blending in two quite distinct application domains, namely theory blending in mathematics and the blending of harmonies in music. As can be seen from the results described in the individual chapters, these goals have been met; and in doing so, a widely visible proof of concept for the power and applicability of conceptual blending as theory and corresponding mechanism for concept invention has been given.

Of course, as is often the case with research projects, much is left to be done: the models and methods have to be applied to further domains, the mechanisms and implementations have to be refined and brought to maturation, and the functionalities have to be further developed, put to use in actual application systems, and rolled out to a general audience. Still, these are by no means shortcomings of the project. To the contrary, these points constitute great opportunities: by showing that conceptual blending can serve as basis for a formally well-founded and implementable model of concept invention, a door has been opened and the way has been cleared for many ambitious follow-up projects. What are the prospects for:

- software frameworks performing blending-based concept invention across domains?
- implementations combining different representations within a perceptual domain, blending speech with music, or text with images?
- multi-modal systems generating novel concepts across different sensory modalities, combining vision, touch, audition, and taste?
- programs co-creatively interacting with designers and artists during the different stages of ideation in the creation process?
- software supporting human agents in developing our own creative abilities and training our imagination?

The range of possibilities seems almost unlimited. Endeavors to answer these questions will lead to insights into computational models of conceptual blending and concept invention, and into the corresponding human faculties and cognitive theory.

We are excited to see these lines of research grow and prosper. We look forward to the advancement of our understanding and use of conceptual blending-based concept invention in the years to come.

Cleveland, Ohio, USA in March 2017   *Mark Turner*
Bremen, Germany in March 2017   *Tarek R. Besold*
Bozen-Bolzano, Italy in March 2017   *Roberto Confalonieri*

Preface

This book, *Concept Invention: Foundations, Implementation, Social Aspects and Applications*, introduces a computationally feasible, cognitively-inspired formal model of concept invention, drawing on Fauconnier and Turner's theory of conceptual blending—a fundamental cognitive operation underlying much of everyday thought and language, and Goguen's Unified Concept Theory—a computational characterisation of conceptual blending using category theory. It also presents the cognitive and social aspects of concept invention. It describes concrete implementations and applications in the fields of musical and mathematical creativity, and further discusses the evaluation of creative systems.

The book contains ten chapters edited by leading researchers in formal systems, cognitive science, artificial intelligence, computational creativity, mathematical reasoning and cognitive musicology, who contributed to advancing the state-of-the-art of conceptual blending in the European research project Concept Invention Theory (COINVENT). The book presents the results developed, the lesson learned and the perspectives drawn within the COINVENT project in such a way that the reader can get a deep understanding of conceptual blending from the formal, social, cognitive, and applied points of view.

Many excellent books that explore how creativity can be enacted using conceptual blending, and that look at creativity in general, already exist. We can refer to titles such as *Creativity and Artificial Intelligence: A Conceptual Blending Approach* (edited by F. Pereira, Mouton de Gruyter, 2007), and *Computers and Creativity* (edited by J. McCormack and M. d'Inverno, Springer, 2012), just to mention a few of them. This book differentiates itself from other books on creativity and conceptual bending because it elaborates on a knowledge-representation independent formalism which makes it more general and more widely applicable; moreover, it describes cognitive models that relate to conceptual blending such as image schemas and analogical reasoning, and provides examples of application in the domains of mathematics and music. Furthermore, it examines and provides insights on the evaluation of computational creative systems, a widely recognised area of research in machine-enhanced creativity by itself. *Concept Invention* will appeal to any reader interested in how conceptual blending can be precisely characterised and implemented for the development of creative computational systems.

Summary of the contributions

The book is organised in four parts. Part I introduces the mathematical and computational foundations of concept invention. Part II discusses its cognitive and social aspects. Part III describes concrete implementations and applications of concept invention in mathematical discovery and music harmonisation. Finally, Part IV constitutes an epilogue on the topic of evaluating computational concept invention and, generally, computational creativity systems.

The first three chapters in Part I are devoted both to the theoretical and computational foundations of concept invention. The concrete implementations described in Part III build on these foundations.

Chapter 1 by Félix Bou, Enric Plaza and Marco Schorlemmer provides a deep theoretical analysis of Goguen's Unified Concept Theory (UCT) for conceptual blending. Starting from this analysis, the authors outline a strategy for concept invention that extends UCT with amalgams, a knowledge transfer method proposed in case-based reasoning. In this chapter, the notion of amalgams is generalised and related to the notion of colimit in category theory, making amalgams a computationally feasible concept that form the basis for many of the subsequent chapters.

Chapter 2, by Roberto Confalonieri, Enric Plaza and Marco Schorlemmer, presents a concept invention process supporting the development of creative applications. This process considers two dimensions, origin and destination, in addition to the blending operation itself. These dimensions are typically not considered in the theory of conceptual blending, nor in existing computational frameworks and implementations. On the one hand, origin describes where the creation starts, and is concerned with how the input concepts to be blended are created. Origin is enacted through a Rich Background—intended as a finite but complex, diverse, and heterogenous set of concepts—from which input concepts are discovered according to the user demands. Whilst origin encompasses the discovery and construction of input spaces, the destination dimension is related to blend evaluation. Blend evaluation is conceived as an argument-based decision making framework in which an artificial agent creates arguments in favor or against a blend by taking values and audiences into account. The Rich Background also provides the means to evaluate newly-created concepts through the notion of conceptual coherence, for which the authors give an account in description logic.

The workflow of a system that facilitates ontology-based blending is presented in the last chapter of Part I (Chapter 3), by Mihai Codescu, Fabian Neuhaus, Till Mossakowski, Oliver Kutz and Danny de Jesús Gómez-Ramírez. Given two input ontologies, the workflow creates and evaluates several blended ontologies. To ensure that all generated blends are consistent, the workflow includes a stage where conflicts within concept elements are identified and resolved by generalising some axioms in the input ontologies. This workflow is enacted using the Distributed Ontology, Model and Specification Language (DOL), an international ontology interoperability standard. DOL provides a unified metalanguage for employing an openended number of formal logics, such as CASL, and ontologies, via the Ontology Web Language (OWL).

The theory of conceptual blending, and of creativity it general, is related to theories of human cognition. Part II discusses some cognitive and social aspects of concept invention through three chapters that focus on image schemas, the relationship between conceptual blending and analogical reasoning and the social aspects in the invention of mathematical and musical concepts. These chapters help put the computational theories of conceptual blending on a cognitively realistic basis.

Chapter 4 by Maria M. Hedblom, Oliver Kutz and Fabian Neuhaus focuses on image schemas that are, according to cognitive linguistics, fundamental patterns of cognition learned by humans in early infancy. The utilisation of image schemas presented in this chapter incorporates the identification of the common abstract keyelement of two input spaces, expressed as an image schema, and the formulation of the generic space based on that. Since image schemas are conceptual building blocks, they appear to be essential to the meaning of concepts and, therefore, they are expected to minimise the number of non-sense blends when applied to conceptual blending processes.

Tarek R. Besold in Chapter 5 outlines a perspective on conceptual blending from the point of view of the cognitive mechanism of analogy-making. In this study, the generalisation of the input spaces that lead to the generic space is analysed under the prism of analogy, where the common elements of the inputs are retrieved as meaningful similarities that are extracted through analogical reasoning. This chapter shows how analogy, amalgams, and conceptual blending are related. The explicit availability of similarities between the input concepts—obtained by analogy using the Heuristic-Driven Theory Projection (HDTP) engine—to an amalgam benefits the overall blending process, since the basic structure introduced by the analogy process is maintained in the creation of new concepts.

Some social aspects of creativity are surveyed in Chapter 6, by Joseph Corneli, Alison Pease and Danae Stefanou. This chapter also gives a succint overview of a formal, computationally feasible model that can describe real-world, social creativity. The chapter surveys approaches to understanding mathematical dialogues. Several example dialogues are marked up with tags that describe the flow of conversation. These tags enable the computational analysis of the exchange of ideas that aim at solving specific problems and, for example, the specification of a protocol that formalises Lakatos's theory of dialogical creativity.

Part III presents the concept invention system, which was developed based on the theoretical background presented in Part I, and two application domains. Chapter 7 by Roberto Confalonieri, Tarek Besold, Mihai Codescu and Manfred Eppe describes COBBLE—a creative, flexible and modular computational prototype that materialises conceptual blending in a generative way—and its enabling technologies. COBBLE makes use of technologies based on notions from the fields of ontologies, analogical reasoning, logic programming, and formal methods. The system allows a user to select input spaces and different techniques for generalisation, outputting the resulting blends as colimits of algebraic specifications. The input spaces are modelled using DOL (described in Chapter 3) that allows for the formulation of blending diagrams encoded in the CASL and OWL languages.

Chapter 8 by Danny de Jesús Gómez-Ramírez and Alan Smaill discusses and shows, with practical examples, the role that conceptual blending plays in the development of new mathematical concepts. This is demonstrated with the reconstruction of existing abstract mathematical theories, e.g., Commutative Algebra, Number Theory, fields and Galois Theory, and also the extension to new equivalences that characterise the notion of Dedekind domain.

The application of concept invention through conceptual blending in harmony is presented in Chapter 9, by Maximos Kaliakatsos-Papakostas, Asterios Zacharakis and Emilios Cambouropoulos. This chapter presents several aspects of the CHAMELEON melodic harmonisation assistant, which allows a user to provide a melody as input, and select two input harmonic spaces learned from data; then CHAMELEON blends the selected spaces, generating a new harmonic style, and harmonises the input melody. The blending module of this system is based on the blending algorithms used in COBBLE, here applied on the level of chord transitions. The new harmonic styles that are invented are judged as new styles that either encompass mixed characteristics of the input spaces, or entirely new elements. Additionally, pilot studies indicate that when composers use CHAMELEON they have a palette of many diverse automatically composed harmonies from which they can draw ideas, a process that potentially enhances their creativity—even though additional formal studies need to be carried out in order to firmly validate this claim.

Part IV is an epilogue that includes Chapter 10, which provides an in depth discussion on the evaluation of computational creativity.

This book presents a wide spectrum of studies that focus on computational concept invention through conceptual blending. Therefore, we hope that this book will constitute a valuable tool for the reader who is interested in the theoretical and computational foundations of concept invention, the cognitive aspects behind and around it, the implementation of a creative system that exhibits creative behaviour, and how such a system can be evaluated.

Bozen-Bolzano, Italy in March 2017   *Roberto Confalonieri*
Thessaloniki, Greece in March 2017   *Maximos Kaliakatsos-Papakostas*

Acknowledgements

We would like to express our gratitude to all the authors for the quality and insights of their contributions. In this book each chapter was reviewed by two independent scholars in addition to our review as editors. We would like thank the reviewers (who include many of the authors of this book) for their constructive comments and thorough evaluation.

The research presented in this book was supported by the COINVENT project, which was funded by the Future and Emerging Technologies (FET) programme within the Seventh Framework Programme for Research of the European Commission, under FET-Open grant number 611553.

Contents

Part I Mathematical and Computational Foundations

1 Amalgams, Colimits, and Conceptual Blending 3
Félix Bou, Enric Plaza, and Marco Schorlemmer
  1.1 Introduction 3
  1.2 Category Theory Preliminaries 6
        1.2.1 Categories and Morphisms 7
        1.2.2 Diagrams, Cocones, and Colimits 8
        1.2.3 Partial Morphisms 11
  1.3 Conceptual Blending as Colimits 12
        1.3.1 Ordered Categories 13
        1.3.2 Colimits in Ordered Categories 14
        1.3.3 $\frac{3}{2}$-Colimits 16
  1.4 Conceptual Blending as Amalgams 19
        1.4.1 Amalgams 20
        1.4.2 Asymmetric Amalgams and Analogy 22
  1.5 Relating Colimits and Amalgams 22
        1.5.1 Preliminaries 23
        1.5.2 A Category-Theoretical Account of Amalgams 23
  1.6 Conclusion 24
  References 26

2 Computational Aspects of Concept Invention 31
Roberto Confalonieri, Enric Plaza, and Marco Schorlemmer
  2.1 A Process Model for Concept Invention 32
  2.2 Rich Background and Discovery 34
        2.2.1 Rich Background 34
        2.2.2 Similarity-Based Discovery 36
  2.3 Blends as Amalgams 37
  2.4 Arguments, Values and Audiences 39
  2.5 Coherence Theory 41

	2.5.1	Coherence Graphs	42
	2.5.2	Blend Evaluation by Means of Coherence	43
2.6	Exemplifying the Process Model		44
	2.6.1	Creating Computer Icon Concepts	45
	2.6.2	Coherent Conceptual Blending	52
2.7	Related Work		60
2.8	Conclusion and Future Perspectives		62
References			64

3   Conceptual Blending in DOL: Evaluating Consistency and Conflict Resolution 69
Mihai Codescu, Fabian Neuhaus, Till Mossakowski, Oliver Kutz, and Danny de Jesús Gómez-Ramírez

3.1	Introduction		70
3.2	Towards the Computational Generation of Blends		71
	3.2.1	COINVENT Model	72
	3.2.2	Conceptual Blending Workflow	74
3.3	Blending with DOL		76
	3.3.1	Foundations of DOL	77
	3.3.2	Features of DOL	79
	3.3.3	Tool Support for DOL	82
	3.3.4	Workflow Formalisation in DOL	83
3.4	Examples of Conceptual Blending in DOL		85
	3.4.1	Creating Monsters	85
	3.4.2	Goldbach Rings	89
3.5	Summary		91
3.6	Conclusion and Future Perspectives		92
References			93

Part II Cognitive and Social Aspects

4   Image Schemas and Concept Invention 99
Maria M. Hedblom, Oliver Kutz, and Fabian Neuhaus

4.1	Introduction		99
4.2	Conceptual Blending		100
	4.2.1	Formalising Conceptual Blending	101
4.3	Image Schemas		103
	4.3.1	Defining "Image Schema"	105
	4.3.2	Formalising Image Schemas	106
4.4	Image Schemas as Families of Theories		108
	4.4.1	The Image Schema Family PATH-Following	108
	4.4.2	Formalising Image Schema Families	112
	4.4.3	Example: Axiomatising the PATH-Following Family	114
4.5	Guiding Conceptual Blending with Image Schemas		117
	4.5.1	Blending with Image Schemas	117
	4.5.2	Similes Revisited	118

      4.5.3   Blending with Families of Image Schemas 122

      4.5.4   The PATH-Following Family at Work 123

  4.6   Conclusion and Future Perspectives 126

  References 127

5   The Relationship Between Conceptual Blending and Analogical

**   Reasoning** 133

  Tarek R. Besold

  5.1   Analogy and Cognition 133

  5.2   Computational Models of Analogy 135

  5.3   Generalisation-Based Analogy and Conceptual Blending 137

      5.3.1   Combining Conceptual Theories Using Amalgams 139

      5.3.2   An Analogy-Rooted Model of Conceptual Blending 140

      5.3.3   Implementing the Model 141

      5.3.4   Example: (Re)Making Pegasus 144

  5.4   Related Work 147

  5.5   Summary 147

  5.6   Conclusion and Future Perspectives 148

  References 149

6   Social Aspects of Concept Invention 153

  Joseph Corneli, Alison Pease, and Danae Stefanou

  6.1   Introduction 153

  6.2   Social Creativity in Mathematics 154

      6.2.1   Core Theories 159

      6.2.2   Survey of Analytic Frameworks 161

      6.2.3   Pilot Study 166

      6.2.4   Direct Extensions 173

      6.2.5   Additional Frameworks from Music Theorists.......... 174

  6.3   Related Work: Social Creativity on Computers 176

      6.3.1   A Formal Representation of Lakatosian Creativity 176

      6.3.2   Patterns of Peeragogy 177

      6.3.3   The Search for Computational Intelligence 178

  6.4   Summary 179

  6.5   Conclusion and Future Perspectives 179

  References 181

Part III Concept Invention System and Applications

7   Enabling Technologies for Concept Invention 189

  Roberto Confalonieri, Tarek Besold, Mihai Codescu, and Manfred Eppe

  7.1   Introduction 189

  7.2   System Architecture and Enabling Technologies 191

  7.3   Generalising Algebraic Specifications Using ASP 193

      7.3.1   Modeling Input Spaces Using CASL 194

      7.3.2   Finding the Generic Space 195

7.4   Finding Generalisations Between Logical Theories Using HDTP . 203
        7.4.1   The Rutherford Analogy Between Atom and Solar
                  System 205
        7.4.2   The Computational Complexity of HDTP 207
7.5   Colimit Computation Using HETS 208
7.6   Conclusion and Future Perspectives 214
References 215

8   Formal Conceptual Blending in the (Co-)Invention of (Pure)
    Mathematics 221
    Danny de Jesús Gómez-Ramírez and Alan Smaill
    8.1   Introduction 221
    8.2   Basic Terminology 222
    8.3   Specific Mathematical Concepts 224
    8.4   Defining the Blends 228
            8.4.1   The Generic Space 228
            8.4.2   The 'Blending' Morphisms 228
            8.4.3   The Resulting Axiomatisation 228
    8.5   Generation of Fundamental Notions of Fields and Galois Theory . 230
    8.6   Summary 231
    8.7   Conclusion and Future Perspectives 235
            8.7.1   Artificial Mathematical Intelligence (AMI) 235
            8.7.2   A Formal Vision 236
    References 237

9   Conceptual Blending in Melodic Harmonisation: Development and
    Empirical Evaluation in the Case of the CHAMELEON System 241
    Maximos Kaliakatsos-Papakostas, Asterios Zacharakis, and Emilios
    Cambouropoulos
    9.1   Introduction 241
    9.2   Representing and Learning Harmonies for the Automated
            Harmonisation of Melodies 244
    9.3   Blending Harmonic Spaces in the CHAMELEON System 246
            9.3.1   Blending and Rating Chord Transitions 247
            9.3.2   Constructing a Compound Chord Transition Matrix of
                      Two Idioms Using Blended Transitions 250
    9.4   Empirical Evaluation of Musical Creativity via Conceptual
            Blending 254
            9.4.1   Empirical Evaluation of a Formal Model for Cadence
                      Blending 255
            9.4.2   Empirical Evaluation of the Output of the
                      CHAMELEON System 263
    9.5   Summary 267
    9.6   Conclusion 268
    References 269

Part IV Epilogue

10 Evaluation of Creativity 277
Alison Pease and Joseph Corneli
10.1   Introduction 277
10.2   A Short Historical Survey of Evaluation in Computational
            Creativity 279
            10.2.1   Other Perspectives 281
10.3   Evaluation Frameworks 282
10.4   Evaluating the Evaluation Frameworks 283
            10.4.1   Methods 283
            10.4.2   Findings 284
            10.4.3   Discussion 284
10.5   Summary 290
10.6   Conclusion and Future Perspectives 292
References 292

List of Contributors

Tarek R. Besold
Digital Media Lab, Center for Computing and Communication Technologies (TZI),
University of Bremen, Bibliothekstr. 5, 28359 Bremen, Germany.
e-mail: tbesold@uni-bremen.de

Félix Bou
Department of Philosophy, University of Valencia, Avda. Blasco Ibáñez 30, 46010
Valencia, Spain.
e-mail: felix.bou@uv.es

Emilios Cambouropoulos
Department of Music Studies, Aristotle University of Thessaloniki, Greece.
e-mail: emilios@mus.auth.gr

Mihai Codescu
Free University of Bozen-Bolzano, Faculty of Computer Science, Dominikanerplatz 3, 39100 Bozen-Bolzano, Italy.
e-mail: Mihai.Codescu@unibz.it

Roberto Confalonieri
Free University of Bozen-Bolzano, Faculty of Computer Science, Dominikanerplatz 3, 39100 Bozen-Bolzano, Italy.
e-mail: Roberto.Confalonieri@unibz.it

Joseph Corneli
Goldsmiths College, University of London, London, UK.
e-mail: j.corneli@gold.ac.uk

Danny de Jesús Gómez-Ramírez
Vienna University of Technology, Wiedner Hauptstrasse 8-10, 1040 Vienna,
Austria.
e-mail: dagomez1982@gmail.com

Maria M. Hedblom
Institute for Intelligent Cooperative Systems, Otto-von-Guericke University of
Magdeburg, Universitätsplatz 2, 39106, Magdeburg, Germany.
e-mail: hedblom@iws.cs.uni-magdeburg.de

Maximos Kaliakatsos-Papakostas
Department of Music Studies, Aristotle University of Thessaloniki, Greece.
e-mail: maxk@mus.auth.gr

Oliver Kutz
Free University of Bozen-Bolzano, Faculty of Computer Science, Dominikanerplatz 3, 39100 Bozen-Bolzano, Italy.
e-mail: Oliver.Kutz@unibz.it

Till Mossakowski
Institute for Intelligent Cooperative Systems, Otto-von-Guericke University of
Magdeburg, Universitätsplatz 2, 39106, Magdeburg, Germany.
e-mail: till@iks.cs.ovgu.de

Fabian Neuhaus
Institute for Intelligent Cooperative Systems, Otto-von-Guericke University of
Magdeburg, Universitätsplatz 2, 39106, Magdeburg, Germany.
e-mail: fneuhaus@iks.cs.ovgu.de

Alison Pease
Department of Computing, University of Dundee, Scotland, UK.
e-mail: a.pease@dundee.ac.uk

Enric Plaza
Artificial Intelligence Research Institute (IIIA-CSIC), C/ Can Planes 2, Campus
UAB, 08193 Bellaterra (Cerdanyola del Vallès), Spain.
e-mail: enric@iiia.csic.es

Marco Schorlemmer
Artificial Intelligence Research Institute (IIIA-CSIC), C/ Can Planes 2, Campus
UAB, 08193 Bellaterra (Cerdanyola del Vallès), Spain.
e-mail: marco@iiia.csic.es

Alan Smaill
School of Informatics, University of Edinburgh, Scotland, UK.
e-mail: A.Smaill@ed.ac.uk

Danae Stefanou
Department of Music Studies, Aristotle University of Thessaloniki, Greece.
e-mail: dstefano@mus.auth.gr

Asterios Zacharakis
Department of Music Studies, Aristotle University of Thessaloniki, Greece.
e-mail: aszachar@mus.auth.gr

Part I
Mathematical and Computational Foundations

Chapter 1
Amalgams, Colimits, and Conceptual Blending

Félix Bou, Enric Plaza, and Marco Schorlemmer

Abstract This chapter is a theoretical exploration of Joseph Goguen's category-theoretic model of conceptual blending and presents an alternative proposal to model blending as *amalgams*, which were originally proposed as a method for knowledge transfer in case-based reasoning. The chapter concludes with a generalisation of the amalgam-based model by relating it to the notion of colimit, thus providing a category-theoretic characterisation of amalgams that is ultimately computationally realisable.

1.1 Introduction

The notion of *amalgam* in a lattice of generalisations was developed in the framework of modelling analogical inference, and case amalgamation in case-based reasoning (CBR) (Ontañón and Plaza, 2010). Case amalgamation models the process of combining two different cases into a new *blended* case to be used in the CBR problem-solving process. As such, the notion of amalgam seems related to but not identical to the notions of *conceptual blending*, also known as conceptual integration (Fauconnier and Turner, 1998). These related notions have in common that there is some combination or fusion of two different sources into a new entity that encompasses selected parts of the sources, but they differ in the assumptions on the entities upon which they work: amalgams work on *cases* (expressed as terms in some language), while conceptual blending works on *mental spaces*.

Félix Bou
Department of Philosophy, University of Valencia, Avda. Blasco Ibáñez 30, 46010 Valencia, Spain.
e-mail: `felix.bou@uv.es`

Enric Plaza · Marco Schorlemmer
Artificial Intelligence Research Institute (IIIA-CSIC), C/ Can Planes 2, Campus UAB, 08193 Bellaterra (Cerdanyola del Vallès), Spain. e-mail: `{enric,marco}@iiia.csic.es`

© Springer Nature Switzerland AG 2018
R. Confalonieri et al. (eds.), *Concept Invention*, Computational Synthesis and Creative Systems, https://doi.org/10.1007/978-3-319-65602-1_1

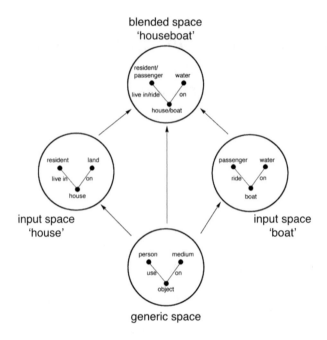

Fig. 1.1: 'Houseboat' blend, adapted from Goguen and Harrell (2010)

Fauconnier and Turner proposed conceptual blending as the fundamental cognitive operation underlying much of everyday thought and language. They model it as
a process by which people subconsciously combine particular elements and their relations of originally separate input mental spaces—which do, however, share some
common structure modelled as a generic space—into a blended space, in which
new elements and relations emerge, and new inferences can be drawn. For instance,
a 'houseboat' or a 'boathouse' are not simply the intersection of the concepts of
'house' and 'boat'. Instead, the concepts 'houseboat' and 'boathouse' selectively
integrate different aspects of the source concepts in order to produce two new concepts, each with its own distinct internal structure (see Figure 1.1 for the 'houseboat'
blend).

Although the cognitive, psychological and neural basis of conceptual blending
has been extensively studied (Fauconnier and Turner, 2002; Gibbs, Jr., 2000; Baron
and Osherson, 2011) and Fauconnier and Turner's theory has been successfully applied for describing existing blends of ideas and concepts in a varied number of
fields, such as linguistics, music theory, poetics, mathematics, theory of art, political science, discourse analysis, philosophy, anthropology, and the study of gesture
and of material culture, their theory has been used only in a more constrained way
for implementing creative computational systems. Since Fauconnier and Turner did

not aim at computer models of cognition, they did not develop the sufficient details for conceptual blending to be captured algorithmically.

Nevertheless, a number of researchers in the field of computational creativity have recognised the potential value of Fauconnier and Turner's theory for guiding the implementation of creative systems, and some computational accounts of conceptual blending have already been proposed (Veale and O'Donoghue, 2000; Pereira, 2007; Goguen and Harrell, 2010; Thagard and Stewart, 2011). They attempt to concretise some of Fauconnier and Turner's insights, and the resulting systems have shown interesting and promising results in creative domains such as interface design, narrative style, poetry generation, or visual patterns. All of these accounts, however, are customised realisations of conceptual blending, which are strongly dependent on hand-crafted representations of domain-specific knowledge, and are limited to very specific forms of blending. The major obstacle for a general account of computational conceptual blending is currently the lack of a mathematically precise theory that is suitable for the rigorous development of creative systems based on conceptual blending.

The only attempt so far to provide a general and mathematically precise account of conceptual blending has been put forward by Goguen, initially as part of algebraic semiotics (Goguen, 1999), and later in the context of a wider theory of concepts that he named Unified Concept Theory (UCT) (Goguen, 2005a); he has also shown its aptness for formalising information integration (Goguen, 2004b) and reasoning about space and time (Goguen, 2006). As it stands, Goguen's account is still very abstract and lacks concrete algorithmic descriptions. There are several reasons, though, that make it an appropriate candidate theory on which to ground the formal model we are aiming at:

- It is an important contribution towards the unification of several formal theories of concepts, including the geometrical conceptual spaces of Gärdenfors (2004), the symbolic conceptual spaces of Fauconnier (1994), the information flow of Barwise and Seligman (1997), the formal concept analysis of Ganter and Wille (1999), and the lattice of theories of Sowa (2000). This makes it possible to potentially draw from existing algorithms that have already been developed in the scope of each of these frameworks.
- It covers any formal logic, even multiple logics, supporting thus the integration and processing of concepts under various forms of syntactic and semantic heterogeneity. This is important, since we cannot assume conceptual spaces to be represented in a homogeneous manner across diverse domains. Current tools for heterogeneous specifications such as HETS (Mossakowski et al., 2007) allow parsing, static analysis and proof management incorporating various provers and different specification languages.

In this chapter we take the approach of generalising the original notion of amalgam from CBR to be used in the development of a theory of conceptual blending that is close to, and even compatible with, Goguen's work on blending. This means taking a category-theoretic approach to model amalgams in the framework of conceptual blending.

By developing a formal, amalgam-based model of conceptual blending building on Goguen's initial account, we aim at providing general principles that will guide the design of computer systems capable of inventing new higher-level, more abstract concepts and representations out of existing, more concrete concepts and interactions with the environment, and to do so based on the sound reuse and exploitation of existing computational implementations of closely related models such as those for analogical and metaphorical reasoning (Falkenhainer et al., 1989), semantic integration (Schorlemmer and Kalfoglou, 2008), or cognitive coherence (Thagard, 2000). With such a formal, but computationally feasible model we shall ultimately bridge the existing gap between the theoretical foundations of conceptual blending and their computational realisations.

Category theory, although initially designed to describe mathematical entities, has proven to be a successful cornerstone in many computer science applications; a trend which has attracted a lot of attention and researchers, and which has been nicely advocated in Goguen's manifesto paper (Goguen, 1991). One of the most interesting advantages of categorical approaches to computational theories is precisely the fact of being independent of any particular implementation. For this very reason, it is very appealing to search for a categorical framework where a computational theory of conceptual blending based on Fauconnier and Turner's ideas can be developed. In particular, Goguen developed his category-theoretic approach to blending based on colimits, following this basic insight:

> Given a species of structure, say widgets, then the result of interconnecting a system of widgets to form a super-widget corresponds to taking the *colimit* of the diagram of widgets in which the morphisms show how they are interconnected.   (Goguen, 1991, Section 6)

In this chapter—after first providing some category theory preliminaries—we shall revisit Goguen's approach that models conceptual blending by means of a certain kind of colimit in ordered categories. Then we present our alternative proposal to model conceptual blending as *amalgams* and conclude the chapter by relating it to the notion of colimit, thus providing a category-theoretic characterisation of amalgams that is computationally realisable.

1.2 Category Theory Preliminaries

In this section, no attempt of being completely self-contained is made, so we suggest the reader supplement the information here provided, whenever necessary, with any standard category theory textbook (e.g., (Barr and Wells, 1990; Pierce, 1991; McLarty, 1992; Mac Lane, 1998)) or short introductions to the subject (e.g., (Diaconescu, 2008, Chapter 2) and (Sannella and Tarlecki, 2012, Chapter 3)).

1.2.1 Categories and Morphisms

Definition 1.1 (Category). A *category* **C** consists of the following items:

- A collection obj(**C**) of *objects*.
- A collection hom(**C**) of *morphisms* (sometimes also called homomorphisms, arrows or maps) satisfying that each morphism f has associated a *source* object denoted by src(f), and a *target* object denoted by tg(f). The expression $f: A \rightarrow B$ is used as a shorthand for claiming that f is a morphism with source A and target B. The collection of all such morphisms is denoted by either $\mathbf{C}(A,B)$ or hom(A,B).
- For all objects A, B, C, there is a binary associative operation called *composition* from hom(A,B) $\times$ hom(B,C) into hom(A,C). Composition of two morphisms f, g is denoted by writing either

$$f;g \quad \text{(diagrammatic notation)} \qquad \text{or} \qquad g \circ f \quad \text{(functional notation)}$$

  to refer to the composition of morphisms $f: A \rightarrow B$ and $g: B \rightarrow C$.
- For every object A, there is an *identity* morphism id_A belonging to hom(A,A) which is a neutral element of composition. This neutrality means that

  - $\mathrm{id}_A; f = f$ (for every morphism f with source A)
  - $f; \mathrm{id}_A = f$ (for every morphism f with target A).

Concerning notation to be used later, we point out that hom($A,$-) will denote the collection of all morphisms with source A and hom(-,A) will denote the collection of morphisms with target A.

Example 1.1 (The categories **Set** *and* **Pfn***).* Among the plethora of examples, there are two well-known categories that are relevant for this chapter (for instance, see (Calugareanu and Purdea, 2011)).

- The category **Set** has sets as objects and (total) functions as morphisms (endowed with the usual composition of functions).[1]
- The category **Pfn** has sets as objects and partial functions as morphisms (endowed also with the usual composition of functions).

Let us point out that if A and B are finite sets with cardinality n and m, respectively, then **Set**(A,B) has cardinality m^n while **Pfn**(A,B) has cardinality $(m+1)^n$. In case we have a partial function f, we will use the notation Dom(f) to refer to its set-theoretical domain and Im(f) for its set-theoretical image.

Besides using the previously introduced notation $f: A \rightarrow B$ to refer to morphisms, it is common to use different kinds of graphical arrows to emphasise whether the arrow satisfies some particular property. Thus, we will use

---

[1] It is worth noticing that, by definition of a category, the collections hom(A_1,B_1) and hom(A_2,B_2) must be disjoint unless both $A_1 = A_2$ and $B_1 = B_2$ hold. Thus, for technicality issues it is better to think that a morphism in **Set** is given by an ordered triple (A, f, B) where f is a function from A to B.

- $f\colon A \twoheadrightarrow B$ for *epimorphisms* (i.e., for every $h_1, h_2 \in \text{hom}(B, -)$, if $f; h_1 = f; h_2$ then $h_1 = h_2$).
- $f\colon A \rightarrowtail B$ for *monomorphisms*, (i.e., for every $h_1, h_2 \in \text{hom}(-, A)$, if $h_1; f = h_2; f$ then $h_1 = h_2$).
- $f\colon A \hookrightarrow B$ only for some very special monomorphisms, i.e., those that live in a category whose morphisms are (set-theoretic) functions preserving some structure and which correspond to inclusions.
- $f\colon A \xrightarrow{\sim} B$ for *isomorphisms* (i.e., there exists some $h \in \text{hom}(B, A)$ such that $f; h = \text{id}_A$ and $h; f = \text{id}_B$).

In the particular cases of **Set** and **Pfn** it is well-known that epimorphisms correspond to being exhaustive on the target object, monomorphisms to injectivity and isomorphisms to bijectivity. Thus, two sets are isomorphic iff they have the same cardinality.

1.2.2 Diagrams, Cocones, and Colimits

Colimits (and also limits) in a category **C** are introduced via diagrams. A *diagram* $\mathscr{D}$ is a functor from a category **J** to the category **C**, and in such a case it is said that $\mathscr{D}$ is **J**-*shaped*. In other words, a *diagram $\mathscr{D}$ in* **C** consists of

- a directed graph (where nodes are objects and edges are morphisms in **J**),[2]
- a family (indexed by the set Nodes of nodes of the graph) of objects in **C**, i.e., every node $X \in$ Nodes of the graph is associated with an object in **C**,
- a family (indexed by the set Edges of edges of the graph) of morphisms in **C** satisfying that: for an edge $f \in$ Edges between nodes X and Y, the associated morphism has the object associated with X as source, and the object associated with Y as target.

We are mostly interested in the case of *finite diagrams*, i.e., when **J** has a finite number of objects and morphisms. In most such examples, instead of defining the category **J** in words, we will simply draw a directed graph.

Before introducing colimits of a diagram $\mathscr{D}$ in a category **C** we introduce cocones.

Definition 1.2 (Cocone). A *cocone* $\mathfrak{c}$ over a diagram $\mathscr{D}$ in a category **C** is an object O in **C** together with a family (indexed by the nodes in the graph associated with $\mathscr{D}$) $\{\mathfrak{c}_X\}_{X \in \text{Nodes}}$ of morphisms in **C** such that:

- $\mathfrak{c}_X$ has source $\mathscr{D}(X)$, for every node X;
- $\mathfrak{c}_X$ has target O, for every node X;
- $\mathscr{D}(f); \mathfrak{c}_Y = \mathfrak{c}_X$, for every edge f from node X to node Y.

---

[2] Strictly speaking **J** is the free category generated over the directed graph, but for the purpose of this chapter it is not necessary to worry about this detail.

We refer to the pointed object O, which is called the *apex of* $\mathfrak{c}$, as $\mathrm{apex}(\mathfrak{c})$. The collection of all cocones over $\mathscr{D}$ is denoted by $\mathrm{Cocones}(\mathscr{D}, \text{-})$.

Notice that the third condition in Definition 1.2 is expressing a family (one for every edge) of commutativity conditions for triangular graphs; this fact is sometimes emphasised using the terminology *commutative cocone* instead of just saying cocone.

It is rather trivial noticing that every cocone $\mathfrak{c}$ over a diagram $\mathscr{D}$ induces a function $\mathsf{H}_{\mathfrak{c}}$ defined by

$$\mathsf{H}_{\mathfrak{c}} : \mathrm{hom}(\mathrm{apex}(\mathfrak{c}), \text{-}) \longrightarrow \mathrm{Cocones}(\mathscr{D}, \text{-})$$
$$h \longmapsto \mathfrak{c}; h$$

With the notation $\mathfrak{c}; h$ we obviously refer to the family $\{g; h\}_{g \text{ is a morphism in } \mathfrak{c}}$, i.e., $\{\mathfrak{c}_X; h\}_{X \in \mathrm{Nodes}}$. These induced functions can be used to define that two cocones $\mathfrak{c}$ and $\mathfrak{d}$ (over the same diagram) are *isomorphic* when there is some isomorphism h in $\mathbf{C}$ such that $\mathfrak{d} = \mathsf{H}_{\mathfrak{c}}(h)$.

Definition 1.3 (Colimit). A cocone $\mathfrak{c}$ over a diagram $\mathscr{D}$ in a category $\mathbf{C}$ is said to be a *colimit* if the function $\mathsf{H}_{\mathfrak{c}}$ is a bijection. We write $\mathrm{colim}(\mathscr{D}, \mathbf{C})$, or simply $\mathrm{colim}(\mathscr{D})$, to refer to a colimit; and we will use $\mathrm{colim}(\mathscr{D}, \mathbf{C})$ or $\mathrm{colim}(\mathscr{D})$ for the apex in the cocone $\mathrm{colim}(\mathscr{D}, \mathbf{C})$.

It is worth noticing that Definition 1.3 can be rephrased as claiming that every cocone over $\mathscr{D}$ is of the form $\mathfrak{c}; h$ for some unique morphism h. This remark allows us to rewrite the existence of a colimit as saying that: for every cocone over the same diagram, there is exactly one solution for a univariate system, using the cocone as parameters, of morphism equations. As an example, we illustrate this fact for the case of a colimit of a span (a V-shaped diagram), which is also called *pushout*.

Definition 1.4 (Pushout). Given a diagram $B \xleftarrow{f} A \xrightarrow{g} C$ —called *span* or V-shaped diagram—a *pushout* of this span is a colimit (see Definition 1.3), i.e., it is a

cocone $\begin{array}{ccc} & \mathrm{apex}(\mathfrak{c}) & \\ {}^{\mathfrak{c}_B}\nearrow & \uparrow{\scriptstyle \mathfrak{c}_A} & \nwarrow{}^{\mathfrak{c}_C} \\ B & & C \\ & {\scriptstyle \mathfrak{c}_A}\uparrow & \\ & A & \end{array}$ such that whenever $\begin{array}{ccc} & D & \\ {}^{\mathfrak{d}_B}\nearrow & \uparrow{\scriptstyle \mathfrak{d}_A} & \nwarrow{}^{\mathfrak{d}_C} \\ B & \mathfrak{d}_A & C \\ {}^{f}\nwarrow & | & \nearrow{}_{g} \\ & A & \end{array}$ commutes, it holds

that the univariate system

$$\mathfrak{c}_B; h = \mathfrak{d}_B \qquad\qquad \mathfrak{c}_A; h = \mathfrak{d}_A \qquad\qquad \mathfrak{c}_C; h = \mathfrak{d}_C$$

of morphism equations has a unique solution for h.

For each categorical construct such as cocones, colimits, pushouts and spans, there exists also a dual notion with morphsims pointing in the opposite direction, such as cones, limits, pullbacks and cospans. We refer the reader to the literature for a thorough discussion of these (e.g., (Pierce, 1991)).

It is always the case that two colimits over the same diagram are isomorphic cocones, i.e., *colimits are unique up to isomorphism*. Indeed, if c is a colimit, then the collection of all colimits is exactly $\{c;h \mid h$ is an ismorphism with $\mathrm{src}(h) = \mathrm{apex}(c)\}$. On the other hand, the existence of a colimit is, in general, not guaranteed; it depends very much on the diagram $\mathscr{D}$ and the category **C**.

Let us now mention two facts that restrict which cocones can be a colimit. The first fact is a trivial consequence of the injectivity of the function H_c: all colimits c have to be *jointly epimorphic*, which means that whenever h_1 and h_2 are two morphisms with source $\mathrm{apex}(c)$ and such that "$c_X;h_1 = c_X;h_2$ for every node X", then $h_1 = h_2$.[3] The second fact, also obvious from Definition 1.3, is that for every object E, the set $\mathrm{Cocones}(\mathscr{D},E)$ (i.e., the collection of cocones over $\mathscr{D}$ with apex E) must have the same cardinality as the set $\mathrm{hom}(\mathrm{apex}(c),E)$. These two facts are, in general, very powerful tools to recognise possible candidates as a colimit over a diagram. In the particular cases of **Set** and **Pfn** the second fact can be used to completely determine the possible apexes of colimits (since all objects with the same cardinal are isomorphic). Remark 1.1 describes the method for the case of **Pfn**.

Remark 1.1 (Cardinality trick for **Pfn***).* Consider the natural number m of cocones over $\mathscr{D}$ with apex $\{①\}$ (i.e., a singleton set). Then, the cardinal of an object $\mathrm{colim}(\mathscr{D},\mathbf{Pfn})$ has to be the only natural number n such that $m = 2^n$.

Definition 1.5. A category is said to be *cocomplete* in case that for all diagrams in **C** there is a colimit. Analogously, *complete* refers to the existence of all limits; and *bicomplete* refers to being both complete and cocomplete.

The categories **Set** and **Pfn** introduced in Example 1.1 are well-known to be bicomplete. Moreover, it is also known that if all morphisms of a diagram $\mathscr{D}$ in **Pfn** are total functions (i.e., the diagram lives inside **Set**) then $\mathrm{colim}(\mathscr{D},\mathbf{Set}) = \mathrm{colim}(\mathscr{D},\mathbf{Pfn})$, i.e., it does not matter whether one computes the colimit in **Set** or in **Pfn**. Let us mention that this last remark is known to be false for the case of limits.[4]

---

[3] Is is worth pointing out that when **C** has coproducts, the following (i) and (ii) are equivalent. (i) $\{c_X\}_{X\in\mathrm{Nodes}}$ is jointly epimorphic; (ii) the single morphism $\bigoplus\{c_X\}_{X\in\mathrm{Nodes}}$ is epimorphic. This relationship explains the intuition behind this "jointly" terminology.

[4] An easy counterexample can be obtained considering the categorical product of two singleton sets, for example, $A := \{⊹\}$ and $B := \{⇸\}$. A quick way to convince oneself that the categorical product computed in **Set** is different than in **Pfn** is to use the cardinality trick described in Remark 1.1 (but dualised, in order to use it for limits instead of colimits). The fact that there are exactly four cones in **Pfn** with apex $\{①\}$ (i.e., a singleton) forces that the product in **Pfn** must have three elements; on the other hand, using that there is exactly one cone in **Set** with apex $\{①,②\}$ one deduces that the product in **Set** must have one element.

Indeed, the content of the previous paragraph is generalised in the following well-known statement (see (Poigné, 1986, p. 20)):

- the product in **Set** of A and B is given by the cone $\begin{array}{ccc} A & & B \\ & \nwarrow_{\pi_A} \quad \nearrow_{\pi_B} & \\ & O & \end{array}$ where O is the Cartesian

  product of A and B (i.e., $O := A \times B$), and the morphisms π_A and π_B are the "projections" from the Cartesian product.

1.2.3 Partial Morphisms

To finish this section about category theory preliminaries we introduce a category that will play a role in Section 1.5, where we discuss the relationship between colimits and amalgams, and their role in modelling conceptual blending. Our aim with this category is to capture the notion of *partial morphism*, which models the selective projection, in conceptual blending, of parts of the input spaces into the blend space.

Definition 1.6. Let $\mathbf{C}$ be a category that is closed under pullbacks, i.e., the limits of all cospans exist. The category $\mathbf{Pfn}(\mathbf{C})$ has the same objects as $\mathbf{C}$, and a morphism from an object A to an object B is the isomorphism class[5] of the *mono spans* from A to B, which are defined to be the spans $A \xleftarrow{f} D \xrightarrow{g} B$ where f is a monomorphism in $\mathbf{C}$. Composition of spans $A \xleftarrow{f} D \xrightarrow{g} B$ and $B \xleftarrow{h} E \xrightarrow{l} C$ is defined (up to isomorphism) using the cone

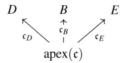

$$\text{apex}(\mathfrak{c})$$

obtained as the pullback of $D \xrightarrow{g} B \xleftarrow{h} E$. The result of the composition is by definition the span $A \xleftarrow{\mathfrak{c}_D;f} \text{apex}(\mathfrak{c}) \xrightarrow{\mathfrak{c}_E;l} C$. A *partial morphism* from A to B is defined as the isomorphism class of a mono span $A \xleftarrow{f} D \xrightarrow{g} B$. Thus, the morphisms in $\mathbf{Pfn}(\mathbf{C})$ are nothing else than the partial morphisms.

It is well known that $\mathbf{Pfn}(\mathbf{Set})$ is (categorically) equivalent to the category $\mathbf{Pfn}$ (and also equivalent to the category of pointed sets). Even more, $\mathbf{Pfn}(\mathbf{Set})$ and $\mathbf{Pfn}$ are isomorphic categories: there is an obvious bijection between partial morphisms in $\mathbf{Set}$ and morphisms in $\mathbf{Pfn}$. Thus, $\mathbf{Pfn}(\mathbf{C})$ can be considered as a natural candidate for generalising the category $\mathbf{Pfn}$ of partial functions.

- the product in $\mathbf{Pfn}$ of A and B is given by the cone $\begin{smallmatrix} A & & B \\ & \nwarrow_{\mathfrak{c}_A} \; \nearrow_{\mathfrak{c}_B} & \\ & O & \end{smallmatrix}$ where $O := (A \times B) \oplus A \oplus B$

  (here $\oplus$ refers, as above, to the disjoint union), the morphism $\mathfrak{c}_A$ is $\pi_A \oplus \text{id}_A \oplus \emptyset$, and the morphism $\mathfrak{c}_B$ is $\pi_B \oplus \emptyset \oplus \text{id}_B$.

The last statement is providing the intuition that for the product in $\mathbf{Pfn}$ of two sets one needs to consider the ordered pairs in the Cartesian product, but also add those ordered pairs that are missing one element of the pair.

[5] In other words, the spans $A \xleftarrow{f} D \xrightarrow{g} B$ and $A \xleftarrow{f'} D' \xrightarrow{g'} B$ are considered equal when

there is an isomorphism $h : D \to D'$ such that $\begin{smallmatrix} & D & \\ f \swarrow & \downarrow & \searrow g \\ A & \; h \; & B \\ f' \nwarrow & \downarrow & \nearrow g' \\ & D' & \end{smallmatrix}$ commutes.

Among partial morphisms from A to B there are some outstanding ones which we call *total*. They are, by definition, the isomorphism classes of mono spans $A \xleftarrow{f} D \xrightarrow{g} B$ where f is an isomorphism. It is obvious that the total morphisms form a subcategory (i.e., total morphisms are closed under composition and the identities are total) of **Pfn(C)**, and this subcategory is equivalent to **C**.

The categories **Pfn(C)** of partial morphisms are well known in the literature. They were first considered in (Robinson and Rosolini, 1988) within an even more general setting; there the authors introduce for every class $\mathscr{M}$ of monomorphisms satisfying certain constraints (see (Hayman and Heindel, 2014, Definitions 6 and 7) for a modern presentation) a category **Pfn(C, $\mathscr{M}$)**. Our category **Pfn(C)** corresponds to choosing $\mathscr{M}$ as the class of all monomorphisms. As for now, we have decided to avoid this more general framework for the sake of simplicity.

1.3 Conceptual Blending as Colimits

The aim of this section is to explain Goguen's framework for conceptual blending. This framework is developed in (Goguen, 1999) (mainly in Section 5 and Appendix B), and instead of using plain categories it is based on categories enriched with a partial order on morphisms.

Kutz et al. (2012) and Kutz et al. (2014) use Goguen's categorical framework, but without ordered categories, i.e., only plain categories are considered. The proposed framework uses the category of CASL theories, which is known to be cocomplete (Mossakowski, 1998), and whose computation of colimits is supported in HETS.[6] Besides this, the authors of (Kutz et al., 2012, 2014) also advocate for using the distributed ontology language DOL as a metalanguage for specifying categorical diagrams (i.e., families of morphisms). When computing colimits, they point out (indeed Goguen already did) that in some case it might be interesting (for blending purposes) to ignore some of the morphisms in the diagram, and consider them just as auxiliary morphisms.

An important difference between (Kutz et al., 2012) and (Kutz et al., 2014) is that in (Kutz et al., 2014) the authors only focus on input diagrams given by total functions, while in the previous version (Kutz et al., 2012) the same authors consider a more general setting allowing for partial morphisms. This simplification has deep consequences, because the colimits of diagrams formed by total functions are, in most cases, although computed in categories of partial morphisms, formed only by total functions (see Page 10).

---

[6] Colimits are available in HETS without problems in the homogeneous case of reasonable institutions (which include most cases: first-order logic, description logics, etc.), but things are not so simple in the heterogeneous case; for such a case only the colimits of certain diagrams (the 'connected thin inf-bounded' ones) (Codescu and Mossakowski, 2008) are computed.

1.3.1 Ordered Categories

Definition 1.7 (Ordered category). An *ordered category* is a category **C** such that

- for every two objects A and B, there is a partial order $\sqsubseteq_{A,B}$ on the set $\hom(A,B)$;
- composition is monotonic with respect to $\sqsubseteq$ in both arguments (i.e., if $f_1 \sqsubseteq g_1$ and $f_2 \sqsubseteq g_2$, then $f_1;f_2 \sqsubseteq g_1;g_2$).

Concerning notation, it is customary to omit indices and simply use $\sqsubseteq$ (see second item), i.e., $\sqsubseteq$ can be considered to be $\bigcup\{\sqsubseteq_{A,B} | A,B \in \mathrm{obj}(\mathbf{C})\}$.

Ordered categories are a special case of so-called 2-categories (see (Leinster, 2002; Johnstone, 2002; Lack, 2010)). Here, there is at most one 2-cell between two 1-cells (i.e., morphisms). Thus, ordered categories lie between plain 1-categories and 2-categories. For this reason, Goguen (1999) introduces the term $\frac{3}{2}$-*categories* to refer to ordered categories.[7] Other names have also been used in the literature, such as locally partially ordered categories, locally posetal categories, Pos-enriched categories, order-enriched categories, etc. We refer to (Kahl, 2010) for a detailed approach to ordered categories, without considering all the difficulties that arise when dealing with general 2-categories.

Example 1.2. The categories **Pfn**(**C**) are ordered categories in the following sense: consider two partial morphisms from A to B, given respectively by the isomorphism classes of the mono spans

$$A \xleftarrow{f} D \xrightarrow{g} B \qquad \text{and} \qquad A \xleftarrow{f'} D' \xrightarrow{g'} B \ .$$

We say that the first partial morphism is *below* the second one (denoted $\sqsubseteq$) if there is a morphism $h : D \to D'$ such that

$$
\begin{array}{ccc}
 & D & \\
f \nearrow & \big| \, h & \searrow g \\
A & \downarrow & B \\
f' \nwarrow & \big\uparrow & \nearrow g' \\
 & D' &
\end{array}
$$

commutes. In such a case, h is also a monomorphism, and $\sqsubseteq$ is a partial order: antisymmetry is obtained using the cancellativity property given by monomorphisms. Moreover, the partial morphisms that are total are the maximal elements of the partial order $\sqsubseteq$ just defined. We will refer to this partial order $\sqsubseteq$ as the *extension partial order*.

Example 1.2 tells us, in particular, that **Pfn**(**Set**) is an ordered category; for this case it holds that

---

[7] The definition given in (Goguen, 1999, Definition 6) also states that the identity morphism id_A has to be maximal in $\hom(A,A)$. We do not require this last condition in the definition we ultimately decided to adopt, but this property also holds for the most natural examples of ordered categories (see Example 1.2).

$f \sqsubseteq g$ iff   whenever f is defined, g is also defined and it agrees with f.

Moreover, the structure of the partial order $\sqsubseteq$ resembles (but is not) a lattice because:

- for every two partial morphisms f_1 and f_2 (with the same sources and targets), there is also a partial morphism $f_1 \sqcap f_2$ which is the infimum in $\sqsubseteq$;
- for every two partial morphisms f_1 and f_2, if they are *compatible* (i.e., if there is some g such that $f_1 \sqsubseteq g$ and $f_2 \sqsubseteq g$) then there is also a partial morphism $f_1 \sqcup f_2$ which is the supremum in $\sqsubseteq$.

It is also worth noticing that the partial orders $\sqsubseteq_{A,B}$ are *directed-complete partial orders* (*dcpo*), which means that every directed subset has a supremum (which we will denote using the symbol $\bigsqcup$). And the composition function can be checked to be *Scott-continuous*, which means that, for every directed family $\{g_i \mid i \in I\}$ of partial functions and every partial function f,

- $\{f; g_i \mid i \in I\}$ is also directed and its supremum is $f; \bigsqcup \{g_i \mid i \in I\}$;
- $\{g_i; f \mid i \in I\}$ is also directed and its supremum is $\bigsqcup \{g_i \mid i \in I\}; f$.

Notice also that **Set** is equivalent to the subcategory of **Pfn(Set)** given by total morphisms.

1.3.2 Colimits in Ordered Categories

In the context of ordered categories there are, at least, two very natural alternative possibilities concerning colimits (see (Kahl, 2010, Chapter 4)). One of them produces a strengthening of the plain notion of colimit, and we will refer to them as *ordered colimits*. The other one accepts a more general class of diagrams, which instead of considering functors considers so-called *lax functors*, where commutativity is replaced with semicommutativity. The latter follows a very similar pattern than the one given for colimits in Definition 1.3, and the respective colimits are called *lax colimits*.

Definition 1.8 (Ordered colimit, see (Kahl, 2010, Definition 4.1.2)). A cocone $\mathfrak{c}$ over a diagram $\mathscr{D}$ in an ordered category **C** is said to be an *ordered colimit* in case that the function $\mathsf{H}_\mathfrak{c}$ introduced on Page 9 is an order-isomorphism (and therefore also a bijection) between the partial orders $\langle \mathrm{hom}(\mathrm{apex}(\mathfrak{c}), -), \sqsubseteq \rangle$ and $\langle \mathrm{Cocones}(\mathscr{D}, -), \sqsubseteq^* \rangle$. The order $\sqsubseteq^*$ considered among cocones is the one defined component-wise, that is, given two cocones $\mathfrak{c} := \{\mathfrak{c}_X\}_{X \in \mathrm{Nodes}}$ and $\mathfrak{d} := \{\mathfrak{d}_X\}_{X \in \mathrm{Nodes}}$ with the same apex, it holds that

$$\mathfrak{c} \sqsubseteq^* \mathfrak{d} \qquad \text{iff} \qquad \mathfrak{c}_X \sqsubseteq \mathfrak{d}_X \text{ for every node } X \in \mathrm{Nodes}.$$

From Definition 1.8 it is obvious that, if c is an ordered colimit, then: whenever h_1 and h_2 are two morphisms with source apex(c) and '$c_X; h_1 \sqsubseteq c_X; h_2$ for every node X', then $h_1 \sqsubseteq h_2$. We will refer to such condition as being *jointly semiepimorphic*.[8]

In the particular case of the ordered category **Pfn** (with the extension partial order described in Example 1.2), one can check that colimits are also ordered colimits.

Next, in order to introduce lax colimits we need to firstly introduce lax diagrams and lax cocones. The only difference between a functor $\mathscr{D} : \mathbf{J} \longrightarrow \mathbf{C}$ and a lax functor $\mathscr{D} : \mathbf{J} \longrightarrow \mathbf{C}$ is that instead of equality one only requires

$$\mathrm{id}_{\mathscr{D}(A)} \sqsubseteq \mathscr{D}(\mathrm{id}_A) \qquad \text{and} \qquad \mathscr{D}(f); \mathscr{D}(g) \sqsubseteq \mathscr{D}(f;g).$$

The second condition is known as *semicommutativity*, and it is common to represent it graphically as follows:

$$
\begin{array}{ccc}
 & & \mathscr{D}(C) \\
\mathscr{D}(g) \nearrow & & \uparrow \mathscr{D}(f;g) \\
\mathscr{D}(B) \quad \sqsubseteq & & \\
\mathscr{D}(f) \nwarrow & & \\
 & & \mathscr{D}(A)
\end{array}
$$

Notice that if the ordered category satisfies that the identity morphisms are maximal, then the first condition $\mathrm{id}_{\mathscr{D}(A)} \sqsubseteq \mathscr{D}(\mathrm{id}_A)$ can be rewritten as saying $\mathrm{id}_{\mathscr{D}(A)} = \mathscr{D}(\mathrm{id}_A)$. A *lax diagram* in an ordered category $\mathbf{C}$ is defined to be a lax functor $\mathscr{D} : \mathbf{J} \longrightarrow \mathbf{C}$. Here $\mathbf{J}$ is just a category (not necessarily an ordered category).

A *lax cocone* c over a lax diagram $\mathscr{D}$ in a category $\mathbf{C}$ is an object O in $\mathbf{C}$ together with a family (indexed by the nodes in the graph associated with $\mathscr{D}$) $\{c_X\}_{X \in \text{Nodes}}$ of morphisms in $\mathbf{C}$ such that:

- c_X has source $\mathscr{D}(X)$, for every node X;
- c_X has target O, for every node X;
- $\mathscr{D}(f); c_Y \sqsubseteq c_X$ for every edge f from node X to node Y.

Thus, lax cocones are capturing the intuition of *semicommutative cocones*. As expected we will refer to the apex object as apex(c). The collection of all lax cocones over $\mathscr{D}$ will be denoted by laxCocones$(\mathscr{D}, \text{-})$.

It is rather trivial noticing that every lax cocone c over a lax diagram $\mathscr{D}$ induces a function[9] H_c defined by

$$
\begin{array}{rcl}
H_c : \mathrm{hom}(\mathrm{apex}(c), \text{-}) & \longrightarrow & \mathrm{laxCocones}(\mathscr{D}, \text{-}) \\
h & \longmapsto & c; h
\end{array}
$$

---

[8] When there are ordered coproducts (in the sense of Definition 1.8) it is obvious that this definition also follows the same intuition explained in Section 1.2.2. That is, $\{c_X\}_{X \in \text{Nodes}}$ is jointly semiepimorphic iff the single morphism $\bigoplus \{c_X\}_{X \in \text{Nodes}}$ is so.

[9] We use the same notation H_c as for the case of plain categories and colimits, but this is not a problem because the context always clarifies which one we refer to.

Definition 1.9 (Lax colimit, see (Kahl, 2010, Definition 4.3.2)). A lax cocone c over a lax diagram $\mathcal{D}$ in an ordered category $\mathbf{C}$ is said to be a *lax colimit* when the recently introduced function H_c is an order-isomorphism (and hence a bijection) between the partial orders $\langle \mathrm{hom}(\mathrm{apex}(c),\text{-}), \sqsubseteq \rangle$ and $\langle \mathrm{laxCocones}(\mathcal{D},\text{-})), \sqsubseteq^* \rangle$. The ordered $\sqsubseteq^*$ considered among lax cocones is the one defined component-wise (see Definition 1.8).

It is again obvious that lax colimits must be jointly semiepimorphic. Notice also that in case of considering a diagram $\mathcal{D}$ (instead of an arbitrary lax diagram), the notions of lax colimit and ordered colimit collapse (up to isomorphism) if and only if all lax cocones are cocones. Thus, whenever semicommutativity is not trivially reduced to commutativity, the two recently introduced notions of colimits can be different.

1.3.3 $\frac{3}{2}$-Colimits

It is well-known that the cocone of an ordered colimit is unique up to isomorphism. And the same happens for the lax cocone of a lax colimit. Goguen considers these facts to show that they might not be adequate notions for the formalisation of conceptual blending, since one expects more than one way to blend concepts. For this reason he proposes the following alternative notion.[10]

Definition 1.10 ($\frac{3}{2}$-Colimit, see (Goguen, 1999, Definition 12)). A lax cocone c over a lax diagram $\mathcal{D}$ in an ordered category $\mathbf{C}$ is said to be a $\frac{3}{2}$-*colimit* in case that, for every lax cocone $\mathfrak{d}$ (with apex D) over $\mathcal{D}$, it holds that the set

$$\{h \mid H_c(h) \sqsubseteq^* \mathfrak{d}\} \qquad \text{(which is a subset of } \mathrm{hom}(\mathrm{apex}(c),D))$$

has a maximum element on $\sqsubseteq$.

Notice that this last definition is equivalent to just saying that the function

$$H_c : \langle \mathrm{hom}(\mathrm{apex}(c),\text{-}), \sqsubseteq \rangle \longrightarrow \langle \mathrm{laxCocones}(\mathcal{D},\text{-}), \sqsubseteq^* \rangle$$
$$h \longmapsto c;h$$

fulfills that the anti-image of principal downsets (i.e., downsets of an element) are also principal downsets.[11] This last restatement of the notion of $\frac{3}{2}$-colimits has the advantage of providing an easier comparison with Definition 1.9. In particular, it becomes obvious that if c is a lax colimit over $\mathcal{D}$, then it is also a $\frac{3}{2}$-colimit.

When the ordered category involves partial orders that are dcpos and composition is Scott-continuous, then it is worth noticing that the following statements are equivalent:[12]

---

[10] In (Goguen, 2001, Section 3.1) the expression "lax pushouts" is used in a naive way: this has not to be understood as a particular case of lax colimits in ordered categories.

[11] The downset of an element h is the set of all $g \sqsubseteq h$.

[12] The assumptions just stated are only necessary to prove the implication $2 \Rightarrow 1$; the reverse implication always holds.

1. The set $\{h \mid H_c(h) \sqsubseteq^* \partial\}$ has a maximum element on $\sqsubseteq$.
2. The set $\{f \mid H_c(h) \sqsubseteq^* \partial\}$ is directed, i.e., whenever $H_c(h_1) \sqsubseteq^* \partial$ and $H_c(h_2) \sqsubseteq^* \partial$ then there is some g such that $h_1 \sqsubseteq g$, $h_2 \sqsubseteq g$ and $H_c(g) \sqsubseteq^* \partial$.

Notice that the first condition is the one involved in Definition 1.10, and also that **Pfn** satisfies the hypotheses for such equivalence.

For the case of the diagram $B_1 \xleftarrow{f_1} A \xrightarrow{f_2} B_2$, Definition 1.10 provides the notion of $\frac{3}{2}$-*pushouts*, which is Goguen's proposal for a formalisation of blending. We restate his proposal in Definition 1.11.

Definition 1.11 ($\frac{3}{2}$-Pushout). A $\frac{3}{2}$-pushout of a span $B_1 \xleftarrow{f_1} A \xrightarrow{f_2} B_2$ is given by a lax cocone

$$
\begin{array}{ccc}
 & C & \\
 \overset{g_1}{\nearrow} \uparrow {\scriptstyle g} \underset{g_2}{\nwarrow} & & \\
B_1 \quad \sqsubseteq \quad \sqsupseteq \quad B_2 & & \\
\nwarrow_{f_1} \quad \nearrow_{f_2} & & \\
 & A &
\end{array}
$$

satisfying that whenever
$$
\begin{array}{ccc}
 & D & \\
\overset{h_1}{\nearrow} \uparrow {\scriptstyle h} \underset{h_2}{\nwarrow} & & \\
B_1 \quad \sqsubseteq \quad \sqsupseteq \quad B_2 & & \\
\nwarrow_{f_1} \quad \nearrow_{f_2} & & \\
 & A &
\end{array}
$$
semicommutes, it holds that the uni-

variate system

$$
g;\lambda \sqsubseteq h \qquad\qquad g_1;\lambda \sqsubseteq h_1 \qquad\qquad g_2;\lambda \sqsubseteq h_2
$$

of morphism equations has a maximum solution for the indeterminate λ.

The formulation given in Definition 1.11 for presenting $\frac{3}{2}$-pushouts exhibits an obvious relationship with the one given in Definition 1.4; the main difference is that instead of looking for unique solutions to a family of morphism equations one looks for the best (i.e., largest) solution to a family of morphism inequations. For the particular inequations given in Definition 1.11, the family of morphism inequations is the one stating that the three triangles

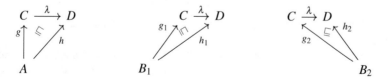

semicommute.

It is worth saying that whenever the category **C** has ordered coproducts (in the sense of Definition 1.8) the system $\{c_X;h \sqsubseteq \partial_X \mid X \in \mathsf{Node}\}$ of morphism inequations (that is, the one which appears in Definition 1.10) is equivalent to the following single inequation: $(\bigoplus\{c_X \mid X \in \text{Node}\}); h \sqsubseteq \bigoplus\{\partial_X \mid X \in \text{Node}\}$.

Let us assume now that c is a $\frac{3}{2}$-colimit (with apex C) over a lax diagram $\mathscr{D}$ and that $h \in \text{hom}(C, D)$. Then, by monotonicity it holds that $c; h$ is also a lax cocone (with apex D). Therefore, by definition of $\frac{3}{2}$-colimit the univariate inequational system $c; \lambda \sqsubseteq^* c; h$ has a maximum solution for λ. In other words, the inequational system

$$c_X; \lambda \sqsubseteq c_X; h \qquad \text{for every node } X$$

has a maximum solution for λ. We denote such a maximum solution g. Considering that h is also trivially a solution to the very system, we obtain that $h \sqsubseteq g$. Thus, by monotonicity it must hold that $c_X; h \sqsubseteq c_X; g$ for every node X. Therefore, g is also the largest solution to the equational system $c; \lambda = c; h$.

Thus, we have demonstrated that for every $\frac{3}{2}$-colimit c (with object C) over a lax diagram $\mathscr{D}$ and every $h \in \text{hom}(C, -)$, there exists $\max_{\sqsubseteq}\{g \mid \mathsf{H}_c(g) = \mathsf{H}_c(h)\}$ that coincides with $\max_{\sqsubseteq}\{g \mid \mathsf{H}_c(g) \sqsubseteq \mathsf{H}_c(h)\}$. Thus, for every $\frac{3}{2}$-colimit c over a lax diagram $\mathscr{D}$, we can define the *expansion* function

$$\begin{aligned} \text{xpan}_c : \text{hom}(\text{apex}(c), -) &\longrightarrow \text{hom}(\text{apex}(c), -) \\ h &\longmapsto \text{xpan}_c(h) := \max_{\sqsubseteq}\{g \mid \mathsf{H}_c(g) = \mathsf{H}_c(h)\} = \\ &\qquad\qquad \max_{\sqsubseteq}\{g \mid \mathsf{H}_c(g) \sqsubseteq \mathsf{H}_c(h)\} \end{aligned}$$

It is obvious that $\mathsf{H}_c(h) = \mathsf{H}_c(\text{xpan}_c(h))$. Moreover, this function xpan_c is

- extensive, i.e., $h \sqsubseteq \text{xpan}_c(h)$;
- increasing, i.e., if $h_1 \sqsubseteq h_2$ then $\text{xpan}_c(h_1) \sqsubseteq \text{xpan}_c(h_2)$;
- idempotent, i.e., $\text{xpan}_c(\text{xpan}_c(h)) = \text{xpan}_c(h)$.

Consequently, every $\frac{3}{2}$-colimit c induces a closure operator (or closure system) (Burris and Sankappanavar, 2012, Section I.5) on the set $\text{hom}(\text{apex}(c), -)$.

On Page 10 we point out that colimits are jointly epimorphic. Unfortunately, in the arbitrary case it not so clear whether this property also holds for $\frac{3}{2}$-colimits. However, as is obvious from the definitions of xpan_c, it holds that

$$\text{if } h_1 \text{ and } h_2 \text{ satisfy that } \mathsf{H}_c(h_1) = \mathsf{H}_c(h_2), \text{ then } \text{xpan}_c(h_1) = \text{xpan}_c(h_2).$$

In other words, the following property (which resembles the definition of jointly epimorphic) holds for $\frac{3}{2}$-colimits c:

$$\begin{aligned} &\text{if } h_1 \text{ and } h_2 \text{ satisfy that } `c_X; h_1 = c_X; h_2 \text{ for every node } X\text{', then} \\ &\qquad\qquad \text{xpan}_c(h_1) = \text{xpan}_c(h_2). \end{aligned}$$

It is worth noticing that $\text{xpan}_c(h_1) = \text{xpan}_c(h_2)$ implies, in particular, that h_1 and h_2 are compatible.

Goguen's proposal is to use $\frac{3}{2}$-pushouts as a computational method for finding conceptual blends (see Figure 1.1). In the easiest case (i.e., the blend of two concepts), this framework assumes that we have previously chosen

- a morphism f_1 from the generic space G into input space I_1 (i.e., $f_1 : G \to I_1$), and also

- a morphism f_2 from the generic space G into input space I_2 (i.e., $f_2 : G \to I_2$).

Furthermore, Goguen suggests to consider all $\frac{3}{2}$-pushouts of the span $I_1 \xleftarrow{f_1} G \xrightarrow{f_2} I_2$ as candidates for blending of the two initial concepts. In the examples provided in (Goguen, 1999)[13] this is done using ordered categories whose objects are algebraic theories (using the formal specification language OBJ), morphisms correspond to partial functions preserving the structure, and the partial order corresponds to being an extension.

There are several difficulties in order to provide a computational framework to conceptual blending following Goguen's categorical proposal. Some of them are as follows.

- While there are several available software packages for dealing with "algebraic theory" categories and colimits (like HETS (Mossakowski et al., 2007; Codescu et al., 2010)) this is not the case in the context of ordered categories.
- Although (Goguen, 1999) contains a first theoretical study of $\frac{3}{2}$-colimits, the theoretical framework still needs to be improved before considering computational implementations. For example, can we characterise all $\frac{3}{2}$-pushouts in the ordered category **Pfn**? What about more complex diagrams that are still in **Pfn**? What about considering other well-known ordered categories? Can we get rid of the ordered category **C** appealing to some particular plain category built from **C**?

For this reason we propose an alternative proposal to model conceptual blending, basing it on the notion of *amalgam*.

1.4 Conceptual Blending as Amalgams

An amalgam is a description that combines parts of two other descriptions as a new coherent whole. There are notions that are related to amalgams in addition to conceptual blending, notions such as merging operation or information fusion. They all have in common that they deal with combining information from more than one 'source' into a new integrated and coherent whole; their differences reside on the assumptions they make on the sources characteristics and the way in which the combination of the sources takes place.

The notion of amalgams was developed in the context of Case-Based Reasoning (CBR), where new problems are solved based on previously solved problems or cases, residing on a case base (Ontañón and Plaza, 2010). Solving a new problem often requires more than one case from the case base, so their content has to be combined in some way to solve the new problem. The notion of amalgam of two cases—two descriptions of problems and their solutions, or situations and their

---

[13] It is also worth looking at `http://cseweb.ucsd.edu/~goguen/papers/blend.html` because this site has more recent examples.

outcomes—is a proposal to formalise this process of the ways in which they can be combined to produce a new, coherent case.

Formally, the notion of amalgams can be defined in any representation language $\mathscr{L}$ for which a subsumption relation $\sqsubseteq$ between the terms (or descriptions) of $\mathscr{L}$ can be defined. We say that a term ψ_1 subsumes another term ψ_2 ($\psi_1 \sqsubseteq \psi_2$) when ψ_1 is more general than (or equal to) ψ_2.[14]

Additionally, we assume that $\mathscr{L}$ contains the infimum element $\bot$ (or 'any') and the supremum element $\top$ (or 'none') with respect to the subsumption order.

Next, for any two terms ψ_1 and ψ_2 we can define their *unification*, ($\psi_1 \sqcup \psi_2$), which is the *most general specialisation* of two given terms, and their *anti-unification*, defined as the *least general generalisation* of two terms, representing the most specific term that subsumes both. Intuitively, a unifier (if it exists) is a term that has all the information in both the original terms, and an anti-unifier is a term that contains only all that is common between two terms. Also, notice that, depending on $\mathscr{L}$, anti-unifier and unifier might be unique or not.

1.4.1 Amalgams

The notion of *amalgam* can be conceived of as a generalisation of the notion of unification over terms. The unification of two terms (or descriptions) ψ_a and ψ_b is a new term $\phi \equiv \psi_a \sqcup \psi_b$, called unifier. All that is true for ψ_a or ψ_b is also true for ϕ; e.g., if ψ_a describes 'a red vehicle' and ψ_b describes 'a German minivan' then their unification yields the description 'a red German minivan.' Two terms are not unifiable when they represent incompatible or contradictory information; for instance 'a red French vehicle' is not unifiable with 'a blue German minivan'. The strict definition of unification means that any two descriptions with only one item with contradictory information cannot be unified.

An *amalgam* of two terms (or descriptions) is a new term that contains *parts from these two terms*. For instance, an amalgam of 'a red French vehicle' and 'a blue German minivan' would be 'a red German minivan'; clearly there are always multiple possibilities for amalgams, since 'a blue French minivan' is another possible amalgam. The notion of amalgam, as a form of 'partial unification', was formally introduced by Ontañón and Plaza (2010).

Definition 1.12 (Amalgam). The set of *amalgams* of two terms ψ_a and ψ_b is the set of terms such that:

$$\psi_a \curlyvee \psi_b = \{\phi \in \mathscr{L} \setminus \{\top\} \mid \exists \alpha_a, \alpha_b \in \mathscr{L} : \alpha_a \sqsubseteq \psi_a \wedge \alpha_b \sqsubseteq \psi_b \wedge \phi \equiv \alpha_a \sqcup \alpha_b\}$$

Thus, an amalgam of two terms ψ_a and ψ_b is a term that has been formed by unifying two generalisations α_a and α_b, whenever this unification is not inconsistent, i.e.,

---

[14] In Machine Learning, $A \sqsubseteq B$ usually means that A is more general than B, unlike in description logics, for instance, where it has the opposite meaning, since it is seen as 'set inclusion' of their interpretations.

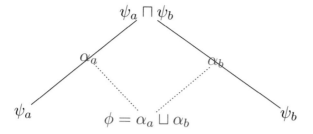

Fig. 1.2: A diagram of an amalgam ϕ from inputs ψ_a and ψ_b where $\chi = \alpha_a \sqcap \alpha_b$

$\alpha_a \sqcup \alpha_b \not\equiv \top$. Thus, an amalgam is a term resulting from combining some of the information in ψ_a with some of the information from ψ_b. Formally, $\psi_a \curlyvee \psi_b$ denotes the set of all possible amalgams; however, whenever it does not lead to confusion, we will use $\psi_a \curlyvee \psi_b$ to denote one specific amalgam of ψ_a and ψ_b.

Ontañón and Plaza (2010) give a slightly different definition of amalgam, for which not all generalisations are taken into account, only those that are less general than $\psi_a \sqcap \psi_b$ (the anti-unification of the inputs). We rephrase this definition here introducing the notion of *bounded amalgam*:

Definition 1.13 (Bounded amalgam). Let $\chi \in \mathcal{L}$. The set of χ-*bounded amalgams* of two terms ψ_a and ψ_b is the set of terms such that:

$$\psi_a \curlyvee_\chi \psi_b = \{\phi \in \mathcal{L} \setminus \{\top\} \mid \exists \alpha_a, \alpha_b \in \mathcal{L} : \chi \sqsubseteq \alpha_a \sqsubseteq \psi_a \wedge \chi \sqsubseteq \alpha_b \sqsubseteq \psi_b \wedge \phi \equiv \alpha_a \sqcup \alpha_b\}$$

A particularly interesting case (the one studied by Ontañón and Plaza (2010)) is when $\chi \equiv \psi_a \sqcap \psi_b$, the anti-unification of the inputs, as illustrated in Figure 1.2. The intuitive reason is that the anti-unification represents what is common or shared between the two inputs and, thus, generalising beyond $\psi_a \sqcap \psi_b$ would eliminate compatible information that is already present in both inputs.

The terms α_a and α_b are called the *transfers* or *constituents* of an amalgam $\psi_a \curlyvee \psi_b$. They represent all the information from ψ_a and ψ_b, respectively, which is *transferred* to the amalgam. As we will see later, this idea of transfer is akin to the idea of *transferring* knowledge from the source to target in CBR, and also in computational analogy (Falkenhainer et al., 1989).

Usually we are interested only in maximal amalgams of two input terms, i.e., those amalgams that contain maximal parts of their inputs that can be unified into a new coherent description. Formally, an amalgam $\phi \in \psi_a \curlyvee \psi_b$ is maximal if there is no $\phi' \in \psi_a \curlyvee \psi_b$ such that $\phi \sqsubset \phi'$. In other words, if more properties of an input were added, the combination would be no longer consistent. The reason why we might be interested in maximal amalgams is very simple: consider an amalgam ϕ' such that $\phi' \sqsubset \phi$; clearly ϕ', being more general than ϕ, has less information than ϕ and thus combines less information from the inputs ψ_a and ψ_b. Since ϕ has more information while being consistent, ϕ' or any amalgam that is a generalisation of ϕ, is trivially derived from ϕ by generalisation.

1.4.2 Asymmetric Amalgams and Analogy

There is a special case of amalgams of special interest: asymmetric amalgams, where the two input terms do not play a symmetrical role. The case of asymmetric amalgams, as we will show, is related to the notion of analogy and case-based inference, where one of the inputs (called the *source*) has much more information that the other input (called the *target* or *problem*). Asymmetric amalgams can be used to model the process by which knowledge from the source can be transfered to the target.

Definition 1.14 (Asymmetric amalgam). The χ-bounded *asymmetric amalgams* $\psi_s \overrightarrow{\curlyvee} \psi_t$ of two terms ψ_s (*source*) and ψ_t (*target*) is the set of terms such that:

$$\psi_s \overrightarrow{\curlyvee}_\chi \psi_t = \{\phi \in \mathscr{L} \setminus \{\top\} \mid \exists \alpha_s \in \mathscr{L} : \chi \sqsubseteq \alpha_s \sqsubseteq \psi_s \wedge \phi \equiv \alpha_s \sqcup \psi_t\}$$

In an asymmetric amalgam, the target term is transferred completely into the amalgam, while the source term is generalised. The result is a form of partial unification that retains all the information in ψ_t while relaxing ψ_s by generalisation and then unifying one of those more general terms with ψ_t itself. As before, we would be usually interested only in the asymmetric amalgams that are maximal.

This model of asymmetric amalgam can be used to model case-based inference in CBR, as explained in (Ontañón and Plaza, 2012), and analogical reasoning (Besold and Plaza, 2015; Besold et al., 2015). Essentially, this model clarifies what knowledge is transferred from source description to target, namely the transfer term α_s captures which case-based inference conjectures are applicable to (are consistent with) the target. In the case of a maximal amalgam, α_s represents as much information as can be transferred from the source to the target ψ_t such that $\alpha_s \sqcup \psi_t$ is consistent.

1.5 Relating Colimits and Amalgams

In Section 1.1 we mentioned that it is very appealing to model blending as a colimit in some category **C** of conceptual spaces and their structure-preserving mappings. When blending two input spaces, however, not everything is included into the blend because there may be incompatibilities between the input spaces. In general, conceptual blending is based on selective projections from the input spaces into the blend (Fauconnier and Turner, 2002).

Consequently, the classical colimit construct in **C** is inadequate for modelling blending. Goguen suggested $\frac{3}{2}$-colimits in ordered categories instead, where structure-preserving mappings between conceptual spaces are based on partial functions. We discussed this approach thoroughly in Section 1.3.

In Definition 1.6 we introduced an alternative way in which selective projection can be modelled categorically, without getting into the subtlety of dealing with ordered categories. In this section we shall focus on **Pfn**(**C**)— the category of iso-morphism classes of mono spans in **C**—and show that the cocone constructs in **Pfn**(**C**) can be seen as an abstraction, into the category-theoretical setting, of amalgams as introduced in Section 1.4.1. Furthermore, this construct might be also suitable for modelling and computing conceptual blends, as we shall illustrate in Chapter 2. First, however, we recall some basic notions of category theory not introduced in Section 1.1 that we are going to need in this section, and we introduce also some additional notation.

1.5.1 Preliminaries

Let **C** be a category and $f : A \to C$ be a morphism in **C**. We say that f *factors* through some morphism $g : B \to C$ if there exists $h : A \to B$ such that $f = h; g$. If g is a monomorphism, then h is the pullback of f along g.[15] Let $A \xrightarrow{f} C \xleftarrow{g} B$ be a diagram in **C**. If there is a pullback over this diagram we shall write $\bar{f}$ for the pullback of morphism f along morphism g.

Remember from Definition 1.6 that a morphism $f : A \to B$ in **Pfn**(**C**) is, in particular, an isomorphism class of a span in **C**. Without loss of generality, we will represent this class with a representative span $A \xleftarrow{f^-} A^0 \xrightarrow{f^+} B$. Recall that f^- is a monomorphism, i.e., the span is a mono span.

1.5.2 A Category-Theoretical Account of Amalgams

A poset $\langle \mathscr{L}, \sqsubseteq \rangle$ as the one considered in Section 1.4 can be seen as a category such that objects are the elements of $\mathscr{L}$, and there is a unique morphism from ϕ to ψ whenever $\phi \sqsubseteq \psi$. Consequently, we can propose a category-theoretical account of the notion of amalgam as given in Definitions 1.12 and 1.13.

Let **C** be a category and let C be an object in **C**. We will say that the *general isations* of C are all monomorphisms with target C. Let $f : A \to C$ be a morphism in **C**. We will say that the *f-bounded generalisations* of C are all monomorphisms $g : B \rightarrowtail C$ such that f factors through g.

Now, let **C** be a category with pullbacks, and let $I_1 \xleftarrow{a_1} G \xrightarrow{a_2} I_2$ be a V-shaped diagram in the category **Pfn**(**C**) such that $a_1^- = a_2^- = id_G$. (Note that we can see it also as a V-shaped diagram $I_1 \xleftarrow{a_1^+} G \xrightarrow{a_2^+} I_2$ in **C**.) Recall that for

---

[15] Following is a proof of this claim: Let $m : D \to A$ and $n : D \to B$ such that $m; f = n; g$. The morphism m is also the unique morphism from D to the apex A of the pullback such that $m; id_A = m$ and $m; h = n$. The first equality is trivial. For the second, we know that $m; f = n; g$ and $f = h; g$, consequently $m; h; g = n; g$. But g is a monomorphism, so $m; h = n$. And if k is any other morphism from D to the apex A satisfying these properties we would have that $k; id = m$, hence $k = m$.

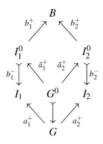

Fig. 1.3: Representation in **C** of a cocone in **MSpan** (**C**) over $I_1 \xleftarrow{a_1} G \xrightarrow{a_2} I_2$

$I_1 \xrightarrow{b_1} B \xleftarrow{b_2} I_2$ to be a cocone over this V-shaped diagram in **Pfn**(**C**) we need that $a_1;b_1 \rightsquigarrow a_2;b_2$. This amounts to saying that, in the **C**-diagram of Figure 1.3, the pullbacks of $I_i^0 \xrightarrow{b_i^-} I_i \xleftarrow{a_i^+} G$ are isomorphic (G^0 denotes the apex of these isomorphic objects, without loss of generality), and $\bar{a}_1^+;b_1^+ = \bar{a}_2^+;b_2^+$. This brings us to the categorical notion of amalgam.

Definition 1.15 (Amalgam). Let $a_1^+ : G \to I_1$ and $a_2^+ : G \to I_2$ be two morphisms in a category **C** with pullbacks. An *amalgam* $\langle b_1^+, b_2^+ \rangle$ of a_1^+ and a_2^+ is a cocone with apex B over $I_1^0 \xleftarrow{\bar{a}_1^+} G^0 \xrightarrow{\bar{a}_2^+} I_2^0$, where $\bar{a}_i^+$ are the pullbacks of a_i^+ along generalisations $b_i^- : I_i^0 \to I_i$ of I_i (for $i \in \{1,2\}$), such that G^0 is the common (up to isomorphism) apex of these pullbacks (see Figure 1.3).

In the particular case when **C** is the poset $\langle \mathscr{L}, \sqsubseteq \rangle$ of Section 1.4 the definition above amounts to Definition 1.12 (taking as G the infimum element $\bot$). If we focus on a_i-bounded generalisations of I_i instead, we get Definition 1.13, where G plays the role of the element χ. This is so because in this case the apex G^0 of the pullback is isomorphic to G.

Definition 1.15 provides us a way to characterise conceptual blending in a manner that is faithful to the description given by Fauconnier and Turner (2002) and is independent of any particular choice of representation formalism for conceptual spaces and of any implementation thereof. Furthermore, the definition points to a possible way to compute blends via the classical colimit construct as implemented in HETS.

1.6 Conclusion

The theory of conceptual blending as put forward by Fauconnier and Turner in cognitive linguistics has been keenly adopted by researchers in the computing sciences for guiding the implementation of computational systems that aim at exhibiting creative capabilities, particularly when taking into consideration the invention of new concepts.

As is common with these early adoptions, each system has made its own choices of interpretation of the core elements that constitute Fauconnier and Turner's theory. They provide a formalisation of some fragment of theory that on the one hand attempts to be as faithful as possible to the intuitions stated by Fauconnier and Turner, and on the other hand would be feasible to implement in a computational system.

What has become evident from these early implementations of conceptual blending is that they have been designed in a very system-specific manner, without a clear separation of system-independent issues from those that are more system-specific. This makes it difficult to gain a deeper insight into the computational aspect of conceptual blending and hence to favour the reuse of blending technology to domains other than those envisioned by the system implementors.

In this chapter we have chosen to pursue a more domain- and system-independent approach to the development of a formal and computational theory of blending. In particular, we have taken the basic insight of Goguen that a blend might be adequately modelled as some kind of category-theoretical colimit, and we have expounded on the details of this insight in order to fully grasp its relationship with Fauconnier and Turner's theory.

Goguen himself proposed the framework of ordered categories to flesh out a mathematical account of conceptual blending, but he never fully worked out the implications of this proposal, nor did he show—other than with some small examples—how concrete acts of conceptual blending actually fit into his framework. The intuitions seemed convincing, but a thorough analysis was still missing. This is what we have started to do and what we have reported in this chapter.

What has become clear from our analysis is that dealing with Goguen's framework is much more subtle than originally expected. His notion of $\frac{3}{2}$-colimit as a way to model blending is quite complicated to grasp conceptually, in particular as a guide for the implementation of computational blending systems. Although the notion of colimit is, in our view, still a powerful notion to be exploited theoretically for the purpose of giving a precise characterisation of conceptual blending, we have considered alternative ways to do so, for instance, exploiting the notion of colimit in a category of spans. The advantage of such an approach is that it nicely covers also a generalisation of the notion of amalgam, originally proposed as a method for knowledge merging or integration in case-based reasoning. Indeed, the notion of amalgam is very reminiscent of that of blending, and by modelling blending as colimits in a category of spans we have become capable of bringing blending and amalgamation to the same theoretical footing.

The theoretical exploration carried out in this chapter will guide our subsequent work to carry out a computational realisation of blending that clearly distinguishes the domain-independent elements of blending such as amalgamation and colimit construction from the domain-specific realisations thereof. The uniformity provided by our model makes it possible to relate it with the mathematical model of the creative process proposed by Mazzola et al. (2011) and Andreatta et al. (2013). They propose to take the insights offered by the Yoneda lemma of category theory as a metaphor for the process by which an open question may be solved in a creative way. Schorlemmer et al. (2016) show by means of the Buddhist monk riddle (Koestler, 1964) that Mazzola et al.'s metaphor for the creative process can be useful to make explicit the external structure of the concept or idea we want to creatively explore. This metaphor likens the creative process to the task of finding a canonical diagram that externalises the structure of a categorical object. In particular we have focussed on the image-schematic structure in such a way that the solution to the riddle can be found by conceptual blending, using an amalgam-based process such as the one put forward in our model.

As future work, we intend to further explore our approach in other domains, validating the hypothesis that a relevant collection of image schemas should be sufficient to model diagrams that, via generalisation and colimit computation, yield novel and useful blends. Moreover, we surmise that for complex situations we will have not a blend but a web of blends, for example, situations where one or both input mental spaces are recursively blended. Such a web of blends is called Hyper-Blending Web (Turner, 2014). We intend to explore the span of the hypothesis that the input concepts in such a web of blends are image schemas and their specialisations, while the blend concepts are created by generalisation and colimit computation of image schemas and previous blends in the web.

References

M. Andreatta, A. Ehresmann, R. Guitart, and G. Mazzola. Towards a categorical theory of creativity for music, discourse, and cognition. In J. Yust, J. Wild, and J. A. Burgoyne, editors, *Mathematics and Computation in Music. 4th International Conference, MCM 2013. Montreal, QC, June 2013. Proceedings*, volume 7937 of *Lecture Notes in Artificial Intelligence*, 2013.

S. G. Baron and D. Osherson. Evidence for conceptual combination in the left anterior temporal lobe. *Neuroimage*, 55(4):1847–1852, 2011.

M. Barr and C. Wells. *Category Theory for Computing Science*. Prentice Hall International Series in Computer Science. Prentice Hall International, New York, 1990. ISBN 0-13-120486-6.

J. Barwise and J. Seligman. *Information Flow: The Logic of Distributed Systems*, volume 44 of *Cambridge Tracts in Theoretical Computer Science*. Cambridge University Press, 1997.

T. R. Besold and E. Plaza. Generalize and blend: Concept blending based on generalization, analogy, and amalgams. In *Proceedings of the Sixth International Conference on Computational Creativity (ICCC 2015)*, 2015.

T. R. Besold, K.-U. Kühnberger, and E. Plaza. Analogy, amalgams, and concept blending. In *Proceedings of the Third Annual Conference on Advances in Cognitive Systems*, 2015.

S. Burris and H. P. Sankappanavar. *A Course in Universal Algebra*. The Millennium, 2012 update edition, 2012. URL http://www.math.uwaterloo.ca/~snburris/htdocs/ualg.html.

G. Calugareanu and I. Purdea. Examples in category theory, 2011. URL http://math.ubbcluj.ro/~calu/BOO-0-14.pdf. Unpublished book.

M. Codescu and T. Mossakowski. Heterogeneous colimits. In *Proceedings of the 2008 IEEE International Conference on Software Testing Verification and Validation Workshop*, ICSTW '08, pages 131–140, Washington, DC, USA, 2008. IEEE Computer Society.

M. Codescu, F. Horozal, M. Kohlhase, T. Mossakowski, F. Rabe, and K. Sojakova. Towards logical frameworks in the heterogeneous tool set HETS. In T. Mossakowski and H. Kreowski, editors, *Recent Trends in Algebraic Development Techniques — 20th International Workshop, WADT 2010, Etelsen, Germany, July 1–4, 2010, Revised Selected Papers*, volume 7137 of *Lecture Notes in Computer Science*, pages 139–159. Springer, 2010.

R. Diaconescu. *Institution-independent model theory*. Studies in Universal Logic. Birkhäuser Verlag, Basel, 2008. ISBN 978-3-7643-8707-5.

B. Falkenhainer, K. D. Forbus, and D. Gentner. The structure-mapping engine: Algorithm and examples. *Artificial Intelligence*, 41(1):1–63, 1989.

G. Fauconnier. *Mental Spaces*. Cambridge University Press, 1994.

G. Fauconnier and M. Turner. Conceptual integration networks. *Cognitive Science*, 22(2):133–187, 1998.

G. Fauconnier and M. Turner. *The Way We Think: Conceptual Blending and the Mind's Hidden Complexities*. Basic Books, 2002. ISBN 978-0-465-08785-3.

B. Ganter and R. Wille. *Formal Concept Analysis*. Springer, 1999.

P. Gärdenfors. *Conceptual Spaces*. A Bradford Book, 2004.

R. W. Gibbs, Jr. Making good psychology out of blending theory. *Cognitive Linguistics*, 11(3–4):347–358, 2000.

J. Goguen. An introduction to algebraic semiotics, with applications to user interface design. In C. L. Nehaniv, editor, *Computation for Metaphors, Analogy, and Agents*, volume 1562 of *Lecture Notes in Computer Science*, pages 242–291. Springer, 1999.

J. Goguen. Towards a design theory for virtual worlds: Algebraic semiotics and scientific visualization as a case study. In C. Landauer and K. Bellman, editors, *Proceedings Conference on Virtual Worlds and Simulation (Phoenix AZ, 7–11 January 2001)*, pages 298–303. Society for Modelling and Simulation, 2001.

J. Goguen. What is a concept? In F. Dau, M.-L. Mugnier, and G. Stumme, editors, *Conceptual Structures: Common Semantics for Sharing Knowledge. 13th International Conference on Conceptual Structures, ICCS 2005, Kassel, Germany, July 17–22, 2005. Proceedings*, volume 3596, pages 52–77. Springer, 2005a.

J. Goguen. Information integration in institutions. In L. Moss, editor, *Jon Barwise Memorial Volume*, Bloomington, IN: Indiana University Press. Available at http://www.cs.ucsd.edu/users/goguen/pps/ifi04.pdf, 2004.

J. Goguen. Mathematical models of cognitive space and time. In D. Andler, Y. Ogawa, M. Okada, and S. Watanabe, editors, *Reasoning and Cognition*, volume 2 of *Interdisciplinary Conference Series on Reasoning Studies*. Keio University Press, 2006.

J. A. Goguen. A categorical manifesto. *Mathematical Structures in Computer Science*, 1:49–68, 1991.

J. A. Goguen and D. F. Harrell. Style: A computational and conceptual blending-based approach. In S. Argamon, K. Burns, and S. Dubnov, editors, *The Structure of Style. Algorithmic Approaches to Understanding Manner and Meaning*. Springer, 2010.

J. Hayman and T. Heindel. On pushouts of partial maps. In H. Giese and B. König, editors, *Graph Transformation — 7th International Conference, ICGT 2014, Held as Part of STAF 2014, York, UK, July 22–24, 2014. Proceedings*, volume 8571 of *Lecture Notes in Computer Science*, pages 177–191. Springer, 2014.

P. T. Johnstone. *Sketches of an Elephant: A Topos Theory Compendium. 2 Volumes*, volume 44 of *Oxford Logic Guides*. The Clarendon Press, Oxford University Press, Oxford, 2002.

W. Kahl. Collagory notes, version 1. SQRL Report 57, Software Quality Research Laboratory, McMaster University, 2010. URL http://www.cas.mcmaster.ca/sqrl/papers/SQRLreport57.pdf.

A. Koestler. *The Act of Creation*. Hutchinson & Co., 1964.

O. Kutz, T. Mossakowski, J. Hois, M. Bhatt, and J. Bateman. Ontological blending in DOL. In *Computational Creativity, Concept Invention, and General Intelligence — 1st International Workshop. International Workshop on Computational Creativity, Concept Invention, and General Intelligence (C3GI-12), First, located at ECAI 2012, August 27, Montpellier, France*. Publication Series of the Institute of Cognitive Science, 2012.

O. Kutz, F. Neuhaus, T. Mossakowski, and M. Codescu. Blending in the Hub — towards a collaborative concept invention platform. In *Proceedings of the Fifth International Conference on Computational Creativity ICCC 2014*, 2014.

S. Lack. A 2-categories companion. In *Towards higher categories*, volume 152 of *IMA Vol. Math. Appl.*, pages 105–191. Springer, New York, 2010. DOI: 10.1007/978-1-4419-1524-5_4.

T. Leinster. A survey of definitions of *n*-category. *Theory Appl. Categ.*, 10:1–70 (electronic), 2002.

S. Mac Lane. *Categories for the Working Mathematician*, volume 5 of *Graduate Texts in Mathematics*. Springer-Verlag, New York, second edition, 1998. ISBN 0-387-98403-8.

G. Mazzola, J. Park, and F. Thalmann. *Musical Creativity*. Computational Music Science. Springer, 2011.

C. McLarty. *Elementary Categories, Elementary Toposes*, volume 21 of *Oxford Logic Guides*. The Clarendon Press Oxford University Press, New York, 1992. ISBN 0-19-853392-6; 0-19-851473-5. Oxford Science Publications.

T. Mossakowski. Colimits of order-sorted specifications. In *Recent Trends in Algebraic Development Techniques (Tarquinia, 1997)*, volume 1376 of *Lecture Notes in Computer Science*, pages 316–332. Springer, Berlin, 1998.

T. Mossakowski, C. Maeder, and K. Lüttich. The Heterogeneous Tool Set. In O. Grumberg and M. Huth, editors, *Tools and Algorithms for the Construction and Analysis of Systems. 13th International Conference, TACAS 2007, Held as Part of the Joint European Conferences on Theory and Practice of Software, ETAPS 2007 Braga, Portugal, March 24 – April 1, 2007. Proceedings*, volume 4424 of *Lecture Notes in Computer Science*, pages 519–522. Springer, 2007.

S. Ontañón and E. Plaza. Amalgams: A formal approach for combining multiple case solutions. In I. Bichindaritz and S. Montani, editors, *Case-Based Reasoning. Research and Development, 18th International Conference on Case-Based Reasoning, ICCBR 2010, Alessandria, Italy, July 19–22, 2010. Proceedings*, volume 6176 of *Lecture Notes in Computer Science*, pages 257–271. Springer, 2010.

S. Ontañón and E. Plaza. Toward a knowledge transfer model of case-based inference. In *Proceedings of the Fifteenth International Florida Artificial Intelligence Research Society (FLAIRS)*. AAAI Press, 2012.

F. C. Pereira. *Creativity and Artificial Intelligence: A Conceptual Blending Approach*, volume 4 of *Applications of Cognitive Linguistics*. Mouton de Gruyter, 2007.

B. C. Pierce. *Basic Category Theory For Computer Scientists*. Foundations of Computing Series. MIT Press, Cambridge, MA, 1991. ISBN 0-262-66071-7.

A. Poigné. Elements of categorical reasoning: Products and coproducts and some other (co-)limits. In D. Pitt, S. Abramsky, A. Poigné, and D. Rydeheard, editors, *Category Theory and Computer Programming (Guildford, 1985)*, volume 240 of *Lecture Notes in Computer Science*, pages 16–42. Springer, Berlin, 1986. DOI: 10.1007/3-540-17162-2_114.

E. Robinson and G. Rosolini. Categories of partial maps. *Information and Computation*, 79(2):95–130, 1988.

D. Sannella and A. Tarlecki. *Foundations of Algebraic Specification and Formal Software Development*. Monographs in Theoretical Computer Science. An EATCS Series. Springer, 2012.

M. Schorlemmer and Y. Kalfoglou. Institutionalising ontology-based semantic integration. *Applied Ontology*, 3(3):131–150, 2008.

M. Schorlemmer, R. Confalonieri, and E. Plaza. The Yoneda path to the Buddhist monk blend. In *Proceedings of the Joint Ontology Workshops 2016 Episode 2: The French Summer of Ontology* co-located with the 9th International Conference on Formal Ontology in Information Systems (FOIS 2016), Annecy, France, July 6–9, 2016.

J. F. Sowa. *Knowledge Representation: Logical, Philosophical, and Computational Foundations*. Brooks/Cole, 2000.

P. Thagard. *Coherence in Thought and Action*. Life and Mind: Philosophical Issues in Biology and Psychology. MIT Press, 2000.

P. Thagard and T. C. Stewart. The AHA! experience: Creativity through emergent binding in neural networks. *Cognitive Science*, 35:1–33, 2011.

M. Turner. *The Origin of Ideas*. Oxford University Press, 2014.

T. Veale and D. O'Donoghue. Computation and blending. *Cognitive Linguistics*, 11 (3/4):253–281, 2000.

Chapter 2
Computational Aspects of Concept Invention[*]

Roberto Confalonieri, Enric Plaza, and Marco Schorlemmer

Abstract In this chapter, we present a computational framework that models concept invention. The framework is based on and extends conceptual blending. Apart from the blending mechanism modeling the creation of new concepts, the framework considers two extra dimensions, namely, origin and destination. For the former, we describe how a Rich Background supports the discovery of input concepts to be blended. For the latter, we show how arguments, promoting or demoting the values of an audience, to which the invention is headed, can be used to evaluate the candidate blends created. We also address the problem of how newly invented concepts are evaluated with respect to a Rich Background so as to decide which of them are to be accepted into a system of familiar concepts, and how this, in turn, may affect the previously accepted conceptualisation. As technique to tackle this problem we explore the applicability of Paul Thagard's computational theory of coherence, in particular, his notion of *conceptual coherence*. The process model is exemplified using two structured representation languages, namely, order-sorted feature terms and description logic.

Roberto Confalonieri
Free University of Bozen-Bolzano, Faculty of Computer Science, Dominikanerplatz 3, 39100, Bozen-Bolzano, Italy. e-mail: Roberto.Confalonieri@unibz.it

Enric Plaza · Marco Schorlemmer
Artificial Intelligence Research Institute, Spanish National Research Council (IIIA-CSIC), Campus UAB, c/ Can Planes s/n, 08193, Bellaterra, Catalonia (Spain). e-mail: enric@iiia.csic.es, marco@iiia.csic.es

[*] This chapter draws on material published in (Confalonieri et al., 2016b) and (Schorlemmer et al., 2016).

© Springer Nature Switzerland AG 2018
R. Confalonieri et al. (eds.), *Concept Invention*, Computational Synthesis
and Creative Systems, https://doi.org/10.1007/978-3-319-65602-1_2

2.1 A Process Model for Concept Invention

Existing computational models for concept invention (see Section 2.7 for an overview) especially focus on the core mechanism of blending, that is, how blends are created, and re-interpret the optimality principles to evaluate the blends. In this chapter, we propose that a computational model also needs to deal with two extra dimensions to which we refer as the *origin* and *destination* of concept invention. The origin considers from where and how input spaces are selected, whereas the destination considers to whom the creation is headed.

A first assumption is that there is no creation *ex nihilo*. This is a widely held assumption in human creativity, be it scientific or artistic; we apply this assumption to any creative agent be it human or artificial. Specifically, combinatorial creativity depends on the experience and expertise of the creative agent (human or artificial) in a given domain, which in turn depends on the externally established 'state of the art' and prevalent assumptions, biases, and preferences on that domain. We express this assumption by claiming that every creative process has an *origin*, where the notion of origin is intended to capture and contain these individual and social preexisting tenets and assets that can potentially be used in a creative process. Specifically, we will model the notion of origin in a particular instance of a creative process as the Rich Background possessed by a creative agent on a particular domain.

The second assumption is that a given creative process has usually a purpose in creating something new. We express this assumption by saying that a creative process has a *destination*. A destination is different from a goal as usually understood in problem solving and Artificial Intelligence systems, where goals are related to the notion of satisfaction of specified sets of requirements or properties. A destination, in our approach, is a notion that is related, for instance in artistic domains, to the notions of audience or genre; different audiences or genres value different sets of properties or aspects as being worthy or even indispensable. Although we do not assume that a creative process has a specific goal, we do assume that a creative process is purposeful in producing an output that is destined to some 'target' audience, be it jazz aficionados in music, or academic colleagues in science. Specifically, we will model the notion of destination as the collection of values held dear by an intended audience. This approach gives us enough concretion to be able to talk about adequacy, significance, or interest of a creative outcome (if those are values held by an audience), while having enough leeway to encompass differences in subjective or individual appreciation or evaluation of a creative outcome by members of an actual audience.

To this end, we propose the following process model of concept invention (Figure 2.1):

- **Rich Background and Discovery**: The origin consists of a Rich Background, the set of concepts available to be blended. This set is finite but complex, diverse, polymathic and heterogeneous. Concepts are associated with a background, understood as the education, experience, and social circumstances of

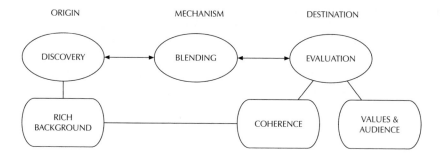

ORIGIN   MECHANISM   DESTINATION

Fig. 2.1: A process model for concept invention

a (creative) individual. The Rich Background supports a discovery process that finds pairs of concepts that can be blended.

- **Blending**: Conceptual blending is the mechanism according to which two concepts are combined into a blended concept. Blending is here characterised in terms of amalgams, a notion that was developed for combining cases in case-based reasoning (Ontañón and Plaza, 2010). Conceptual blending is modeled in terms of an amalgam-based workflow. The blending of two concepts may result in a large number of blends, that need to be evaluated.
- **Arguments, Values, Audiences and Evaluation**: Values are properties expected from a good blend. Values are considered as points of view and can be of different kinds, e.g., moral, aesthetic, etc. A destination or audience is characterised by a preference relation over these values.[2] Arguments in favor or against a blend are built to evaluate the generated blends. An argument can promote or demote a value. In this way, the blends are evaluated depending on the audience for which they are created.
- **Conceptual Coherence and Evaluation**: The notion of coherence developed by Thagard (2000), when used to explain human reasoning, proposes that humans *accept* or *reject* a cognition (a percept, image, proposition, concept, etc.) depending on how much it contributes to maximising the number of constraints, that are imposed by situational context and other relevant cognitions. Among the different types of coherence proposed by Thagard (2000), conceptual coherence can be used to evaluate conceptual blends by measuring to what extent a blend coheres or incoheres with the Rich Background.

The rest of the chapter is organised as follows. The first four sections develop a general model that enacts the concept invention process depicted above. In Section 2.2, we model the notion of Rich Background and similarity-based discovery. In Section 2.3 we characterise a blend in terms of amalgams. In Section 2.4, we propose an argumentation framework based on values and audiences that can be used to

---

[2] Therefore, if the values are for example {*jazz,classical*}, then two audiences can be defined, one where *jazz* is preferred to *classical*, and another one, where *classical* is preferred to *jazz*. We will formalise these notions in Section 2.4.

evaluate conceptual blends by means of decision-criteria. Section 2.5 describes the computational coherence theory by Thagard (2000) and how it can be used in blend evaluation. In Section 2.6, we describe two instantiations of the process model by using two structured representation languages, feature-terms and description logic. Section 2.7 presents a survey of existing computational models for concept invention and how our concept invention process relates. Finally, Section 2.8 concludes the chapter.

2.2 Rich Background and Discovery

In cognitive theories of conceptual blending, input spaces to be blended are givens that represent how humans package some relevant information in the context in which the blend is created.

In our process model, an input space is a concept belonging to a library of concepts that we call Rich Background. Concepts can be represented by means of structured representations such as feature terms (Smolka and Aït-Kaci, 1989; Carpenter, 1992) or description logics (Baader et al., 2003), as we shall see in Section 2.6. The packaging of some relevant information corresponds to a discovery process that takes certain properties, which the blends need to satisfy, into account. The discovery takes a query as input, looks for concepts in the Rich Background, and returns an ordered set of pairs of concepts that can be blended.

2.2.1 Rich Background

The Rich Background consists of a finite set of concepts $\mathscr{C} = \{\psi_1, \psi_2, \ldots, \psi_n\}$ specified according to a language $\mathscr{L}$ for which a *subsumption* relation between formulas (or descriptions) of $\mathscr{L}$ can be defined.

Intuitively, the subsumption between formulas captures the idea of generality or specificity between two concepts. We say that a concept ψ_1 is subsumed by a concept ψ_2, denoted as $\psi_1 \sqsubseteq \psi_2$, if all information in ψ_1 is also in ψ_2. The subsumption relation induces a partial order on the set of all concept descriptions that can be formed using $\mathscr{L}$, i.e., the pair $\langle \mathscr{L}, \sqsubseteq \rangle$ is a *poset* for a given set of formulas. Additionally, $\mathscr{L}$ contains the elements $\bot$ and $\top$ representing the infimum element or supremum element w.r.t. the subsumption order, respectively.

Given the subsumption relation, for any two concepts ψ_1 and ψ_2, we can define the *anti-unification* and *unification* as their *least general generalisation* (LGG) and *most general specialisation* (MGS) respectively. These operations are relevant for defining both a similarity measure for comparing concepts, and the blend of two concepts as an amalgam (Confalonieri et al., 2018, 2016b).

Definition 2.1 (Least General Generalisation). The least general generalisation of two concepts ψ_1 and ψ_2, denoted as $\psi_1 \sqcap \psi_2$, is defined as the most specific concept that subsumes both:

$$\psi_1 \sqcap \psi_2 = \{\psi \mid \psi_1 \sqsubseteq \psi \wedge \psi_2 \sqsubseteq \psi \text{ and } \nexists \psi' : \psi' \sqsubset \psi \wedge \psi_1 \sqsubseteq \psi' \wedge \psi_2 \sqsubseteq \psi'\}$$

The least general generalisation encapsulates all the information that is common to both ψ_1 and ψ_2. For this reason, it is relevant for defining a similarity measure. If two concepts have nothing in common, then $\psi_1 \sqcap \psi_2 = \bot$. The complementary operation to the least general generalisation is the most general specialisation of two descriptions.

Definition 2.2 (Most General Specialisation). The most general specialisation of two concepts ψ_1 and ψ_2, denoted as $\psi_1 \sqcup \psi_2$, is defined as the most general concept that is subsumed by both:

$$\psi_1 \sqcup \psi_2 = \{\psi \mid \psi \sqsubseteq \psi_1 \wedge \psi \sqsubseteq \psi_2 \text{ and } \nexists \psi' : \psi \sqsubset \psi' \wedge \psi' \sqsubseteq \psi_1 \wedge \psi' \sqsubseteq \psi_2\}$$

If two descriptions have contradictory information, then they do not have a most general specialisation.

The least general generalisation and the most general specification can be characterised as operations over a refinement graph of descriptions. The *refinement graph* is derived from the poset $\langle \mathscr{L}, \sqsubseteq \rangle$ as the poset $\langle \mathscr{G}, \prec \rangle$, where $\psi_1 \prec \psi_2$ denotes that ψ_2 is a generalisation refinement of ψ_1 (or equivalently ψ_1 is a specialisation refinement of ψ_2).

The refinement graph is defined by means of a *generalisation refinement operator* γ.

$$\gamma(\psi) \subseteq \{\psi' \in \mathscr{L} \mid \psi \sqsubseteq \psi'\}$$

The above definition states that γ is an operation that generalises a description to a set of descriptions. The refinement graph, then, is a directed graph whose nodes are descriptions, and for which there is an edge from a description ψ_1 to a description ψ_2, whenever $\psi_2 \in \gamma(\psi_1)$.

The refinement graph can be more or less complex depending on the representation language adopted and the type of refinement operator used.

A refinement operator γ can be characterised according to some desirable properties (van der Laag and Nienhuys-Cheng, 1998). We say that γ is:

- *locally finite*, if the number of generalisations generated for any given element by the operator is finite, that is, $\forall \psi \in \mathscr{L} : \gamma(\psi)$ is finite;
- *proper*, if an element is not equivalent to any of its generalisations, i.e., $\forall \psi_1, \psi_2 \in \mathscr{L}$, if $\psi_2 \in \gamma(\psi_1)$, then ψ_1 and ψ_2 are not equivalent;
- *complete*, if there are no generalisations that are not generated by the operator, i.e., $\forall \psi_1, \psi_2 \in \mathscr{L}$ it holds that if $\psi_1 \sqsubseteq \psi_2$, then $\psi_2 \in \gamma^*(\psi_1)$ (where $\gamma^*(\psi_1)$ denotes the set of all elements which can be reached from ψ_1 by means of γ in zero or a finite number of steps).

Designing a generalisation refinement operator that fulfills all the above properties is not possible in general, because one usually has to sacrifice completeness for finiteness, and let the computation of the operator terminate. This is the case also for the generalisation refinement operators that we design for the ordered-sorted feature terms and description logic (see Section 2.6.1 and Section 2.6.2 respectively).

2.2.2 Similarity-Based Discovery

The main idea behind the similarity-based discovery is that, for each concept ψ_i in the Rich Background, we measure how ψ_i and a concept ψ_q—modeling a query— are similar and we use this measure to rank the results. The similarity between two descriptions can be defined by means of their LGG.

As previously stated, the least general generalisation of two descriptions $\psi_1 \sqcap \psi_2$ is a symbolic representation of the information shared by ψ_1 and ψ_2. It can be used to measure the similarity between concepts in a quantitative way. The refinement graph allows us to estimate the quantity of information of any description ψ. It is the length of the (minimal) *generalisation path* that leads from ψ to the most general term $\top$.

Definition 2.3 (Generalisation Path). A finite sequence of descriptions $\langle \psi_1, \dots, \psi_m \rangle$ is a generalisation path $\psi_1 \overset{\gamma}{\to} \psi_m$ between ψ_1 and ψ_m when for each $1 \leq i \leq m$, $\psi_{i+1} \in \gamma(\psi_i)$. The length of $\langle \psi_1, \dots, \psi_m \rangle$ is denoted as $\lambda(\psi_1 \overset{\gamma}{\to} \psi_m)$.

Therefore, the length $\lambda(\psi_1 \sqcap \psi_2 \overset{\gamma}{\to} \top)$ estimates the informational content that is common to ψ_1 and ψ_2. In order to define a similarity measure, we need to compare what is common to ψ_1 and ψ_2 with what is not common. To this end, we take the lengths $\lambda(\psi_1 \overset{\gamma}{\to} \psi_1 \sqcap \psi_2)$ and $\lambda(\psi_2 \overset{\gamma}{\to} \psi_1 \sqcap \psi_2)$ into account (see Figure 2.2). Then a similarity measure can be defined as follows.

Definition 2.4 (LGG-Based similarity). The LGG-based similarity between two descriptions ψ_1 and ψ_2, denoted by $S_\lambda(\psi_1, \psi_2)$, is:

$$S_\lambda(\psi_1, \psi_2) = \frac{\lambda(\psi_1 \sqcap \psi_2 \overset{\gamma}{\to} \top)}{\lambda(\psi_1 \sqcap \psi_2 \overset{\gamma}{\to} \top) + \lambda(\psi_1 \overset{\gamma}{\to} \psi_1 \sqcap \psi_2) + \lambda(\psi_2 \overset{\gamma}{\to} \psi_1 \sqcap \psi_2)}$$

The measure S_λ estimates the ratio between the amount of information that is shared and the total information content. From a computational point of view, S_λ requires to compute two things: the LGG and the three lengths defined in the above equation. The computation of the LGG depends on the language representation used (see Section 2.6).

Given the above definitions, the discovery of concepts can be implemented by the following discovery algorithm.

Algorithm Discovery($\mathscr{C}, \gamma, \psi_q$)
  ForEach ($\psi_j \in \mathscr{C}$) Do
    $\lambda_i = S_\lambda(\psi_j, \psi_q)$
    $\mathscr{T} = \mathscr{T} \,\dot{\cup}\, \langle \psi_j, \lambda_j \rangle$

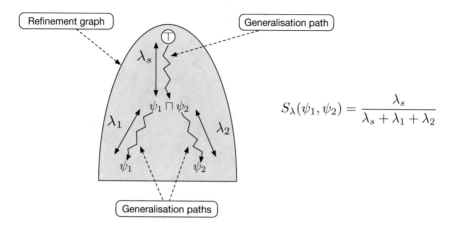

Fig. 2.2: Illustration of the LGG-based similarity, adapted from (Ontañón and Plaza, 2012)

EndForEach
$\mathscr{P} = conceptsPairs(\mathscr{T})$
Return $\mathscr{P}$
EndAlgorithm

The algorithm accepts a Rich Background of concepts $\mathscr{C}$, a query ψ_q, and a generalisation operator γ as inputs. $\cup$ ranks the concepts discovered according to their similarity value λ_j.

The algorithm returns a ranked set of pairs of concepts. This ranking can be done according to different strategies. One way is to build all pairs of concepts and to rank them in a lexicographical order. The function *conceptsPairs* builds $\mathscr{P}$, as the set of pairs of concepts $\langle(\psi_j, \lambda_j), (\psi_k, \lambda_k)\rangle$ in which $\lambda_j \geq \lambda_k$ $(j \neq k)$.

2.3 Blends as Amalgams

The computational model of concept blending is based on the notion of *amalgams* (Ontañón and Plaza, 2010). This notion was proposed in the context of case-based reasoning. Amalgams have also been used to model analogy (Besold and Plaza, 2015). According to this approach, input concepts are generalised until a generic space is found, and pairs of generalised input concepts are 'unified' to create blends.

Formally, the notion of amalgams can be defined in any representation language $\mathscr{L}$ for which a subsumption relation $\sqsubseteq$ between formulas (or descriptions) of $\mathscr{L}$ can be defined, together with the least general generalisation operation—playing the role of the generic space—and a most general specialisation (see Definitions 2.1 and 2.2).

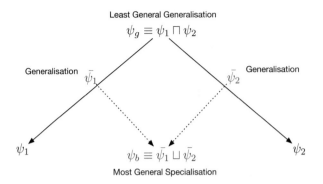

Fig. 2.3: A diagram of a blend ψ_b from inputs ψ_1 and ψ_2

A *blend* of two descriptions is a new description that contains *parts from these two descriptions*. For instance, an amalgam of 'a red French sedan' and 'a blue German minivan' is 'a red German sedan'; clearly, there are always multiple possibilities for amalgams, like 'a blue French minivan'.

For our purposes, we define a *blend* of two input descriptions as follows:

Definition 2.5 (Blend as Amalgam). A description $\psi_b \in \mathscr{L}$ is a blend of two inputs ψ_1 and ψ_2 (with LGG $\psi_g = \psi_1 \sqcap \psi_2$) if there exist two generalisations $\bar{\psi}_1$ and $\bar{\psi}_2$ such that:

1. $\psi_g \sqsubseteq \bar{\psi}_1 \sqsubseteq \psi_1$,
2. $\psi_g \sqsubseteq \bar{\psi}_2 \sqsubseteq \psi_2$, and
3. $\psi_b \equiv \bar{\psi}_1 \sqcup \bar{\psi}_2$.

The above definition is illustrated in Figure 2.3, where the LGG of the inputs is indicated as ψ_g, and the blend ψ_b is the unification of two concrete generalisations $\bar{\psi}_1$ and $\bar{\psi}_2$ of the inputs. Equality ($\equiv$) here should be understood as $\sqsubseteq$-equivalence, that is, $\psi_1 \equiv \psi_2$ iff $\psi_1 \sqsubseteq \psi_2$ and $\psi_2 \sqsubseteq \psi_1$.

Usually one is interested only in *maximal blends*, i.e., in those blends that contain the maximal information of their inputs. A blend ψ_b of two inputs ψ_1 and ψ_2 is maximal if there is no other blend ψ_b' of ψ_1 and ψ_2 such that $\psi_b \sqsubset \psi_b'$. The reason why one is interested in maximal blends is that a maximal blend captures as much information as possible from the inputs. Moreover, any non-maximal blend can be obtained by generalising a maximal blend.

However, the number of blends that satisfies the above definition can still be very large and selection criteria for filtering and ordering them are therefore needed. Fauconnier and Turner (2002) discussed optimality principles, however, the computational realisation of these principles lacks some flexibility, especially if we think that blend evaluation should not be limited to a merely accept or reject affair. It should be the output of a more open discussion, and the reasons that lead to that decision need to be made explicit.

To this end, we propose two alternative tools for blend evaluation. On the one hand, by taking the notion of argument into account, we define an argument-based decision making framework that allows us to select the best blend w.r.t. some values and audiences. On the other hand, we explore how coherence theory can serve for guiding the process of conceptual blending and for evaluating conceptual blends.

2.4 Arguments, Values and Audiences

An argument is a central notion in several frameworks for reasoning about defeasible information (Dung, 1995; Pollock, 1992), decision making (Amgoud and Prade, 2009; Bonet and Geffner, 1996), practical reasoning (Atkinson et al., 2004), and modelling different types of dialogues such as persuasion (Bench-Capon, 2003). In most existing works on argumentation, an argument is a reason for believing a statement, choosing an option, or doing an action. Depending on the application domain, an argument is either considered as a purely abstract entity, or it is a logical proof for a statement where the proof is built from a knowledge base.

In our model, arguments are reasons for accepting or rejecting a given blend. They are built by the agent when calculating the different values associated with a blend. Values are considered as points of view, and can have different origins, e.g., they can be moral, aesthetic, etc.

Generally, there can be several values $\mathscr{V} = \{v_1, \ldots, v_k\}$. Each value is associated with a degree that belongs to the scale $\Delta = (0, \ldots, 1]$, where 0 and 1 are considered the worst and the best degree respectively.

Values play a different role depending on the target or audience towards which the creation is headed. Audiences are characterised by the values and by preferences among these values. Given a set of values $\mathscr{V}$, there are potentially as many audiences as there are orderings on $\mathscr{V}$.

Definition 2.6 (Audience). An audience is a binary relation $\mathscr{R} \subseteq \mathscr{V} \times \mathscr{V}$ which is irreflexive, asymmetric, and transitive. We say that v_i is preferred to v_j in the audience $\mathscr{R}$, denoted as $v_i \succ_{\mathscr{R}} v_j$, if $\langle v_i, v_j \rangle \in \mathscr{R}$.

Definition 2.7 (Cover Relation). We say that a value v_j covers v_i in the audience $\mathscr{R}$, denoted as $v_i \succ\!\!\succ_{\mathscr{R}} v_j$, if $v_i \succ_{\mathscr{R}} v_j$ and $\not\exists v_{i'}$ such that $v_i \succ_{\mathscr{R}} v_{i'} \succ_{\mathscr{R}} v_j$.

Given a blend, an argument is generated for each value. The degree of the value characterises the 'polarity' of the argument which can be *pro* or *con* a blend. Arguments pro promote a blend whereas arguments con demote it. Given a set of blends $\mathscr{B}$, the tuple $\langle \mathscr{B}, \mathscr{V}, \Delta \rangle$ will be called an argumentation framework.

Definition 2.8 (Argument). Let $\langle \mathscr{B}, \mathscr{V}, \Delta \rangle$ be an argumentation framework. Then:

- An *argument pro* a blend b is a tuple $\langle (v, \delta), b \rangle$ where $v \in \mathscr{V}$, $\delta \in \Delta$ and $0.5 \leq \delta \leq 1$
- An *argument con* b is a pair $\langle (v, \delta), b \rangle$ where $v \in \mathscr{V}$, $\delta \in \Delta$ and $0 < \delta < 0.5$

A function Val returns the value v associated with an argument and a function Deg returns δ.

The blend evaluation can be formulated as a decision problem in which one has to decide an order relation $\succeq_{\mathscr{B}}$ on the set of candidate blends $\mathscr{B}$. The definition of this relation is based on the set of arguments pro and con associated with the candidate blends. Depending on the kind of arguments that are considered and how they are handled, different decision criteria can be defined (Amgoud and Prade, 2009):

- **Unipolar decision criteria:** they focus either only on arguments pro or arguments con;
- **Bipolar decision criteria:** they take both arguments pro and con into account;
- **Meta-criteria:** they aggregate arguments pro and con into a meta-argument.

In what follows, we denote the set of arguments pro and con as $\mathscr{A}_p = \{\alpha_1, \ldots, \alpha_n\}$ and $\mathscr{A}_c = \{\alpha_1, \ldots, \alpha_m\}$ respectively. Besides, we assume to have the following functions: $\mathscr{M}_p : \mathscr{B} \to 2^{\mathscr{A}_p}$ and $\mathscr{M}_c : \mathscr{B} \to 2^{\mathscr{A}_c}$ that return the set of arguments pro and the set of arguments con associated with a blend respectively; $\mathscr{M} : \mathscr{B} \to 2^{\mathscr{A}_p \cup \mathscr{A}_c}$ that returns all arguments associated with a blend.

A basic decision criterion for comparing candidate blends can be defined by comparing the number of arguments pro associated with them.

Definition 2.9. Let $b_1, b_2 \in \mathscr{B}$. $b_1 \succeq_{\mathscr{B}} b_2$ if and only if $|\mathscr{M}_p(b_1)| \geq |\mathscr{M}_p(b_2)|$.

Notice that the above criterion guarantees that any pair of blends can be compared.

When the audience is taken into account, one may think of preferring a blend that has an argument pro whose value is preferred to the values of any argument pro the other blends.

Definition 2.10. Let $b_1, b_2 \in \mathscr{B}$. $b_1 \succeq_{\mathscr{B}} b_2$ if and only if $\exists \alpha \in \mathscr{M}_p(b_1)$ such that $\forall \alpha' \in \mathscr{M}_p(b_2)$, $\mathrm{Val}(\alpha) \succ_{\mathscr{R}} \mathrm{Val}(\alpha')$.

In the above definition, $\succeq_{\mathscr{B}}$ depends on the relation $\succ_{\mathscr{R}}$. Since $\succ_{\mathscr{R}}$ is a preference relation, some of the values of the arguments can be incomparable. In this case, b_1 and b_2 will not be comparable, either. This definition can be relaxed, for instance, by ignoring these arguments.

The counter-part decision criteria of Definitions 2.9-2.10 for the case of arguments con can be defined in a similar way.

Definition 2.11. Let $b_1, b_2 \in \mathscr{B}$. $b_1 \succeq_{\mathscr{B}} b_2$ if and only if $|\mathscr{M}_c(b_1)| \leq |\mathscr{M}_c(b_2)|$.

Definition 2.12. Let $b_1, b_2 \in \mathscr{B}$. $b_1 \succeq_{\mathscr{B}} b_2$ if and only if $\exists \alpha \in \mathscr{M}_c(b_1)$ such that $\forall \alpha' \in \mathscr{M}_c(b_2)$, $\mathrm{Val}(\alpha) \succ_{\mathscr{R}} \mathrm{Val}(\alpha')$.

In the case of bipolar decision criteria, we can combine the criterion dealing with arguments pro with the criterion dealing with arguments con.

Definition 2.13. Let $b_1, b_2 \in \mathscr{B}$. $b_1 \succeq_{\mathscr{B}} b_2$ if and only if $|\mathscr{M}_p(b_1)| \geq |\mathscr{M}_p(b_2)|$ and $|\mathscr{M}_c(b_1)| \leq |\mathscr{M}_c(b_2)|$.

Unfortunately, the above definition does not ensure that we can compare all the blends.

Finally, meta-criteria for deciding which blends are preferred can be defined by aggregating arguments pro and con into a meta-argument. Then, comparing two blends amounts to comparing the resulting meta-arguments. A simple criterion can be defined by aggregating the degrees of the arguments associated with a blend.

Definition 2.14. Let $b_1, b_2 \in \mathcal{B}$. $b_1 \succeq_{\mathcal{B}} b_2$ if and only if

$$\sum_{\alpha \in \mathcal{M}(b_1)} \text{Deg}(\alpha) \geq \sum_{\alpha' \in \mathcal{M}(b_2)} \text{Deg}(\alpha')$$

This definition can be extended to take the audience into account. To this end, we consider a rank function that maps each value of $\mathcal{R}$ to an integer. The rank function is defined as follows:

$$\text{Rank}_{\mathcal{R}}(v) = \begin{cases} 1 & \text{if } \nexists v' \text{ s.t. } v' \succ_{\mathcal{R}} v \\ \max_{v' \succ_{\mathcal{R}} v} \{\text{Rank}_{\mathcal{R}}(v')\} + 1 & \text{otherwise} \end{cases}$$

Essentially, Rank counts how many values a certain value covers. This ranking is then used to define the following audience-based aggregation decision criterion.

Definition 2.15. Let $b_1, b_2 \in \mathcal{B}$. $b_1 \succeq_{\mathcal{B}} b_2$ if and only if

$$\sum_{\alpha \in \mathcal{M}(b_1)} \frac{\text{Deg}(\alpha)}{\text{Rank}_{\mathcal{R}}(\text{Val}(\alpha))} \geq \sum_{\alpha' \in \mathcal{M}(b_2)} \frac{\text{Deg}(\alpha')}{\text{Rank}_{\mathcal{R}}(\text{Val}(\alpha'))}$$

This last definition is based on an audience-based aggregation that sums the arguments' degrees by taking the preference order over values into account. This definition also guarantees that all the blends are comparable.

2.5 Coherence Theory

Thagard addresses the problem of determining which pieces of information, such as hypotheses, beliefs, propositions or concepts, should be accepted and which should be rejected based on the relationships of coherence and incoherence among them. That is, when two elements cohere, they tend to be accepted together or rejected together, and when two elements incohere, one tends to be accepted while the other tends to be rejected (Thagard, 2000).

This can be reformulated as a constraint satisfaction problem as follows. Pairs of elements that cohere form positive constraints, and pairs of elements that incohere form negative constraints. If we partition the set of pieces of information we are dealing with into a set of accepted elements and a set of rejected elements, then a positive constraint is satisfied if both elements of the constraint are either among the accepted elements or among the rejected ones; and a negative constraint is satisfied if one element of the constraint is among the accepted ones and the other is among the rejected ones. The coherence problem is to find the partition that maximises the number of satisfied constraints.

Note that in general we may not be able to partition a set of elements so as to satisfy *all* constraints, thus ending up accepting elements that incohere between them or rejecting an element that coheres with an accepted one. The objective is to minimise these undesired cases. The coherence problem is known to be NP-complete, though there exist algorithms that find good enough solutions of the coherence problem while remaining fairly efficient.

Depending on the kind of pieces of information we start from, and on the way the coherence and incoherence between these pieces of information is determined, we will be dealing with different kinds of coherence problems. So, in *explanatory coherence* we seek to determine the acceptance or rejection of hypotheses based on how they cohere and incohere with given evidence or with competing hypotheses; in *deductive coherence* we seek to determine the acceptance or rejection of beliefs based on how they cohere and incohere due to deductive entailment or contradiction; in *analogical coherence* we seek to determine the acceptance or rejection of mapping hypotheses based on how they cohere or incohere in terms of structure; and in *conceptual coherence* we seek to determine the acceptance or rejection of concepts based on how they cohere or incohere as the result of the positive or negative associations that can be established between them. Thagard discusses these and other kinds of coherence.

Although Thagard provides a clear technical description of the coherence problem as a constraint satisfaction problem, and he enumerates concrete principles that characterise different kinds of coherences, he does not clarify the actual nature of the coherence and incoherence relations that arise between pieces of information, nor does he suggest a precise formalisation of the principles he discusses. Joseph et al. (2010) have proposed a concrete formalisation and realisation of deductive coherence, which they applied to tackle the problem of norm adoption in a normative multi-agent system. Here, we will focus on the problem of conceptual coherence and its applicability to conceptual blending as we shall see in Section 2.6.2.

2.5.1 Coherence Graphs

In this section we give precise definitions of the concepts intuitively introduced in the previous section.

Definition 2.16. A *coherence graph* is an edge-weighted, undirected graph $G = \langle V, E, w \rangle$, where:

1. V is a finite set of nodes representing pieces of information.
2. $E \subseteq V^{(2)}$ (where $V^{(2)} = \{\{u,v\} \mid u,v \in V\}$) is a finite set of edges representing the coherence or incoherence between pieces of information.

3. $w : E \rightarrow [-1,1] \setminus \{0\}$ is an edge-weighted function that assigns a value to the coherence between pieces of information.

Edges of coherence graphs are also called *constraints*.

When we partition the set V of vertices of a coherence graph (i.e., the set of pieces of information) into a set A of accepted elements and a set $R = V \setminus A$ of rejected elements, then we can say when a constraint—an edge between vertices—is satisfied or not by the partition.

Definition 2.17. Given a coherence graph $G = \langle V, E, w \rangle$, and a partition (A, R) of V, the set of *satisfied constraints* $C_{(A,R)} \subseteq E$ is given by:

$$C_{(A,R)} = \left\{ \{u,v\} \in E \; \middle| \; \begin{array}{l} u \in A \text{ iff } v \in A, \text{ whenever } w(\{u,v\}) > 0 \\ u \in A \text{ iff } v \in R, \text{ whenever } w(\{u,v\}) < 0 \end{array} \right\}$$

All other constraints (i.e., those in $E \setminus C_{(A,R)}$) are said to be *unsatisfied*.

The coherence problem is to find the partition of vertices that satisfies as many constraints as possible, i.e., to find the partition that maximises the coherence value defined as follows, which makes coherence independent of the size of the coherence graph.

Definition 2.18. Given a coherence graph $G = \langle V, E, w \rangle$, the *coherence of a partition* (A, R) of V is given by

$$\kappa(G, (A,R)) = \frac{\displaystyle\sum_{\{u,v\} \in C_{(A,R)}} |w(\{u,v\})|}{|E|}$$

Notice that there may not exist a unique partition with a maximum coherence value. Actually, at least two partitions have the same coherence value, since $\kappa(G, (A,R)) = \kappa(G, (R,A))$ for any partition (A, R) of V.

2.5.2 Blend Evaluation by Means of Coherence

This section describes how coherence is used to evaluate blends. The overall idea is to compute the coherence graph and maximising partitions for each blend, and use the maximal coherence degree of the coherence graphs to rank the blends.

The process of evaluating blends according to conceptual coherence can be described as follows:

1. Given two input concepts, we generate a candidate blend according to Definition 2.5.

2. We form the coherence graph using the input concepts and the blend.[3]
3. We compute the coherence maximising partitions according to Definition 2.18 and we associate it to the blend.
4. We repeat this procedure for all the blends that can be generated from the mental spaces.
5. "Good" blends are those with maximal coherence degree.

Once the maximising partitions are computed, the coherence of the blend could be measured in terms of the coherence value of the coherence-maximising partitions. The degree of the coherence graph directly measures how much a blend coheres with the Rich Background.

Definition 2.19. Let $G = \langle V, E, w \rangle$ be the coherence graph of a blend B and let $\mathscr{P}$ be the set of partitions of G. The maximal coherence value of B of G is $\deg(B) = \max_{P \in \mathscr{P}} \{\kappa(G, P)\}$.

This maximal coherence value can be used to rank blends as follows.

Definition 2.20. For each $b_1, b_2 \in \mathscr{B}$, we say that b_1 is preferred to b_2 ($b_1 \succeq_{\mathscr{C}} b_2$) if and only if $\deg(b_1) \geq \deg(b_2)$.

The above criterion guarantees that any pair of blends can be compared.

2.6 Exemplifying the Process Model

In this section, we exemplify the process of concept invention making use of two use-cases, modeled according to two structured representation languages, i.e., feature terms and description logic.

First, we show how a Rich Background of concepts representing computer icons is modeled in terms of feature terms and how conceptual blending can be used to model the creation of new computer icons. Following the process model, computer icons belonging to a Rich Background of icons are retrieved using a similarity measure (see Section 2.2); new blended icons are generated as amalgams (see Section 2.3), and evaluated by means of the argumentation framework introduced in Section 2.4.

Second, we exemplify how a certain form of coherence of Thagard, namely conceptual coherence, can be used to evaluate how new conceptual blends cohere w.r.t. a Rich Background of concepts. To this end, we propose a formalisation of conceptual coherence for concepts represented in the $\mathscr{AL}$ description logic, and explore by means of an illustrative example the role coherence may play in blend evaluation.

---

[3] This depends on the representation language used and the type of coherence considered. In Section 2.6, we show how a coherence graph for conceptual coherence can be built from a Rich Background of $\mathscr{AL}$ concepts.

$$x_1 : \text{ICON} \begin{bmatrix} form = \left\{ \begin{array}{l} x_2 : \text{MAGNIFYINGGLASS} \begin{bmatrix} action = x_4 \\ on = x_3 \end{bmatrix} \\[2ex] x_3 : \text{HARDDISK}\begin{bmatrix} objectType = x_5 \end{bmatrix} \end{array} \right\} \\[4ex] meaning = \left\{ \begin{array}{l} x_4 : \text{SEARCH} \\ x_5 : \text{HARDDRIVE} \end{array} \right\} \end{bmatrix}$$

(a) Feature term representation of a computer icon

(b) Examples of computer icons

Fig. 2.4: Rich Background about computer icons

2.6.1 Creating Computer Icon Concepts

We assume that concept blending is the implicit process which governs the creative behavior of icon designers who *create* new icons by blending existing icons and signs. To this end, we propose a simple semiotic system for modeling computer icons. We consider computer icons as combinations of signs (e.g., document, magnifying glass, arrow, etc.) that are described in terms of *meanings*. Meanings convey *actions-in-the-world* or *types of objects* and are associated to signs. Signs are related by sign-patterns modeled as qualitative spatial relations such as *on*, *left*, etc.

2.6.1.1 A Rich Background of Computer Icons

Let the Rich Background be a collection of computer icons. We assume that computer icons are described in terms of *form* and a *meaning*. The form consists of a finite set of signs which are related by spatial relationships. Figure 2.4b(I) shows an example of an icon in which two signs, a MAGNIFYINGGLASS and a HARDDISK, are related by relation *on*. The meaning, on the other hand, is the interpretation that is given to an icon. For instance, a possible meaning associated to the icon in Figure 2.4b(I) is SEARCH-HARDDRIVE. We allow a sign to have different interpretations depending on the icons in which it is used.

We shall model the Rich Background by means of a finite set $\mathscr{C}$ of feature terms (Smolka and Aït-Kaci, 1989; Carpenter, 1992), each representing a concept. Here, feature terms are defined over a signature $\Sigma = \langle \mathscr{S}, \mathscr{F}, \preceq, \mathscr{X} \rangle$, where $\mathscr{S}$ is finite set of sort symbols, including $\top$ and $\bot$, which represent the most specific and the most general sort, respectively; $\mathscr{F}$ is a finite set of feature symbols; $\preceq$ is an order relation inducing an inheritance hierarchy such that $\bot \preceq s \preceq \top$, for all $s \in \mathscr{S}$; and $\mathscr{X}$ is a denumerable set of variables. Then, a feature term ψ has the form:

$$\psi := x : s[f_1 = \Psi_1, \dots, f_n = \Psi_n]$$

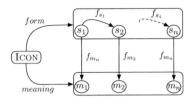

Fig. 2.5: Feature term representation of a computer icon

with $n \geq 0$, and where $x \in \mathcal{X}$ is called the root variable of ψ (denoted as root(ψ)), $s \in \mathcal{S}$ is the sort of x (denoted as sort(x)), and, for all j with $1 \leq j \leq n$, $f_j \in \mathcal{F}$ are the features of x (denoted as features(x)) and the values[4] Ψ_j of the features are finite, non-empty sets of feature terms and/or variables (provided they are root variables of feature terms occurring in ψ). When the set of values of a feature is a singleton set, we will omit the curly brackets in our notation. We will write vars(ψ) to denote the set of variables occurring in a feature term ψ.

We choose to model icons as concepts represented by feature terms over the signature with the following sort hierarchy $\mathcal{S}$:[5]

ICON
SIGN $\prec$ {ARROW, MAGNIFYINGGLASS, DOCUMENT,
          PEN, HARDDISK, CLOUD}
MEANING $\prec$ {ACTION, OBJECTTYPE}
ACTION $\prec$ {MODIFY, VIEWSEARCH, TRANSFER}
MODIFY $\prec$ {EDIT, WRITE}
VIEWSEARCH $\prec$ {SEARCH, FIND, ANALYSE}
TRANSFER $\prec$ {UPLOAD, DOWNLOAD}
OBJECTTYPE $\prec$ {INFOCONTAINER, DATACONTAINER}
INFOCONTAINER $\prec$ {PAGE, DOC, FILE}
DATACONTAINER $\prec$ {HARDDRIVE, CLOUD}

and features $\mathcal{F} = \{form, meaning, on, below, left, right, action, objectType\}$.

In addition, feature terms representing icons need to have the structure represented in Figure 2.5. Root variables are of sort ICON and have at most two features *form* and *meaning*, modelling the signs ($s_1, \ldots, s_n$) and the meaning ($m_1, \ldots, m_n$) of these signs in the context of the icon. Each sign is again represented by means of a feature term whose root variable is of sort $s \succeq$ SIGN, and each meaning by means of feature terms whose root variable is of sort $s \succeq$ MEANING.

Features of sign terms ($f_{s_1}, \ldots f_{s_n}$ in the schema above) are at most one of *on*, *left*, *right*, or *below*, specifying the spatial relationship between signs; and at most one of *action* or *objectType*, specifying the meaning of signs ($f_{m_1}, \ldots f_{m_n}$ in the schema above). The values of spatial relation features are root variables of feature terms

---

[4] The meaning of 'values' in this section is different from the idea of 'values' in the argumentation framework presented in Section 2.4.

[5] The notation $s \prec \{s_1, \ldots, s_n\}$ denotes that $s_1, \ldots, s_n$ are sub-sorts of s.

that are in the value of the *form* feature; and those of features *action* and *objectType* are root variables of feature terms that are in the value of the *meaning* feature. In addition the root variables in the value of the *action* feature are of sort $s \succeq$ ACTION, while those of the *objectType* feature are of sort $s \succeq$ OBJECTTYPE. Figure 2.4a shows the feature term representation of the icon in Figure 2.4b(I).

A fundamental relation between feature terms is that of subsumption ($\sqsubseteq$). Intuitively, a feature term ψ_1 subsumes a feature term ψ_2 (ψ_1 is more general than ψ_2), if all the information in ψ_1 is also in ψ_2.[6] We write $\psi_1 \sqsubseteq \psi_2$ to denote that ψ_1 subsumes ψ_2. We omit the formal definition of subsumption, which can be found in (Ontañón and Plaza, 2012) for feature terms as represented here. The subsumption relation induces a partial order on the set of all features terms $\mathscr{L}$ over a given signature, that is, $\langle \mathscr{L}, \sqsubseteq \rangle$ is a poset.

2.6.1.2 Discovery

The discovery takes a query over the meaning of an icon concept as input, looks for concepts in the Rich Background, and returns an ordered set of pairs of concepts that can be blended. The query is modeled as a feature term ψ_q in which only the meaning part of an icon is specified. For instance, a query asking for an icon with meaning SEARCH-DOC is modeled as:

$$\psi_q := x_1 : \text{ICON} \left[meaning = \left\{ \begin{array}{l} x_2 : \text{SEARCH} \\ x_3 : \text{DOC} \end{array} \right\} \right] \qquad (2.1)$$

The matching of the query is not always a perfect match, since icon concepts in the Rich Background can have only one part of the meaning or similar meanings w.r.t. the meaning searched. To this end, the query resolution is modeled as a *similarity-based search*.

As seen in Section 2.2, the similarity between two concepts can be defined using the similarity measure S_λ. From a computational point of view, S_λ requires two things to be computed: the LGG and the three lengths defined in Eq. 2.4.

The algorithms for computing S_λ can be found in (Ontañón and Plaza, 2012). They implement the generalisation refinement operator shown in Figure 2.6. It consists of the following operations:

Sort generalisation, which generalises a term by substituting the sort of one of its variables by a more general sort;

Variable elimination, which generalises a term by removing the value of one of the features in one variable of the term (a variable is removed only when the variable does not have any features);

---

[6] Notice that, in Description Logics, $A \sqsubseteq B$ has the inverse meaning "A is subsumed by B", since subsumption is defined from the set inclusion of the interpretations of A and B. Also, this is the way in which we understand $\sqsubseteq$ in all the chapter apart from this section, in which we adopt the feature-term interpretation for $\sqsubseteq$.

(γ_s) SORT GENERALISATION:

$$\begin{bmatrix} s_1 \prec s \wedge \nexists s_2 : s_1 \prec s_2 \prec s \wedge \\ \forall x.f = y \in \phi\ \exists s_1.f = s_3 \in O \wedge \\ \mathsf{sort}(y) \preceq s_3 \end{bmatrix} \quad \frac{\phi\ \&\ x : s}{\phi\ \&\ x : s_1}$$

(γ_v) VARIABLE ELIMINATION:

$$\begin{bmatrix} s.f = s' \in O \wedge \\ \mathsf{features}(y) = \emptyset \end{bmatrix} \quad \frac{\phi\ \&\ x : s\ \&\ x.f = y\ \&\ y : s'}{\phi\ \&\ x : s}$$

(γ_e) VARIABLE EQUALITY ELIMINATION:

$$\begin{bmatrix} z_1 \notin \mathsf{vars}(\phi) \end{bmatrix} \quad \frac{\phi\ \&\ x.f = z\ \&\ y.f' = z}{\phi\ \&\ z.f = z\ \&\ y.f' = z_1\ \&\ z_1 : \mathsf{sort}(z)}$$

(γ_r) ROOT VARIABLE EQUALITY ELIMINATION:

$$\begin{bmatrix} z_1 \notin \mathsf{vars}(\phi) \wedge \\ \mathsf{root}(\psi) = z \end{bmatrix} \quad \frac{\phi\ \&\ x.f = z}{\phi\ \&\ x.f = z_1\ \&\ z_1 : \mathsf{sort}(z)}$$

Fig. 2.6: Generalisation operators for feature terms (Ontañón and Plaza, 2012), in which feature terms are represented in clause notation. The term form of any feature term $\psi := x : s[f_1 = \psi_1, \ldots, f_n = \psi_n]$ can be rewritten into the equivalent clause form $\phi := x : s\ \&\ x.f_1 = x_1\ \&\ \ldots\ \&\ x.f_n = x_n$. Notice that these operators ensure that it is possible to reach $\perp$ from any feature term in the language.

Variable equality elimination, which generalises a term by removing a variable equality and ensuring that $\perp$ can be reached from any term.

It is worth noticing that, in case of variable equalities, it is not possible to define a generalisation operator for feature terms that is complete and still locally finite. However, for the purpose of defining a least general generalisation-based similarity, an operator which ensures that $\perp$ is reachable in a finite number of steps will suffice.

Example 2.1 (LGG example). Let us consider the feature terms ψ_q in Eq. 2.1 and ψ_1 in Figure 2.4a. The LGG $\psi_q \sqcap \psi_1$ is:

$$x_1 : \text{ICON}\left[meaning = \left\{ \begin{array}{l} x_2 = \text{SEARCH} \\ x_3 = \text{OBJECTTYPE} \end{array} \right\} \right]$$

$\psi_q \sqcap \psi_1$ captures the information shared among the icon concept ψ_1 and the query ψ_q. Both of them have two meanings. According to the ontology previously defined, the most general sorts for variables x_2 and x_3 are SEARCH and OBJECTTYPE respectively. The *form* feature of ψ_1 is removed, since ψ_q does not contain this information.

The measure S_λ estimates the ratio between the amount of information that is shared and the total information content.

Example 2.2 (Similarity example). Let us consider the feature terms ψ_q in Eq. 2.1, ψ_1 in Figure 2.4a and their LGG in Example 2.1. Lengths $\lambda_1 = \lambda(\psi_1 \sqcap \psi_q \xrightarrow{\gamma} \bot) = 8$, $\lambda_2 = \lambda(\psi_1 \xrightarrow{\gamma} \psi_1 \sqcap \psi_q) = 12$, and $\lambda_3 = \lambda(\psi_q \xrightarrow{\gamma} \psi_1 \sqcap \psi_q) = 2$. Notice that λ_3 is very small (two generalisations), while λ_2 is larger since ψ_1 has more generalised content. Therefore, the similarity between ψ_q and ψ_1 is:

$$S_\lambda(\psi_1, \psi_q) = \frac{8}{12 + 2 + 8} = 0.36$$

$S_\lambda(\psi_1, \psi_q)$ expresses that these two concepts share 36% of their information.

This measure is used to retrieve and rank input concepts as shown in the following example.

Example 2.3. Let us imagine an agent that has access to a Rich Background $\mathscr{C} = \{\psi_1, \psi_2, \psi_3, \psi_4\}$ consisting of four of the icons depicted in Figures 2.4b(I-II-III-IV). As previously described, ψ_1 is a feature term representing an icon with meaning SEARCH-HARDDISK. ψ_2 represents an icon that consists of two sorts of type SIGN, an ARROW and a CLOUD, whose meaning is DOWNLOAD-CLOUD. ψ_3 represents an icon with two sorts of type SIGN, a PEN and a DOCUMENT, whose meaning is EDIT-DOC; finally, ψ_4 is a feature term that consists of three sorts, ARROW, DOCUMENT and CLOUD with the intended meaning of DOWNLOAD-DOC-CLOUD.

The agent receives as input a query asking for an icon with meaning SEARCH-DOC, ψ_q (Eq. 2.1). The discovery retrieves the following pairs of concepts:

$$\{\langle(\psi_1, 0.36), (\psi_3, 0.36)\rangle\}, \{\langle(\psi_1, 0.36), (\psi_2, 0.27)\rangle\}$$

$$\{\langle(\psi_3, 0.36), (\psi_2, 0.27)\rangle\}, \{\langle(\psi_1, 0.36), (\psi_4, 0.25)\rangle\}$$

$$\{\langle(\psi_3, 0.36), (\psi_4, 0.25)\rangle\}, \{\langle(\psi_2, 0.27), (\psi_4, 0.25)\rangle\}$$

The agent proceeds to blend the first pair in the list. To this end, it applies the amalgam-based blending.

2.6.1.3 Blending Computer Icons

The least general generalisation of ψ_1 and ψ_3 is an icon with two sorts of type SIGN, one *on* the other one, and with meaning ACTION and OBJECTTYPE respectively. The agent explores the space of generalisations and finds two maximal blends; a blend ψ_{b_1} describing an icon with two sorts of type MAGNIFYINGGLASS and DOCUMENT whose meaning is SEARCH-DOC; another blend ψ_{b_2} describing an icon with sorts of type PEN and HARDDISK whose meaning is EDIT-HARDDRIVE. Since ψ_{b_2} does not satisfy the query, it is discarded, and only ψ_{b_1} is kept. The creation of ψ_{b_1} is illustrated in Figure 2.7.

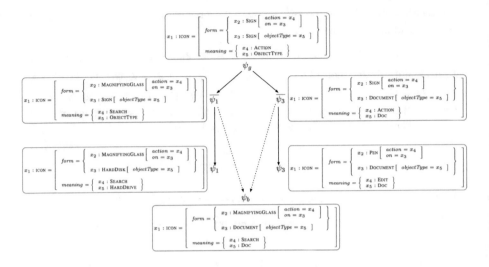

Fig. 2.7: A blend of feature terms ψ_1 and ψ_3

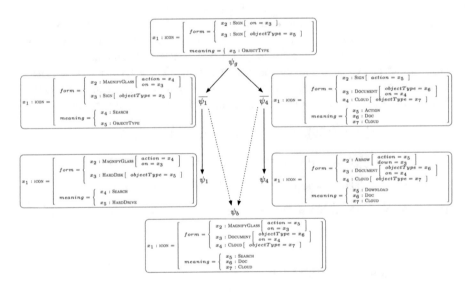

Fig. 2.8: A blend of feature terms ψ_1 and ψ_4

The agent repeats the above procedure for each pair discovered. Finally, it finds another blend, which satisfies ψ_q, by blending the pair ψ_1 and ψ_4. It is a blend describing an icon with three sorts of type MAGNIFYINGGLASS, DOCUMENT, and CLOUD whose meaning is SEARCH-DOC-CLOUD. Intuitively, this blend can be obtained by generalising HARDDISK from ψ_1 and ARROW from ψ_4, and by keeping the other input icons' specifics (see Figure 2.8). We denote this blend as ψ_{b_2}. The set of blends is $\mathscr{B} = \{\psi_{b_1}, \psi_{b_2}\}$. A representation of ψ_{b_1} and ψ_{b_2} is given in Figures 2.4b(V-VI).

2.6.1.4 Evaluating Conceptual Blends by Means of Arguments

The agent evaluates newly created concepts on the basis of some values and the audience to which these blends are headed.

In the case of evaluating blends representing new computer icons, we can imagine that the agent is equipped with values such as *simplicity* and *unambiguity*.

The main idea behind simplicity is that the agent estimates how simple an icon is from a representation point of view. This can be done by counting the quantity of information used in the feature term describing an icon. We can assume that simple icons are those described with less information. Therefore, simplicity is defined to be inversely proportional to the total number of features and sorts used in the variables of a feature term ψ_b.

$$\text{Simplicity}(\psi_b) = \frac{1}{\sum\limits_{x \in \text{vars}(\psi_b)} \text{features}(x) + \text{sorts}(x)}$$

Unambiguity, on the other hand, measures how many interpretations an icon has w.r.t. the Rich Background. Since icons are *polysemic*—they can be interpreted in different ways—there can be icons that contain the same sign but the sign is associated with a different meaning. To define the unambiguity value, let us first define the polysemic set of ψ_b as:

$$\text{Pol}(\psi_b) = \{\psi_j \in \mathscr{C} \mid \exists s \in \text{form}(\psi_j) \cap \text{form}(\psi_b) \\ \wedge \text{meaning}(\psi_j, s) \neq \text{meaning}(\psi_b, s)\}$$

where $\text{form}(\psi_j)$ is a function that returns the value of feature *form*, i.e., the set of signs used in the icon represented by feature term ψ_j; and $\text{meaning}(\psi_j, s)$ is a function that returns the sort of the variable that is the value of feature *action* or *objectType* of the variabe of sort s, i.e., the meaning used for the sign represented by sort s in feature term ψ_j. Then, the unambiguity value is defined to be inversely proportional to the cardinality of Pol.

$$\text{Unambiguity}(\psi_b) = \begin{cases} 1/|\text{Pol}(\psi_b)| & \text{if } |\text{Pol}(\psi_b)| \neq 0 \\ 1 & \text{otherwise} \end{cases}$$

Example 2.4. The agent evaluates the set of blends $\mathcal{B} = \{\psi_{b_1}, \psi_{b_2}\}$ by means of the values above. The blend ψ_{b_1} contains 10 variables whereas ψ_{b_2} contains 14. Therefore, the simplicity value's degrees of ψ_{b_1} and ψ_{b_2} are 0.1 and 0.07 respectively. Their unambiguity, on the other hand, is 1, since the Rich Background does not contain icons with the same signs used in ψ_{b_1} and ψ_{b_2}, but with a different meaning. The arguments built by the agent are:

	Simplicity	Unambiguity
ψ_{b_1}	0.1	1
ψ_{b_2}	0.07	1

Therefore, both blends have an argument pro regarding their simplicity and an argument con w.r.t. their unambiguity value. It is easy to see that the blends are ranked in different ways when using the criteria we defined. For instance, ψ_{b_1} and ψ_{b_2} are equally preferred when counting their arguments pro (or con) (Definition 2.9), and when considering both arguments pro and con (Definition 2.13).

Instead, when considering the audience Simplicity $\succ_{\mathscr{R}}$ Unambiguity, ψ_{b_1} is preferred to ψ_{b_2} (Definition 2.15).

2.6.2 Coherent Conceptual Blending

The process model introduced in Section 2.1 can be instantiated in another formal structured representation language such as Description Logics (DLs).

Description logics play an important role in conceptual blending, as witnessed by other approaches (see Chapter 3) that make use of ontological descriptions as formal backbones for modelling conceptual blending in a computational way.

In the following, we will focus on how a specific description logic, namely $\mathcal{AL}$, can be used to model concepts belonging to a Rich Background, amalgam-based blending and conceptual coherence. The main reason for choosing $\mathcal{AL}$ is that it is a subset of OWL 2, the Web Ontology Language recommended by the World Wide Web Consortium (W3C, http://www.w3.org), and supported by the DOL metalanguage (see Chapter 3). In this way, our approach could be integrated in the DOL-based computational blending framework presented in the next chapter rather straightforwardly.

2.6.2.1 Rich Background in $\mathcal{AL}$

In DLs, concept and role descriptions are defined inductively by means of concept and role constructors over a finite set N_C of concept names, a finite set N_R of role names, and (possibly) a finite set N_I of individual names. As is common practice, we shall write A, B for concept names, C, D for concept descriptions, r, s for role names, and a, b, for individual names.

concept description	interpretation
$\top$	$\Delta^{\mathscr{I}}$
$\bot$	$\emptyset$
A	$A^{\mathscr{I}} \subseteq \Delta^{\mathscr{I}}$
$\neg A$	$\Delta^{\mathscr{I}} \backslash A^{\mathscr{I}}$
$C \sqcap D$	$C^{\mathscr{I}} \cap D^{\mathscr{I}}$
$\forall r.C$	$\{x \in \Delta^{\mathscr{I}} \mid \forall y \in \Delta^{\mathscr{I}}.(x,y) \in r^{\mathscr{I}} \wedge y \in C^{\mathscr{I}}\}$
$\exists r.\top$	$\{x \in \Delta^{\mathscr{I}} \mid \exists y \in \Delta^{\mathscr{I}}.(x,y) \in r^{\mathscr{I}}\}$

Table 2.1: Syntax and semantics of $\mathscr{AL}$ contructors

House $\sqsubseteq$ Object	Resident $\sqsubseteq$ Person
Boat $\sqsubseteq$ Object	Passenger $\sqsubseteq$ Person
Land $\sqsubseteq$ Medium	Person $\sqcap$ Medium $\sqsubseteq \bot$
Water $\sqsubseteq$ Medium	Object $\sqcap$ Medium $\sqsubseteq \bot$
Water $\sqcap$ Land $\sqsubseteq \bot$	Object $\sqcap$ Person $\sqsubseteq \bot$

Fig. 2.9: The Rich Background for the House and Boat

The $\mathscr{AL}$ language was introduced by Schmidt-Schauß and Smolka (1991) as a minimal language of practical interest. Concept descriptions in $\mathscr{AL}$ are formed according to the syntax rules shown in the left column in Table 2.1.

The semantics of concept and role descriptions is defined in terms of an interpretation $\mathscr{I} = (\Delta^{\mathscr{I}}, \cdot^{\mathscr{I}})$, where $\Delta^{\mathscr{I}}$ is a non-empty domain and $\cdot^{\mathscr{I}}$ is an interpretation function assigning a set $A^{\mathscr{I}} \subseteq \Delta^{\mathscr{I}}$ to each concept name $A \in N_C$, a set $r^{\mathscr{I}} \subseteq \Delta^{\mathscr{I}} \times \Delta^{\mathscr{I}}$ to each role name $r \in N_r$, and an element $a^{\mathscr{I}} \in \Delta^{\mathscr{I}}$ for each individual name $a \in N_I$, which is extended to general concept and role descriptions. Table 2.1 shows the interpretation of the constructors of the description logic $\mathscr{AL}$.

The bottom concept $\bot$, in combination with general concept inclusions (GCIs), allows one to express disjointness of concept descriptions, e.g., $C \sqcap D \sqsubseteq \bot$ tells that C and D are disjoint. In $\mathscr{AL}$, and generally speaking in any description logic, there are two sets of axioms, namely, a TBox and an ABox.

The TBox, denoted as $\mathscr{T}$, consists of terminological axioms that describe intensional knowledge defining the main notions relevant to the domain of discourse. The ABox, denoted as $\mathscr{A}$, consists of assertional axioms that describe extensional knowledge about individual objects of the domain.

An interpretation $\mathscr{I}$ is a model of a TBox $\mathscr{T}$ if and only if it satisfies all axioms in $\mathscr{T}$. The basic reasoning task in $\mathscr{AL}$ is subsumption. Given a TBox $\mathscr{T}$ and two concept descriptions C and D, we say that C is (strictly) subsumed by D w.r.t. $\mathscr{T}$, denoted as $C \sqsubseteq_{\mathscr{T}} D$ ($C \sqsubset_{\mathscr{T}} D$), iff $C^{\mathscr{I}} \subseteq D^{\mathscr{I}}$ ($C^{\mathscr{I}} \subseteq D^{\mathscr{I}}$ and $C^{\mathscr{I}} \neq D^{\mathscr{I}}$) for every model $\mathscr{I}$ of $\mathscr{T}$.

In what follows, a Rich Background in $\mathscr{AL}$ is a TBox, containing terminological axioms of the form $C \sqsubseteq D$, i.e., GCIs, and disjointness axioms. By $\mathscr{L}(\mathscr{T})$ we refer to the set of all $\mathscr{AL}$ concept descriptions we can form with the concept and role names occurring in $\mathscr{T}$.

To illustrate an example of Rich Background, we use the classical conceptual blending example of the *house-boat* (Fauconnier and Turner, 2002; Goguen, 1999). In Figure 2.9, we depict the set of axioms, necessary for defining the mental spaces of the House and Boat. The precise formalisation is not critical at this point, different ones exist (Goguen and Harrell, 2010; Pereira, 2007), but all provide similar distinctions.

The Rich Background for the house and boat consists of a taxonomy of concepts, concept descriptions, and restrictions among them. For instance, Land and Water are atomic concepts, both of type Medium, and the axiom Water $\sqcap$ Land $\sqsubseteq \bot$ captures the idea that any object of type Water cannot be of type Land at the same time.

Atomic roles such as usedBy and on are used to define concept relations. The mental spaces representing the concept of a house and boat can be modeled as follows:

$$\text{House} \sqsubseteq \forall \text{usedBy.Resident} \sqcap \forall \text{on.Land}$$
$$\text{Boat} \sqsubseteq \forall \text{usedBy.Passenger} \sqcap \forall \text{on.Water}$$

The above axioms denote that a *house is an object that is only used by residents and is located only on land*. Similarly, *boat is an object that is only used by passengers and is located only on water*.

In principle, the House and Boat theory could not be directly blended (they generate an inconsistency due to the disjointness axiom Water $\sqcap$ Land $\sqsubseteq \bot$), but the blended specification is still to be considered an interesting option—from a creative point of view—that needs to be assessed. We will do it by means of conceptual coherence, as we shall see. First, we define a blend as an amalgam in the $\mathcal{AL}$ language.

2.6.2.2 Blending in $\mathcal{AL}$

As said earlier, the notion of blend as an amalgam can be defined in any representation language $\mathcal{L}$ for which a subsumption relation between formulas is defined, therefore, also in the set of all $\mathcal{AL}$ concept descriptions, which can be formed with the concept and role names occurring in an $\mathcal{AL}$ TBox $\mathcal{T}$, with the subsumption relation $\sqsubseteq_{\mathcal{T}}$. The process of conceptual blending in $\mathcal{AL}$ can be described as follows:

1. We take a Rich Background of concepts (see Figure 2.9).
2. A mental space of an atomic concept A is modelled, for the purpose of conceptual blending, by means of a subsumption $A \sqsubseteq C$ specifying the necessary conditions we are focusing on.
3. The new concept to be invented is represented by the concept description that conjoins the atomic concepts to be blended.
4. With amalgams we generalise the input spaces based on the taxonomy in our Rich Backgroud until a satisfactory blend is generated.

The definitions of most general specialisation, least general generalisation, and amalgam in $\mathcal{AL}$ follow by replacing the subsumption relation ($\sqsubseteq$) with subsumption in $\mathcal{AL}$ ($\sqsubseteq_{\mathcal{T}}$) in a straightforward way; therefore, we omit them.

The least general generalisation and the generalised descriptions, needed to compute an amalgam (see Definition 2.5), are obtained by means of a generalisation refinement operator that allows us to find generalisations of $\mathcal{AL}$ concept descriptions.

Generalising $\mathcal{AL}$ descriptions

Roughly speaking, a generalisation operator takes a concept C as input and returns a set of descriptions that are more general than C by taking a Tbox $\mathcal{T}$ into account.

In order to define a generalisation refinement operator for $\mathcal{AL}$, we need some auxiliary definitions.

Definition 2.21. Let $\mathcal{T}$ be a TBox in $\mathcal{AL}$. The set of *non-trivial subconcepts* of $\mathcal{T}$ is given as

$$\mathsf{sub}(\mathcal{T}) = \bigcup_{C \sqsubseteq D \in \mathcal{T}} \mathsf{sub}(C) \cup \mathsf{sub}(D)$$

where sub is defined over the structure of concept descriptions as follows:

$$\mathsf{sub}(A) = \{A\}$$
$$\mathsf{sub}(\bot) = \{\bot\}$$
$$\mathsf{sub}(\top) = \{\top\}$$
$$\mathsf{sub}(\neg A) = \{\neg A, A\}$$
$$\mathsf{sub}(C \sqcap D) = \{C \sqcap D\} \cup \mathsf{sub}(C) \cup \mathsf{sub}(D)$$
$$\mathsf{sub}(\forall R.C) = \{\forall R.C\} \cup \mathsf{sub}(C)$$
$$\mathsf{sub}(\exists R.\top) = \{\exists R.\top\}$$

We next define the upward cover set of atomic concepts. In the following definition, the definition of $\mathsf{sub}(\mathcal{T})$ guarantees that the upward cover set is finite.

Definition 2.22. Let $\mathcal{T}$ be an $\mathcal{AL}$ TBox with concept names from N_C. The *upward cover set* of an atomic concept $A \in N_C \cup \{\top, \bot\}$ with respect to $\mathcal{T}$ is given as:

$$\mathsf{UpCov}(A) := \{C \in \mathsf{sub}(\mathcal{T}) \mid A \sqsubseteq_{\mathcal{T}} C \tag{2.2}$$
$$\text{and there is no } C' \in \mathsf{sub}(\mathcal{T})$$
$$\text{such that } A \sqsubseteq_{\mathcal{T}} C' \sqsubseteq_{\mathcal{T}} C\}$$

We can now define our generalisation refinement operator for $\mathcal{AL}$ as follows.

Definition 2.23. Let $\mathcal{T}$ be an $\mathcal{AL}$ TBox. We define the *generalisation refinement operator* γ inductively over the structure of concept descriptions as follows:

$$\gamma(A) = \mathsf{UpCov}(A)$$
$$\gamma(\top) = \mathsf{UpCov}(\top) = \emptyset$$
$$\gamma(\bot) = \mathsf{UpCov}(\bot)$$
$$\gamma(C \sqcap D) = \{C' \sqcap D \mid C' \in \gamma(C)\} \cup \{C \sqcap D' \mid D' \in \gamma(D)\} \cup \{C, D\}$$
$$\gamma(\forall r.C) = \begin{cases} \{\forall r.C' \mid C' \in \gamma(C)\} & \text{whenever } \gamma(C) \neq \emptyset \\ \{\top\} & \text{otherwise.} \end{cases}$$
$$\gamma(\exists r.\top) = \emptyset$$

We should note at this point that our definition of UpCov only considers the set of subconcepts present in a Tbox $\mathscr{T}$. On the one hand, this guarantees that γ is finite, since at each generalisation step, the set of possible generalisations is finite. On the other hand, however, this implies that γ is not complete, since it cannot find all possible upward covers of a concept w.r.t. subsumption in $\mathscr{AL}$.[7] Besides, γ can return concept descriptions that are equivalent to the concept being generalised; consequently, γ is not a proper generalisation operator. One possible way to avoid this situation is to discard these generalisations. This can be achieved by an additional semantic test that can be found in (Confalonieri et al., 2018).

Given a generalisation refinement operator γ, $\mathscr{AL}$ concepts are related by refinement paths as described next.

Definition 2.24. A finite sequence $C_1, \ldots, C_n$ of $\mathscr{AL}$ concepts is a *concept refinement path* $C_1 \xrightarrow{\gamma} C_n$ from C_1 to C_n of the generalisation refinement operator γ iff $C_{i+1} \in \gamma(C_i)$ for all $i : 1 \leq i < n$. $\gamma^*(C)$ denotes the set of all concepts that can be reached from C by means of γ in a finite number of steps.

The repetitive application of the generalisation refinement operator allows us to find a description that represents the properties that two or more $\mathscr{AL}$ concepts have in common. This description is a common generalisation of $\mathscr{AL}$ concepts, the so-called *generic space* that is used in conceptual blending.

Definition 2.25. An $\mathscr{AL}$ concept description G is a generic space of the $\mathscr{AL}$ concept descriptions $C_1, \ldots, C_n$ if and only if $G \in \gamma^*(C_i)$ for all $i = 1, \ldots, n$.

The House-Boat Blend

The $\mathscr{AL}$ theories for House and Boat introduce the axioms modelling the mental spaces for *house* and *boat*.

$$\text{House} \sqsubseteq \forall \mathsf{usedBy.Resident} \sqcap \forall \mathsf{on.Land}$$
$$\text{Boat} \sqsubseteq \forall \mathsf{usedBy.Passenger} \sqcap \forall \mathsf{on.Water}$$

---

[7] For instance, if $\mathscr{T}$ contains two axioms $A \sqsubseteq B$, $A \sqsubseteq C$, and we generalise A (in the domain knowledge), then $\gamma(A) = \{B, C\}$ while a possible generalisation of A w.r.t. $\sqsubseteq_{\mathscr{T}}$ is $B \sqcap C$.

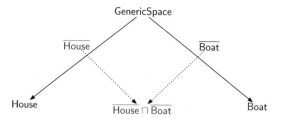

Fig. 2.10: A diagram of an amalgam from descriptions House and Boat and their respective generalisations $\overline{\text{House}}$ and $\overline{\text{Boat}}$. Arrows indicate the subsumption of the target by the source of the arrow

The House and Boat theories cannot be directly blended since they generate an inconsistency. This is due to the background ontology stating that the medium on which an object is situated cannot be *land* and *water* at the same time (Figure 2.9). Therefore, some parts of the House and Boat descriptions need to be generalised in a controlled manner before these concepts can be blended. The generic space between a house and a boat—an object that is on a *medium* and *used-by* a *person*— is a lower bound in the space of generalisations that need to be explored in order to generalise these concepts and to blend them into a *house-boat*. The generic space is obtained according to Definition 2.25 by applying the refinement operator γ.

Example 2.5. Let us consider the House and Boat concepts. Their generic space is: ∀usedBy.Person⊓ ∀on.Medium and is obtained as follows. In the House concept, the subconcepts ∀usedBy.Resident and ∀on.Land are generalised to ∀usedBy.Person and ∀on.Medium respectively. In the Boat concept, the subconcepts ∀usedBy. Passenger and ∀on.Water are generalised in a similar way.

From a conceptual blending point of view, the *house-boat* blend can be created when the medium on which a house is situated (land) becomes the medium on which boat is situated (water), and the resident of the house becomes the passenger of the boat. This blend can be obtained when the input concepts house and boat are generalised as follows:

$$\overline{\text{House}} \sqsubseteq \forall \text{usedBy.Resident} \sqcap \forall \text{on.Medium}$$
$$\overline{\text{Boat}} \sqsubseteq \forall \text{usedBy.Person} \sqcap \forall \text{on.Water}$$

The *house-boat* blend is obtained by conjoining the generalised mental spaces $\overline{\text{House}}$ and $\overline{\text{Boat}}$ (Figure 2.10). It is easy to see that $\overline{\text{House}} \sqcap \overline{\text{Boat}}$ is an amalgam according to Definition 2.5.

2.6.2.3 Conceptual Coherence in $\mathcal{AL}$

Thagard (2000) characterises conceptual coherence with these principles:

Symmetry: Conceptual coherence is a symmetric relation between pairs of concepts.

Association: A concept coheres with another concept if they are positively associated, i.e., if there are objects to which they both apply.

Given Concepts: The applicability of a concept to an object may be given perceptually or by some other reliable source.

Negative Association: A concept incoheres with another concept if they are negatively associated, i.e., if an object falling under one concept tends not to fall under the other concept.

Acceptance: The applicability of a concept to an object depends on the applicability of other concepts.

To provide a precise account of these principles we shall formalise *Association* and *Negative Association* between concepts expressed in $\mathscr{A L}$, since these are the principles defining coherence and incoherence. We shall assume coherence between two concept descriptions when we have explicitly stated that one subsumes the other ("there are objects to which both apply"); and we shall assume incoherence when we have explicitly stated that they are disjoint ("an object falling under one concept tends not to fall under the other concept").

Definition 2.26. Given a Tbox $\mathscr{T}$ in description logic $\mathscr{A L}$ and a pair of concept descriptions $C, D \notin \{\top, \bot\}$, we will say that:

- C coheres with D if $C \sqsubseteq D \in \mathscr{T}$, and that
- C incoheres with D if $C \sqsubseteq \neg D \in \mathscr{T}$ or $C \sqcap D \sqsubseteq \bot \in \mathscr{T}$.

In addition, coherence and incoherence between concept descriptions depend on the concept constructors used, and we will say that, for all atomic concepts A, atomic roles R, and concept descriptions $C, D \notin \{\top, \bot\}$:

- $\neg A$ incoheres with A;
- $C \sqcap D$ coheres both with C and with D;
- $\forall R.C$ coheres (or incoheres) with $\forall R.D$ if C coheres (or incoheres) with D.[8]

Symmetry follows from the definition above, and *Acceptance* is captured by the aim of maximising coherence in a coherence graph. For this we need to define how a TBox determines a coherence graph, and, in order to keep the graph finite, we express coherence and incoherence only between non-trivial concept descriptions (i.e., excluding $\top$ and $\bot$) that are explicitly stated in the TBox. This set can be computed based on Definition 2.21:

$$\mathsf{sub}'(\mathscr{T}) = \mathsf{sub}(\mathscr{T}) \backslash \{\bot, \top\}$$

Definition 2.27. The *coherence graph of a TBox* $\mathscr{T}$ is the edge-weighted, undirected graph $G = \langle V, E, w \rangle$ whose vertices are non-trivial subconcepts of $\mathscr{T}$ (i.e.,

---

[8] Note that since $\mathscr{A L}$ allows only for limited existential quantification we cannot provide a general rule for coherence between concept descriptions of the form $\exists R.\top$.

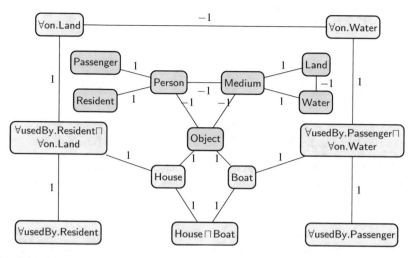

Fig. 2.11: The coherence graph of the House ⊓ Boat blend, showing the main concepts and their coherence relations. Blue and green coloured boxes represent concepts belonging to the background ontology and to the input mental spaces respectively

$V = \mathsf{sub}'(\mathcal{T}))$, whose edges link subconcepts that either cohere or incohere according to Definition 2.26, and whose edge-weight function w is given as follows:

$$w(\{C,D\}) = \begin{cases} 1 & \text{if } C \text{ and } D \text{ cohere} \\ -1 & \text{if } C \text{ and } D \text{ incohere} \end{cases}$$

2.6.2.4 Evaluating the Coherence of Conceptual Blends

To exemplify how the coherence degree can be used to evaluate blends, we consider the *house-boat* example. According to the amalgam-based process of conceptual blending described in the previous section, several blends can be generated by blending the mental space of House and Boat. In particular, the concept House ⊓ Boat is a valid blend.

The coherence graph blending the House and Boat directly is shown in Figure 2.11. As expected the concepts House and Boat positively cohere with the axioms representing the mental spaces and with the concept House ⊓ Boat, which is representing the blend. The incoherence relation between ∀on.Land and ∀on.Water is due to the fact that the concepts Water and Land incohere, since the background ontology contains the disjointness axiom Water ⊓ Land ⊑ ⊥. The coherence graph of House and Boat has a maximal coherence value of 0.84.

For the sake of our example, we generate new blends by generalising the axioms modelling our mental spaces. For instance, by applying the generalisations seen in

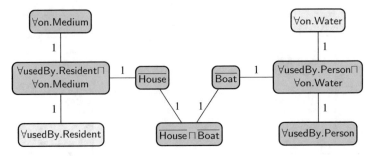

Fig. 2.12: The coherence graph of the $\overline{\text{House} \sqcap \text{Boat}}$ blend, showing the main concepts and coherence relations. Generalised concepts are displayed in a darker tone

the previous section that lead to the creation of the *house-boat* blend, we obtain the coherence graph in Figure 2.12.[9] The coherence graph of blending $\overline{\text{House}}$ and $\overline{\text{Boat}}$ has a maximal coherence value of 0.9. This graph yields a higher coherence degree since generalising ∀on.Land to ∀on.Medium prevents the appearance of the incoherence relation between ∀on.Land and ∀on.Water.

By Definition 2.20, it is easy to see that the blend $\overline{\text{House} \sqcap \text{Boat}}$ is preferred to House ⊓ Boat since it has a maximal coherence degree that is higher.

2.7 Related Work

Several approaches of formal and computational models for concept invention have been proposed (Eppe et al., 2018, 2015a,b; Kutz et al., 2014; Goguen and Harrell, 2006; Veale and Donoghue, 2000; Pereira, 2005, 2007; Goguen and Harrell, 2010; Guhe et al., 2011). Many of these models are inspired by the work of Fauconnier and Turner (2002), but there are also other approaches emanating from analogical reasoning (Schwering et al., 2009) and neuroscience (Thagard, 2010).

Amalgam-based conceptual blending have been developed to blend $\mathcal{ELL}^{++}$ concepts in (Confalonieri et al., 2018). In this work, the generalisation of an $\mathcal{ELL}^{++}$ concept is achieved by means of a generalisation refinement operator. The refinement operator is implemented in ASP as a step-wise transition process—similar to the one presented in this paper— that looks for a generic space between two (or more) concepts. The operator generalises a concept by taking the TBox knowledge into account. Good blends are selected by re-interpreting some optimality principles. Blending ontologies rather than concepts has been explored in the ontological blending framework of Kutz et al. (2014), where blends are computed as *colimits* of blending diagrams specified according to the Distributed Ontology Language (DOL) (Mossakowski et al., 2015), a recent OMG international ontology interoperability standard. In that framework, the blending process is not characterised

---

[9] Concepts belonging to the background ontology are omitted.

in terms of amalgams, nor are input concepts generalised syntactically. Rather, the generic space is assumed to be given and mapped to the input ontologies via theory interpretations.

The Alloy algorithm for conceptual blending by Goguen and Harrell (2006) is based on the theory of algebraic semiotics (Goguen, 1999). Alloy has been integrated in the Griot system for automated narrative generation (Goguen and Harrell, 2006; Harrell, 2007, 2005). The input spaces of the Alloy algorithm are theories defined in the algebraic specification language OBJ (Malcolm, 2000). In the Alloy algorithm, input spaces are assumed to be given, hence there is no discovery. The optimality principles proposed by Fauconnier and Turner (2002) are re-interpreted as *structural* optimality principles, and serve to prune the space of possible blends.

Sapper was originally developed by Veale and Keane (1997) as a computational model of metaphor and analogy. It computes a mapping between two separate domains—understood as graphs of concepts—that respects the relational structure between the concepts in each domain. Sapper can be seen as a computational model for conceptual blending, because the pairs of concepts that constitute its output can be manipulated as blended concepts (Veale and Donoghue, 2000). Strictly speaking, Sapper does not work with *a priori* given input spaces. It is the structure mapping algorithm itself which determines the set of concepts and relations between these concepts. In Sapper, most of the optimality principles are captured and serve to rank and filter the correspondences that comprise the mappings computed by the algorithm.

The research in (Pereira and Cardoso, 2002, 2003a,b) led to the development of Divago (Pereira, 2005; Pereira and Cardoso, 2006; Pereira, 2007), probably the first complete implementation of conceptual blending. Pereira draws the terminology and definitions for his formal and computational model from Wiggins' formalisation of creative systems (Wiggins, 2006). The implementation of Divago is realised in Prolog. Divago's architecture includes different modules. A knowledge base contains different micro-theories and their instantiations. Of these, two are selected for the blending by the user or randomly, thus, no discovery is taken into account. A mapper then generates the generic space between the inputs, and passes it to a blender module which generates the 'blendoid', i.e., a projection that defines the space of possible blends. A factory component is used to select the best blends among the blendoid by means of a genetic algorithm. A dedicated module implements the optimality principles. Given a blend, this module computes a measure for each principle. These measures yield a preference value of the blend that is taken as the fitness value of the genetic algorithm.

The combinatorial kind of creativity (Boden, 1996) that we are interested in has been investigated from a neurological perspective by Thagard and Stewart (2011). The major motivation of their approach is to explain and to model the *Aha!* or *Eureka!* effect that occurs when humans make serendipitous discoveries by means of creative thinking. The authors build their work on findings from neuroscience and approaches to realise human thinking with neural networks (Thagard, 2010). The key idea is to represent mental concepts as activity patterns of vectors of neurons and to perform a convolution operation to combine these patterns. Activity patterns are mathematically represented as vectors of numbers that represent the firing rate of neurons. According to Thagard and Stewart (2011), a mental concept can then be represented as a huge but finite vector of such numbers. The blend is generated by mathematical convolution of vectors. The underlying mathematical model is based on the so-called LIF model of neuronal activity (see e.g., Thagard (2010)). It accounts for various details on the neuronal level, such as neuron voltage, input current, membrane time, direction vector of neuron patterns, and synaptic connection weights. Thagard and Stewart (2011) do not use Fauconnier and Turner's optimality principles to distinguish reasonable blends within the huge space of possible blends. Instead, they combine the blend of two input spaces with another space representing emotional reaction to assess blends. However, the authors do not provide a detailed description of how to model the emotional input spaces computationally.

Finally, works that relate to ours are (Confalonieri et al., 2015; Kaliakatsos-Papakostas et al., 2016). Confalonieri et al. (2015) use Lakatosian reasoning to model dialogues in which users engage to discuss the intended meaning of an invented concept. The main difference between that effort and the current work lies in the way in which arguments are generated and used. Here, an argument is a reason for choosing a blend and it is generated automatically, whereas in (Confalonieri et al., 2015) an argument is a reason to refine the meaning of a blend and is provided by the user. In (Kaliakatsos-Papakostas et al., 2016), arguments are specified by musicologists to drive the harmonic blending process. Refinement operators presented here were further extended to work with the $\mathcal{ALC}$ language, and they were used to conceive axiom weakening, a technique that was developed to repair inconsistent ontologies (Troquard et al, 2018; Porello et al, 2018).

2.8 Conclusion and Future Perspectives

In this chapter, we described a process model for concept invention that is based on and extends the conceptual blending theory of Fauconnier and Turner (2002). According to this process, concept invention is characterised by different sub-processes—discovery, blending, and evaluation—that together account for concept invention.

Apart from the blending mechanism modelling the creation of new concepts, we focused on two extra dimensions that are typically not addressed in computational approaches of concept blending. On the one hand, we described how a Rich Background supports the discovery of input concepts to be blended. On the other hand, we showed how arguments promoting or demoting the values of an audience (to which the invention is headed) can be used to evaluate candidate blends.

We also showed how the evaluation of new blended concepts can be achieved by taking the computational theory of conceptual coherence due to Thagard (2000) into account. In this setting, newly invented concepts are evaluated with respect to a Rich Background conceptual knowledge so as to decide which of them are to be accepted into a system of familiar concepts.

We described two instantiations of the process model using two structured languages, namely, feature terms and description logics. This allowed us to capture the concept invention process in terms of well-defined operators such as least general generalisation—for computing a generic space—and most general specialisation—for computing a blend. Pairs of input concepts are retrieved from a Rich Background by means of a discovery process that takes a similarity measure into account. Blending is realised according to the notion of amalgam, and blend evaluation is achieved by means of arguments, values and audience and conceptual coherence. An implementation of conceptual coherence presented in this chapter using the OWL API and Answer Set Programming is available at: `https://rconfalonieri@bitbucket.org/rconfalonieri/coinvent-coherence.git`.

We exemplified the computational framework in these two languages but the framework is general enough to be instantiated in other representation languages in which a subsumption relation between formulas or descriptions holds.

We aim at extending the current work from different perspectives. First, here, we presented a discovery method based on a similarity measure based on the structure of the refinement space, but other similarity methods, considering more nuanced aspects of the domain, are envisioned to be needed and useful. Particularly, having a subset of the concepts in a Rich Background activated as salient but lacking a clear second concept that can be used to yield an interesting blend is an interesting avenue of research.

Then, generating other kinds of arguments than the ones seen in this chapter, opens also a wide area of research related not only to computational argumentation, but also to human level argumentation. For instance, social arguments applying to an invented concept could be considered as an open-ended process—that is to say a collection of arguments that can always increase, since the members of an audience may change and the values (and their social prevalence) may also change in time. This, for instance, has also been the approach of Confalonieri et al. (2015) when modeling blend evaluation using Lakatosian reasoning. In this way, a given invented concept may, for instance, first be divisive and at later times reach an overlapping consensus in an audience (be it positive or negative). This open-endedness also highlights the relationship between subjective and social values in a given domain, in the sense that a large disagreement between a traditional (consensued) set of values of an audience and the idiosyncratic values of a creative agent should be able to model disruptive or groundbreaking inventions.

We aim at employing a richer DL, such as $\mathscr{SROIQ}$ (Horrocks et al., 2006), enacting the concept invention process, and allowing degrees of coherence and incoherence relations. Usually, coherence and incoherence are not treated only in binary terms, but it is also natural to take certain degrees of coherence or incoherence into account. This, for instance, has also been the approach of Joseph et al. (2010) when formalising deductive coherence.

Finally, we will need to discuss yet another important aspect of coherence theory, namely how to interpret the two parts of a coherence-maximising partition: the set of accepted and of rejected concepts. The information that a particular concept description falls in the set of accepted concepts or in the set of rejected concepts could also be taken into account to decide the acceptance or rejection of newly invented concepts; or even of already existing concepts in the Rich Background, in the light of newly invented concepts. This aspect might become clearer as a wider range of concept representation languages is explored.

References

L. Amgoud and H. Prade. Using arguments for making and explaining decisions. *Artificial Intelligence*, 173:413–436, 2009.

K. Atkinson, T. Bench-Capon, and P. McBurney. Justifying practical reasoning. In *Proc. of the Fourth Workshop on Computational Models of Natural Argument (CMNA'04)*, pages 87–90, 2004.

F. Baader, D. Calvanese, D. L. McGuinness, D. Nardi, and P. F. Patel-Schneider, editors. *The Description Logic Handbook: Theory, Implementation, and Applications*. Cambridge University Press, New York, NY, USA, 2003.

T. J. M. Bench-Capon. Persuasion in practical argument using value-based argumentation frameworks. *Journal of Logic and Computation*, 13(3):429–448, 2003.

T. R. Besold and E. Plaza. Generalize and blend: Concept blending based on generalization, analogy, and amalgams. In *Proceedings of the 6th International Conference on Computational Creativity, ICCC15*, 2015.

M. A. Boden. Creativity. In M. A. Boden, editor, *Artificial Intelligence (Handbook of Perception and Cognition)*, pages 267–291. Academic Press, 1996.

B. Bonet and H. Geffner. Arguing for decisions: A qualitative model of decision making. In *Proc. of the 12th Conf. on Uncertainty in Artificial Intelligence (UAI'96)*, pages 98–105, 1996.

B. Carpenter. *The Logic of Typed Feature Structures*. Cambridge University Press, New York, NY, USA, 1992. ISBN 0-521-41932-8.

R. Confalonieri, J. Corneli, A. Pease, E. Plaza, and M. Schorlemmer. Using argumentation to evaluate concept blends in combinatorial creativity. In *Proc. of the 6th International Conference on Computational Creativity, ICCC15*, pages 174–181, 2015.

R. Confalonieri, M. Eppe, M. Schorlemmer, O. Kutz, R. Peñaloza, and E. Plaza. Upward refinement operators for conceptual blending in $\mathcal{ELL}^{++}$. *Annals of Mathematics and Artificial Intelligence*, 82(1):69–99, 2018. DOI: 10.1007/s10472-016-9524-8.

R. Confalonieri, E. Plaza, and M. Schorlemmer. A process model for concept invention. In *Proc. of the 7th International Conference on Computational Creativity, ICCC16*, pages 338–345, 2016.

P. M. Dung. On the acceptability of arguments and its fundamental role in nonmonotonic reasoning, logic programming and *n*-person games. *Artificial Intelligence Journal*, 77:321–357, 1995.

M. Eppe, E. Maclean, R. Confalonieri, O. Kutz, M. Schorlemmer, E. Plaza, and K.-U. Kühnberger. A computational framework for conceptual blending. *Artificial Intelligence* 256:105–129, 2018. DOI: 10.1016/j.artint.2017.11.005

M. Eppe, R. Confalonieri, E. Maclean, M. A. Kaliakatsos-Papakostas, E. Cambouropoulos, W. M. Schorlemmer, M. Codescu, and K. Kühnberger. Computational invention of cadences and chord progressions by conceptual chord-blending. In Q. Yang and M. Wooldridge, editors, *Proceedings of the Twenty-Fourth International Joint Conference on Artificial Intelligence, IJCAI 2015*, Buenos Aires, Argentina, July 25-31, 2015, pages 2445–2451. AAAI Press, 2015a.

M. Eppe, E. Maclean, R. Confalonieri, O. Kutz, W. M. Schorlemmer, and E. Plaza. ASP, amalgamation, and the conceptual blending workflow. In F. Calimeri, G. Ianni, and M. Truszczynski, editors, *Proceedings of the 13th International Conference on Logic Programming and Nonmonotonic Reasoning, LPNMR 2015*, Lexington, KY, USA, September 27-30, 2015, pages 309–316, 2015b.

G. Fauconnier and M. Turner. *The Way We Think: Conceptual Blending and the Mind's Hidden Complexities*. Basic Books, 2002. ISBN 978-0-465-08785-3.

J. Goguen. An introduction to algebraic semiotics, with application to user interface design. In C. L. Nehaniv, editor, *Computation for Metaphors, Analogy, and Agents*, volume 1562 of *Lecture Notes in Computer Science*, pages 242–291. 1999.

J. Goguen and D. F. Harrell. Style: A computational and conceptual blending-based approach. In S. Argamon, K. Burns, and S. Dubnov, editors, *The Structure of Style: Algorithmic Approaches to Understanding Manner and Meaning*, pages 291–316. Springer, 2010.

J. A. Goguen and D. F. Harrell. Foundations for active multimedia narrative: Semiotic spaces and structural blending. *Available at* `https://cseweb.ucsd.edu/~goguen/pps/narr.pdf`, 2005. Last accessed, 2016.

M. Guhe, A. Pease, A. Smaill, M. Martínez, M. Schmidt, H. Gust, K.-U. Kühnberger, and U. Krumnack. A computational account of conceptual blending in basic mathematics. *Cognitive Systems Research*, 12(3-4):249–265, 2011.

D. F. Harrell. Shades of computational evocation and meaning: The GRIOT system and improvisational poetry generation. *6th Digital Arts and Culture Conference*, 2005. URL `http://groups.csail.mit.edu/icelab/sites/default/files/pdf/Harrell-DAC2005.pdf`.

D. F. Harrell. *Theory and technology for computational narrative: an approach to generative and interactive narrative with bases in algebraic semiotics and cognitive linguistics*. Ph.D. thesis, University of California, San Diego, 2007.

I. Horrocks, O. Kutz, and U. Sattler. The even more irresistible $\mathcal{SROIQ}$. In P. Doherty, J. Mylopoulos, and C. A. Welty, editors, *Proceedings, Tenth International Conference on Principles of Knowledge Representation and Reasoning*, Lake District of the United Kingdom, June 2-5, 2006, pages 57–67. AAAI Press, 2006.

S. Joseph, C. Sierra, M. Schorlemmer, and P. Dellunde. Deductive coherence and norm adoption. *Logic Journal of the IGPL*, 18(1):118–156, 2010.

O. Kutz, J. Bateman, F. Neuhaus, T. Mossakowski, and M. Bhatt. E pluribus unum: Formalisation, use-cases, and computational support for conceptual blending. In T. R. Besold, M. Schorlemmer, and A. Smaill, editors, *Computational Creativity Research: Towards Creative Machines*, Thinking Machines. Atlantis/Springer, 2014.

G. Malcolm. *Software Engineering with OBJ: Algebraic specification in action.* Kluwer, 2000.

M. A. Kaliakatsos-Papakostas, R. Confalonieri, J. Corneli, A. I. Zacharakis, and E. Cambouropoulos. An argument-based creative assistant for harmonic blending. In *Proc. of the 7th International Conference on Computational Creativity, ICCC16*, pages 330–337, 2016.

T. Mossakowski, M. Codescu, F. Neuhaus, and O. Kutz. *The Road to Universal Logic—Festschrift for 50th birthday of Jean-Yves Beziau, Volume II.* Studies in Universal Logic. Birkhäuser, 2015.

S. Ontañón and E. Plaza. Similarity measures over refinement graphs. *Machine Learning*, 87(1):57–92, Apr. 2012.

S. Ontañón and E. Plaza. Amalgams: A formal approach for combining multiple case solutions. In I. Bichindaritz and S. Montani, editors, *Proceedings of the International Conference on Case Base Reasoning*, volume 6176 of *Lecture Notes in Computer Science*, pages 257–271. Springer, 2010. ISBN 978-3-642-14273-4.

F. C. Pereira. *A Computational Model of Creativity*. Ph.D. thesis, Universidade de Coimbra, 2005.

F. C. Pereira. *Creativity and Artificial Intelligence: A Conceptual Blending Approach*. Mouton de Gruyter, 2007.

F. C. Pereira and A. Cardoso. The boat-house visual blending experiment. In *Proceedings of the 2nd Workshop on Creative Systems: Approaches to Creativity in AI and Cognitive Science. ECAI 2002, Lyon, France*, 2002.

F. C. Pereira and A. Cardoso. Optimality principles for conceptual blending: A first computational approach. *AISB Journal*, 1(4):351–370, 2003a.

F. C. Pereira and A. Cardoso. The horse-bird creature generation experiment. *AISB Journal*, 1(3):257–280, 2003b.

F. C. Pereira and A. Cardoso. Experiments with free concept generation in Divago. *Knowledge-Based Systems*, 19(7):459–470, 2006.

J. Pollock. How to reason defeasibly. *Artificial Intelligence Journal*, 57:1–42, 1992.

D. Porello, N. Troquard, R. Peñaloza, R. Confalonieri, P. Galliani, O. Kutz. Two approaches to ontology integration based on axiom weakening. *Proceedings of the Twenty-Seventh International Joint Conference on Artificial Intelligence, IJCAI-18*, 1942–1948, 2018. DOI: 10.24963/ijcai.2018/268

M. Schmidt-Schauß and G. Smolka. Attributive concept descriptions with complements. *Artificial Intelligence*, 48(1):1–26, Feb. 1991. ISSN 0004-3702.

M. Schorlemmer, R. Confalonieri, and E. Plaza. Coherent concept invention. In T. R. Besold, O. Kutz, and C. Leon, editors, *Proceedings of the Workshop on Computational Creativity, Concept Invention, and General Intelligence (C3GI 2016)*, Bozen-Bolzano, Italy, August 20-22, 2016, volume 1767 of *CEUR Workshop Proceedings*. CEUR-WS.org, 2016.

A. Schwering, U. Krumnack, K.-U. Kühnberger, and H. Gust. Syntactic principles of heuristic-driven theory projection. *Cognitive Systems Research*, 10(3):251–269, 2009.

G. Smolka and H. Aït-Kaci. Inheritance hierarchies: Semantics and unification. *Journal of Symbolic Computation*, 7(3–4):343—370, 1989.

P. Thagard. *Coherence in Thought and Action*. The MIT Press, 2000. ISBN 978-0-262-20131-5.

P. Thagard. *The Brain and the Meaning of Life*. Princeton University Press, 2010.

P. Thagard and T. C. Stewart. The AHA! experience: Creativity through emergent binding in neural networks. *Cognitive Science*, 35(1):1–33, 2011.

N. Troquard, R. Confalonieri, P. Galliani, R. Peñaloza, D. Porello, O. Kutz. Repairing ontologies via axiom weakening. *Proceedings of the Thirty-Second AAAI Conference on Artificial Intelligence, AAAI-18*, 1981–1988, 2018.

P. R. van der Laag and S.-H. Nienhuys-Cheng. Completeness and properness of refinement operators in inductive logic programming. *The Journal of Logic Programming*, 34(3):201 – 225, 1998. ISSN 0743-1066.

T. Veale and D. O. Donoghue. Computation and blending. *Cognitive Linguistics*, 11(3-4):253–282, 2000. DOI: 10.1515/cogl.2001.016.

T. Veale and M. Keane. The competence of sub-optimal theories of structure mapping on hard analogies. In *International Joint Conference in Artificial Intelligence*, pages 232–237, 1997.

G. A. Wiggins. A preliminary framework for description, analysis and comparison of creative systems. *Knowledge-Based Systems*, 19(7):449–458, 2006.

Chapter 3
Conceptual Blending in DOL: Evaluating Consistency and Conflict Resolution[*]

Mihai Codescu[†], Fabian Neuhaus[†], Till Mossakowski, Oliver Kutz, and Danny de Jesús Gómez-Ramírez

Abstract In cognitive science the theory of *conceptual blending* provides an explanation of the human ability to invent concepts. This cognitive theory provides an inspiration for computational concept invention theory, which has the goal of building creative systems that generate new concepts automatically. In Chapter 3 we discuss a workflow for a system that (a) creatively blends two concepts into a new concept, (b) identifies conflicts, (c) resolves conflicts by generalising the input spaces, and (d) evaluates the new concept against requirements.

One critical question for the development of such a system is the choice of an appropriate representation of the conceptual blend and the other steps in the workflow. For this purpose we use the Distributed Ontology, Model and Specification Language (DOL). DOL is a metalanguage that enables the reuse of existing ontologies as building blocks for new ontologies and, further, allows the specification of intended relationships between ontologies. One important feature of DOL is the ability to combine (blend) ontologies that are written in different languages without changing their semantics.

Fabian Neuhaus, Till Mossakowski

Institute for Intelligent Cooperative Systems, Otto-von-Guericke University of Magdeburg, Universitätsplatz 2, 39106, Magdeburg, Germany. e-mail: `fneuhaus@iks.cs.ovgu.de, till@iks.cs.ovgu.de`

Oliver Kutz, Mihai Codescu

KRDB Research Centre for Knowledge and Data, Free University of Bozen-Bolzano, Dominikanerplatz 3, 39100, Bozen-Bolzano, Italy. e-mail: `Oliver.Kutz@unibz.it, Mihai.Codescu@unibz.it`

Danny de Jesús Gómez-Ramírez

Vienna University of Technology, Wiedner Hauptstrasse 8-10, 1040 Vienna, Austria. e-mail: `dagomez1982@gmail.com`

[*] This chapter is based on the following works: (Neuhaus et al., 2014), (Kutz et al., 2014), (Kutz et al., 2014b), and (Mossakowski et al., 2015).

[†] These authors contributed equally to this work.

R. Confalonieri et al. (eds.), *Concept Invention*, Computational Synthesis and Creative Systems, https://doi.org/10.1007/978-3-319-65602-1_3

69

3.1 Introduction

Conceptual blending in the spirit of Fauconnier and Turner operates by combining two input 'conceptual spaces', construed as rather minimal descriptions of some thematic domains, in a manner that creates new 'imaginative' configurations (Fauconnier and Turner, 2003; Turner, 2014). A classic example for this is the blending of the concepts *house* and *boat*, yielding as most straightforward blends the concepts of a *houseboat* and a *boathouse*, but also an *amphibious vehicle*. These examples illustrate that, typically, the blended spaces inherit some features from both spaces and combine them to something novel. The blending of the input spaces involves a base space (also called 'generic space'), which contains shared structures between both input spaces. The structure in the base space is preserved in the blended space (the *blendoid*).

For Fauconnier and Turner, conceptual blending is a cognitive ability, and not a symbolic process. Nevertheless, it inspired researchers to search for computational representations of conceptual blending.

Goguen defines an approach that he terms *algebraic semiotics* in which certain structural aspects of semiotic systems are logically formalised in terms of algebraic theories, sign systems, and their mappings (Goguen, 1999). In Goguen and Harrell (2010), algebraic semiotics has been applied to user interface design and conceptual blending. Algebraic semiotics does not claim to provide a comprehensive formal theory of blending – indeed, Goguen and Harrell admit that many aspects of blending cannot be captured formally. However, the structural aspects *can* be formalised and provide insights into the space of possible blends. The formalisation of these blends has been formulated using the algebraic specification language OBJ3 (Goguen and Malcolm, 1996). Since OBJ3 has been invented as a language for algebraic specification and programming, it is not best-suited for knowledge representation due to the lack of predicates, full Boolean connectives and existential quantifiers. Therefore, we will consider other logical languages below.

For the purpose of implementing conceptual blending as a model for computational creativity there are two significant challenges:

First, the literature on conceptual blending typically discusses examples that illustrate how a given concept may be understood as the blend of two (or more) existing concepts. Thus, the literature is usually focussed on the *reconstructive analysis* of blends. However, for the purpose of computational creativity we need to go far beyond that and achieve *creative blends*. In order for a system to be creative, it needs to generate some new, useful, and ideally surprising concepts (Boden, 1998). As Colton and Wiggins (2012) argue, one important aspect for a creative system is the ability of the system to evaluate the output it generates and to select candidates itself (low curation factor).

Second, conceptual blending is a process that is applicable to a wide range of domains and even across domains. However, the languages that are used to represent knowledge vary often significantly across domains; e.g., mathematical knowledge is usually represented using first-order formulas, much biological knowledge is represented in the Web Ontology Language (OWL), and music is often represented

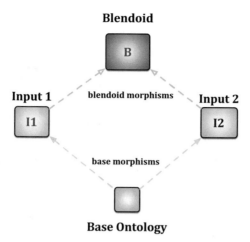

Fig. 3.1: The basic integration network for blending: concepts in the base ontology are first refined to concepts in the input ontologies and then selectively blended into the blendoid

as notes on staves. Hence, one challenge is to develop a knowledge representation framework that enables the representation of the blending processes and that supports knowledge sources that are provided in a diverse set of knowledge representation languages.

In this chapter, we address both of these challenges. In Section 3.2, we discuss a workflow that implements conceptual blending in a computational system. Further, in Section 3.3, we introduce the Distributed Ontology, Model, and Specification Language (DOL), a knowledge representation language that supports the representation of conceptual blending. In Section 3.4, we illustrate the use of DOL for conceptual blending with the help of two examples.

3.2 Towards the Computational Generation of Blends

As mentioned above, we follow in the footsteps of Goguen and Harrell (2010)'s approach to computational conceptual blending. Their main insight has been the following: Semiotic systems and conceptual spaces may be represented as logical theories or ontologies. If two such theories are related via *morphisms* to a third space (the base ontology), then the blending of the input spaces is comparable to a *colimit computation*. This construction is comparable to a disjoint union modulo the identification of certain parts. In particular, the blending of two concepts is often a *pushout*, also called a *blendoid* in this context. (See Figure 3.1.)

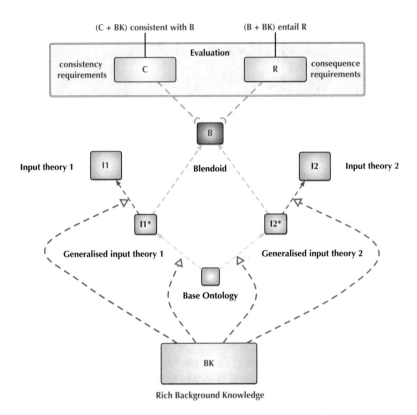

Fig. 3.2: The core COINVENT model for computational blending enriched with evaluation and background layers

3.2.1 COINVENT Model

A variant of the Goguen and Harrell approach has been proposed within the COIN-VENT research project (see Figure 3.2 and www.coinvent-project.eu). In the next sections we discuss the various elements of this revised blending approach which we will refer to as the *COINVENT model*. The model is discussed in more technical detail in Chapter 1 of this book.

The COINVENT model differs from the model proposed in (Goguen and Harrell, 2010) by introducing an extra step: the ontologies *I*1 and *I*2 are not blended directly, but are first generalised to two theories $I1^*$ and $I2^*$ (see Figure 3.2).[3] There are different strategies that can be used to generate the generalised theories from the input ontologies; e.g., by amalgams (see Chapter 1) and refinement operators (Confalonieri et al., 2018). The only constraint is that input ontologies logically entail their generalised counterparts. The purpose of this extra step is to remove some of the information from the input spaces that is undesired for the blend. There are several reasons why such a step might be necessary. Firstly, when blending a concept from a given ontology, typically large parts of the ontology are in fact off-topic. Logically speaking, when extracting a module for the concept in question, large parts of the ontology turn out to be logically irrelevant (module extraction is typically based on conservative extensions, see e.g., Konev et al. (2008)). Secondly, when running the blend it may become obvious that the blendoid preserved too many properties from the input spaces — it may even become inconsistent. In this case, generalising the input spaces will lead to a better result.

The generalised input ontologies $I1^*$ and $I2^*$ are used to generate the base ontology. The base ontology is identifying some structure that is shared across $I1^*$ and $I2^*$. Or, to put it differently, the base ontology contains some theory, which can be found in both the input spaces, but it abstracts from the peculiarities of the input spaces and generalises the theory in some domain-independent way.

From the perspective of a blending workflow the base ontology is a more general theory that is generated from the (generalised) input ontologies. From a logical point of view, there exist two theory morphisms (interpretations of theories) which embed the base ontology into $I1^*$ and $I2^*$. (In Figure 3.2 these are represented by the thinly dotted connectors between the base and $I1^*$ and $I2^*$.) These interpretations are a key element to make the automatic blending process work.

The ontologies $I1^*$ and $I2^*$ together with the base ontology and the two theory morphisms (interpretations) that connect the base to $I1^*$ and $I2^*$ determine the blendoid. Informally, what happens is that the blendoid is a disjoint union of $I1^*$ and $I2^*$, where the shared structure from the base is identified. Technically, this is a colimit computation, a construction that abstracts the operation of disjoint unions modulo the identification of certain parts specified by the base and the theory morphisms, as discussed in detail in (Goguen, 2003; Kutz et al., 2010, 2012). For a formal definition, see Chapter 1.

The COINVENT model guarantees that for any two input theories $I1, I2$ there are many blendoids. In the most trivial case the base ontology is empty, in which case the blendoid consists just of the disjoint union of the inputs. One slightly less trivial approach is to use the shared symbols as the base ontology and the inclusions of the shared symbols in the input theories as morphisms from the base to the input theories. In this case, the blendoid is the union of both input theories. Another option would be to relate the two input spaces via alignment relations: this covers not only the case of the intersections (the symbols match only if they have the same name), but handles the case where we would like to identify synonyms

---

[3] Note that Goguen and Harrell achieved a similar effect by considering morphisms that do not preserve all axioms. However, we think that our solution is conceptually easier and also provides a cleaner basis for blend evaluation.

across the input spaces, and it allows moreover for finer semantic relations between the entities of the two ontologies, for example subsumption between concepts. DOL provides support for declarative specification of alignments between ontologies (see Section 3.3.2 for more technical detail). In general there exists a plethora of options for generalising the input theories, for possible base ontologies and for the morphisms between the base ontology and the generalised input theories. However, most of these combinations lead to undesirable blendoids. The blendoid may be incoherent, because it includes conflicting information from the input spaces. Alternatively, the blendoid may contain too little information to be considered a coherent concept or just combine the wrong ideas to be of any use in a particular context. For instance, one possible conceptual blend of a Rubik's Cube and a computer keyboard is an object where the keys of a keyboard are arranged in the shape of a cube and may change their locations. This blendoid may be a new concept, but it will be of little use if the goal is to develop ergonomic keyboards. Thus, two major challenges for the implementation of a framework for conceptual blending are to (1) find heuristics for generalising the input theories, selecting base ontologies, and selecting the morphisms between them (2) develop methods for automating evaluating candidate blendoids that are generated by the system.

While there is a wide range of evaluation methods possible, we consider here two important strategies. Both depend on a rich background theory, which provides knowledge to drive the selection heuristics and the evaluation. One strategy is to evaluate the blendoid B against ontological constraints, i.e., a set C of axioms that express conditions that the blendoid is not supposed to violate. Whether the ontological constraints C are met can be determined by checking the logical consistency of the blendoid with the union of the constraints C and the background knowledge BK. The other strategy is to consider consequence requirements R, i.e., a collection of conjectures that represent desired properties that the blendoid should have. These requirements may be evaluated by automatic theorem provers, which check whether the requirements in R are entailed by the blendoid B together with the background knowledge BK. If the blendoid is rejected according to these criteria, the next cycle is started with different generalised input spaces and/or a different base. Ideally, the results of the evaluation are supposed to guide the changes in the next cycle.

Figure 3.2 captures the conceptual blending model that we discussed in this section in a static view. However, this perspective is somewhat misleading, since conceptual blending is an iterative process and previous attempts influence new attempts. Thus, we will now discuss a workflow for conceptual blending.

3.2.2 Conceptual Blending Workflow

Since there is a vast number of potential blends of two concepts, most of which are poor, computational concept blending is an iterative process. This ideas lead us to the evaluation-based blending workflow depicted in Figure 3.3.

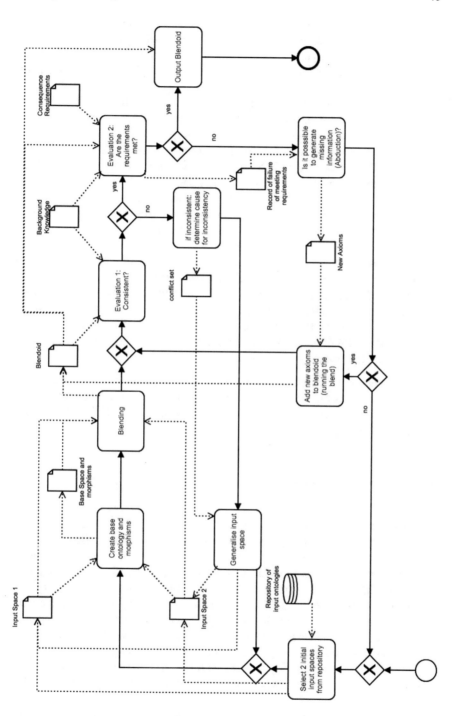

Fig. 3.3: A Blending Workflow

We assume the existence of a library of potential input spaces; and, further, that the requirements for the blended concepts are provided as *consequence requirements*. Consequence requirements are logical propositions that are supposed to be logically entailed by the blended concepts (given the available background knowledge).[4]

The input spaces for the blending process are selected from the library of input spaces. They are then used in a one-step blending loop: a base ontology and base morphisms are generated, and based on that a blendoid is computed. We now come to evaluating the blendoid. First, the ontology resulting from the union of the blendoid with the background knowledge and ontological constraints is evaluated for logical consistency. Should the consistency check fail, we analyse the inconsistency proof to extract the involved axioms. One of these axioms is either removed or replaced by a logically weaker version, thereby generalising one of the input spaces. By iterating this process, we eliminate all inconsistencies, and finish with a blendoid consistent with the background knowledge.

If the consistency test is successful, then it is evaluated whether it meets the consequence requirements for the blending process. If this second test is successful, then the blending process is considered successful. Otherwise, there are two options: if it is possible to identify information that could be added in order to successfully meet the requirements, then new axioms can be added to the blendoid. This step requires some form of abductive reasoning and is often called 'running the blend'. Alternatively, the process is started over.

The processes in Figure 3.3 involve operations on documents that contain logical theories. This raises the question about the appropriate representation of these operations, and their semantics. For this purpose we developed DOL, which will be discussed in the next section.

3.3 Blending with DOL

Any implementation of the workflow that is presented in the previous section requires a language that is suitable to represent a wide range of operations on representations of concepts. Since these concepts may be part of any domain, we cannot assume that they are represented in a particular language. The Distributed Ontology, Model, and Specification Language DOL is a formal language for specifying both ontologies, input networks, and their blends. DOL is a metalanguage in the sense that it enables the reuse of existing ontologies (written in some ontology language like OWL or Common Logic) as building blocks for new ontologies and, further, allows the specification of intended relationships between ontologies. One important feature of DOL is the ability to combine ontologies that are written in different languages without changing their semantics. DOL has been adopted as a standard

---

[4] This technique for the evaluation of concepts corresponds to the technique of competency questions in ontology engineering (Grüninger and Fox, 1995; Ren et al., 2014).

by the Object Management Group.[5] DOL is supported by the Heterogeneous Tool Set HETS (Mossakowski et al., 2007), presented in more detail in Chapter 7, and the Ontohub platform (Mossakowski et al., 2014) discussed briefly below.

In this section, we introduce DOL only informally. A formal specification of the language and its model-theoretic semantics can be found in (Mossakowski et al., 2013a, 2015).

3.3.1 Foundations of DOL

A large variety of logical languages in use can be captured at an abstract level using the concept of *institutions* (Goguen and Burstall, 1992). This allows us to develop results independently of the particularities of a logical system and to use the notions of institution and logical languages interchangeably throughout the rest of this chapter. The main idea is to collect the non-logical symbols of the language in signatures and to assign to each signature the set of sentences that can be formed with its symbols. Signature morphisms are mappings between signatures. We do not assume any details except that signature morphisms can be composed and that there are identity morphisms; this amounts to a category of signatures.[6]

Institutions also provide a model theory, which introduces semantics for the language and gives a satisfaction relation between the models and the sentences of a signature. The only restriction imposed is the satisfaction condition, which captures the idea that truth is invariant under change of notation (and enlargement of context) along signature morphisms. This relies on two further components of institutions: the translation of sentences along signature morphisms, and the reduction of models against signature morphisms (generalising the notion of model reduct known from logic).

It is also possible to complement an institution with a proof theory, introducing a derivability relation between sentences, formalised as an *entailment system* (Meseguer, 1989). In particular, this can be done for all logics that have so far been in use in DOL.

To sum up, an institution provides notions of signature and signature morphism (formally, this is given by a category **Sign**), and for each signature Σ in **Sign**, a set of sentences $Sen(\Sigma)$, a class of models $Mod(\Sigma)$ and a binary satisfaction relation $\models_\Sigma$ between models and sentences. Furthermore, given a signature morphism $\sigma : \Sigma_1 \to \Sigma_2$, an institution provides sentence translation along σ, written $\sigma(\varphi)$, and model reduct against σ, written $M|_\sigma$, in a way that satisfaction remains invariant:

$$M'|_\sigma \models_{\Sigma_1} \varphi \text{ iff } M' \models_{\Sigma_2} \sigma(\varphi)$$

---

[5] http://www.omg.org/spec/DOL/; see also http://dol-omg.org/ for more material about DOL.

[6] Readers unfamiliar with category theory may replace this with a partial order (signature morphisms are then just inclusions). See Mossakowski et al. (2013b) for details of this simplified foundation.

for each $\varphi \in Sen(\Sigma_1)$ and $M' \in Mod(\Sigma_2)$.

DOL and HETS support a variety of different logics; the most important and currently most frequently used logics for conceptual blending within COINVENT are the following:

OWL 2 is the Web Ontology Language recommended by the World Wide Web Consortium (W3C);[7] see OWL Working Group (2009). It is used for knowledge representation on the Semantic Web (Berners-Lee et al., 2001). HETS supports OWL 2 DL and the provers Fact++ and Pellet.

FOL/TPTP is an untyped first-order logic with equality,[8] underlying the interchange language TPTP (Sutcliffe, 2010).[9] HETS offers several automated theorem proving (ATP) systems for TPTP, namely SPASS (Weidenbach et al., 2002), Vampire (Riazanov and Voronkov, 2002), Eprover (Schulz, 2002), Darwin (Baumgartner et al., 2005), E-KRHyper (Pelzer and Wernhard, 2007), and MathServe Broker (which chooses an appropriate ATP upon a classification of the FOL problem) (Zimmer and Autexier, 2006).

CFOL is many-sorted first-order logic with so-called sort generation constraints, expressing that each value of a given sort is the interpretation of some term involving certain functions (called constructors). This is equivalent to an induction principle and allows the axiomatisation of lists and other datatypes, using the usual Peano-style axioms (such an axiomatisation is called a *free type*). CFOL is a sublogic of the Common Algebraic Specification Language CASL, see (Mosses, 2004; Bidoit and Mosses, 2004). Proof support for CFOL is available through a simple induction scheme in connection with automated first-order provers like SPASS (Lüttich and Mossakowski, 2007), or via a logic translation to HOL. A connection to the induction prover KIV (Balser et al., 1998) is under development.

HOL is typed higher-order logic (Borzyszkowski, 1999). HETS actually supports several variants of HOL, among them THF0 (the higher-order version of TPTP (Benzmüller et al., 2008b)), with automated provers LEO-II (Benzmüller et al., 2008a) and Satallax (Brown, 2012) and an automated interface to Isabelle (Nipkow et al., 2002), as well as the logic of Isabelle, with an interactive interface.

HETS supports the input languages of these logics directly. This is achieved by representing these logics within the framework of institutions. As illustration we informally sketch in the following how OWL is described as institution:

---

[7] http://www.w3.org

[8] There is also SoftFOL, extending first-order logic with equality with a softly typed logic used by SPASS; however, here we will only use the sublanguage corresponding to FOL.

[9] http://www.tptp.org

> OWL **as institution:** OWL *signatures consist of sets of atomic classes,*
> *individuals and properties. OWL signature morphisms map classes to*
> *classes, individuals to individuals, and properties to properties. For an*
> *OWL signature Σ, sentences are subsumption relations between classes or*
> *properties, membership assertions of individuals in classes and pairs of in-*
> *dividuals in properties, complex role inclusions, and some more things. Sen-*
> *tence translation along a signature morphism simply replaces non-logical*
> *symbols with their image along the morphism. The kinds of symbols are*
> *class, individual, object property and data property, respectively, and the*
> *set of symbols of a signature is the union of its sets of classes, individuals*
> *and properties. Models are (unsorted) first-order structures that interpret*
> *concepts as unary and properties as binary predicates, and individuals as*
> *elements of the universe of the structure, and satisfaction is the standard*
> *satisfaction of description logics. This gives us an institution for OWL.*

In this framework, a basic ontology O over an institution I is a pair (Σ, E) where Σ is a signature and E is a set of Σ-sentences. Given a basic ontology O, we denote by $\text{Sig}(O)$ the signature of the ontology. A theory morphism $\sigma : (\Sigma_1, E_1) \rightarrow (\Sigma_2, E_2)$ is a signature morphism $\sigma : \Sigma_1 \rightarrow \Sigma_2$ such that $\sigma(E_1)$ is a logical consequence of E_2.

Several notions of *translations* between institutions can be introduced. The most frequently used variant is *institution comorphisms* (Goguen and Roşu, 2002). A comorphism from institution L_1 to institution L_2 maps L_1-signatures to L_2-signatures along a functor Φ and Σ-sentences in L_1 to $\Phi(\Sigma)$-sentences in L_2, for each L_1-signature Σ, while $\Phi(\Sigma)$-models are mapped to Σ-models. Again, a satisfaction condition has to be fulfilled. For *institution morphisms*, the directions of the translation of sentences and models are reversed. See Goguen and Roşu (2002) for full details.

3.3.2 Features of DOL

An essential novelty introduced in DOL is that a user can specify the ontological input diagram (network) in DOL, from which the colimit and other blendoids can then be computed.[10] This is a crucial task, as the computed colimit ontology depends on the dependencies between symbols that are stored in the network. Ontohub, a DOL-enabled repository discussed further in Section 3.3.3, is able to use the specification of an input network to automatically generate the colimit ontology.

For the purpose of ontology blending the following features of DOL are relevant:

---

[10] While OBJ3 already provides the possibility to write down theory morphisms, only DOL provides means to collect them into a formally defined diagram; see the **network** construct below. While in the blending literature, the term "diagram" is used, in DOL they are called networks in order to avoid confusion with UML diagrams.

1. a *basic ontology* O written inline, in a conforming ontology language and serialisation. The semantics is inherited from the ontology language. O can also be an ontology fragment, which means that some of the symbols or axioms may refer to symbols declared outside O (i.e., in an imported ontology). This is mainly used for extensions and equivalences. Here are two sample ontologies in OWL (using Manchester syntax) and CFOL:

```
Class: Woman EquivalentTo: Person and Female
ObjectProperty: hasParent

ontology PreOrder =
 sort Elem
 pred __<=__ : Elem * Elem
 . forall x : Elem . x <= x
 . forall x, y, z : Elem . x <= y /\ y <= z => x <= z
```

2. an ontology qualified with the ontology *language* that is used to express it (written **language** $l : O$, where l identifies a language). Similarly, qualifications can also be by *logic* (written **logic** $l : O$), and/or *serialisation* (written **syntax** $s : O$).[11]

3. an IRI reference to an ontology existing on the Web,[12] possibly abbreviated using prefixes.[13] For example:

```
%prefix(
expl:<http://example.org/ontologies/>)%
http://example/ontologies/pizza.owl
expl:pizza.owl
```

4. an *extension* of an ontology by new symbols and axioms, written O_1 **then** O_2, where O_2 is an ontology (fragment) in a conforming ontology language. The resulting signature is that of O_1, augmented with the symbols in O_2. A model of an extension ontology is a model over this signature that satisfies the axioms of O_2 and is (when appropriately reduced) a model of O_1. In case that O_2 does not introduce any new symbols, the annotation %implies can be used instead of %ccons or %mcons; the extension then merely states intended logical consequences. The following OWL ontology is an example:

```
   Class Person
   Class Female
then
   Class: Woman EquivalentTo: Person and Female
```

5. a *union* of two self-contained ontologies (not fragments), written O_1 **and** O_2. Models of this union are those models that are (perhaps after appropriate reduction) models of both O_1 and O_2. For example, the class of commutative monoids can be expressed as

---

[11] Some of the following listings omit obvious qualifications for readability.

[12] Note that not all ontologies can be downloaded by dereferencing their IRIs. Implementing a catalogue mechanism in DOL-aware applications might remedy this problem.

[13] Some of the following listings abbreviate IRIs using prefixes but omit the prefix bindings for readability.

```
algebra:Monoid and algebra:Commutative
```

6. a *translation* of an ontology to a different signature (written O **with** σ, where
σ is a signature morphism) or into some ontology language (written O **with**
translation ρ, where ρ is an institution comorphism). For example, we can
combine an OWL ontology with a first-order axiom as follows:

```
ObjectProperty: isProperPartOf
  Characteristics: Asymmetric
  SubPropertyOf: isPartOf
with translation OWL22CASL
then
  . forall x, y : Thing
   . isProperPartOf(x, y) /\ isProperPartOf(y, z)
     => isProperPartOf(x, z)
```

Note that OWL can express transitivity, but not together with asymmetry.

7. a *filtering* of an ontology, written O **select** (Σ, Δ) which selects those sentences
from O that have signature Σ, plus those in Δ, where Δ is a subset of $Ax(O)$.
It can also be written O **reject** (Σ, Δ) where Σ is the set of symbols and Δ the
set of axioms to be hidden. For example, we can select all axioms of GALEN[14]
involving Drugs, Joints, or Bodyparts by:

```
logic OWL
ontology myGalen =
<http://example.org/GALEN/galen.owl>
select Drugs, Joints, Bodyparts
end
```

8. a module *extracted* from an ontology, written O **extract** Σ. Here, Σ is a restriction signature, which needs to be a subsignature of $Sig(O)$. The extracted
module is a subontology of O with signature larger than (or equal to) Σ, such
that O is a conservative extension of the extracted module. Dually, O **remove** Σ
extracts w.r.t. the signature $Sig(O) \setminus \Sigma$.[15]

```
Pizza remove
  VegetarianTopping
```

9. a *network*: the syntax for specifying networks (= diagrams of ontologies and
morphisms) in DOL is

```
network N = N1,...,Nm,O1,...,On,M1,...,Mp,A1,...,Ak
```

where N_i are networks, O_i are ontologies, M_i are morphisms and A_i are alignments. The user specifies a network N formed with existing networks N_i, extended with ontologies O_i and the morphisms M_i and the networks of the alignments A_i (full details regarding alignments is given in Codescu et al. (2014)).
Models of networks are families of models for the involved individual ontologies that are compatible along the morphisms in the network.

---

[14] We assume here that GALEN is available as an OWL ontology.

[15] Note that the resulting module can still contain symbols from Σ, because the resulting signature
may be enlarged.

10. a *combination* of ontologies: DOL also provides means for combining a network into a new ontology, such that the symbols related in the network are identified. The syntax of combinations is `ontology O = combine N`, where *N* is a network, named or specified as above. The semantics of a combination *O* is the class of models of the colimit ontology of the network specified in the combination. Under rather mild technical assumptions, this model class captures exactly the models of the network.

The simplest example of a combination is a disjoint union (we here translate OWL ontologies into many-sorted OWL in order to be able to distinguish between different universes of individuals):

```
ontology Publications1 =
  Class: Publication
  Class: Article SubClassOf: Publication
  Class: InBook SubClassOf: Publication
  Class: Thesis  SubClassOf: Publication
  ...

ontology Publications2 =
  Class: Thing
  Class: Article SubClassOf: Thing
  Class: BookArticle SubClassOf: Thing
  Class: Publication SubClassOf: Thing
  Class: Thesis  SubClassOf: Thing
  ...

ontology Publications_Combined =
combine
  1 : Publications1 with translation trans:OWL2MS-OWL,
  2 : Publications2 with translation trans:OWL2MS-OWL
  %% implicitly: Article ↦ 1:Article ...
  %%            Article ↦ 2:Article ...
end
```

3.3.3 Tool Support for DOL

Currently, DOL is supported by two tools: Ontohub and the Heterogeneous Tool Set (HETS). Ontohub is a web-based repository engine for ontologies that are written either in DOL or in some specific ontology language.[16]

Ontohub provides means for organising ontologies into repositories. The distributed nature enables communities to share and exchange their contributions easily. The heterogeneous nature makes it possible to integrate ontologies written in various ontology languages. Ontohub supports a wide range of DOL-conforming ontology languages building on DOL and also supports DOL's interpretations, equivalences

---

[16] Ontohub is available at `http://ontohub.org`. Ontohub's sources are freely available at `https://github.com/ontohub/ontohub`.

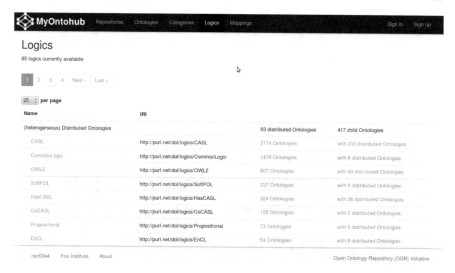

Fig. 3.4: Overview of logics in Ontohub

and alignments. Users of Ontohub can upload, browse, search and annotate ontologies and ontology libraries in various languages via a web front end. Figure 3.4 shows an excerpt of the 25 logics currently available in Ontohub.

The parsing and inference back end is the Heterogeneous Tool Set (HETS), available at hets.eu (Mossakowski et al., 2007). HETS supports a large number of ontology languages and logics, as well as the DOL metalanguage as described here.[17]

The structural information extracted by HETS from ontologies and ontology libraries is stored in the Ontohub database and exposed to human users via a web interface and to machine clients as linked data, a set of best practices for publishing structured data on the Web in a machine-friendly way (Berners-Lee, 2006). DOL and Ontohub conform with linked data.

3.3.4 Workflow Formalisation in DOL

The input network can be formally specified in DOL in the following way. The two input spaces, $I1$ and $I2$, are named ontologies that can make use of the DOL structuring in an arbitrarily complex way. In practice, since the methods for computing the base space from two given input ontologies take as arguments two logical theories, it is reasonable to require that the input spaces are flattenable. The base ontology G (which represents the generic space) is also a named ontology, usually computed

---

[17] Some (but only few) of DOL's features are still being implemented at the time of the writing of this chapter.

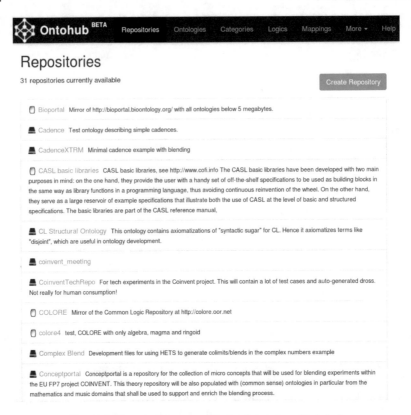

Fig. 3.5: Some of the repositories hosted on Ontohub

with some external tool that returns a basic ontology as well as two signature morphisms from the generic space to the two input spaces. These are represented in DOL using theory morphisms (interpretations):

```
ontology I1 = ... %% DOL structured specification
ontology I2 = ... %% DOL structured specification
ontology  G = ... %% DOL basic specification
interpretation V1 : G to I1 = ... %% signature morphism
interpretation V2 : G to I2 = ... %% signature morphism
```

The elements of the input network are then collected in DOL as follows:

```
network N = V1, V2
```

Notice that here it suffices to add the two interpretations to the network, as their source and target ontologies are included in the network by default.

The blendoid is then obtained as the colimit of the input network, using DOL combinations:

```
ontology B = combine N
```

HETS provides an interface to theorem provers and model finders. For example, one can postulate that the blendoid should be consistent with some ontological constraints C from some background knowledge ontology BK using the semantic annotation **%consistent**:

```
ontology BlendConsistent = %consistent
  B and BK and C
```

This gives rise to a consistency obligation in HETS, which can be discharged by calling a consistency checker for the logic of the blendoid. If the blendoid is inconsistent, one possible way of generalising the input spaces is by filtering axioms. HETS can deliver the axioms that generate an inconsistency or that are used in a proof of falsity and one of these can be removed from the input spaces it originates from as below

```
ontology I1* = I1 reject Ax1, Ax2
```

where we assume that the axioms named Ax1 and Ax2 are removed from the first input space.

Finally, if the consequence requirements R are given as a DOL ontology that contains conjectures over the signature of the blendoid *B* and the background knowledge *BK*, we can use the following DOL construction to express that the conjectures in *R* are proof obligations:

```
ontology BlendRequirements =
    {B and BK}
  then %implied
    R
```

These proof obligations may be validated via HETS, which calls an automatic theorem prover that supports the logic of the blendoid.

3.4 Examples of Conceptual Blending in DOL

In Section 3.3.4, we described how DOL may be utilised in the formal representation of conceptual blending networks. In this section, we illustrate this point with the help of two examples.

3.4.1 Creating Monsters

We illustrate our blending workflow with the example of blending animals into monsters. The background knowledge consists of an ontology about animals, their body parts, habitats, and other features of animals. (Figure 3.6 shows small fragments of the background knowledge.)

The input spaces consist of descriptions of animal concepts. These can be thought of as prototypical individuals. Each of these specifications extends the background

```
Class: Tiger
        SubClassOf: Carnivore, has_habitat some Jungle, Quadruped,
                    Mammal, has_part exactly 1 Tail
Class: Cobra
        SubClassOf: Reptile, Poisonous, Carnivore,
                    has_habitat some Forest, SnakeShapedOrganism
Class: Quadruped
        SubClassOf: has_part some QuadrupedTrunk,
                    has_part some Head, has_part exactly 4 Leg
```

Fig. 3.6: Fragments of background knowledge

knowledge, thus the concepts from the background knowledge may be reused. This particular representation focusses on the body parts of the animal and their connections. Figure 3.7 shows one example.

```
ontology cobraInput = backgroundKnowledge then {

Individual: thisConcept
    Types: Cobra
Individual: t
        Types: CobraTrunk
        Facts: part_of thisConcept, has_fiat_boundary t_nb,
               has_fiat_boundary t_tlb
Individual: t_nb
        Types: NeckBoundary
Individual: t_tlb
        Types: TailBoundary
Individual: h
        Types: CobraHead
        Facts: part_of thisConcept, has_fiat_boundary h_nb
Individual: h_nb
        Types: ProximalBoundary
        Facts: meets t_nb
Individual: tl
        Types: CobraTail
        Facts: part_of thisConcept,  has_fiat_boundary tl_pb
Individual: tl_pb
        Types: ProximalBoundary
        Facts: meets t_tlb
}
```

Fig. 3.7: Example of an input space

For the sake of this example, let us assume that the ontologies cobraInput and tigerInput have been selected as the input spaces _I_1 and _I_2, respectively. In the following, we show how the results of the individual steps in Figure 3.3 may be represented in DOL.

3.4.1.1 Generating the Base Ontology

As discussed in Section 3.2, the blending of two input spaces relies on a base ontology, which represents the shared structure. If the base ontology is empty, then nothing is blended, hence in our example the resulting blendoid consists of a theory that contains both a tiger and a cobra. Identifying the shared structure is a complex problem, which is discussed in other chapters of this volume.

While our workflow assumes that the base ontology is generated by some tool, DOL actually provides an operation that generates a base ontology, which may serve as a touchstone for other blends. This approach presupposes that the same terminology is used consistently across the animal ontologies; which is the case in our example since the ontologies have been hand-crafted. We use DOL's theory intersections for this: if *I*1 and *I*2 are two ontologies, then *I*1 intersect *I*2 is the ontology whose signature is the intersection of the signatures of *I*1 and *I*2 and whose sentences are the sentences that are common to *I*1 and *I*2. This automatically generates theory morphisms (interpretations) from the intersection to *I*1 and respectively to *I*2, labelled with the inclusions of the corresponding signatures.

Figure 3.8 shows the specification of the input network for our running example. Notice that the two generated theory morphisms are implicitly added to the input network.

```
ontology Base   =  cobraInput intersect tigerInput

ontology monsterblend  =  combine Base,  cobraInput, tigerInput
```

Fig. 3.8: Specification of the input network

The input network ensures that entities in the different input spaces are identified if they share the same name. The monsterblend ontology that is specified in Figure 3.8 contains a new concept that inherits all properties from cobras and tigers. Typically, such a blend will be inconsistent. For instance, in our example the blended concept would be a reptile and a mammal and have both four legs and no legs. This is why the input spaces need to be generalised (see below).

While the intersection operation of DOL provides a useful baseline for creating blends, this approach limits the number of interesting blends, because the similar entities are identified across the conceptual spaces. However, conceptual blends may combine entities in more unexpected ways. For example, a conceptual blend of a tiger and a cobra may lead to a monster where the cobra is the tiger's tail. This may be achieved by identifying the tail in the tigerInput ontology and the animal in the

cobra ontology via some entity in the base ontology that is mapped to both entities
(see Figure 3.9).

```
ontology BaseB = { Individual: ts }
interpretation BaseB2tiger : BaseB to tigerInput = {ts |-> t}
interpretation BaseB2cobra : BaseB to cobraInput =
                                              {ts |-> thisconcept}
ontology monsterblend2 = combine BaseB2tiger, BaseB2cobra
```

Fig. 3.9: Specification of the input network

3.4.1.2 Generalising the Input Spaces

As mentioned above, the conceptual blending of two input spaces often leads to a
new concept where incompatible properties are combined. For instance, in our case
the straightforward blend in Figure 3.8 leads to a blended theory monsterblend,
where the new concept is both a reptile and a mammal. One way to identify these
conflicts automatically is by evaluating the newly blended concepts for consistency
(see 'Evaluation' step in Figure 3.3). The quality of this kind of evaluation depends
on the richness of the available background knowledge.

If an inconsistency is detected, it is necessary to generalise the input spaces until
the inconsistencies are resolved. There are different heuristics that are available, but,
in general, the goal is to remove axioms that are causing the inconsistency, but not
lose too much information. For example, one way to resolve the Mammal-Reptile-
inconsistency in our running example is by rejecting the axiom that the concept in
cobraInput is a cobra. However, there are many features of cobras that are not
causing any conflicts and may be interesting to retain; e.g., that cobras are poisonous.

DOL enables the generalisation of input spaces. This is achieved by removing
axioms or by replacing them with certain of their logical consequences. (See Figure 3.10)

```
ontology generalisedCobraInput = cobraInput reject {
    Individual: thisConcept Types: Cobra } then {
    Individual: thisConcept Types: Poisonous, Carnivore,
                has_habitat some Forest              }
```

Fig. 3.10: Example of a generalised input space

3.4.1.3 Expressing and Evaluating Requirements

The second evaluation step in Figure 3.3 is about the evaluation of the blendoid against requirements. One requirement for a good blendoid is that it needs to combine information from both input spaces. In other words, if the information in the blendoid is contained in one of the input ontologies, then the blendoid is not a good conceptual blend. This is particularly important to check, since it may happen that one of the input ontologies is generalised so strongly that it no more contributes anything significant to the blendoid.

However, typically a blending process is done with more specific requirements in mind. For instance, in our example we look for monsters that are blended from animals. Thus, we may expect that our monsters combine body parts from different animals. We may also have more abstract requirements, which can be broken down into more specific ones. If we are expecting monsters to be scary, then this leads to additional requirements. In particular, a monster is only scary if it is has the ability to attack people, and it is only able to do that if it has features that enable it to hurt people; e.g., it is poisonous or has fangs or claws or stings.

These requirements can be stated in DOL as proof obligations that have to be proven from the blendoid (potentially involving some additional background knowledge). The proof obligations are marked by the `%implies` keyword; see Figure 3.11.

```
ontology requirementEval = monsterblend then {
    Class Scary
        EquivalentTo  Poisonous  or
                      has_part some (Fang or Claw or Sting)
    } then %implied {
    Individual: thisConcept Types: Scary }
```

Fig. 3.11: Example for expressing requirements

3.4.2 Goldbach Rings

In the previous section, we showed how DOL is able to express the individual steps in a computational blending workflow. As example we used the creation of monsters by blending animal ontologies written in the Web Ontology Language (OWL). In this section we illustrate the blending process with a mathematical example written in the Common Algebraic Specification Language (CASL).

One of the most famous open problems in number theory states that each even natural number $m \geq 4$ can be written as the sum of two prime numbers. Now, with Goldbach's conjecture as motivation, let us define a non-trivial Goldbach structure as a set A with two binary operations $+$ and $*$, neutral elements 0 (for $+$) and 1 (for $*$) for the two operations, a divisibility relation $|$ (defined in terms of the operation $*$), and a unary relation P in A describing all the prime numbers in this structure:

```
ontology Goldbach =
  sort A
  ops __+__, __*__ : A * A -> A
  ops 0, 1 : A
  pred __|__ : A * A
  pred P : A

  forall a : A
    . 0 + a = a
    . a + 0 = a
    . a * 1 = a
    . 1 * a = a

  .forall c : A
    . P(a) <=>
        forall a, b : A
        . c | a * b => (c | a \/ c | b)

    . exists a, b : A
      . not a + a = b + b %(nonTriviality)%

  forall a, b, c : A
    . a * (b + c) = (a * b) + (a * c)
    . (b + c) * a = (b * a) + (c * a)


  forall a: A
    . exists p1, p2 : A
    . P(p1) /\ P(p2) /\ (a + 1) + (a + 1 )= p1 + p2
end
```

The last three axioms guarantee that the collection of even numbers is not trivial and that each sufficiently large even number can be expressed as the sum of two prime numbers.

The second input space is a specification of groups of torsion 2. A set B with a binary operation $++$ and neutral element e is a group of torsion 2 if $(G, ++, e)$ is a group. Besides, each element has order (torsion) at most 2:

```
ontology GroupTorsionTwo =
  sort B
  op e : B
  op __++__ : B * B -> B

  forall a : B
    . a ++ e = a
    . e ++ a = a
    . a ++ a = e
    . exists b : B
        . (a ++ b = e) /\ (b ++ a = e)
  forall a, b, c : B
```

```
        .  (a ++ b)  ++ c = a ++ (b ++ c)
end
```

Let us define the generic space consisting of a set G with a binary operation $+$ and a neutral element n. The theory morphisms (interpretations) from the generic space to the two input spaces are the expected ones:

```
interpretation V1 : Generic to Goldbach =
    __+__ |-> __+__, n |-> 0
```

```
interpretation V2 : Generic to GroupTorsionTwo
```

Now, if we check the consistency of the blendoid obtained as the colimit of the diagram formed by V1 and V2, we obtain an inconsistency because, on the one hand, the non-triviality axiom for even numbers guarantees that there exists at least one non-trivial (non-neutral) even number, and, on the other hand, the torsion-2 condition states that each even number (i.e., of the form $x + x$) is trivial (the neutral element).

However, if the non-triviality condition is erased from the first space, we get a consistent theory. This blend can be specified as follows:

```
ontology GoldbachGeneralised = Goldbach reject nonTriviality
```

```
interpretation V1' : Generic to GoldbachGeneralised =
    __+__ |-> __+__, n |-> 0
```

```
ontology ConsistentBlend = combine V1', V2
```

The conceptual blend `ConsistentBlend` can be computed by HETS; the resulting theory is shown in Figure 3.12. The new concept is an enriched Goldbach Ring due to the fact that the binary operation $+$ fulfils the axioms of a group and the Goldbach space satisfied the distributivity and neutral conditions for $+, *$ and 1, respectively. In fact, the ring of integers module 6 ($\mathbb{Z}/6\mathbb{Z}$) with the natural operations and constants is a model for this blend.

3.5 Summary

In this chapter, we showed how key ideas of the cognitive theory of conceptual blending may be utilised in computational creativity. The goal is to develop a system that automatically creates a new concept based on existing input spaces by blending them with the help of some base space. In the COINVENT model, the input spaces and the base space are represented as ontologies, which are connected by morphisms (interpretations). The blending process is modelled as a colimit operation. The resulting blendoid is evaluated in several ways.

One way to evaluate the blendoid is to check its consistency with a set of background knowledge axioms. In the case of an inconsistency, the relevant axioms can be identified, and this drives the generalisation of the input spaces until a consistent blend is achieved. In addition, we can check whether the resulting (consistent)

```
sorts G
op 1 : G
op __*__ : G * G -> G
op __+__ : G * G -> G
op n : G
pred P : G
pred __|__ : G * G
```

```
forall a : G . n + a = a                                    %(Ax1)%
forall a : G . a * 1 = a                                    %(Ax3)%
forall a : G . 1 * a = a                                    %(Ax4)%
forall a, c : G. P(a) <=>
       forall a, b : G . c | a * b => c | a \/ c | b %(Ax5)%
forall a, b, c : G . a * (b + c) = (a * b) + (a * c) %(Ax7)%
forall a, b, c : G . (b + c) * a = (b * a) + (c * a) %(Ax8)%
forall a : G . exists p1, p2 : G .
       P(p1) /\ P(p2) /\ (a + 1) + (a + 1) = p1 + p2 %(Ax9)%
forall a : G . a + n = a                                    %(Ax1_9)%
forall a : G . a + a = n                                    %(Ax3_11)%
forall a : G . exists b : G . a + b = n /\ b + a = n %(Ax4_12)%
forall a, b, c : G . (a + b) + c = a + (b + c)       %(Ax5_13)%
```

Fig. 3.12: The blended theory ConsistentBlend

blendoid satisfies some desired properties. If this is not the case, the search for a blend starts again with different generalisations of the input spaces. We have organised this as an evaluation-based conceptual blending workflow. The workflow can be formally represented using DOL, which provides constructions for each of the involved steps and has the advantage of being generic in the underlying logic of the input spaces. Thus, we can apply the same workflow to different domains. We presented DOL's features directly relevant for blending and showed how the blending workflow can be generically represented in DOL. We illustrated our approach with two examples: one involving combining features of animals to create monsters and another about re-creating Goldbach rings as a blend of generalised Goldbach structures with groups of torsion 2.

3.6 Conclusion and Future Perspectives

The main contribution of this chapter is the introduction of a workflow for a conceptual blending system and the illustration how the individual steps of the workflow may be represented in DOL. While we characterised the workflow in broad strokes, we did not discuss the individual steps in much detail. In particular, the generation of the base ontology, the generation of the morphisms from the base ontology to the input spaces, and the generalisations of the input spaces all require heuristics that were not in scope of this chapter.

An initial experimental implementation allowed us to test our ideas by automatically generating monsters from animal ontologies. The prototype showed us that the workflow works, but also indicated limitations. One important issue is that the evaluation of the blendoids depends highly on the availability of rich background knowledge as ontologies. Further, these ontologies need to fit the terminology that is used in the input spaces. For this reason we will consider a semi-automatic approach to the evaluation problem of blendoids in the future.

A promising idea is to interactively generate competency questions (cf. Grüninger and Fox (1995); Ren et al. (2014)) from justifications for inconsistencies (Kalyanpur et al., 2007). Here, a user can steer the generation of new blends by rejecting certain ways to fix an inconsistent blendoid. A similar debugging workflow has recently been proposed by Shchekotykhin et al. (2014), although only for the debugging of single inconsistent ontologies. In the case of blending, such approaches need to be adapted to a revision procedure covering networks of ontologies, where several ontologies (i.e., input and base ontologies) as well as the mappings between them are subject to revision.

References

M. Balser, W. Reif, G. Schellhorn, and K. Stenzel. KIV 3.0 for provably correct systems. In D. Hutter, W. Stephan, P. Traverso, and M. Ullmann, editors, *FM-Trends*, volume 1641 of *Lecture Notes in Computer Science*, pages 330–337. Springer, 1998.

P. Baumgartner, A. Fuchs, and C. Tinelli. Implementing the model evolution calculus. *Special Issue of the International Journal of Artificial Intelligence Tools (IJAIT)*, 15(1):21–52, 2005.

C. Benzmüller, L. C. Paulson, F. Theiss, and A. Fietzke. LEO-II: A cooperative automatic theorem prover for classical higher-order logic (System Description). In A. Armando, P. Baumgartner, and G. Dowek, editors, *IJCAR*, volume 5195 of *LNCS*, pages 162–170. Springer, 2008a.

C. Benzmüller, F. Rabe, and G. Sutcliffe. THF0: The core of the TPTP language for higher-order logic. In A. Armando, P. Baumgartner, and G. Dowek, editors, *IJCAR 2008*, volume 5195 of *Lecture Notes in Computer Science*, pages 491–506. Springer, 2008b.

T. Berners-Lee. Design Issues: Linked Data, 2006.

T. Berners-Lee, J. Hendler, and O. Lassila. The Semantic Web. *Scientific American*, May 2001.

M. Bidoit and P. D. Mosses. CASL *User Manual*, volume 2900 of *LNCS*. Springer, 2004.

M. A. Boden. Creativity and artificial intelligence. *Artificial Intelligence*, 103(1): 347 – 356, 1998.

T. Borzyszkowski. Higher-order logic and theorem proving for structured specifications. In D. Bert, C. Choppy, and P. D. Mosses, editors, *WADT*, volume 1827 of *LNCS*, pages 401–418. Springer, 1999.

C. E. Brown. Satallax: An automatic higher-order prover. In B. Gramlich, D. Miller, and U. Sattler, editors, *IJCAR*, volume 7364 of *LNCS*, pages 111–117. Springer, 2012.

M. Codescu, T. Mossakowski, and O. Kutz. A categorical approach to ontology alignment. In *Proc. of the 9th International Workshop on Ontology Matching (OM-2014)*, ISWC-2014, Riva del Garda, Trentino, Italy, 2014. CEUR-WS.

S. Colton and G. A. Wiggins. Computational creativity: The final frontier? In *Proceedings of the 20th European Conference on Artificial Intelligence*, ECAI 2012, pages 21–26, Amsterdam, The Netherlands, The Netherlands, 2012. IOS Press.

R. Confalonieri, M. Eppe, M. Schorlemmer, O. Kutz, R. Peñaloza, and E. Plaza. Upward refinement operators for conceptual blending in the description logic $\mathcal{ELL}^{++}$. *Annals of Mathematics and Artificial Intelligence*, 82(1–3):69–99, 2018. DOI: 10.1007/s10472-016-9524-8.

G. Fauconnier and M. Turner. *The Way We Think: Conceptual Blending and the Mind's Hidden Complexities*. Basic Books, 2003.

J. A. Goguen. An introduction to algebraic semiotics, with applications to user interface design. In *Computation for Metaphors, Analogy and Agents*, number 1562 in LNCS, pages 242–291. Springer, 1999.

J. A. Goguen. Semiotic morphisms, representations and blending for interface design. In *Proc. of the AMAST Workshop on Algebraic Methods in Language Processing*, pages 1–15. AMAST Press, 2003.

J. A. Goguen and R. M. Burstall. Institutions: Abstract model theory for specification and programming. *Journal of the Association for Computing Machinery*, 39 (1):95–146, 1992. Predecessor in: LNCS 164, 221–256, 1984.

J. A. Goguen and D. F. Harrell. Style: A computational and conceptual blending-based approach. In S. Argamon and S. Dubnov, editors, *The Structure of Style: Algorithmic Approaches to Understanding Manner and Meaning*, pages 147–170. Springer, Berlin, 2010.

J. A. Goguen and G. Malcolm. *Algebraic Semantics of Imperative Programs*. MIT Press, 1996.

J. A. Goguen and G. Roşu. Institution morphisms. *Formal aspects of computing*, 13:274–307, 2002.

M. Grüninger and M. S. Fox. The role of competency questions in enterprise engineering. In *Benchmarking—Theory and Practice*, pages 22–31. Springer, 1995.

A. Kalyanpur, B. Parsia, M. Horridge, and E. Sirin. Finding all justifications of OWL DL entailments. In *Proc. of ISWC/ASWC 2007*, volume 4825 of *LNCS*, pages 267–280. Springer, 2007.

B. Konev, C. Lutz, D. Walther, and F. Wolter. Semantic modularity and module extraction in description logics. In *18th European Conf. on Artificial Intelligence (ECAI-08)*, 2008.

O. Kutz, T. Mossakowski, and D. Lücke. Carnap, Goguen, and the Hyperontologies: Logical pluralism and heterogeneous structuring in ontology Design. *Logica Universalis*, 4(2):255–333, 2010. Special Issue on 'Is Logic Universal?'.

O. Kutz, T. Mossakowski, J. Hois, M. Bhatt, and J. Bateman. Ontological blending in DOL. In T. Besold, K.-U. Kuehnberger, M. Schorlemmer, and A. Smaill, editors, *Computational Creativity, Concept Invention, and General Intelligence, Proc. of the 1st Int. Workshop C3GI@ECAI*, volume 01-2012, Montpellier, France, August 27 2012. Publications of the Institute of Cognitive Science, Osnabrück.

O. Kutz, J. Bateman, F. Neuhaus, T. Mossakowski, and M. Bhatt. E pluribus unum: Formalisation, use-cases, and computational support for conceptual blending. In T. R. Besold, M. Schorlemmer, and A. Smaill, editors, *Computational Creativity Research: Towards Creative Machines*, Thinking Machines. Atlantis/Springer, 2014a.

O. Kutz, F. Neuhaus, T. Mossakowski, and M. Codescu. Blending in the Hub: Towards a collaborative concept invention platform. In *Proc. of the 5th International Conference on Computational Creativity (ICCC-2014)*, Ljubljana, Slovenia, June 10–13 2014b.

K. Lüttich and T. Mossakowski. Reasoning support for CASL with automated theorem proving systems. In J. Fiadeiro, editor, *WADT 2006*, number 4409 in LNCS, pages 74–91. Springer, 2007.

J. Meseguer. General logics. In *Logic Colloquium 87*, pages 275–329. North Holland, 1989.

T. Mossakowski, C. Maeder, and K. Lüttich. The Heterogeneous Tool Set. In *TACAS*, volume 4424 of *LNCS*, pages 519–522. Springer, 2007.

T. Mossakowski, O. Kutz, M. Codescu, and C. Lange. The Distributed Ontology, Modeling and Specification Language. In C. Del Vescovo et al., editor, *Proc. of the 7th Int. Workshop on Modular Ontologies (WoMO-13)*, volume 1081. CEUR-WS, 2013a.

T. Mossakowski, O. Kutz, and C. Lange. Semantics of the distributed ontology language: Institutes and institutions. In N. Martí-Oliet and M. Palomino, editors, *Recent Trends in Algebraic Development Techniques, 21th International Workshop, WADT 2012*, volume 7841 of *Lecture Notes in Computer Science*, pages 212–230. Springer, 2013b.

T. Mossakowski, O. Kutz, and M. Codescu. Ontohub: A semantic repository for heterogeneous ontologies. In *Proc. of the Theory Day in Computer Science (DACS-2014)*, Satellite workshop of ICTAC-2014, University of Bucharest, September 15–16, 2014.

T. Mossakowski, M. Codescu, F. Neuhaus, and O. Kutz. *The Road to Universal Logic–Festschrift for 50th birthday of Jean-Yves Beziau, Volume II*, chapter The distributed ontology, modelling and specification language - DOL. Studies in Universal Logic. Birkhäuser, 2015.

P. D. Mosses, editor. CASL *Reference Manual*, volume 2960 of *Lecture Notes in Computer Science*. Springer, 2004.

F. Neuhaus, O. Kutz, M. Codescu, and T. Mossakowski. Fabricating monsters is hard: Towards the automation of conceptual blending. In *Proc. of Computational Creativity, Concept Invention, and General Intelligence (C3GI at ECAI-14), Prague, 2014*. 2014.

T. Nipkow, L. C. Paulson, and M. Wenzel. *Isabelle/HOL — A proof assistant for higher-order logic*. Springer Verlag, 2002.

OWL Working Group. OWL 2 Web Ontology Language: Document Overview. W3C recommendation, World Wide Web Consortium (W3C), Oct. 2009.

B. Pelzer and C. Wernhard. System description: E-KRHyper. In F. Pfenning, editor, *CADE*, volume 4603 of *Lecture Notes in Computer Science*, pages 508–513. Springer, 2007.

Y. Ren, A. Parvizi, C. Mellish, J. Z. Pan, K. van Deemter, and R. Stevens. Towards competency question-driven ontology authoring. In *The Semantic Web: Trends and Challenges*, pages 752–767. Springer, 2014.

A. Riazanov and A. Voronkov. The design and implementation of VAMPIRE. *AI Communications*, 15(2-3):91–110, 2002.

S. Schulz. E – A brainiac theorem prover. *Journal of AI Communications*, 15(2/3): 111–126, 2002.

K. Shchekotykhin, G. Friedrich, P. Rodler, and P. Fleiss. Interactive ontology debugging using direct diagnosis. In *Proc. of the Third International Workshop on Debugging Ontologies and Ontology Mappings (WoDOOM-14), May 26, 2014, ESWC, Anissaras/Hersonissou, Greece*, 2014.

G. Sutcliffe. The TPTP world – Infrastructure for automated reasoning. In E. M. Clarke and A. Voronkov, editors, *LPAR (Dakar)*, volume 6355 of *LNCS*, pages 1–12. Springer, 2010.

M. Turner. *The Origin of Ideas: Blending, Creativity, and the Human Spark*. Oxford University Press, 2014.

C. Weidenbach, U. Brahm, T. Hillenbrand, E. Keen, C. Theobalt, and D. Topic. SPASS version 2.0. In A. Voronkov, editor, *Automated Deduction – CADE-18*, LNCS 2392, pages 275–279, 2002.

J. Zimmer and S. Autexier. The MathServe system for semantic web reasoning services. In U. Furbach and N. Shankar, editors, *3rd IJCAR*, LNCS 4130. Springer, 2006.

Part II
Cognitive and Social Aspects

Chapter 4
Image Schemas and Concept Invention[*]

Maria M. Hedblom, Oliver Kutz, and Fabian Neuhaus

Abstract In cognitive linguistics, image schemas are understood as conceptual building blocks that are learned in early infancy and which shape not only language but conceptualisation as a whole. In this chapter, we discuss the role that image schemas play in concept invention, with a focus on computational conceptual blending. Moreover, we motivate and outline a formalisation approach to image schemas representing them as interlinked families of theories.

4.1 Introduction

Cognitive psychology and developmental linguistics have yet to provide an explanation of the human capacity to learn concepts and from these generate new ones. Naturally, it is therefore a challenge to model these cognitive abilities computationally. In this chapter this challenge will be approached by looking at two cognitive theories: *conceptual blending* and *image schemas*. Built on the cognitive mechanisms driving analogical thinking and embodied cognition, these theories are hypothesised to provide some of the fundamental parts to the puzzle of human concept formation.

Conceptual Blending is considered to be a cognitive process behind creative thinking and generation of novelty (Turner, 2014). The underlying idea is that novel

Maria M. Hedblom, Fabian Neuhaus
Institute for Intelligent Cooperating Systems (IKS), Otto-von-Guericke University of Magdeburg, Germany. e-mail: {hedblom, fneuhaus}@iws.cs.uni-magdeburg.de

Oliver Kutz
Research Centre for Knowledge and Data (KRDB), Free University of Bozen-Bolzano, Italy, Dominikanerplatz 3, 39100 Bozen-Bolzano, Italy. e-mail: oliver.kutz@unibz.it

[*] This chapter draws on material published in (Hedblom et al., 2015) and (Hedblom et al., 2016)

© Springer Nature Switzerland AG 2018
R. Confalonieri et al. (eds.), *Concept Invention*, Computational Synthesis and Creative Systems, https://doi.org/10.1007/978-3-319-65602-1_4

concepts are created by merging already known (and potentially conflicting) conceptual spaces[2] into a new conceptual space, which, due to the unique combination of information, exhibits new properties.

As prominently discussed in several other chapters of this book, two critical steps in blending are the generalisation of input spaces and the identification of shared structure across the different input spaces. While humans perform these tasks more or less automatically, it is challenging to represent these aspects of conceptual blending computationally. The main hypothesis of this chapter is that image schemas may play a vital role in generalising input spaces and identifying shared structure.

Image schemas are hypothesised to capture abstractions that model affordances[3] related to spatio-temporal processes and relationships (Kuhn, 2007). In the cognitive sciences, *image schemas* are identified as the fundamental patterns for the cognition of objects, which are perceived, conceptualised and manipulated in space and time (Mandler and Pagán Cánovas, 2014). Examples of image schemas, proposed in the literature, are CONTAINER, SUPPORT and SOURCE_PATH_GOAL (see Section 4.3).

In this chapter, we present a methodological framework on how to formally represent image schemas in terms of family resemblance and argue that combining conceptual blending with image schemas may not only shed light on the phenomenon of concept generation and creative thinking in humans, but also provide a useful tool for computational concept invention in computational creativity (Schorlemmer et al., 2014; Kutz et al., 2014; Eppe et al., 2018).

The chapter is structured as follows: In Section 4.2, we give a brief motivation for the theory of conceptual blending as an approach to concept invention, and outline the formalisation approach pursued in the COINVENT project.[4] In Section 4.3 we introduce the theory of image schemas and the problem with defining them as well as some previous formalisation approaches. This is followed by our own suggestion on how to formally structure image schemas as families of theories in Section 4.4. Our method of formalising image schemas is joined by our proposal on how to integrate image schemas into a formal framework of conceptual blending in Section 4.5, where we apply our method to a few examples.

4.2 Conceptual Blending

The theory of *Conceptual Blending* was introduced during the 1990s as the cognitive machinery for novel concept generation (Fauconnier and Turner, 1998). The theory aims to explain the process behind creative thinking. It has support from research in

---

[2] These are also called mental spaces in Fauconnier and Turner (1998) and are not to be confused with the 'conceptual spaces' in the sense of Gärdenfors (2000).

[3] Affordance theory was introduced by Gibson (1977). The term 'affordance' is typically understood to refer to a potentiality for action (or inaction) offered to an agent by some feature of the environment, see Galton (2010).

[4] www.coinvent-project.eu

cognitive psychology and linguistics (Gibbs, 2001; Grady, 2001; Yang et al., 2012) as well as in more computational areas (Veale, 2012; Goguen and Harrell, 2010).

According to conceptual blending theory, generation of novel concepts occurs via the combination of already existing ideas and knowledge. It is suggested that such novel concepts are selective and 'compressed' combinations, or blends, of previously formed concepts, building on the notion that all novel generation builds from already existing knowledge. This cognitive process is thought to happen as two, or more, input domains, or information sources, are combined into a new domain, the blended domain. The blend inherits some of the attributes and relationships from each source domain while at the same time is built on the common structure present in all input spaces. This mixing of information allows the blends to have emergent properties that are unique to each particular blend.

Conceptual blending has many similarities to the cognitive mechanisms behind analogical reasoning. In analogical reasoning information flows from a source domain to a target domain by using cognitive structure-mapping mechanisms. Conceptual blending is comparable insofar as it employs a search for shared structure in the two input domains. This shared structure is the *generic space*, also called the *base ontology*.[5] The base ontology provides the backbone of the newly blended space. Simultaneously some characteristics from each input are included in the blended space, which allows for creative combinations.

For humans conceptual blending is effortless. We are able to create new blends spontaneously and have no difficulty to understand new conceptual blends when we encounter them. This includes the selection of suitable input spaces, the identification of a relevant generic space, the identification of irrelevant features of the input spaces, the performance of the blend, and the evaluation of the usefulness of the blend. In contrast, for an automated system each of these steps provides a significant challenge. In the upcoming section we discuss a formal, logic-based model for conceptual blending.[6]

4.2.1 Formalising Conceptual Blending

We formalise conceptual blending following an approach based on Goguen (1999)'s work on *algebraic semiotics* in which certain structural aspects of semiotic systems are logically formalised in terms of algebraic theories, sign systems, and their mappings. In (Goguen and Harrell, 2010) algebraic semiotics has been applied to user interface design and conceptual blending. Algebraic semiotics does not claim to provide a comprehensive formal theory of blending – indeed, Goguen and Harrell admit that many aspects of blending, in particular concerning the meaning of the involved notions, as well as the optimality principles for blending, cannot be captured

---

[5] Introduced by Fauconnier and Turner as *generic space*, the notion carries the name *base space* or *base ontology* in formal approaches.

[6] For a more detailed description on formalised conceptual blending and DOL, check out Chapter 3 in this edition.

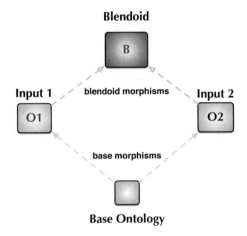

Fig. 4.1: The blending process as described by Goguen and Harrell (2010)

formally. However, the structural aspects *can* be formalised and provide insights into the space of possible blends. The formalisation of these blends can be formulated using languages from the area of algebraic specification, e.g., OBJ3 (Goguen and Malcolm, 1996).

In (Hois et al., 2010; Kutz et al., 2012, 2014b), an approach to computational conceptual blending was presented, which is in the tradition of Goguen's proposal. In these earlier papers, it was suggested to represent the input spaces as ontologies, e.g., in the OWL Web Ontology Language[7]. The structure that is shared across the input spaces, i.e., the generic space, is also represented as an ontology, which is linked by mappings to the input spaces. As proposed by Goguen, the blending process is modelled by a colimit computation, a construction that abstracts the operation of disjoint unions modulo the identification of certain parts specified by the base and the interpretations, as discussed in detail in (Goguen, 2003; Kutz et al., 2010, 2012).

The inputs for a blending process (input concepts, generic space, mappings) can be formally specified in a *blending diagram* in the Distributed Ontology, Model, and Specification Language (DOL).

DOL is a metalanguage that allows the specification of (1) new ontologies based on existing ontologies, (2) relations between ontologies, and (3) networks of ontologies, including networks that specify blending diagrams. These diagrams encode the relationships between the base ontology and the (two or more) input spaces. The blending diagrams can be executed by the *Heterogeneous Tool Set* (HETS) system, a proof management system. HETS is integrated into Ontohub,[8] an ontology repository which allows users to manage and collaboratively work on ontologies. DOL,

---

[7] With 'OWL' we refer to OWL 2 DL, see http://www.w3.org/TR/owl2-overview/
[8] www.ontohub.org

HETS, and Ontohub provide a powerful set of tools, which make it easy to specify and computationally execute conceptual blends, as demonstrated by Neuhaus et al. (2014). An extensive introduction to the features and the formal semantics of DOL can be found in (Mossakowski et al., 2015).

One important theory in analogical research is the Structure Mapping Theory (Gentner, 1983). It claims that analogical reasoning is characterised by the relationships between objects rather than their attributes. Similarly, but relying on generalisations rather than direct mappings between the domains, is the analogy engine Heuristic Driven Theory Projection, HDTP (Schmidt et al., 2014a). HDTP computes a 'least general generalisation' B of two input spaces $O1$ and $O2$. This is done by anti-unification to find common structure in both input spaces $O1$ and $O2$. HDTP's algorithm for anti-unification is, analogously to unification, a purely syntactical approach that is based on finding matching substitutions.[9]

While this is an interesting approach, it has a major disadvantage. Typically, for any two input spaces there exists a large number of potential generalisations. Thus, the search space for potential base spaces and potential conceptual blends is vast. HDTP implements heuristics to identify interesting anti-unifiers; e.g., it prefers anti-unifiers that contain rich theories over anti-unifiers that contain weak theories. However, since anti-unification is a purely syntactical approach, there is no way to distinguish cognitively relevant from irrelevant information. As a result, an increase of the size of the two input ontologies leads to an explosion of possibilities for anti-unifications.

In order to minimize this problem we suggest to introduce image schemas as the conceptual building blocks found in the generic space. In the upcoming sections we introduce image schemas followed by our suggestion on how image schemas can be formally structured and approached by making a proof of concept using the image schema of PATH-following.

4.3 Image Schemas

Embodied theories of cognition (Shapiro, 2011) emphasise bodily experiences as the prime source for concept formation. Based on this cognitively supported view (Gallese and Lakoff, 2005), the theory of image schemas suggests that our conceptual world is grounded in the perceivable spatio-temporal relationships between objects.

A well studied image schema is CONTAINMENT, capturing the notion that an object can be within a border (two-dimensional), or inside a container (three-

---

[9] There are several other methods for finding generalisations. One example is the Analogical Thesaurus (Veale, 2003) which uses WordNet to identify common categories for the source and target spaces.

dimensional) (Johanson and Papafragou, 2014). The temporal aspect of CONTAIN-MENT includes the notions of 'entering' and 'exiting'.[10]

One important aspect of image schemas is that they can be combined with one another. The image schema PATH can easily merge with the image schema LINK, leading to the more complex image-schematic concept LINKED_PATH. As PATH illustrates a movement through space, and LINK illustrates the causal relationship between two (or more) objects, a LINKED_PATH represents joint movement of two objects on two linked paths; e.g., a truck and trailer moving along a highway, or the joint movement of two separate magnets.

The cognitive benefit of image schemas is to provide a means for information transfer. The conceptual abstraction that constitutes the image schema can be util-ised to explain unknown relationships and affordances of objects. The core idea is that after an image schema has been formed, it can be generalised and the struc-ture can be transferred through analogical reasoning to other domains with similar characteristics (Mandler, 1992). In concrete situations this means that the informa-tion such as 'a table offers SUPPORT' can be transferred to similar domains such as 'a desk also offers SUPPORT'. That is, an image schema structure may be used as a conceptual skeleton in an analogical transfer from the concrete spatial domain of the image schema to another domain. Often the target domains are abstract concepts, which are conceptualised by relying on metaphors that are based on sensory-motor experiences and, thus, involve image schemas. Evidence for the image schematic roots of these concepts is often provided by the lexicalisations of these concepts, which reuse terminology from concrete spatial domains to describe the abstract tar-get spaces.

For example, the phrase *support a family* expresses the concept of 'providing the financial means for a family' with the help of the SUPPORT image schema. An analogous example is *support of an argument*. Further, processes and time are often conceptualised as objects and spatial regions. Expressions such as 'we meet *on* Thursday' map information from a concrete situation such as 'a book *on* a table' to the abstract process and time period. Another example is our conceptualisation of relationships like love or marriage, which also are often based on spatial metaphors. For example, one way to view a marriage is as LINKED_PATH, where the PATH represents how two spouses move together through time and the LINK between them is the bond they share. A sentence like *Their marriage chains them together* works only if one conceptualises the relationship as a LINKED_PATH, because it reinterprets the LINK as an element that constrains the movements of both lovers. Alternatively, marriage may also be conceptualised as CONTAINER. This is reflected by metaphors like 'marriage is a prison', 'marriage is a safe harbour', and 'having an open marriage'. Depending on whether one chooses CONTAINER or LINKED_PATH as a base for the conceptualisation of marriage, a different vocabulary and different metaphors are supported.

The examples illustrate how image schemas may be used to conceptualise an abstract domain. As mentioned above, the first image schemas are developed at

---

[10] It can be argued that IN and OUT are by themselves image schemas, or spatial primitives. For now we include them under the umbrella schema of CONTAINER.

the early stages of infancy when abstract thinking is not yet fully developed. This illustrates how concrete reasoning involving physical objects can provide the basis for the conceptualisation of the world and the formation of more abstract concepts.

4.3.1 Defining "Image Schema"

The term "Image schema" is hard to define properly. Image schemas are studied in several disciplines and from various perspectives, including neuroscience (Rohrer, 2005), developmental psychology (Mandler, 1992), cognitive linguistics (Hampe and Grady, 2005) and formal approaches (St. Amant et al., 2006). This broad range of research has lead to incoherence in the use of terminology. Also, the disputed relationship between socio-cultural aspects and the neurobiology of embodied cognition (Hampe, 2005) complicates the literature on image schema research.

Oakley defines an image schema as *"... a condensed re-description of perceptual experience for the purpose of mapping spatial structure onto conceptual structure"* (Oakley, 2010, p. 215). Johnson describes it as *"... a recurring, dynamic pattern of our perceptual interactions and motor programs that gives coherence and structure to our experience"* (Johnson, 1987, p. xiv). Kuhn (2007) considers image schemas as the pre-linguistic structures of object relations in time and space.

One issue of these explanations of image schemas is that they do not provide individuation criteria. Hence, it is hard to evaluate whether a proposed image schema qualifies as such or not. The situation is complicated by the fact that image schemas may change and become more specialised during the development of a child (Mandler and Pagán Cánovas, 2014). Therefore, it is sometimes not obvious whether two conceptual structures are just variants of the same image schema or whether they are different image schemas.

Mandler and Pagán Cánovas (2014) presented a three level hierarchy of image schemas: (1) 'Spatial primitives': basic spatial building blocks, (2) 'image schemas': simple spatial events using the primitives, and (3) 'conceptual integrations': image schemas blended with non-spatial elements such as force or emotions.

From our perspective, this terminology provides the benefit of clearly distinguishing between image schemas and their building blocks (the spatial primitives). An image schema always represents an event and, thus, has some temporal dimension. The spatial primitives are the components that are participating in the event. For instance, according to this terminology PATH is not an image schema but a spatial primitive. In contrast, MOVEMENT_ON_PATH is an image schema. Another benefit is that it provides a clear criterion for distinguishing two image schemas (or Mandler's schematic integrations): if x and y involve different spatial primitives, then x and y are different.[11]

Mandler and Pagán Cánovas (2014)'s approach provides a useful way to explain how conceptualisations are refined: an image schema is a representation of some

---

[11] Note that this is a sufficient condition, but not a necessary one, since two different representations may involve the same spatial primitives arranged in different ways.

kind of spatial event involving a number of spatial primitives. Hence, an image schema may be enriched by adding spatial primitives, yielding a more complex image schema. For instance, by adding the spatial primitives CONTAINER and INTO to the image schema MOVEMENT ON PATH, we obtain the schema MOVEMENT ON PATH INTO CONTAINER. This new image schema is more specific and less universally applicable. However, it provides more specific information when it is utilised conceptualising analogous situations. It follows that image schemas can be ordered into a hierarchy ranging from general image schemas, which contain only few spatial primitives, to more specific image schemas, which contain more spatial primitives.[12] Hence, image schemas do not exist in isolation but can be organised (at least) with respect to their (shared) spatial primitives. This observation is discussed further in Section 4.4.

In the following, we will continue to use "image schema" as the umbrella term for the three levels of conceptualisations. To avoid any confusion with the usage of image schemas in the sense of Mandler and Pagán Cánovas, we will refer to their image schemas as *spatial schemas*.

One major advantage of partitioning image schemas into spatial primitives, spatial schemas, and conceptual integration is that it enables a more fine-grained analysis of connections between image schemas. We believe that the change from one spatial schema to another can be accomplished by providing or detailing more spatial information, e.g., by adding additional spatial primitives.

4.3.2 Formalising Image Schemas

Lakoff and Núñez (2000) used image schemas extensively in their reconstruction of abstract mathematical concepts using blending and image schemas. Working from the perspective that all of mathematics can be eventually derived from the body's interactions with its environment, they give a detailed account on how image schemas provide some of the conceptual principles that provide a grounding of abstract concepts.

While Lakoff and Núñez (2000)'s work is not primarily focused on a formalisation of image schemas, their attempt to ground mathematics in embodied cognition has been further developed and formalised. Guhe et al. (2011) account for the ideas by Lakoff and Núñez (2000) by formalising in first-order logic some basic mathematical constructs such as the *measuring stick*, *motion along a path*, and *object construction*. Using the mentioned analogy engine HDTP (Schmidt et al., 2014a), they illustrate how generalisations such as image schemas could help to transfer information in a computational system. Their system is based on anti-unification to identify the common structure in both source and target domain. This common structure is used to transfer information to the target domain from the source.

---

[12] In their list of spatial primitives, Mandler and Pagán Cánovas (2014) include MOVE, ANIMATED MOVE, and BLOCKED MOVE. This seems to suggests that the spatial primitives are ordered into a subtype hierarchy, since both animated movement and blocked movement are a kind of movement.

Looking at how image schemas can be computationally acquired, there are studies that attempt to model early cognitive development and learn from perceptual input. The connectionist model proposed by Regier (1996) learns to linguistically classify visual stimuli in accordance with the spatial terms of various natural languages. Similarly, the *Dev E-R* system by Aguilar and Pérez y Pérez (2015) is a computer model that simulates the first sensorimotor stages in cognitive development. Their system learns to distinguish and fine-tune visual clues such as nuances of colour, as well as different sizes of objects and directions of movement. Both approaches demonstrate how an artificial agent can develop cognitive abilities and language development from perceptual input.

Another study using perceptual input to simulate the development of image schemas was made by Nayak and Mukerjee (2012). They fed video material of OBJECTs moving IN and OUT of boxes into an unsupervised statistical model in order to capture the dynamic aspects of the CONTAINMENT schema. From this, the system learned how to categorise different CONTAINMENT contexts and could in combination with a linguistic corpus generate simple CONTAINMENT-related language constructions.

These are examples of systems that learn image schemas and object relationships from perceptual input. Working with already defined image schemas, Kuhn (2002, 2007) argues that image schemas capture abstractions in order to model affordances. Working top-down rather than bottom-up as above, he uses WordNet to define noun words and connects them to spatial categorisations related to image schemas based on affordance-related aspects of meaning.

Walton and Worboys (2009) build further on Kuhn's work by visualising and formalising the connections between different image schemas using bigraphs. By visually representing the topological and 'physical' image schemas relevant in built environments, they demonstrate how more complex dynamic image schemas such as BLOCKAGE could be generated using sequences of bigraph reaction rules on top of simpler static image schemas. Besold et al. (2017) also presented work on how combinations of image schemas can be used to explain increasingly complex image schemas by looking at simple events such as 'bouncing'

St. Amant et al. (2006) present what they call the *Image Schema Language*, ISL. In their paper, they provide a set of diagrams that illustrate how combinations of image schemas can lead to more complex image schemas, and provide some real life examples.

Brugman and Lakoff (1988) discuss how image schema transformations form networks that capture the relationships in polysemous words; in particular the preposition 'over' is investigated. This relates to our own approach of how to formalise and formally represent image schemas. Namely to use the hierarchical structure of image schemas demonstrated previously to represent image schemas as families of theories.

Acquired from natural language, Bennett and Cialone (2014) formally represented several different kinds of CONTAINER schemas. They distinguish eight different spatial CONTAINER relationships and their mappings to natural language constructs.

Their work also demonstrates the non-trivial nature of formalising image schemas, and that there are many closely related variants of any given image schema.

4.4 Image Schemas as Families of Theories

The primary goal of our research is to develop a computational system for concept invention by combining a formal representation of image schemas with the framework of conceptual blending. One of the major obstacles for implementing such a system is that image schemas are, typically, not crisply defined in the literature, but rather presented as mouldable concepts. Their adaptability is indeed part of the explanatory success of image schemas. Hence, to realise our goal of a computational system using image schemas in conceptual blending, we need to develop a formal representation of image schemas that captures their inherent complexity.

In this section we suggest that image schemas should be considered as members of tightly connected image schema families, where the connecting relation is based on the notion of family resemblance. In particular, each of the image schemas covers a particular conceptual-cognitive scenario within the scope of the schema family. An image schema family may be formally represented as a set (i.e., a *family*) of interlinked theories. As a proof of concept, we look closer at the classic image schema SOURCE_PATH_GOAL and identify the specifications through the presence of different spatial primitives. We call the network the PATH-following family.

4.4.1 The Image Schema Family PATH-*Following*

MOVEMENT_ALONG_PATH is one of the first image schemas to be acquired in early infancy as children are immediately exposed to movement from a range of objects Rohrer (2005). However, in order to understand how the PATH-following family is fine-tuned and in 'more completion' internally structured, experiments with children have provided some insights on distinguishing how the different spatial schemas may develop.

Firstly, already at an early age children pay more attention to moving objects than resting objects. Trivial as it may seem, it requires children to detect the spatial primitive OBJECT (or THING) and the spatial schema MOVEMENT_OF_OBJECT.[13] Secondly, children tend to remember the PATH of the movement of the object. The

---

[13] OBJECT is understood here in a very wide sense that includes not only solid material objects but entities like waves on a pond or shadows. Mandler and Pagán Cánovas (2014) also discuss MOVE as a spatial primitive of its own. We consider MOVEMENT_OF_OBJECT to be a spatial schema, since movement necessarily involves a temporal dimension and, further, it always involves at least one spatial primitive, since any movement, necessarily, involves at least one OBJECT that moves.

PATH is a spatial primitive, which is different from the movement and the moving object.[14].

In addition to these two basic spatial primitives and as the child becomes more and more familiar with PATH-following, image schemas that contain more spatial information are learned. This means that in more advanced stages, image schemas may include beyond MOVEMENT_OF_OBJECT and the spatial PATH itself also the spatial primitive END_PATH, and later also a START_PATH (Mandler and Pagán Cánovas, 2014). Already at five months infants can distinguish PATH-following that has an END_PATH (the image schema PATH_GOAL) from the initial PATH, while the START_PATH is less interesting until the end of the first year of life. This is further supported by linguistic analyses in which an END_PATH is initially more interesting than a START_PATH (Johanson and Papafragou, 2014).

A more specified example of the PATH-following family is presented by Lakoff and Núñez (2000). In accordance with other linguistic literature on image schemas they are focussed on the SOURCE_PATH_GOAL schema, see Figure 4.2. Here, the object, called trajector following cognitive linguistic standard terminology, moves from a source to a goal. END_PATH and START_PATH are not identical to the SOURCE and GOAL found in the SOURCE_PATH_GOAL schema. In SOURCE_PATH_GOAL, a direction and a purpose are implied in the image schema, which changes the conceptual nature of the movement. Lakoff and Núñez (2000) make the distinction of 'elements', or roles, that to some extent correspond to the spatial primitives discussed above, but additional distinctions are added. Most importantly, they make the clear distinction between end location and goal, as they distinguish between 'path', the actual trajectory of a movement, and 'route', the expected movement.

The distinction, made by Lakoff and Núñez (2000), between the *expected* movement and the *actual* movement is primarily interesting for a description of how new image schemas relate to actual events and how new image schemas are learned. Consider, for example, a situation where a child observes the movement of a billiard ball and is surprised that the ball stops because it is blocked by another billiard ball. In this case, a given instance of the MOVEMENT_ALONG_PATH spatial schema formed the expectations of the child, which were disappointed by the actual physical movement, because the expected END_PATH (the goal) does not correspond to the actual END_PATH (end location). Given a repeated exposure to similar events, the child may develop the new spatial schema BLOCKAGE. After learning BLOCKAGE, the child will no longer be surprised by blocked movement since the expected END_PATH (the goal) will correspond to the actual END_PATH (end location). While the terminological distinction between *expected trajectory* and *actual trajectory* is useful, these do not necessarily need to constitute two different spatial primitives. Indeed, spatial primitives are parts of image schemas and, thus, always parts of conceptualisations, and not parts of actual events. In order to ground the different levels of the PATH-following family in real world scenarios we will look closer at a few concepts present in everyday language.

---

[14] This spatial primitive is not to be confused with the image schema family PATH-following.

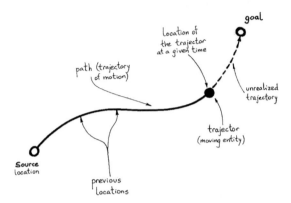

Fig. 4.2: The SOURCE_PATH_GOAL schema as illustrated by Lakoff and Núñez (2000)

4.4.1.1 Concepts That Involve PATH-Following

The most straightforward examples of concepts that involve PATH-following are concepts that are about the spatial relationship of movement between different points. Prepositions such as *from, to, across* and *through* all indicate a kind of PATH-following.[15] This also includes key verbs that describe movement, e.g., *coming* and *going*. Another example, here for the spatial schema SOURCE_PATH_GOAL, is *Going from Berlin to Prague*. Note that in many cases we do not provide information about START_PATH and END_PATH of a movement; e.g., *leaving Berlin* and *travelling to Berlin* are examples for the spatial schemas SOURCE_PATH and PATH_GOAL, respectively. *Meandering* is an example for a concept that realises MOVEMENT_ALONG_PATH, which involves a PATH but neither a START_PATH nor an END_PATH. In contrast, no discernible PATH is involved in *roaming the city*, which is an example for MOVEMENT_OF_OBJECT. These examples illustrate that spatial schemas may be ordered hierarchically with respect to their content: SOURCE_PATH_GOAL contains more spatial primitives and more information than, for example, MOVEMENT_ALONG_PATH, which is the root of the PATH-following family. And MOVEMENT_ALONG_PATH is more specific than MOVEMENT_OF_OBJECT.

Beyond concepts that involve movement, PATH-following plays an important role in many abstract concepts and conceptual metaphors.

The concept of *"going for a joy ride"* realises the spatial schema SOURCE_PATH, since it has a START_PATH and a PATH but no END_PATH. Similarly, the expression *"running for president"* describes the process of trying to get elected as president

---

[15] Some prepositions include other image schemas at the same time. For instance, 'through' involves apart from PATH also some notion of CONTAINMENT.

metaphorically as a PATH_GOAL. In this metaphor the PATH consists of the various stages of the process (e.g., announcing a candidacy and being nominated by a party) with the inauguration as END_PATH.

Another metaphor *"life is a journey"*, studied by Ahrens and Say (1999), makes an analogical mapping between the passing of time in life, to the passing of spatial regions on a journey. As in the example mentioned above, where the concept of "being in love" acquired information from the CONTAINMENT schema, this metaphor gains information from the spatial primitives connected to the image schema SOURCE_PATH_GOAL. Here, the most important spatial primitives are START_PATH and END_PATH – in this metaphor they are mapped to the moments of birth and death, as well as the PATH itself, illustrating how "life goes on" in a successive motion.

A different perspective on life and death is expressed in the metaphorical expression *"the circle of life"*. Implied is that life leads to death, but also that death gives rise to life, completing a cyclic movement – the image schema MOVEMENT_IN_LOOPS. This image schema can be considered as a version of PATH-following, in which START_PATH and END_PATH coincide at the same 'location'.

These examples illustrate a general pattern, namely that many conceptual metaphors involving PATHs are about processes, and different events during such processes are treated metaphorically as locations on a path.

The importance of PATH-following image schemas for the conceptualisation of processes can be illustrated by considering *similes*. If we pick from Table 4.1 randomly a target domain X from the first column and a source domain Y from the second column, the resulting simile X *is like* Y will be sensible (of course, depending on the choice of X and Y the simile may be more or less witty). Note that the target domains have little or nothing in common. Thus, at least on first glance, one would not expect that one can compare them meaningfully to one and the same source domain.

Table 4.1: PATH similes: <target> is like <source>

Target Domain	Source Domain
Watching the football game	the swinging of a pendulum
Their marriage	a marathon
The story	escaping a maze
This piece of music	a sail boat during a hurricane
Bob's career	a roller coaster ride
Her thoughts	a Prussian military parade
Democracy in Italy	stroll in the park

The similes work because all of the concepts in the second column involve physical MOVEMENT_ALONG_PATH, which have some pertinent characteristics. These characteristics may concern the shape of the path itself (e.g., the path of a roller coaster involves many ups and downs and tight curves, the path out of a maze involves many turns, the path of a pendulum is regular and between two points), the way the movement is performed (e.g., the movement of a sail boat during a storm is erratic and involuntary, a stroll in the park is done leisurely), and the effects the movement may have (e.g., running a marathon is exhausting, a Prussian military parade may be perceived as threatening). In each of the similes we use some of the pertinent characteristics from the source domain to describe the process from the target domain. For example, in the simile 'Bob's career is like a Prussian military parade' we conceptualise the career as a path along time (with career-related events like promotions as the sites on the path) and transfer characteristics from the movement of a Prussian military parade on this path. Thus, one way to read the simile is that Bob moves through the stages of his career in a exceptionally predictable fashion. The example illustrates how the similes work: first, we conceptualise the process in the target domain as MOVEMENT_ALONG_PATH, where the events of the process are ordered by time, and then we transfer some pertinent characteristics of the MOVEMENT_ALONG_PATH of the source domain to the target domain. This pattern is not just applicable to the concepts in Table 4.1. As we discussed above, any process can be conceptualised as MOVEMENT_ALONG_PATH, thus, any process could be added as target domain in Table 4.1. Further, any concept that involves interesting physical movement along some path could be added as source domain. Hence, the use of the image schema MOVEMENT_ALONG_PATH enables the mechanical generation of similes for processes.

Similes are a particular form of concept generation in which two domains are combined. This phenomenon is strongly connected to conceptual blending that we briefly introduced and discussed in Section 4.2, with a full formal treatment in Chapters 1 and 3 of this book.

4.4.2 Formalising Image Schema Families

In order to discuss the problem of how more complex image schemas can be constructed through a combination of different image schemas (e.g., LINKED_PATH, MOVEMENT_IN_LOOPS), we will discuss the possible interconnection these families of theories allow. Formally, we can represent the idea as a graph[16] of theories in DOL, the *Distributed Ontology, Modeling and Specification Language* (Mossakowski et al., 2015), that we briefly introduced in Section 4.2 on formalised conceptual blending.

This choice is motivated primarily by two general features of DOL: (1) the heterogeneous approach, which allows for a variety of image schematic formalisations without being limited to a single logic, and (2) the focus on linking and modularity. Therefore, DOL provides a rich toolkit to further formally develop the idea of *image schema families* in a variety of directions.

---

[16] These graphs are diagrams in the sense of category theory.

PATH: **the image schema family of moving along paths and in loops**

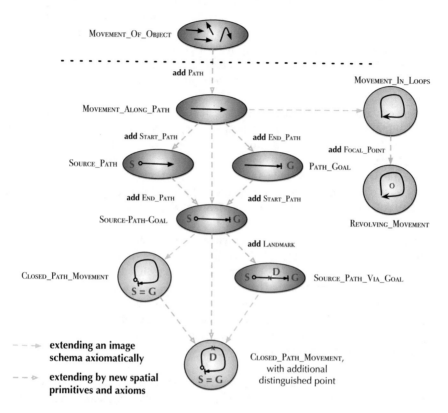

Fig. 4.3: A portion of the family of image schemas related to path following shown as DOL graph

Building on similar ideas to those underlying the first-order ontology repository COLORE[17] (Grüninger et al., 2012), we propose to capture image schemas as interrelated families of (heterogeneous) theories. Similar ideas for structuring common sense notions have also been applied to various notions of time (Van Benthem, 1983; Allen and Hayes, 1985). This approach would also allow for the introduction of non-spatial elements, e.g., 'force', to be included as a basic ingredient of image schemas. This has for instance been argued for by Gärdenfors (2007) and constitutes the core of Mandler and Pagán Cánovas (2014)'s *conceptual integrations*.

In Figure 4.3, some of the first basic stages of the image schema family PATH-following are presented. Ranging from Mandler's general definition presented in Section 4.4.1, of object movement in any trajectory, to more complex constructions.

---

[17] See http://stl.mie.utoronto.ca/colore/

The particular image schema family sketched is organised primarily via adding new spatial primitives to the participating image schemas and/or by refining an image schema's properties (extending the axiomatisation). In general, different sets of criteria may be used depending, for example, on the context of usage, thereby putting particular image schemas (say, REVOLVE_AROUND) into a variety of families. Apart from a selection of spatial primitives, other dimensions might be deemed relevant for defining a particular family, such as their role in the developmental process.

One way MOVEMENT_ALONG_PATH can be specialised is as the image schema of MOVEMENT_IN_LOOPS. Note that this change does not involve adding a new spatial primitive, but just an additional characteristic of the path. The resulting image schema can be further refined by adding the spatial information of a *focal point*, which the path revolves around – this leads to the notion of *orbiting*, or, by continuously moving the orbiting path away from the focal point, to creating the concept of *spirals*. Alternatively, we may change MOVEMENT_ALONG_PATH by adding distinguished points; e.g., the START_PATH, the target END_PATH, or both.

The MOVEMENT_IN_LOOPS image schema may be further specialised by identifying (the location of) the START_PATH and the END_PATH. In this case, the path is closed in the sense that any object which follows the path will end up at the location at where it started its movement. The difference between a closed path and a looping path is that the closed path has a start and an end (e.g., a race on a circular track), while the looping path has neither (like an orbit). It is possible to further refine the schema by adding more designated points (i.e., 'landmarks') or other related spatial primitives as well as extending the PATH-following family as demonstrated in Gromann and Hedblom (2016).

We will now discuss in some more detail one approach to characterising formally the theories of image schemas involved in the PATH-following family, highlighting some of the branching points.

4.4.3 Example: Axiomatising the PATH-*Following Family*

In this section, we present part of an axiomatisation that aims to capture the important differences of the branching points of the PATH-following family represented in Figure 4.3. A more complete axiomatisation is available at an Ontohub repository[18] and in Hedblom et al. (2015).

As discussed in more detail in Besold et al. (2017), the same image-schematic notion, say MOVEMENT_ALONG_PATH, can be axiomatised on different levels of granularity and abstraction (i.e., regarding the reflection of the actual physics of objects, forces, time and movement, etc.), and using a variety of logical formalisms with varying expressivty.

---

[18] https://ontohub.org/repositories/imageschemafamily/

Our axiomatisation presented here is inspired by semantics in the neo-Davidsonian tradition (Davidson, 1967; Parson, 1990). We consider image schemas as a type of event (in generality quite similar to the view defended in (Clausner and Croft, 1999) to view image schemas as a kind of 'domain') and consider spatial primitives as thematic roles of these events. Thus, if a given image schema is enriched by adding a new spatial primitive, this is typically represented by adding a new entity (e.g., site) and a new relation (e.g., has_start_path) that determines the thematic role of the new entity in the event. As representation language we use ISO/IEC 24707 Common Logic. Common Logic is a standardised language for first-order logic knowledge representation, which supports some limited forms of higher-order quantification (Menzel, 2011).

For the axiomatisation of the image schemas in the PATH-following family we assume an image schema MOVEMENT_ALONG_PATH as the root of the family. MOVEMENT_ALONG_PATH is derived from a more general notion, namely MOVEMENT_OF_OBJECT. This is movement of some kind that involves only one spatial primitive, namely an OBJECT. This object plays the role of the *trajector* within the context of the MOVE. This can be formalised in Common Logic as follows:

```
(forall (m)
 (iff
    (MovementOfObject m)
    (exists (o)
      (and
        (Movement m)
        (Object o)
        (has_trajector m o)))))
```

No additional information about what kind of object is moving and how it is moving is assumed.[19]

The schema MOVEMENT_ALONG_PATH is the result of adding a new spatial primitive to MOVEMENT_OF_OBJECT, which plays the role of a PATH.

```
(forall (m)
 (iff
    (MovementAlongPath m)
    (exists (p)
      (and
        (MovementOfObject m)
        (Path p)
        (has_path m p)))))
```

Under a PATH we understand a collection of two or more sites, which are connected by successor relationships. Each of these sites have (relative to the path) at most one successor site. The transitive closure of the successor relation defines a *before* relationship (relative to the path); and for any two different sites x, y of a given

---

[19] From an ontological perspective, MOVEMENT_OF_OBJECT can be seen as a kind of process (or occurrent). Thus, any adequate axiomatisation of MOVEMENT_OF_OBJECT needs to represent change over time in some form. To keep things simple, we here just quantify over time points. We assume that time points are ordered by an `earlier` relationship. Further, we use two other relationships to connect time points to processes: (has_start m t) means *The movement m starts at time point t* and (during t m) means *Time point t lies within the interval during which movement m happens.*

path, either x is before y or y is before x (relative to the path).[20] This axiomatisation provides a representation of a quite abstract notion of MOVEMENT_ALONG_PATH. It needs to be sufficiently abstract, since it serves as the root node for the PATH-following family. All other image schemas in the family are derived from this root by adding additional spatial primitives and/or additional axioms.

Given this notion of PATH, we can axiomatise the relationship between the PATH and the OBJECT, which characterises a MOVEMENT_ALONG_PATH. During the movement, the moving object needs to pass through all sites of the path in a temporal order, which matches the before-relationship between the sites:

```
(forall (p o m s1 s2)
  (if
    (and
      (MovementAlongPath m)
      (has_path m p)
      (has_trajector  m o)
      (before s1 s2 p))
    (exists (t1 t2)
      (and
        (Timepoint t1) (Timepoint t2)
        (during t1 m)  (during t2 m)
        (located_at o s1 t1) (located_at o s2 t2)
        (earlier t1 t2)))))
```

The image schema SOURCE_PATH is the result of adding the spatial primitive SOURCE to MOVEMENT_ALONG_PATH. We represent this with the *has_starts_path* relationship. The SOURCE of a PATH is a site on the path that is before any other site of the path:

```
(forall  (m)                              (forall  (m s1 s2 p)
  (iff                                      (if
    (SourcePathMovement m)                    (and
    (exists  (s)                                (SourcePathMovement m)
      (and                                      (Site s1)
        (MovementAlongPath m)                   (Site s2)
        (has_start_path m s)))))              (not (= s1 s2))
                                              (has_path m p)
                                              (has_start_path m s1)
                                              (part_of s2 p))
                                            (before s1 s2 p)))
```

A completely different branch of the movement image schema family does not involve either SOURCE or END_PATH, but the PATH consists of a loop of sites. One way to represent this is by requiring that the before-relationship is reflexive (with respect to the path of the movement):

```
(forall (m)
  (iff
    (MovementInLoops m)
    (and
      (MovementAlongPath m)
      (forall (p s)
        (if
          (and
            (has_path m p)
            (Site s)
            (part_of s p))
          (before s s p))))))
```

---

[20] The before-relationship is not a total order, since antisymmetry is not postulated.

This demonstration of some of the levels in the axiomatisation show the foundation for how we believe the complexity of image schema notions can be approached formally. This will play a crucial role later in the paper as we discuss how formalised image schemas can be integrated into conceptual blending.

4.5 Guiding Conceptual Blending with Image Schemas

4.5.1 Blending with Image Schemas

Instead of relying on a purely syntactical approach to blending, the semantic content found in image schemas can be employed to help guide the blending process. The basic idea here is that in order to identify common structure sufficient for defining a useful generic space for two (or more) given input spaces, we search for shared image-schematic information rather than *arbitrary* structure. As discussed above, a vast space of blends opens up if we work with more unconstrained or syntax-based shared structure in the generic space. With a similar motivation, Schorlemmer et al. (2016) explored the use of image schemas for generic spaces of blends, focussing on the connections to the Yoneda-based creative process model of Mazzola et al. (2011).

Given the powerful role that image schemas generally seem to play in human conceptual (pre-linguistic) development, the working hypothesis is that the semantic content and cognitive relevance given by identifying shared image schemas will provide valuable information for constructing and selecting the more substantial or interesting possible blends.

To implement computationally the idea of using image schemas as generic spaces, two independent algorithmic problems have to be solved. Namely (1) the **Recognition Problem**: to identify an image-schematic theory within an input theory, and (2) the **Generalisation Problem**: to find the most specific image schema common to both inputs.

To address the recognition problem, suppose a lattice $\mathfrak{F}$ encoding an image schema family is fixed. We here assume for simplicity that elements of $\mathfrak{F}$ will be logical theories in a fixed formal logic, say first-order logic.[21] Given an input theory O_1 and $\mathfrak{F}$, solving the recognition problem means finding a member $f \in \mathfrak{F}$ that can be *interpreted* in O_1, i.e., such that we find a renaming σ of the symbols in f (called a signature morphism) and such that $O_1 \models \sigma(f)$ (also written $O_1 \models_\sigma f$).[22] Note that this is a more general statement than claiming the inclusion of the axioms of f

---

[21] Note that none of the ideas presented here depend on a particular, fixed logic. Indeed, heterogeneous logical specification is central to formal blending approaches, see Kutz et al. (2014).

[22] In more detail: a theory interpretation σ is a signature morphism renaming the symbols of the image schema theory f and induces a corresponding sentence translation map, also written σ, such that the translated sentences of f, written $\sigma(f)$, are logically entailed by O_1. In practice, it may often be sufficient to recognise a part of the image schematic structure in the input theory. In this case, it suffices that σ maps a subset of f to O_1 (i.e., establishes a partial theory interpretation).

(modulo renaming) in O_1 (the trivial inclusion interpretation) since establishing the entailment of the sentences in $\sigma(f)$ from O_1 might indeed be involved.

Computational support for automatic theory-interpretation search in first-order logic is investigated in (Normann, 2008), and a prototypical system was developed and tested as an add-on to the *Heterogeneous Tool Set* system (HETS) (Mossakowski et al., 2007). Experiments carried out in (Normann and Kutz, 2009; Kutz and Normann, 2009) showed that this works particularly well with more complex axiomatisations in first-order logic, rather than with simple taxonomies expressed in OWL, because in the latter case too little syntactic structure is available to control the combinatorial explosion of the search task. From the point of view of interpreting image schemas into non-trivial axiomatised concepts, we may see this as an encouraging fact, as image schemas are, despite their foundational nature, complex objects to axiomatise.

Once the recognition problem has been solved in principle, the given lattice structure of the image schema family $\mathfrak{F}$ gives us a very simple handle on the generalisation problem. Namely, given two input spaces O_1, O_2, and two image schemas f_1, f_2 from the same family $\mathfrak{F}$ (say, 'containment') such that $O_1 \models_{\sigma_1} f_1$ and $O_2 \models_{\sigma_2} f_2$, compute the most specific generalisation $G \in \mathfrak{F}$ of f_1 and f_2, i.e., their least upper bound in $\mathfrak{F}$. Since the signature of G will be included in signatures of both f_1 and f_2, we obtain that $O_1 \models_{\sigma_1} G$ and $O_2 \models_{\sigma_2} G$. $G \in \mathfrak{F}$ is therefore an image schema common to both input spaces and can be used as generic space.

We now proceed to give a formalised version of blending with image schema using the mother ship blend. Here, image schemas play a crucial role, showing that the gulf between the cognitive relevance of image schemas and formal, logic-based concept blending can be bridged.

4.5.2 Similes Revisited

Consider the concepts *Space Ship, North Korea, Universe, Marriage* and *Bank account*. Note that these concepts differ significantly. However, all of them can be construed as various kinds of *containers*. This is obvious in the case of space ships, which may contain passengers and cargo. Geopolitical entities like North Korea instantiate the CONTAINER schema, since they have boundaries and people may be inside and outside of countries. The conceptualisation of the *Universe* as container is a particularly interesting case since it implies the notion of inertial frames of reference, which is arguably inconsistent with the Theory of Relativity. This does not prevent science fiction writers construing a universe as a container for planets, suns and other things; in many fictive stories it is possible to leave and return to the Universe (e.g., by visiting a 'parallel universe'). While the first three examples are physical entities, *Marriage* is a social entity. Thus, in the literal physical sense marriage cannot be a container. Nevertheless, we use vocabulary that is associated with containers to describe marriage. For instance, one can *enter* and *leave* a marriage, some marriages are *open*, others are *closed*, and people may find happiness *in* their

Table 4.2: CONTAINER similes: < target> is like a <source>

Target Domain	Source Domain
This space ship	leaky pot
North Korea	prison
The universe	treasure chest
Their marriage	bottomless pit
My bank account	balloon

marriage. Similarly, a *bank account* may *contain* funds, and if it is *empty* we can put some additional funds *into* the account and take them *out* again later. These linguistic examples provide some evidence that we conceptualise *Marriage* and *Bank account* as kinds of *containers*.

The claim that these five concepts are indeed instantiating CONTAINER is supported by the behaviour of these concepts in *similes*.

The first column ('target domain') of Table 4.2 contains our examples. The second column ('source domain') contains various concepts of physical containers which highlight some possible features of containers: e.g., a container may leak, be hard to get out of, or have a flexible boundary. Let us consider the similes *X is like a Y* that are the result of randomly choosing an element *X* from the first row and combining it with a random element *Y* from the second column. For example, 'The Universe is like a treasure chest', 'Their marriage is like a prison', 'My bank account is like a leaky pot'. Note that all of the resulting similes are meaningful. Some of them will intuitively have more appeal than others, which may only be meaningful within a particular context.[23]

The fact that Table 4.2 can be used to randomly produce similes is linguistically interesting, because the target concepts vary significantly. The concepts *space ship*, *marriage* and *North Korea* seem to have nothing in common. Therefore, the fact that they can all be compared meaningfully to the same concepts needs an explanation. The puzzle is solved if we assume all concepts in the first column share the underlying image schema CONTAINER. For this reason they can be blended with the container concepts from the second column. In each simile we project some feature of the container in the source domain (second column) via analogical transfer onto the container aspect of the target domain (first column). Thus, Table 4.2 provides evidence that image schemas can help us to identify or (construe) shared structure between concepts.

The shared structure between concepts can be utilised in conceptual blending. For example, we can conceptually blend the concepts *universe* and *balloon* to a *balloon-universe*, that is a universe that continuously increases its size and expands. This concept is already lexicalised as *expanding universe* in English. Blending *space ship* with *prison* could lead to various interesting concepts: e.g., to a space ship that

---

[23] For example, 'This space ship is like a bottomless pit' may sound odd in isolation, but in the context of 'I have already 20,000 containers in storage, and there is still empty cargo space' the simile works.

```
Class: Container
    EquivalentTo: MaterialObject and has_proper_part some Cavity

ObjectProperty: contains
    SubPropertyChain: has_proper_part o is_location_of
    DisjointWith: has_proper_part
    Domain: Container
    Range: MaterialObject
```

Fig. 4.4: A (partial) representation of CONTAINER in OWL

is used as a prison – a kind of space age version of the British prison hulks of the 19th century.

How something is conceptualised depends on the context. For example, surgeons may conceptualise people as containers of organs, blood, and various other anatomical entities, but in most contexts we do not conceptualise humans in this way. By choosing the appropriate context an image schema may be pushed from the background into the conceptual forefront. For example, in most contexts a *mother* is probably not conceptualised as a kind of container. However, in the appropriate contexts it is possible to generate similes for *mother* reusing the source domains from Table 4.2; e.g., 'The mother is pregnant with twins, she looks like a balloon' or 'The mother is like a prison for the unborn child'.

The examples that we have discussed in this section show how the CONTAINER image schema can be utilised as generic space in conceptual blending. In the next sections we present the formalisation of the blending of two of our examples, namely *space ship* and *mother*.

4.5.2.1 The 'Mother Ship' Blend

Our thesis is that image schemas provide a useful heuristics for conceptual blending, because shared image schemas are good candidates for the generic space in the blending process.

The concepts *space ship* and *mother* share the CONTAINER schema.

As a first step towards the formalisation of the blending process, we need to represent CONTAINER in some formal language.

For the sake of illustrating the basic ideas, we choose here a simplified representation in OWL (see Figure 4.4). Containers are defined as material objects that have a cavity as a proper part. A container contains an object if and only if the object is located in the cavity that is part of the container.[24]

During the blending of *mother* and *space ship* into *mother ship* the CONTAINER schema structure of both input spaces is preserved (see Figure 4.8). The uterine cavity and the cargo space are both mapped to the docking space. The *mother ship*

---

[24] This is a simplified view on CONTAINER. For instance, a more accurate formalisation of the CONTAINER schema would need to cover notions like moving into or out of the container.

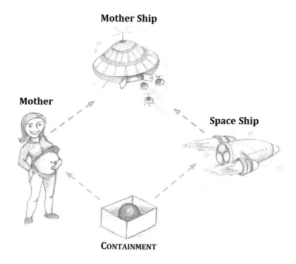

Fig. 4.5: The blending of mother ship

```
Class: Mother
    EquivalentTo: Female and Human and parent_of some (Small and Human)
    SubClassOf: has_proper_part some UterineCavity

Class: SpaceShip
    EquivalentTo: Vehicle and has_capability some Spacefaring
    SubClassOf: has_proper_part some CargoSpace
```

Fig. 4.6: Mother and space ships

inherits some features from both input spaces, while others are dropped. Obviously, a mother ship is a space travelling vessel. But like a mother, it is a 'parent' to some smaller entities of the same type. These smaller vessels can be contained within the mother ship, they may leave its hull (a process analogous to a birth) and are supported and under the authority of the larger vessel.[25]

To summarise, in our example we try to blend the input spaces of "Mother" and "Space ship". Instead of trying to utilise a syntactic approach like anti-unification to search for a base space, we recognise that both input spaces have cavities and, thus, are containers. Using the base space CONTAINER in the blending process yields a blended concept of "Mother ship". Here, the precise mappings from the base space axiomatisation of CONTAINER to the two input spaces regulate the various properties of the blended concept. Figure 4.5 illustrates this blend by populating the generic blending schema shown in Figure 4.1.

---

[25] To represent dynamic aspects like birth and vessels leaving a docking bay adequately, one needs a more expressive language than OWL.

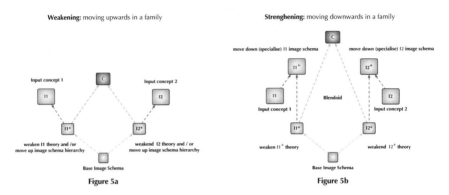

Fig. 4.7: Blending using common image schemas: strengthening vs. weakening

```
Class: MotherShip
    SubClassOf: Vehicle and has_capability some Spacefaring
    SubClassOf: has_proper_part DockingStation
    SubClassOf: parent_of some (Small and Vehicle)
```

Fig. 4.8: Mother ship

The mother ship blend demonstrated the general idea of using image schemas in conceptual blending. However, is it not always possible to directly map the image schema structures in the different input spaces. Often the image schema that are present can be from the same family, but on different levels of specificity/characteristics. In the next section we introduce the idea of how to integrate the idea of image schemas as families of theories into conceptual blending.

4.5.3 Blending with Families of Image Schemas

Figure 4.7 shows the two basic ways of using image schemas within the conceptual blending workflow. In both cases, the image schematic content takes priority over other information the input concepts might contain. On the left, following the core model of blending described above, we first identify different spatial structures within the same image schema family in the input concepts, and then generalise to the most specific common version within the image schema family to identify a generic space, using our pre-determined graph of spatial schemas (i.e., we compute the least upper bound in the lattice). The second case, shown on the right, illustrates the situation where we first want to specialise or complete the (description of the) spatial schemas found in the input concepts, before performing a generalisation step and identifying the generic space. This means moving down in the graph of the image schema family. Of course, also a mix of these two basic approaches is reasonable, i.e., where one input spatial schema is specialised within a family whilst the other is generalised in order to identify a generic space based on image-schematic content.

4.5.4 The PATH-Following Family at Work

In this section, we will illustrate how moving up and down within the image schema family of PATH-following opens up a space of blending possibilities, infused with the respective semantics of the (different versions of the) image schema.

We can explore the basic idea on how to combine the input space of 'thinking process', which involves only an underspecified kind of 'movement of thoughts',[26] with a second input space that carries a clearly defined path-following image schema. This leads intuitively to a number of more or less well known phrases that can be analysed as blends, including: 'train of thought', 'line of reasoning', 'derailment', 'flow of arguments', or 'stream of consciousness', amongst others. Indeed, a central point we want to make in this section is that these blends work well and appear natural because of the effectiveness of the following heuristics:[27] (i) given two input spaces I_1 and I_2, search for the strongest version G of some image schema that is *common to both* (in the sense that a substantial part of G's axiomatisation can be identified in the inputs), according to the organisation of a particular image schema family $\mathfrak{F}$; (ii) use G as generic space; and (iii) use again $\mathfrak{F}$ to identify the stronger version of G, say G', inherent in one of the two inputs, and use the semantic content of G' to steer the overall selection of axioms for the blended concept.[28]

To illustrate this process informally, let us briefly consider the concepts of 'stream of consciousness', 'train of thought', and 'line of reasoning'.[29]

On first inspection, the spatial schema of movement related to 'thinking' might be identified as MOVEMENT_OF_OBJECT, i.e., without necessarily identifying following a PATH at all. Indeed, in Figure 4.3, MOVEMENT_OF_OBJECT is marked as an 'entry point' to the path-following family.

---

[26] As discussed on Page 111, we can conceptualise any process as movement along a path. In this case, we conceptualise the process of *thinking* as movement. Therefore, this input space is already a blended concept.

[27] By 'heuristics' we mean a method that imposes rules on how to select a base (i.e., introduces a preference order on possible generic spaces) and, moreover, rules to decide which axioms to push into the blend. This means that without any heuristics we are left to perform a randomised axiom selection, followed by an evaluation of the resulting blended concept.

[28] As pointed out in Section 4.5.1, since image schemas typically have non-trivial axiomatisations, the possibility of interpreting (a large subset of) such an axiomatisation into an input space puts strong constraints on the structure of the input space.

[29] The examples presented here are chosen to illustrate the basic ideas on how to employ families of image schemas in blending. They do not intend to capture fully the meaning of these terms as they are used in the psychological or linguistic literature, or indeed the subtle meaning they might carry in natural language.

The *stream of consciousness* may be seen as an unguided flow of thoughts, in which topics merge into each other without any defined steps, but rather in a continuous manner. It lacks a clear START_PATH and has no guided movement towards a particular END_PATH. It resembles the more basic forms of PATH-following that, according to Mandler and Pagán Cánovas (2014), is simply movement in any trajectory.

A *train of thought*[30] can be conceptualised in various ways. It differs from a stream of consciousness by having a more clear direction, often with an intended END_PATH. It is possible to say that one "lost their train of thought", or that "their mind got hijacked" or how "it reversed its course". The 'train' may be understood as a chain-like spatial object (in which case 'losing the train' decodes to 'disconnecting the chain') or more plainly as a locomotive.

A *line of reasoning* might be seen as a strengthening of this blend, where the path imposed is linear. Although a 'line', mathematically speaking, has no beginning or end, the way this expression is normally understood is as a discrete succession of arguments (following logical rules) leading to an insight (or truth). This blend might therefore be analysed to correspond to SOURCE_PATH_GOAL in (Lakoff and Núñez, 2000), in which there is a clear direction and trajectory of the 'thought' (the trajector).

In order to understand how blending can result in these concepts, and how image schemas are involved, let us have a closer look at the input spaces and their relationship to the PATH-following image schemas. Relevant input spaces include line (perhaps analysed as 'discrete interval'), stream/river, train/locomotive, and, as secondary input space, 'thinking process'. In opposition to the example with the mother ship, this example will be motivated visually in Figure 4.9.

'Thinking' as an input space is difficult to visualise. However, when 'thinking' is understood as a process it can be easily combined with various PATH-following notions. As thoughts (in the form of OBJECT) are moved around, the simplest form of thinking is MOVEMENT_OF_OBJECT. There is no START_PATH nor an END_PATH. Intuitively, it does not appear to have any particular PATH (in the sense of a spatial primitive).

A stream is characterised by a continuous flow along a PATH. Whilst START_PATH and END_PATH can be part of a stream-like concept, like in the fleshed out concept of a river with a source and mouth, they do not constitute an essential part of the concept of stream.

For a train (understood as 'locomotive'), the concepts of START_PATH and END_PATH have a much higher significance. The affordances found in trains are primarily those concerning going from one place to another. A train ride can also be seen as a discrete movement in the sense that for most train rides, there are more stops than the final destination. This results in a discrete form of the spatial schema SOURCE_PATH_GOAL.

---

[30] The expression 'train of thoughts' appears to have been first used by Thomas Hobbes in his *Leviathan* (1651): "*By 'consequence of thoughts' or 'TRAIN of thoughts' I mean the occurrence of thoughts, one at a time, in a sequence; we call this 'mental discourse', to distinguish it from discourse in words.*"

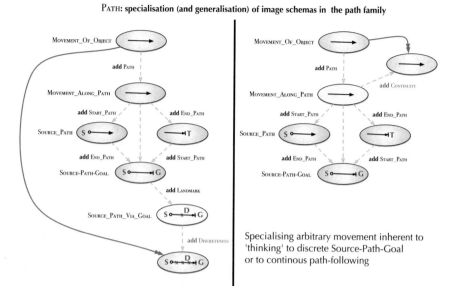

Fig. 4.9: How 'thinking' transforms into 'train of thought' or 'stream of consciousness'

When blending such forms of movement with the thinking process, what happens is that the unspecified form of movement found in 'thinking process' is specialised to the PATH-following characteristics found in the second input space. The result is the conceptual metaphors for the different modes of thinking listed above, where the generic space contains just MOVEMENT_OF_OBJECT, and the blended concepts inherit the more complex PATH-following from 'train', 'stream', or 'line'.

In more detail, Figure 4.9 shows two specialisations of the basic spatial schema of MOVEMENT_OF_OBJECT. The first, shown on the left, specialises to a discrete version of the schema SOURCE_PATH_GOAL with a designated element and discrete movement, supporting the 'train of thought' blend. The second, shown on the right, specialises to a continuous version of MOVEMENT_ALONG_PATH, where an axiom for gapless movement is added to the MOVEMENT_ALONG_PATH spatial schema to support the 'flow of consciousness' blend. As a third possibility, in 'line of reasoning', we would impose additionally a linear (and perhaps discrete) path onto 'thinking'.

4.6 Conclusion and Future Perspectives

In this chapter, we presented an approach to computational concept invention in which image schemas, understood as conceptual building blocks, are utilised in conceptual blending, the suggested cognitive machinery behind concept invention. More specifically, we suggested that image schemas can constitute the generic space that contains the shared structure from all input spaces during the blending process. Based on the idea that image schemas are conceptual building blocks, we argued that they are essential to the meaning of concepts, motivating the claim that their usage will greatly minimise the number of 'nonsense'-blends that are generated in automated conceptual blending systems. As an example, the 'Mother ship' blend is formalised to demonstrate how both input spaces, consequently also the generic space, contain the CONTAINMENT schema, and how this image schema guides the blending process.

In order for this to work, the abstract image schemas need to be formally captured before it is possible to integrate them into a computational system for concept invention. This problem is approached through formalising image schemas as interlinked families of theories. To this end, the PATH-following family is used as a proof of concept showing that the image schema SOURCE_PATH_GOAL cannot be treated as an isolated formal theory, but rather needs to be formally embedded into a rich network of concepts, stretching over a range of different movement types, such as MOVEMENT_ALONG_PATH, SOURCE_PATH_GOAL and MOVEMENT_IN_LOOPS. Following this general strategy, it is hoped that eventually many of the complexities arising from work on image schemas in developmental psychology and cognitive linguistics can be suitably mapped to a formalised library of these notions, enabling new cognitively driven solutions in concept invention and more generally in cognitive AI.

Building on the family representation of image schemas, this chapter also introduced some of the basic ideas on how computational aspects of conceptual blending can be advanced through generalisation and specialisation operators, which allow us to identify common image schematic structures by moving up and down the network of an image schema family.

The benefits of this approach lie not only in the provided structuring of image schemas, but also in how formal systems may use them. By using image schemas in conceptual blending, it is our belief that computational concept invention has taken a step in the right direction. Image schemas provide a cognitively plausible foundation for the idea of a generic space found in the theory of conceptual blending. In analogy engines, or (formal) approaches to conceptual blending (Turner, 2014; Kutz et al., 2014), the presented graph of image schemas can provide a method for theory weakening and strengthening based on the involved image schemas, employing basic ideas of amalgams (Ontañón and Plaza, 2010) and refinement operators (Confalonieri et al., 2018; Troquard et al, 2018; Porello et al, 2018). This approach is therefore substantially different from the more syntactic-driven methods used by the Structure Mapping Engine (SME) (Gentner, 1983; Forbus et al., 1989) or Heuristic-Driven Theory Projection (HDTP) (Schwering et al., 2009; Schmidt et al., 2014b).

To successfully investigate and evaluate the fruitfulness of this idea, a more comprehensive formalisation of image schemas is needed. Formalising image schemas has been a rather recent undertaking in artificial intelligence research as a means to aid computational concept invention and common-sense reasoning (Kuhn, 2002; Walton and Worboys, 2009; Morgenstern, 2001; Goguen and Harrell, 2010; Kutz et al., 2014).

References

W. Aguilar and R. Pérez y Pérez. Dev E-R: A computational model of early cognitive development as a creative process. *Cognitive Systems Research*, 33:17–41, 2015.

K. Ahrens and A. L. Say. Mapping image schemas and traslating metaphors. In *Proceedings of Pacific Asia Conference on Language, Information and Computation*, pages 1–8, February 1999.

J. Allen and P. Hayes. A common-sense theory of time. In *Proceedings of the 9th International Joint Conference on Artificial Intelligence (IJCAI-85)*, pages 528–531, Los Angeles, CA, USA, 1985.

B. Bennett and C. Cialone. Corpus guided sense cluster analysis: A methodology for ontology development (with examples from the spatial domain). In P. Garbacz and O. Kutz, editors, *8th International Conference on Formal Ontology in Information Systems (FOIS)*, volume 267 of *Frontiers in Artificial Intelligence and Applications*, pages 213–226. IOS Press, 2014.

T. R. Besold, M. M. Hedblom, and O. Kutz. A narrative in three acts: Using combinations of image schemas to model events. *Biologically Inspired Cognitive Architectures*, 19:10–20, 2017.

C. Brugman and G. Lakoff. Cognitive topology and lexical networks. In M. T. Stephen Small, Gary Cottrell, editor, *Lexical ambiguity resolution*, pages 477–508. 1988.

T. C. Clausner and W. Croft. Domains and image schemas. *Cognitive Linguistics*, 10(1):1–31, 1999.

R. Confalonieri, M. Eppe, M. Schorlemmer, O. Kutz, R. Peñaloza, and E. Plaza. Upward refinement operators for conceptual blending in the description logic $\mathcal{EL}^{++}$. *Annals of Mathematics and Artificial Intelligence*, 82(1–3):69–99, 2018. DOI: 10.1007/s10472-016-9524-8.

D. Davidson. The logical form of action sentences. In N. Rescher, editor, *The logic of decision and action*, pages 81–94. Pittsburgh, 1967.

M. Eppe, E. Maclean, R. Confalonieri, O. Kutz, M. Schorlemmer, E. Plaza, and K-U. Kühnberger. A computational framework for conceptual blending. Artificial Intelligence 256:105–129, 2018. DOI: 10.1016/j.artint.2017.11.005

G. Fauconnier and M. Turner. Conceptual integration networks. *Cognitive Science*, 22(2):133–187, 1998.

K. Forbus, B. Falkenhainer, and D. Gentner. The structure-mapping engine. *Artificial Intelligence*, 41:1–63, 1989.

V. Gallese and G. Lakoff. The brain's concepts: the role of the sensory-motor system in conceptual knowledge. *Cognitive neuropsychology*, 22(3):455–79, 5 2005.

A. Galton. The formalities of affordance. In *Proceedings of ECAI-2010 Workshop on Spatio-Temporal Dynamics*, pages 1–6, 2010.

P. Gärdenfors. *Conceptual Spaces - The Geometry of Thought*. Bradford Books. MIT Press, 2000.

P. Gärdenfors. *Embodiment in Cognition and Culture*, volume 71 of *Advances in Consciousness Research*, chapter Cognitive semantics and image schemas with embodied forces, pages 57–76. John Benjamins Publishing Company, 2007.

D. Gentner. Structure mapping: A theoretical framework for analogy. *Cognitive Science*, 7(2):155–170, 1983.

J. J. Gibson. The theory of affordances, in perceiving, acting, and knowing. towards an ecological psychology. In R. Shaw and J. Bransford, editors, *Perceiving, Acting, and Knowing: Toward an Ecological Psychology*, pages 67–82. NJ: Lawrence Erlbaum, Hillsdale, 1977.

J. A. Goguen. An introduction to algebraic semiotics, with applications to user interface design. In *Computation for Metaphors, Analogy and Agents*, number 1562 in LNCS, pages 242–291. Springer, 1999.

J. A. Goguen. Semiotic morphisms, representations and blending for interface design. In *Proc. of the AMAST Workshop on Algebraic Methods in Language Processing*, pages 1–15. AMAST Press, 2003.

J. A. Goguen and D. F. Harrell. Style: A computational and conceptual blending-based approach. In S. Argamon and S. Dubnov, editors, *The Structure of Style: Algorithmic Approaches to Understanding Manner and Meaning*, pages 147–170. Springer, Berlin, 2010.

J. A. Goguen and G. Malcolm. *Algebraic Semantics of Imperative Programs*. MIT, 1996.

J. E. Grady. Cognitive mechanisms of conceptual integration. *Cognitive Linguistics*, 11(3-4):335–345, 2001.

D. Gromann and M. M. Hedblom. Breaking down finance: A method for concept simplification by identifying movement structures from the image schema Path-following. In *Proceedings of the Second Joint Ontology Workshops (JOWO)*, volume 1660, Annecy, France, 2016. CEUR-WS online proceedings.

M. Grüninger, T. Hahmann, A. Hashemi, D. Ong, and A. Ozgovde. Modular first-order ontologies via repositories. *Applied Ontology*, 7(2):169–209, 2012.

M. Guhe, A. Pease, A. Smaill, M. Martínez, M. Schmidt, H. Gust, K.-U. Kühnberger, and U. Krumnack. A computational account of conceptual blending in basic mathematics. *Cognitive Systems Research*, 12(3–4):249–265, 2011.

B. Hampe. Image schemas in cognitive linguistics: Introduction. In B. Hampe and J. E. Grady, editors, *From perception to meaning: Image schemas in cognitive linguistics*, pages 1–14. Walter de Gruyter, 2005.

B. Hampe and J. E. Grady. *From perception to meaning: Image schemas in cognitive linguistics*, volume 29 of *Cognitive Linguistics Research*. Walter de Gruyter, Berlin, 2005.

M. M. Hedblom, O. Kutz, and F. Neuhaus. Image schemas as families of theories. In T. R. Besold, K.-U. Kühnberger, M. Schorlemmer, and A. Smaill, editors, *Proceedings of the Workshop "Computational Creativity, Concept Invention, and General Intelligence" 2015*, volume 2 of *Publications of the Institute of Cognitive Science*, pages 19–33. Institute of Cognitive Science, 2015.

M. M. Hedblom, O. Kutz, and F. Neuhaus. Choosing the right path: Image schema theory as a foundation for concept invention. *Journal of Artificial General Intelligence*, 6(1):22–54, 2015.

M. M. Hedblom, O. Kutz, and F. Neuhaus. Image schemas in computational conceptual blending. *Cognitive Systems Research*, 39:42–57, 2016.

J. Hois, O. Kutz, T. Mossakowski, and J. Bateman. Towards ontological blending. In *Proc. of the 14th International Conference on Artificial Intelligence: Methodology, Systems, Applications (AIMSA-2010)*, Varna, Bulgaria, September 8th–10th, 2010.

M. Johanson and A. Papafragou. What does children's spatial language reveal about spatial concepts? Evidence from the use of containment expressions. *Cognitive science*, 38(5):881–910, 2014.

M. Johnson. *The Body in the Mind: The Bodily Basis of Meaning, Imagination, and Reason*. The University of Chicago Press, Chicago and London, 1987.

R. W. Gibbs. Making good psychology out of blending theory. *Cognitive Linguistics*, 11(3-4):347–358, 2001. DOI: 10.1515/cogl.2001.020.

W. Kuhn. Modeling the semantics of geographic categories through conceptual integration. In *Proceedings of GIScience 2002*, pages 108–118. Springer, 2002.

W. Kuhn. An image-schematic account of spatial categories. In S. Winter, M. Duckham, L. Kulik, and B. Kuipers, editors, *Spatial Information Theory*, volume 4736 of *Lecture Notes in Computer Science*, pages 152–168. Springer, 2007.

O. Kutz and I. Normann. Context discovery via theory interpretation. In *Proc. of the IJCAI Workshop on Automated Reasoning about Context and Ontology Evolution, ARCOE-09*, Pasadena, California, 2009.

O. Kutz, T. Mossakowski, and D. Lücke. Carnap, Goguen, and the Hyperontologies: Logical pluralism and heterogeneous structuring in ontology design. *Logica Universalis*, 4(2):255–333, 2010. Special Issue on 'Is Logic Universal?'.

O. Kutz, T. Mossakowski, J. Hois, M. Bhatt, and J. Bateman. Ontological blending in DOL. In T. Besold, K.-U. Kühnberger, M. Schorlemmer, and A. Smaill, editors, *Computational Creativity, Concept Invention, and General Intelligence, Proceedings of the 1st International Workshop C3GI@ECAI*, volume 01-2012, Montpellier, France, August 27 2012. Publications of the Institute of Cognitive Science, Osnabrück.

O. Kutz, J. Bateman, F. Neuhaus, T. Mossakowski, and M. Bhatt. E pluribus unum: Formalisation, use-cases, and computational support for conceptual blending. In T. R. Besold, M. Schorlemmer, and A. Smaill, editors, *Computational Creativ-*

ity Research: Towards Creative Machines, Thinking Machines. Atlantis/Springer, 2014a.

O. Kutz, F. Neuhaus, T. Mossakowski, and M. Codescu. Blending in the Hub— Towards a collaborative concept invention platform. In *Proceedings of the 5th International Conference on Computational Creativity*, Ljubljana, Slovenia, June 10–13 2014b.

G. Lakoff and R. Núñez. *Where Mathematics Comes from: How the Embodied Mind Brings Mathematics Into Being*. Basic Books, New York, 2000.

J. M. Mandler. How to build a baby: II. conceptual primitives. *Psychological review*, 99(4):587–604, 10 1992.

J. M. Mandler and C. Pagán Cánovas. On defining image schemas. *Language and Cognition*, 0:1–23, 2014.

G. Mazzola, J. Park, and F. Thalmann. *Musical Creativity: Strategies and Tools in Composition and Improvisation*. Computational Music Science. Springer, 2011.

C. Menzel. Knowledge representation, the World Wide Web, and the evolution of logic. *Synthese*, 182:269–295, 2011.

L. Morgenstern. Mid-sized axiomatizations of commonsense problems: A case study in egg cracking. *Studia Logica*, 67:333–384, 2001.

T. Mossakowski, C. Maeder, and K. Lüttich. The Heterogeneous Tool Set. In O. Grumberg and M. Huth, editors, *TACAS 2007*, volume 4424 of *Lecture Notes in Computer Science*, pages 519–522. Springer-Verlag Heidelberg, 2007.

T. Mossakowski, M. Codescu, F. Neuhaus, and O. Kutz. *The road to Universal Logic–Festschrift for 50th birthday of Jean-Yves Beziau, Volume II*, chapter The Distributed Ontology, Modelling and Specification Language DOL. Studies in Universal Logic. Birkhäuser, 2015.

S. Nayak and A. Mukerjee. Concretizing the image schema: How semantics guides the bootstrapping of syntax. In *2012 IEEE International Conference on Development and Learning and Epigenetic Robotics, ICDL 2012*, 2012.

F. Neuhaus, O. Kutz, M. Codescu, and T. Mossakowski. Fabricating monsters is hard - Towards the automation of conceptual blending. In *Proc. of Computational Creativity, Concept Invention, and General Intelligence (C3GI-14)*, volume 1-2014, pages 2–5, Prague, 2014. Publications of the Institute of Cognitive Science, Osnabrück.

I. Normann. *Automated Theory Interpretation*. Ph.D. thesis, Department of Computer Science, Jacobs University, Bremen, 2008.

I. Normann and O. Kutz. Ontology correspondence via theory interpretation. In *Workshop on Matching and Meaning, AISB-09, Edinburgh, UK*, 2009.

T. Oakley. Image schema. In D. Geeraerts and H. Cuyckens, editors, *The Oxford Handbook of Cognitive Linguistics*, pages 214–235. Oxford University Press, Oxford, 2010.

S. Ontañón and E. Plaza. Amalgams: A formal approach for combining multiple case solutions. In *Case-Based Reasoning. Research and Development*, pages 257–271. Springer, 2010.

T. Parson. *Events in the Semantics of English: A Study in Subatomic Semantics*. MIT Press, 1990.

D. Porello, N. Troquard, R. Peñaloza, R. Confalonieri, P. Galliani, O. Kutz. Two approaches to ontology integration based on axiom weakening. *Proceedings of the Twenty-Seventh International Joint Conference on Artificial Intelligence, IJCAI-18*, 1942–1948, 2018. DOI: 10.24963/ijcai.2018/268

T. Regier. *The Human Semantic Potential: Spatial Language and Constrained Connectionism*. The MIT Press, 1996.

T. Rohrer. Image schemata in the brain. In B. Hampe and J. E. Grady, editors, *From perception to meaning: Image schemas in cognitive linguistics*, volume 29 of *Cognitive Linguistics Research*, pages 165–196. Walter de Gruyter, 2005.

M. Schmidt, U. Krumnack, H. Gust, and K.-U. Kühnberger. *Computational Approaches to Analogical Reasoning: Current Trends*, volume 548 of *Studies in Computational Intelligence*. Springer Berlin Heidelberg, 2014a.

M. Schmidt, U. Krumnack, H. Gust, and K.-U. Kühnberger. Heuristic-driven theory projection: An overview. In H. Prade and G. Richard, editors, *Computational Approaches to Analogical Reasoning: Current Trends*, Computational Intelligence 548. Springer-Verlag, 2014b.

M. Schorlemmer, A. Smaill, K.-U. Kühnberger, O. Kutz, S. Colton, E. Cambouropoulos, and A. Pease. COINVENT: Towards a computational concept invention theory. In *Proceedings of the 5th International Conference on Computational Creativity*, Ljubljana, Slovenia, June 10–13 2014.

M. Schorlemmer, R. Confalonieri, and E. Plaza. The Yoneda path to the Buddhist monk blend. In O. Kutz, S. de Cesare, M. M. Hedblom, T. R. Besold, T. Veale, F. Gailly, G. Guizzardi, M. Lycett, C. Partridge, O. Pastor, M. Grüninger, F. Neuhaus, T. Mossakowski, S. Borgo, L. Bozzato, C. D. Vescovo, M. Homola, F. Loebe, A. Barton, and J. Bourguet, editors, *Proceedings of the Joint Ontology Workshops 2016, Episode 2: The French Summer of Ontology (JOWO 2016), co-located with the 9th International Conference on Formal Ontology in Information Systems (FOIS 2016), Annecy, France, July 6–9*, volume 1660. CEUR-WS.org, 2016.

A. Schwering, U. Krumnack, K.-U. Kühnberger, and H. Gust. Syntactic principles of Heuristic-Driven Theory Projection. *Cognitive Systems Research, Special Issue on Analogies - Integrating Cognitive Abilities*, 10(3):251–269, 2009.

L. Shapiro. *Embodied Cognition*. New problems of philosophy. Routledge, London and New York, 2011.

R. St. Amant, C. T. Morrison, Y.-H. Chang, P. R. Cohen, and C. Beal. An image schema language. In *International Conference on Cognitive Modeling (ICCM)*, pages 292–297, 2006.

N. Troquard, R. Confalonieri, P. Galliani, R. Peñaloza, D. Porello, O. Kutz. Repairing ontologies via axiom weakening. *Proceedings of the Thirty-Second AAAI Conference on Artificial Intelligence*, 1981–1988, 2018.

M. Turner. *The Origin of Ideas: Blending, Creativity, and the Human Spark*. Oxford University Press, 2014.

J. F. A. K. Van Benthem. *The Logic of Time*. D. Reidel Publishing Company, Dordrecht, Holland, 1983.

T. Veale. The analogical thesaurus. In J. Riedl and R. Hill, editors, *Proceedings of the Fifteenth Innovative Applications of Artificial Intelligence Conference*, pages 137–142. AAAI Press, 2003.

T. Veale. From conceptual "mash-ups" to "bad-ass" blends: A robust computational model of conceptual blending. In M. L. Maher, K. Hammond, A. Pease, R. P. y Pérez, D. Ventura, and G. Wiggins, editors, *Proc. of the 3rd International Conference on Computational Creativity*, pages 1–8, Dublin, Ireland, May 2012.

L. Walton and M. Worboys. An algebraic approach to image schemas for geographic space. In *Proceedings of the 9th International Conference on Spatial Information Theory (COSIT)*, pages 357–370, France, 2009.

F.-P. G. Yang, K. Bradley, M. Huq, D.-L. Wu, and D. C. Krawczyk. Contextual effects on conceptual blending in metaphors: An event-related potential study. *Journal of Neurolinguistics*, 26:312–326, 2012.

Chapter 5
The Relationship Between Conceptual Blending and Analogical Reasoning

Tarek R. Besold

Abstract This chapter connects work on (the modelling of) conceptual blending with research efforts in computational analogy-making. After a high-level introduction to analogy as cognitive capacity, we discuss a computational-level model of conceptual blending between two input theories which combines an approach from generalisation-based analogy-making with the notion of amalgams from Case-Based Reasoning. We then exemplify how the model can be instantiated on the algorithmic level, and by way of example reconstruct the blend between horse and bird which gave rise to Pegasus as a mythological creature.

5.1 Analogy and Cognition

During the course of a day, as humans we use different kinds of reasoning processes for solving puzzles, playing instruments, discussing problems, preparing meals, and the plethora of other everyday activities we perform. Often we will find ourselves in situations in which we apply our knowledge of a familiar situation to the structurally similar novel one—both in highly complex social scenarios such as when organising a March for Science following the example of the Women's March on Washington on January 21, 2017, as well as in the fairly simple case of shortening the description of a task in an instruction manual of a refrigerator (e.g., *"To set the high limit value HL, proceed analogously as described for LL."*, p. 31, Bio (2006)).

Notwithstanding its omnipresence in daily live, for a long time analogy nonetheless was merely considered a special case of reasoning, mostly to be found in application when encountering creative solutions or in arts, as for example in the case of poetic writing. But the scene has changed and today it is mostly undoubted that one of the basic elements of human cognition is the ability to see two a priori distinct

Tarek R. Besold
Digital Media Lab, Center for Computing and Communication Technologies (TZI), University of Bremen, Bibliothekstr. 5, 28359 Bremen, Germany, e-mail: tbesold@uni-bremen.de

© Springer Nature Switzerland AG 2018
R. Confalonieri et al. (eds.), *Concept Invention*, Computational Synthesis and Creative Systems, https://doi.org/10.1007/978-3-319-65602-1_5

domains as similar with respect to certain aspects, based either on their shared relational structure or (to a lesser extent) appearance—i.e., to recognise analogies and often use them for cross-domain transfer of knowledge and reasoning.[1] Some prominent cognitive scientists—with Hofstadter (2001) leading the way—even consider analogy the core of cognition itself.[2]

As more cautiously described, for instance, by Schwering et al. (2009b), key abilities within everyday life, such as communication, social interaction, tool use and the handling of previously unseen situations crucially rely on the use of analogy-based strategies and procedures. Relational matching, one of the key mechanisms underlying analogy-making, is also one of the bases of perception, language, learning, memory and thinking, i.e., the constituent elements of most conceptions of cognition.[3]

Whilst analogies can be quite diverse in appearance and usage, it is widely agreed that on a procedural level at least three steps are indispensable (which also reappear in most, if not all computational models of analogy-making):

1. **Retrieval:** Given the target domain of an analogy (e.g., in form of a problem scenario a reasoner has to confront), the reasoner's memory has to be queried for similar cases encountered in the past. Candidate source domains have to be identified and made available to the analogy process.

2. **Mapping:** Given the target domain and a source domain (i.e., one of the candidate domains found during the retrieval step), respective domain elements which are hypothesised to stand in an analogical relation to each other have to be aligned. This process of pairing up domain elements can possibly give rise to insights about the internal structure of the domains, potentially also triggering domain-internal restructuring and new conceptualisations. (In the case of computational analogy-making, the alignment is mostly based on structural and syntactic properties of the respective representation formalisms applied in the domains, and the process of restructuring the domains is called re-representation. See also Figure 5.1.)

3. **Transfer/evaluation:** Once a mapping has been established between source and target domain, knowledge can be transferred from the (better informed) source to the (more sparse) target domain using the alignments from the mapping phase as guidance for the potentially needed knowledge adaptation during the cross-domain transfer. Once the target domain has been enriched, a final step of evaluation (possibly also involving reasoning within and, once again, restructuring of the target domain) judges the established analogy. This judgement

---

[1] This definition implies a very broad conception of analogy, also covering phenomena such as similarity, metaphor and allegory (and, thus, can partially be seen in the Classical Greek tradition of analogy as shared abstraction described, among others, by Shelley (2003), and as related to the stance taken for example by Gentner and Markman (1997) for similarity and by Gentner et al. (1988) and Gentner et al. (2001) for metaphor).

[2] Even more, it seems that analogy-like capabilities are not exclusive to our species, but that simple manifestations—mostly based on feature or surface similarity, rather than on shared relational structure—can also be observed in other primates (Holyoak et al. (2001)).

[3] For an overview of psychological research on analogy see Gentner and Smith (2013).

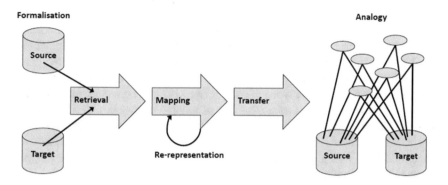

Fig. 5.1: A schematic overview of the standard conceptual approach to computational analogy-making is given by Schwering et al. (2009a)

can then also be used to decide whether the analogy-making was successful, or if another candidate domain should be considered instead of the used source domain—either by returning to the mapping phase and using another candidate from the collection of retrieved cases, or even by returning to the retrieval phase and (taking into account the insights about the target domain gained during restructuring and transfer) starting the entire procedure anew.

5.2 Computational Models of Analogy

Because of the described crucial role of analogy in human cognition researchers on the computational side of cognitive science and in AI also very quickly got interested in the topic and have been creating computational models of analogy-making basically since the advent of computer systems. Although the developed models and implemented systems differ vastly in their precise specifications and computational paradigms (some being symbolic, some connectionist, others hybrid), on the level of procedural abstraction most also adhere to the just outlined retrieval–mapping–transfer/evaluation triad and can be conceptualised as shown in Figure 5.1.

The resulting history of computational analogy systems starts with Reitman et al. (1964)'s ARGUS and Evans (1964)'s ANALOGY in the late 1950s and early 1960s, contains, for instance, Winston (1980)'s work on analogy and learning, and features systems as prominent as Hofstadter and Mitchell (1994)'s Copycat or Falkenhainer et al. (1989)'s famous Structure-Mapping Engine (SME) and Gentner and Forbus (1991)'s MAC/FAC.[4]

---

[4] For an overview of different architectural and conceptual paradigms for computational analogy engines and of well-known implemented systems see, for example, Besold (2011).

The SME and MAC/FAC implement a version of Gentner (1983)'s Structure Mapping Theory (SMT). The theory assigns a crucial role in the process of analogy-making to structural similarities between base and target domains: SMT emphasizes the dependence of rules exclusively on syntactic properties of the knowledge representation, and the possibility of distinguishing analogies from literal similarity statements or other, distinct types of comparison. The corresponding mapping principles can be characterised as a mapping of relations between objects from base to target domain, and a choice of mapped relations based on a certain systematicity, rooted in the existence of some designated higher-order relations. Kokinov and French (2003) gives a short list of conjectures underlying the Structure-Mapping Engine implementation of SMT:

- The mapping part of the process is widely isolated and disjoint from other sub-mechanisms.
- Relational matches get assigned a higher priority than mere property-based matchings.
- In order to be interpreted as corresponding relations in the base and target domains, relations have to be identical.
- Relations which form arguments of higher-order relations, which in turn can also be used for a mapping, get assigned a higher priority than mere isolated relations.

Contrasting this mapping-focused take on analogy, more recently a different approach based on the computation of explicit generalisations has been proposed: Heuristic-Driven Theory Projection (HDTP, Schmidt et al. (2014)). HDTP aims at being a mathematically sound framework for the computation of analogical relations and inferences between domains which are given in form of a many-sorted first-order logic representation. Source domain S and target domain T are handed over to the system in terms of finite axiomatisations, and HDTP tries to align pairs of formulae from the two domains by means of restricted higher-order anti-unification as introduced by Krumnack et al. (2007): Given two terms, one from each domain, HDTP computes an anti-instance in which distinct subterms have been replaced by variables so that the anti-instance can be seen as a meaningful generalisation of the input terms. As already indicated by the name, the class of admissible substitution operations is limited. On each expression, only renamings, fixations, argument insertions, and permutations may be performed. By this process, HDTP tries to find the least general generalisation G of the input terms, which (due to the higher-order nature of the anti-unification) is not unique. In order to solve this problem, current implementations of HDTP rank possible generalisations according to a complexity measure on the chain of substitutions—the respective values of which are taken as the heuristic costs—and return the least expensive solution as the preferred one. HDTP extends the notion of generalisation from terms to formulae by basically treating formulae in clause form and terms alike. Finally, as analogies rarely rely exclusively on one isolated pair of formulae from source and target domain, but usually encompass sets of formulae (possibly completely covering one or even both input domains), a process iteratively selecting pairs of formulae for generalisation has

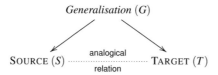

Fig. 5.2: A schematic overview of HDTP's generalisation-based approach to analogy

been included. The selection of formulae is again based on a heuristic component: Mappings in which substitutions can be reused get assigned a lower cost than isolated substitutions, leading to a preference for coherent over incoherent mappings.[5] In summary, when looked at on the theory level, the process of analogy-making in HDTP can be conceptualised as shown in Figure 5.2.

Synoptically comparing both paradigms, SMT and HDTP are very similar in that they are symbolic (i.e., operating on domain theories expressed in logic-based languages) and during the mapping stage heavily rely on syntactical properties of the respective representation languages and domain formalisations for pairing up domain elements. Still, whilst SMT proclaims that the mapping between domains is established directly from elements in the source domain to elements in the target domain, and that the subsequent transfer/evaluation step is exclusively guided by groupings of these individual correspondences, HDTP explicitly computes a generalisation of the source and target domain theories into a least general subsuming theory which later determines the transfer/evaluation phase.[6] As shown in the next section, the explicit availability of a shared generalisation between source and target domain of an analogy is what makes HDTP a good candidate for exemplifying the relationship between analogy (and computational models thereof) and conceptual blending.

5.3 Generalisation-Based Analogy and Conceptual Blending

Following Goguen (2006), conceptual blending can formally be conceptualised as follows: Given two domain theories I_1 and I_2 representing two (possibly complex) concepts, first compute a generalisation G and then construct the blend space B in

---

[5] For an overview of further formal and technical aspects of HDTP (and restricted higher-order anti-unification in particular) see Chapter 7, Section 7.4. For details specifically concerning the heuristic aspects of HDTP see Schwering et al. (2009a) and Schmidt et al. (2011).

[6] Here, subsumption has to be understood in the following sense: The joint generalised theory subsumes the original source theory and target theory in that each of the latter can be re-obtained by applying certain substitution operations to the generalisation (again see Chapter 7, Section 7.4 for additional details). In this way the joint generalisation encompasses both domain theories at a time as more specific variants.

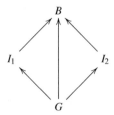

Fig. 5.3: A conceptual overview of Goguen (2006)'s account of conceptual blending

such a way as to preserve the correlations between I_1 and I_2 given by G (see also Figure 5.3).[7]

In this view, the morphisms mapping the axioms of one domain theory to another are induced by signature morphisms over the symbols of the representation languages — an analogical correspondence is assumed to exist between symbols in I_1 and I_2 coming from the same symbol in G. As incompatibilities might exist between the domains, the morphisms from I_1 and I_2 to B are possibly only partial (i.e., not all axioms from the domain theories are mapped to the blend). In Goguen (2006)'s category theory-based framework, B is the smallest theory comprising as much as possible from I_1 and I_2 while reflecting the commonalities of I_1 and I_2 encoded in the generalisation G.

As originally outlined in (Besold and Plaza, 2015)—which serves as basis for this section's presentation of our analogy-rooted computational-level model and the algorithmic implementation of conceptual blending—this approach clearly offers itself to a (re)conceptualisation and (re)implementation using HDTP: Whilst intra-domain reasoning can be performed with classical logic calculi over the many-sorted FOL language, the computation of a generalisation G from two input domains I_1 and I_2 (involving cross-domain generalisation, cross-domain specialisation, and possibly the detection of congruence relations as used, for instance, by Guhe et al. (2011)) is one of HDTP's core functionalities. Thus, basically the entire lower half of Figure 5.3 is naturally covered by the standard mechanisms of HDTP (also compare Figure 5.3 with Figure 5.2).[8] The only additional element needed is a mechanism for using the information provided by the domain theories I_1 and I_2 together with the generalisation G for computing the blend B.

---

[7] In the present setting, the domain theories should be understood as conceptual theories, i.e., as descriptive results of a formalisation process which in most cases represent a certain partial perspective (among several possible ones) on the described concept, providing an instantiation of what Bou et al. (2015) call a conceptual space.

[8] For the purpose of conceptual blending, the distinction between a source domain and a target domain as in the case of computational analogy-making becomes obsolete.

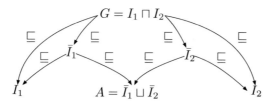

Fig. 5.4: A diagram of an amalgam A from inputs I_1 and I_2 where $A = \bar{I}_1 \sqcup \bar{I}_2$: the anti-unification of the inputs is indicated as G, and the amalgam A is the unification of two concrete generalisations $\bar{I}_1 \sqsubseteq I_1$ and $\bar{I}_2 \sqsubseteq I_2$ of the inputs

5.3.1 Combining Conceptual Theories Using Amalgams

This missing element is provided through the use of Ontañón and Plaza (2010)'s amalgams (as already touched upon in the context of blending in Chapter 2, Section 2.3). Originally conceived of in the context of Case-Based Reasoning, amalgams are a proposal to formalise the ways in which two cases can be combined to produce a new, coherent case.

Amalgams can be defined in any representation language $\mathscr{L}$ for which a subsumption relation $\sqsubseteq$ between the formulae (or descriptions) of $\mathscr{L}$ can be defined, where a description I_1 subsumes another description I_2 ($I_1 \sqsubseteq I_2$) when I_1 is more general than (or equal to) I_2.[9] In this setting, amalgams can then be conceived of as a generalisation of the notion of unification: as 'partial unification' (Ontañón and Plaza, 2010). The unification of two terms (or descriptions) I_1 and I_2 is a new description $U = I_1 \sqcup I_2$, where what is true for I_1 or I_2 is also true for U; e.g., if I_1 describes 'a red vehicle' and I_2 describes 'a German minivan' then their unification yields a common specialisation like 'a red German minivan.' An amalgam A of two descriptions now is a new description that features parts from these two descriptions, even if the two descriptions contain information which would produce an inconsistency when unified in the usual sense. As illustrated in Figure 5.4, the corresponding problem is solved by the intermediate use of suitable generalisations $\bar{I}_1$ and $\bar{I}_2$ of I_1 and I_2, respectively. For instance, an amalgam of 'a red French sedan' and 'a blue German minivan' is 'a red German sedan'; clearly there are always multiple possibilities for amalgams, like 'a blue French minivan'. Usually we are interested only in maximal amalgams of two input descriptions, i.e., those amalgams that contain maximal parts of their inputs that can be unified into a new coherent description. A non-maximal amalgam $\bar{A} \sqsubset A$ would preserve less compatible information from the inputs than the maximal amalgam A, and conversely, any non-maximal amalgam $\bar{A}$ could be obtained by generalising a maximal amalgam A, since $\bar{A} \sqsubset A$.

If the two inputs do not play equal roles in computing the amalgam, the amalgam is called asymmetric. In that case, the inputs are called source and target, and while

---

[9] Additionally, we assume that $\mathscr{L}$ contains the infimum element $\bot$ (or 'any') and the supremum element $\top$ (or 'none') with respect to the subsumption order.

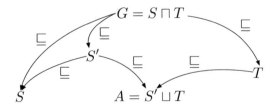

Fig. 5.5: A diagram that transfers content from source S to a target T via an asymmetric amalgam A

the source is allowed to be generalised, the target is not. As shown in Figure 5.5, the content of target T is transferred completely into the asymmetric amalgam, while the source S is generalised. The result is a form of partial unification that preserves all information in T while relaxing S by generalisation and then unifying one of those generalisations S' with T itself. As before, we will usually be interested in maximal amalgams: in this case, a maximal amalgam corresponds to transferring maximal content from S to T while keeping the resulting amalgam A consistent. In a way, asymmetric amalgams can thus be seen as akin to analogical inference: while the source can be relaxed and thus lose information (resulting in the creation of S'), the target is fixed, so all information belonging to the target will be present in the final (asymmetric) amalgam Ontañón and Plaza (2012).

5.3.2 An Analogy-Rooted Model of Conceptual Blending

Taking the notion of generalisation-based analogy as implemented, for instance, by HDTP, and the just described concept of amalgams, conceptual blending can then be phrased as the following task: given two axiomatisations of two domain theories I_1 and I_2, we need first to compute a generalised theory G of I_1 and I_2 (which codes the commonalities between I_1 and I_2) and second to compute the blend theory B in a structure preserving way such that new properties hold in B. Ideally, these new properties in B are considered to be (moderately) interesting properties. In what follows, for reasons of simplicity and without loss of generality we assume that the additional properties are just provided by one of the two domains, i.e., we align the situation with a standard setting in computational analogy-making by renaming I_1 and I_2: the domain providing the additional properties for the concept blend will be called source S, the domain providing the conceptual basis and receiving the additional features will be called target T.[10]

---

[10] In the case where additional properties are provided by both domains the same general principles as described below apply. It just becomes necessary to also treat the target domain T similarly to the current source S, expanding the conceptual overview in Figure 5.6 with a second "generalisation triangle" to the right of the "blending diamond", computing a generalisation of T and using the latter for the blending process (for which only minor and quite straightforward changes become

The conceptual blending process (a schematic overview of which is given in Figure 5.6) is then triggered by the analogy-style computation of the generalisation G between S and T, in which pairs of formulae from the source and target spaces are anti-unified resulting in a generalised theory that reflects common aspects of both spaces. The generalised theory can be projected into the original spaces by substitutions which are computed during anti-unification. In what follows, we will say that a formula is "covered" by the analogy if it is in the image of this projection (T_c and S_c, respectively), otherwise it is "uncovered". Now, while in analogy making the analogical relations are used in the transfer phase to translate additional uncovered knowledge from the source to the target space, conceptual blending combines additional (uncovered) facts from one or both spaces. Therefore the process of blending can build on the generalisation and substitutions provided by the analogy process, but has to include a new mechanism for transfer and concept combination. Here, amalgams naturally come into play: the set of substitutions can be inverted and applied to generalise the original source theory S into a more general version S' (forming a superset of the shared generalisation G, also including previously uncovered knowledge from the source) which then can be combined into an asymmetric amalgam with the target theory T, forming the (possibly underspecified) proto-blend T' of both. In a final step, T' is then completed into the blended theory and output of the process T_B by applying corresponding specialisation steps stored from the generalisation process between S and T.

5.3.3 Implementing the Model

Concerning an implementation of the just sketched model, several elements of the process have to be specified more precisely, such as what the operationalisations of novelty and usefulness are taken to be, how the ordering relationship is to be defined, and how the generalisation and the amalgamation mechanisms are supposed to work. For the implementation example discussed below, these variable aspects have been fixed as follows:

- A blend is taken to be novel if it is not a subset of or equal to the source or the target domain.
- Usefulness is defined as consistency of the resulting theory.
- The generalisation step uses a further constrained variant of restricted higher-order anti-unification (based on a subset of the operations admissible in HDTP), applying only fixations and renamings.
- The amalgamation uses higher-order unification as combination mechanism.
- Logical semantic consequence serves as ordering relationship.

Since a (further restricted) variant of HDTP's higher-order anti-unification has been named as generalisation mechanism of choice, in the following the analogy-

---

necessary, assuring that all terms in the resulting blend are grounded and no variables introduced during the generalisation steps remain uninstantiated).

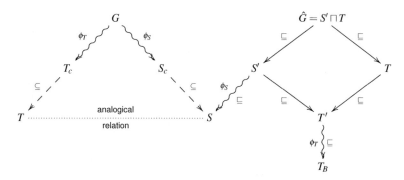

Fig. 5.6: A conceptual overview of our model of concept blending rooted in generalisation-based analogy-making: The shared generalisation G from S and T is computed with $\phi_S(G) = S_c$. The relation ϕ_S is subsequently re-used in the generalisation of S into S', which is then combined in an asymmetric amalgam with T into the proto-blend $T' = S' \sqcup T$ and finally, by application of ϕ_T, completed in the blended output theory T_B. ($\subseteq$ indicates an element-wise subset relationship between sets of axioms and $\sqsubseteq$ indicates subsumption between theories in the direction of the respective arrows. $\sqcap$ and $\sqcup$ refer to semantic overlap (or intersection) and union (or joining) operations, the latter of which are commonly conceptualised as unification)

related part of the system is simply assumed to be run on a correspondingly limited instance of HDTP. The implementation of our analogy-based model of conceptual blending then boils down to the following five algorithmic steps:

1. **Compute common generalisation G of input theories S and T:**
   Given two input domain theories S and T, the (set of) common generalisation(s) $G = \{G_1, G_2, \ldots, G_n\}$ (i.e., the anti-unified forms of sets of axioms which are structurally shared between S and T) is computed using only renamings and fixations as admissible types of unit substitutions. If the anti-unification returns several possible least general generalisations, the system choses one generalisation G_x using HDTP's built-in heuristics.

2. **Generalise entire source theory S to S' using set of higher-order anti-unifications $\phi_{x,S}^{-1}$ from common generalisation:**
   Given the generalised theory G_x, together with the associated two sets of substitutions $\phi_{x,S}$ and $\phi_{x,T}$ respectively corresponding to the covered parts $S_c \subseteq S$ and $T_c \subseteq T$ of the input domain theories, the set of higher-order anti-unifications $\phi_{x,S}^{-1}$ (inversely related to the substitutions $\phi_{x,S}$) is then used to generalise the previous source domain theory S as far as possible into the generalised source theory S' such that $\phi_{x,S}(S') = S$.
   Here, if $S = S_c$, i.e., all axioms from S could be matched and anti-unified with axioms from T in the previous step (constituting a pathological case as S is supposed to provide some additional content over and above T), it holds that $S = \phi_{x,S}(G_x)$ and, thus, $S' = G_x$; otherwise $G_x \subseteq S'$. Notice that, due to the re-

striction to fixations and renamings in the higher-order anti-unifications, it holds that $S \models S' \models G$ in both cases. (Here, $\subseteq$ indicates an element-wise subset relationship between sets of axioms as in Figure 5.6, and $\models$ indicates the classical semantic consequence relation in the logical sense.)

3. **Compute asymmetric amalgam between S' and T and add remaining axioms to obtain proto-blend T':**
   Given S', we can compute the asymmetric amalgam between S' and T (with T staying fixed) using higher-order unification and the semantic consequence relation as subsumption relation for refinement (i.e., given two theories A and B it holds that A is more general than B, $A \sqsubseteq B$, if and only if $B \models A$): axioms from S' and T are unified pairwise as far as possible (i.e., a subset of S' of maximum cardinality is unified with a similar subset of T). Conveniently, for the part of S' which is contained in S_c under $\phi_{x,S}$ this is equal to T_c, so only axioms from $\{a | a \in S' \wedge \phi_{x,S}(a) \notin S_c\}$ and from $T \setminus T_c$, respectively, have to be checked.[11]
   Subsequently, the remaining axioms from both theories are added as additional elements to the resulting unified set of axioms, resulting in an enriched target theory (or proto-blend) T'.[12]

4. **Fully instantiate variables in proto-blend T' into blend T_B using substitutions $\phi_{x,T}$ from common generalisation:**
   Remaining variables not instantiated by the unification step between S' and T' (i.e., imported in axioms from S') in the proto-blend T' are instantiated by applying the set of substitutions $\phi_{x,T}$ from the initial generalisation step to T', resulting in the (fully instantiated) blended theory T_B. (If T' does not contain any variables it trivially holds that $T' = \phi_{x,T}(T') = T_B$ and this step becomes obsolete.)

5. **Check for inconsistencies in blend T_B and trigger repair if needed:**
   A check for consistency of the blended theory T_B is conducted (both internally as well as with respect to potentially available world knowledge). As we are only interested in consistent output theories (since otherwise the amalgam becomes trivial, i.e., equal to the logical $\top$), if an inconsistency is found, clash resolution tries to solve the inconsistency by returning to step 1., removing one or several axioms from S resulting in a new source theory $S_{clash} \subseteq S$, and then re-initiating the procedure.

The resulting blend theory T_B is based on T, (consistently) enriched by imported "unaffected" axioms and (via generalisation from S to S', and re-instantiation from T' to T_B) adapted structural elements from S. This blend forms the (in a certain concept-theoretical sense) "closest" blend to T and can presumably play an important role in different contexts: for instance it can account for the addition of new solution elements to a solution idea at hand in problem-solving scenarios, and in creativity tasks the addition of novel features and elements to existing concepts can be achieved.

---

[11] The maximality of the outcome is rooted in HDTP's heuristics-driven coverage maximisation.

[12] Note that the unifications and addition of axioms conserve the $\models$ relation between theories and, thus, the subsumption ordering as indicated in Figure 5.6.

Clearly, this is a fairly simplistic instantiation of the general model, leaving much to be desired: the inconsistency resolution in the last step can probably be made significantly more efficient by developing heuristics for efficiently selecting axioms for removal, the simple identification between usefulness and consistency might not be enough for many contexts, and methods for assessing the novelty of the resulting blend (also allowing for comparisons between different possible blends) have to be developed and integrated.

5.3.4 Example: (Re)Making Pegasus

One of the best known concept blends is Pegasus, the winged divine stallion and son of Poseidon and the Gorgon Medusa from classical Greek mythology. Using the example introduced in Besold et al. (2015), for illustration purposes we want to reconstruct the Pegasus blend using our just described model. From a concept blending perspective, Pegasus constitutes a blend between a stereotypical horse and a stereotypical bird, maintaining all the horse characteristics but adding bird-like features such as, for instance, the wings and the ability to fly.

We start with the stereotypical characterisations of a horse and a bird in a many-sorted first-order logic representation (as used by HDTP) from Table 5.1. The corresponding formalisations include (some of) the most salient features commonly associated with horses or birds, respectively: The clade to which the respective animal belongs, the most typical body parts (for instance, wings, legs, and the torso in the case of the bird), and common abilities or behaviours (for example a bird's abilities to fly, to walk, and to lay eggs).

Sorts:
  clade, entity, bodypart, ability
Entities:
  mammal, avialae : clade   horse, bird : entity   torso, legs, wings : bodypart   walk, fly, lay_eggs : ability
Predicates:
  is_of_clade : entity × clade,   has_bodypart : entity × bodypart,
  has_ability : entity × ability
Facts of the bird characterisation:
  (α_1) is_of_clade(bird, avialae) (α_2) has_bodypart(bird, legs)
  (α_3) has_bodypart(bird, torso) (α_4) has_bodypart(bird, wings)
  (α_5) has_ability(bird, walk) (α_6) has_ability(bird, fly)
  (α_7) has_ability(bird, lay_eggs)
Facts of the horse characterisation:
  (β_1) is_of_clade(horse, mammal) (β_2) has_bodypart(horse, legs)
  (β_3) has_bodypart(horse, torso) (β_4) has_ability(horse, walk)

Table 5.1: Example formalisations of stereotypical characterisations for a bird S and a horse T

Given these characterisations, HDTP can be used for finding a common generalisation of both (Table 5.2).[13] The resulting theory in general terms describes the common core shared between horse and bird, i.e., the concept of an animal of some clade, having legs and a torso, and being able to walk.

Entities:
  C : clade, E : entity
Facts:
  (γ_1) is_of_clade(E,C) (γ_2) has_bodypart$(E, legs)$
  (γ_3) has_bodypart$(E, torso)$ (γ_4) has_ability$(E, walk)$

Table 5.2: Abbreviated representation of the shared generalisation G based on the stereotypical characterisations for a horse and a bird, constituted by generalisations $\alpha_1 = \phi_S(\gamma_1)/\beta_1 = \phi_T(\gamma_1)$, $\alpha_2 = \phi_S(\gamma_2)/\beta_2 = \phi_T(\gamma_2)$, $\alpha_3 = \phi_S(\gamma_3)/\beta_3 = \phi_T(\gamma_3)$, and $\alpha_5 = \phi_S(\gamma_4)/\beta_4 = \phi_T(\gamma_4)$ (i.e., $S_c = \{\alpha_1, \alpha_2, \alpha_3, \alpha_5\}$ and $T_c = \{\beta_1, \beta_2, \beta_3, \beta_4\}$)

Subsequently, the anti-unifications corresponding to the mapping ϕ_S between the covered part S_c of the source domain and the generalisation are used for generalising the entire source theory S into S' as given in Table 5.3.

Entities:
  C : clade, E : entity
Facts:
  (γ_1) is_of_clade(E,C) (γ_2) has_bodypart$(E, legs)$
  (γ_3) has_bodypart$(E, torso)$ (γ_4) has_ability$(E, walk)$
  (γ_5) has_bodypart$(E, wings)$ (γ_6) has_ability(E, fly)
  (γ_7) has_ability(E, lay_eggs)

Table 5.3: Abbreviated representation of the generalised source theory S' based on the stereotypical characterisations for a horse and a bird, including additional axioms γ_5, γ_6, and γ_7 obtained from generalising the remaining axioms from $S \setminus S_c = \{\alpha_4, \alpha_6, \alpha_7\}$

Then, computing the asymmetric amalgam of S' with the (fixed) target theory T, we obtain the proto-blend T' from Table 5.4. This incomplete (i.e., not yet fully instantiated) blend is made up by the initial characterisation of a horse, together with three axioms describing some undetermined entity having wings and the ability to fly and lay eggs.

Finally, as T' still features axioms containing non-instantiated variables (namely the unspecified entity E in axioms δ_5 to δ_7), the mapping ϕ_T between the covered part T_c of the target domain and the generalisation is applied to T'. In the original

---

[13] As stated previously, when using HDTP the required subsumption relation between theories currently is given by logical semantic consequence $\models$, i.e., $A \sqsubseteq A'$ if $A' \models A$ for any two theories A and A'. In order to make sure that this relationship is preserved by HDTP's syntax-based operations, the range of admissible substitutions for restricted higher-order anti-unifications has to be further constrained to only allow for fixations and renamings.

Entities:
 E : entity
Facts:
 (δ_1) is_of_clade(horse, mammal)   (δ_2) has_bodypart(horse, legs)
 (δ_3) has_bodypart(horse, torso)   (δ_4) has_ability(horse, walk)
 (δ_5) has_bodypart(E, wings)   (δ_6) has_ability(E, fly)
 (δ_7) has_ability(E, lay_eggs)

Table 5.4: Abbreviated representation of the proto-blend T' obtained from computing the asymmetric amalgam between S' and T

generalisation step, E had been obtained from generalising *horse* with *bird*, adding a mapping $E \mapsto horse$ to the set of substitutions ϕ_T corresponding to T. Application of ϕ_T to T' now results in the (with respect to ϕ_T) fully instantiated blend theory T_B from Table 5.5: a horse with wings, which is able to fly and lay eggs.

Facts:
 (δ_1) is_of_clade(horse, mammal)   (δ_2) has_bodypart(horse, legs)
 (δ_3) has_bodypart(horse, torso)   (δ_4) has_ability(horse, walk)
 (δ_5) has_bodypart(horse, wings)   (δ_6) has_ability(horse, fly)
 (δ_7) has_ability(horse, lay_eggs)

Table 5.5: Abbreviated representation of $T_B = \phi_T(T')$

In a concluding step, a consistency check of the blended theory T_B is performed. As already initially expected, taking into account world knowledge about mammals identifies a clash with axiom δ_7 as mammals generally do not lay eggs (except for the subclass Prototheria as a precisely defined special case). Using one of the most naive forms of conflict resolution and consistency restoration, returning to the start of the procedure, the algorithm is re-initiated, for example, with $S_{clash} = S \setminus \{\alpha_7\}$. When this new run of the procedure terminates, we finally obtain the (with respect to ϕ_T fully instantiated and consistent) version of T_B given in Table 5.6 as output: a horse with wings which is able to fly—i.e., a simple conceptualisation of the concept of Pegasus from Greek mythology.

Facts:
 (δ_1) is_of_clade(horse, mammal)   (δ_2) has_bodypart(horse, legs)
 (δ_3) has_bodypart(horse, torso)   (δ_4) has_ability(horse, walk)
 (δ_5) has_bodypart(horse, wings)   (δ_6) has_ability(horse, fly)

Table 5.6: Abbreviated representation of the final blended theory T_B giving a characterisation of Pegasus after inconsistency check and repair (i.e., based on $S_{clash} = S \setminus \{\alpha_7\}$)

5.4 Related Work

As has already become clear from several references given in earlier sections, the present chapter naturally is not the first time the relationship between analogy and conceptual blending has been closely looked at or built upon in conceptualising models and system architectures.

Martinez et al. (2014) presented an approach for the theory-based algorithmic blending of mathematical concepts as basis for concept invention. The approach pursued there also takes inspiration from Goguen (2006)'s ideas and uses HDTP for finding shared generalisations between mathematical input theories. Still, major differences reside in the blending mechanism and the overall conceptual setup: The former implements a step-wise generate-and-test approach, generating increasingly complex logically consistent combinations of the axioms from the input theories. Concerning the latter, working exclusively in the domain of mathematical conceptual theories removes the need for "semantic" consistency checks of the resulting blends within output theories or against world knowledge.

Also Martinez et al. (2012) elaborate on conceptual blending as general cognitive mechanism, again also taking into account Goguen (2006) and computational analogy-making via HDTP. Still, the account described in this chapter goes significantly further by adding amalgams and providing a tightly integrated end-to-end model for conceptual blending, together with a significantly more detailed prototypical algorithm-level specification as compared to the computational-level account in Martinez et al. (2012).

Concerning earlier mentions, the use of an analogy-based mechanism for mapping between elements of the input domains to the blending process was already suggested in Pereira and Cardoso (2003)—where also the Pegasus example of conceptual blending had been discussed. On the cognitive side, Kokinov and Zareva-Toncheva (2001) used his AMBR model of analogical problem solving to establish a connection between blending effects in stories when recalled from memory, and analogical reasoning processes. Finally, among others Nagai et al. (2009) emphasised the importance of analogy-related forms of reasoning in conceptual blending as part of creative concept generation processes in design.

5.5 Summary

Following a general introduction to analogy and its role in human cognition, in this chapter, we outlined a perspective on conceptual blending from the point of view of (mostly computational) research into analogy-making as a related cognitive capacity. More precisely, we introduced a computational-level model of conceptual blending between two input theories, in its overall mechanism combining generalisation-based analogy-making and amalgams. The model then was further illustrated by the description of an algorithmic instantiation thereof, followed by a reconstruction of the Pegasus blend as worked example.

Our account is based on certain foundational assumptions concerning the nature both of conceptual blending, and of several analogy-related mechanisms. For us, blending happens on the knowledge level, relying on knowledge about the input concepts available to the individual. The blending process then does not operate arbitrarily, but is guided by similarities between the input concepts, which define the basic structure of the resulting blend(s). These similarities in turn are accessible via meaningful generalisation between concepts, which, on the level of conceptual theories, can be modeled using the anti-unification of theories. Once generalisation-based analogy-making has identified and subsequently carried over the similarities into the basic structure of the blend, the combination of further properties from both input theories can then be conceived of as generalisation-based amalgamation, maintaining the basic structure introduced by the analogy process.

5.6 Conclusion and Future Perspectives

Traditionally, the concluding section of this type of project summary is reserved for a look ahead, identifying open questions—some of them left unanswered over the course of the reported work, others newly arising from the results—and, wherever possible, hinting at potential answers. Concerning the outlined analogy-based approach to concept blending, at least three lines of future work immediately come to mind:

- Looking at the outlined algorithmic implementation of the model, it would of course be desirable to leverage the full power of HDTP. In order to do so, the present restrictions on substitutions have to be overcome. Among other things, this would for instance require a replacement for the semantic consequence relationship $\models$ as basis for the subsumption ordering so that also permutations and argument insertions over successive generalisation steps can be accounted for.
- Thinking about systems going beyond the current capacities of HDTP, another open question is the further integration of heuristic and knowledge-sensitive methods during blend computation and selection for modelling contextual constraints or (in a cognitive modelling scenario) internal properties of the supposed reasoning agent. Two of the most obvious starting points for this are the generalisation step and the inconsistency resolution: during the generalization stage, conceptually meaningful combinations of elements from the respective input domains could be favoured over more remote ones, and inconsistency resolution could also add content-related aspects as additional criteria next to efficiency in finding a consistent conceptual theory.
- Finally, a more general challenge—not only relevant for our system but for significant parts of computational creativity as a research discipline—concerns the evaluation of systems and outputs concerning criteria such as, for instance, usefulness and novelty. This is of course also the case in the subdomain of conceptual blending, both for judging the outcome of blending processes, but—

directly tying back into the previous paragraph—also for guiding the process itself. While there is work in these directions, either concerning evaluation of creativity in a more general context (as outlined, for instance, in Chapter 10), or for the specific case of conceptual blending (where Chapter 2 provides several proposals), the question for the evaluation of creative systems and their outputs remains one of the big topics future research will have to address.

We are convinced that even partial answers to each of the three overarching questions will significantly advance the respective state of the art, and allow for important further developments concerning both the computational theory and applications of conceptual blending.

References

T. R. Besold. Computational models of analogy-making. An overview analysis of computational approaches to analogical reasoning. Technical Report X-2011-03, FNWI/FGw: Institute for Logic, Language and Computation (ILLC), University of Amsterdam, 2011.

T. R. Besold, K.-U. Kühnberger, and E. Plaza. Analogy, amalgams, and concept blending. In *Proceedings of the Third Annual Conference on Advances in Cognitive Systems (Poster Collection)*. Cogsys.org, 2015.

T. R. Besold and E. Plaza. Generalize and blend: Concept blending based on generalisation, analogy, and amalgams. In *Proceedings of the 6th International Conference on Computational Creativity, ICCC15*, 2015.

Whatman Biometra: Refrigerated Circulator KH-4. Biometra biomedizinische Analytik GmbH, Göttingen, Germany, June 2006.

F. Bou, M. Schorlemmer, J. Corneli, D. Gomez Ramirez, E. Maclean, A. Smaill, and A. Pease. The role of blending in mathematical invention. In *Proceedings of the Sixth International Conference on Computational Creativity (ICCC 2015)*, pages 55–62, Park City, Utah, 2015. Brigham Young University, Brigham Young University.

T. G. Evans. A heuristic program to solve geometric-analogy problems. In *Proceedings of the April 21-23, 1964, Spring Joint Computer conference*, AFIPS '64 (Spring), pages 327–338, New York, NY, USA, 1964. ACM.

B. Falkenhainer, K. Forbus, and D. Gentner. The structure-mapping engine: Algorithm and examples. *Artificial Intelligence*, 41(1):1 – 63, 1989. ISSN 0004-3702.

D. Gentner. Structure-mapping: A theoretical framework for analogy. *Cognitive Science*, 7(2):155–170, 1983.

D. Gentner, B. Bowdle, P. Wolff, and C. Boronat. Metaphor is like analogy. In D. Gentner, K. Holyoak, and B. Kokinov, editors, *The Analogical Mind: Perspectives from Cognitive Science*, pages 199–253. MIT Press, 2001.

D. Gentner, B. Falkenhainer, and J. Skorstad. Viewing metaphor as analogy. In
D. Helman, editor, *Analogical Reasoning*, volume 197 of *Synthese Library*, pages
171–177. Springer Netherlands, 1988.

D. Gentner and K. Forbus. MAC/FAC: A model of similarity-based retrieval. *Cognitive Science*, 19:141–205, 1991.

D. Gentner and A. Markman. Structure mapping in analogy and similarity. *American Psychologist*, 52(1):4 –56, 1997.

D. Gentner and L. A. Smith. Analogical learning and reasoning. In D. Reisberg,
editor, *The Oxford Handbook of Cognitive Psychology*, pages 668–681. Oxford
University Press, New York, NY, USA, 2013.

J. Goguen. Mathematical models of cognitive space and time. In D. Andler,
Y. Ogawa, M. Okada, and S. Watanabe, editors, *Reasoning and Cognition; Proceedings of the Interdisciplinary Conference on Reasoning and Cognition*, pages
125–128, 2006.

M. Guhe, A. Pease, A. Smaill, M. Martinez, M. Schmidt, H. Gust, K.-U. Kühnberger, and U. Krumnack. A computational account of conceptual blending in basic
mathematics. *Journal of Cognitive Systems Research*, 12(3):249–265, 2011.

D. Hofstadter. Epilogue: Analogy as the core of cognition. In D. Gentner,
K. Holyoak, and B. Kokinov, editors, *The Analogical Mind: Perspectives from
Cognitive Science*, pages 499–538, Cambridge, MA, 2001. MIT Press.

D. Hofstadter and M. Mitchell. The copycat project: a model of mental fluidity
and analogy-making. In K. Holyoak and J. Barnden, editors, *Advances in Connectionist and Neural Computation Theory*, volume 2: Analogical Connections,
pages 31–112, New York, NY, USA, 1994. Ablex.

K. J. Holyoak, D. Gentner, and B. N. Kokinov. *The Analogical Mind: Perspectives
from Cognitive Science*, chapter Introduction: The Place of Analogy in Cognition,
pages 1–19. MIT Press, Cambridge, MA, 2001.

B. Kokinov and R. M. French. *Encyclopedia of Cognitive Science*, volume 1,
chapter Computational Models of Analogy Making, pages 113–118. Nature Publishing Group, London, 2003.

Boicho Kokinov and Neda Zareva-Toncheva. Episode blending as result of analogical problem solving. In *Proceedings of the 23rd Annual Conference of the
Cognitive Science Society*, pages 510–515, 2001.

U. Krumnack, A. Schwering, H. Gust, and K. Kühnberger. Restricted higher-order
anti-unification for analogy making. In *Twentieth Australian Joint Conference on
Artificial Intelligence*. Springer, 2007.

M. Martinez, T. R. Besold, A. Abdel-Fattah, H. Gust, M. Schmidt, U. Krumnack,
and K.-U. Kühnberger. Theory blending as a framework for creativity in systems
for general intelligence. In P. Wang and B. Goertzel, editors, *Theoretical Foundations of Artificial General Intelligence*, volume 4 of *Atlantis Thinking Machines*,
pages 219–239. Atlantis Press, 2012.

M. Martinez, U. Krumnack, A. Smaill, T. R. Besold, A. M. Abdel-Fattah,
M. Schmidt, H. Gust, K.-U. Kühnberger, M. Guhe, and A. Pease. Algorithmic aspects of theory blending. In G. Aranda-Corral, J. Calmet, and F. Martín-Mateos,

editors, *Artificial Intelligence and Symbolic Computation*, volume 8884 of *Lecture Notes in Computer Science*, pages 180–192. Springer, 2014.

Yukari Nagai, Toshiharu Taura, and Futoshi Mukai. Concept blending and dissimilarity: factors for creative concept generation process. *Design Studies*, 30(6):648–675, 2009.

S. Ontañón and E. Plaza. Amalgams: A formal approach for combining multiple case solutions. In I. Bichindaritz and S. Montani, editors, *Case-Based Reasoning: Research and Development*, volume 6176 of *Lecture Notes in Computer Science*, pages 257–271. Springer, 2010.

S. Ontañón and E. Plaza. On knowledge transfer in case-based inference. In B. D. Agudo and I. Watson, editors, *Case-Based Reasoning Research and Development*, volume 7466 of *Lecture Notes in Computer Science*, pages 312–326. Springer, 2012.

F. C. Pereira and A. Cardoso. Optimality principles for conceptual blending: A first computational approach. *AISB Journal*, 1(4), 2003.

W. R. Reitman, R. B. Grove, and R. G. Shoup. Argus: An information-processing model of thinking. *Behavioral Science*, 9(3):270–281, 1964. ISSN 1099-1743.

M. Schmidt, H. Gust, K.-U. Kühnberger, and U. Krumnack. Refinements of restricted higher-order anti-unification for heuristic-driven theory projection. In *KI 2011: Advances in Artificial Intelligence, Proceedings of the 34th Annual German Conference on Artificial Intelligence*, volume 7006 of *Lecture Notes in Computer Science*. Springer, 2011.

M. Schmidt, U. Krumnack, H. Gust, and K.-U. Kühnberger. Heuristic-driven theory projection: An overview. In H. Prade and G. Richard, editors, *Computational Approaches to Analogical Reasoning: Current Trends*, pages 163–194. Springer, 2014.

A. Schwering, U. Krumnack, K.-U. Kühnberger, and H. Gust. Syntactic principles of heuristic-driven theory projection. *Journal of Cognitive Systems Research*, 10 (3):251–269, 2009a.

A. Schwering, K.-U. Kühnberger, and B. Kokinov. Analogies: Integrating multiple cognitive abilities - guest editorial. *Journal of Cognitive Systems Research*, 10 (3), 2009b.

C. Shelley. *Multiple Analogies in Science and Philosophy*. John Benjamins Publishing, Amsterdam; Philadelphia, 2003.

P. H. Winston. Learning and reasoning by analogy. *Commun. ACM*, 23(12):689–703, 1980.

Chapter 6
Social Aspects of Concept Invention

Joseph Corneli, Alison Pease, and Danae Stefanou

Abstract This chapter surveys frameworks that describe social creativity. It focuses on mathematics, but includes work which heads in a more general direction: first, by examining social creativity in music, and then turning to a description of several new results that use formal, qualitative, and simulation techniques to theorise social creativity on computers. The chapter includes a pilot study examining the salience of various frameworks for the analysis of mathematical text.

6.1 Introduction

This chapter surveys theoretical frameworks that lie on the spectrum between real-world social creativity and formal theory. We will focus primarily on creativity in mathematics, with brief forays into musical creativity and more general domains to round out the picture. Some of the settings that the frameworks describe are immediately recognisable as places where real-world social creativity happens (but these tend to be less formal); some are more convincingly computational, in the sense that they describe stand-alone simulations (however, these tend to be less obvious examples of what we would understand by social creativity). Relative to our broader research goals, the existing frameworks and efforts all have limitations, which we plan to address through integration.

Joseph Corneli
Goldsmiths College, University of London, UK. e-mail: `j.corneli@gold.ac.uk`

Alison Pease
Department of Computing, University of Dundee, Scotland, UK. e-mail: `a.pease@dundee.ac.uk`

Danae Stefanou
Department of Music Studies, Aristotle University of Thessaloniki, Greece. e-mail: `dstefano@mus.auth.gr`

© Springer Nature Switzerland AG 2018
R. Confalonieri et al. (eds.), *Concept Invention*, Computational Synthesis
and Creative Systems, https://doi.org/10.1007/978-3-319-65602-1_6

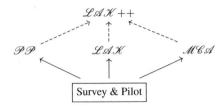

Fig. 6.1: Survey of theoretical frameworks describing social creativity, focusing on mathematics (Section 6.2); $\mathscr{LAK}$: Lakatosian creativity (Section 6.3.1); $\mathscr{PP}$: Patterns of Peeragogy (Section 6.3.2); $\mathscr{MCA}$: Meta-Cellular Automata (Section 6.3.3); and $\mathscr{LAK}++$: Summary of findings and plans for future integration efforts (Section 6.4)

Figure 6.1 presents an overview of the chapter in graphical form. Section 6.2 examines a variety of existing frameworks, and includes a small pilot study that applies these frameworks to analyse mathematical texts. In Section 6.3, we describe, in overview, three directions of research that we have developed:

- $\mathscr{LAK}$ is a formal, implemented system that models social creativity in mathematics at a high level.
- $\mathscr{PP}$ models the "recognisably social domain" of peer learning and peer production using design patterns (but does not have a formal, computational, implementation).
- $\mathscr{MCA}$ is a highly abstract simulation of social creativity that uses a simple evolutionary computing model.

Some take-away points for future integration efforts and steps towards "$\mathscr{LAK}++$" are presented in Section 6.4. Further details on the original work that is summarised in a necessarily abbreviated format here can be found in Pease et al. (2017), Corneli et al. (2015), and Corneli and Maclean (2015).

We see this broad survey of approaches to be highly relevant for our long-term project of building computational systems that can engage meaningfully in varied and diverse mathematical discourses. This chapter can therefore be seen as groundwork for future projects in natural language processing (NLP) and natural language generation (NLG) for mathematics.

6.2 Social Creativity in Mathematics

We will begin with a catalogue of examples of social creativity in mathematics, together with a survey of existing approaches to their socio-linguistic and "metamathematical" interpretation. In Section 6.2.4, we will take a brief look at music as a comparison case that helps to flesh out a theory of social creativity – showing the limitations, for example, of an entirely linguistic approach. Nevertheless, mathematics is seen as a reasonably typical domain. Thurston (1994) offered the following explanation for why social creativity is an important part of mathematical practice:

> *We are not trying to meet some abstract production quota of definitions, theorems and proofs. The measure of our success is whether what we do enables people to understand and think more clearly and effectively about mathematics.*

A long-term goal in our research is to build a systematic, computational account of the way mathematical understanding develops. The examples in which we ground this work can be broadly classed as follows:

(A) Live, in-person mathematical dialogues show how mathematical sociality works in the everyday practice of mathematicians and students. However, recorded examples are somewhat limited, and often contain many extra-mathematical features. These examples are useful for theory development, but can be difficult to systematise.

(B) At another extreme, some recent developments in computer mathematics have produced proofs written in a manner that resembles natural language, while others provide basic examples of computational social intelligence. We would ultimately like to have a system that can incorporate and extend these feature sets.

(C) Perhaps the most central set of examples for this work are an existing catalogue of records from social experiments that incorporate computer-mediated dialogue. These include the Polymath and MiniPolymath projects, which have focused on computer-mediated problem solving at the research and advanced pre-college student level, respectively. For our purposes, the transcripts of these online dialogues are particularly useful, since as researchers we have access to the same material as research subjects (cf. Stahl (2010)).

These thematic areas can be tied together by considering how a relatively informal mathematical discussion corresponds, in an appropriate sense, to some set of formal and computationally meaningful objects, such as *proof plans* (Bundy, 1998). Figure 6.2 presents a general schematic that depicts the overall research situation, translating the sources of examples *A*, *B*, *C* to a parallel set of interlinked research perspectives, **I**-*Discourse*, **II**-*Formalisation* (relative to a hypertextual model), and **III**-*Model* (suitable for embedding in a formal system). We envision the possibility of participants in a discussion directly modifying the state of a running computation (**I**→**II**), and of the computer intervening in the discussion as a participant (**II**→**I**).

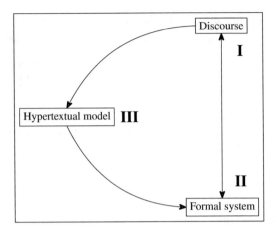

Fig. 6.2: Schematic relationship between (I) discourse, (II) formalisation, and (III) model

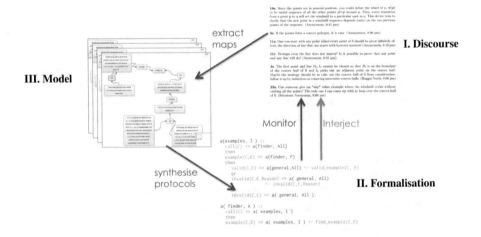

Fig. 6.3: The Online Visualisation of Argument (OVA) system as a bridge between the Minipolymath3 dialogue and a formalisation of the discourse in the Lightweight Social Calculus (graphic by Dave Murray-Rust, used with permission)

Figure 6.3 shows one possible instantiation of this schema, with discourse drawn from one of the MiniPolymath dialogues (see comments above on the general characteristics of Data Source C, above), formalised using the Lightweight Social Calculus, and modelled using the Online Visualisation of Argument (OVA) toolset.

In the typical case, moves in **I** drive moves in **II**, mediated implicitly or explicitly by **III**. The situation as a whole resembles the general case of *heterogeneous reasoning* as described by Barwise (1993), and instantiated, for instance, in his **Hyperproof** system. In **Hyperproof**, **I** would be a graphical puzzle with certain implicit rules governing its structure, and **II** the corresponding logic problem. In a typical mathematics setting, **I** may include some explicit pictorial features, but its basic structure is (implicitly) that of a graph or hypertext that depicts a dialogue. This structure is made explicit as an *argument* in **III**. **III** has the important feature that it reflects all of the structures in **I** that have a recognisable mapping in **II**, and, symmetrically, there are no logical- or language-level features in **II** that do not have an analogue in **III**. As Barwise (1993) puts it: *"Inference, as we understand the term, is the task of extracting information implicit in some explicitly presented information."*

In the broader features of the schematic introduced above, we are inspired by *Inference Anchoring Theory (IAT)* (Reed and Budzynska, 2011; Budzynska and Reed, 2011; Budzynska, 2013), which develops connections between a dialogical context and logical argument by way of illocutionary schemes. In this manner, IAT takes the earlier notion of *dialogue games* from Carlson (1982) and others[1] in a more explicitly computational direction. Prakken (2006) writes: *"[W]hereas logic defines the conditions under which a proposition is true, dialogue systems define the conditions under which an utterance is appropriate."*

Our strategy in what follows examines the parallel between dialogue and the interpretation of dialogue, logic and models of logic, and contextualised discourse and its hypertextual models. We will think of the sets of examples *A* ("live discussion"), *B* ("computer mathematics"), and *C* ("computer-mediated discussion") that were introduced earlier along the schematic lines of analysis suited to perspectives **I**, **II**, and **III**.

Much previous research has often focused on just one of these components, rather than on their interconnections, although there is also precedent for studying just these interconnections. Our overall philosophical perspective on *sociality* derives from that of Mead (1932), witnessed here by the key feature that both **I** and **II** are understood to be evolving works-in-progress. If either is completed, the conversation ends, or the proof is resolved. This is similar to the Meadian (multi)-perspective in which both "organism" and "environment" undergo change together. In this metaphor, **III** corresponds to the sensory interface between "organism" and "environment." Alternatively, from a linguistic point of view, **III** could be seen as a Rosetta stone that defines translations between domains. More formally, it is the existence of satisfactory mappings between discourse on the one hand and the logical description on the other that allow us to think about connections between **I** and **II** in

---

[1] *NB*. Dialogue games are also known as *dialogue systems*.

terms of the *infomorphisms* of Barwise and Seligman (1997). Barwise and Seligman would call **III** the *core* of the information channel.

The work presented here is a preliminary step in a larger programme that aims to identify *dialogical* moves that can be associated with meaningful computational moves.[2] In the mathematics domain, the relevant computations are typically *logical*.[3] Other dualities (e.g., content and expression, genotype and phenotype, organism and environment, etc.) may potentially be treated similarly: the key issue in each case will be their *pragmatic* interplay – i.e., the effect of "context" on the outcome of events.

The role of context is well-studied in linguistics and the philosophy of language, since merely decoding statements is not usually sufficient to determine the intended meaning (Sperber and Wilson, 2002). Context has also been studied in computing, for instance by Sowa (1995), although attempts to formalise the concept are not conclusive – with Hirst (1997) in particular arguing that *"the notion of 'context' can be defined only in terms of its effects in a particular situation."* The notion of context that we rely on here is embedded in **III**. This can be illustrated, for example, with a switch that converts a computer keyboard between the QWERTY and the Dvorak layouts. Whereas both keyboard layouts can model the same discourse (as represented by a flow of characters), flipping the switch influences the practical (stateful, and contextually-meaningful) characteristics of the model.

In the survey that follows we trace the pragmatic and computational features of mathematical discourse. We are inspired by earlier work of Louwerse and Crossley (2006), who examined a specialised linguistic task,[4] and found *n*-grams that were strongly associated with pre-defined speech acts. This survey that we develop here constitutes necessary preliminary work that can help to chart a course for future NLP-based analyses. We emphasise that our present effort is much more theoretical high-level than the work found in contemporary linguistic analyses of mathematical texts, such as that of Ganesalingam (2013) and Wolska and Kruijff-Korbayová (2004). Although mathematics is a fairly specialised domain that is communicated with an array of technical languages, mathematical language is also tremendously expressive. Classifications of speech acts in expressive languages tend to be correspondingly broad and nuanced, as has been pointed out by Leech and Weisser (2003) and Stolcke et al. (2000).

A secondary aim is to develop an approach that can be replicated to model social creativity in other areas. A claim to extensibility derives in part from the generality of the core theories that we build on, as described in Section 6.2.1. Following the survey in Section 6.2.2, Section 6.2.3 presents a pilot study that applies the collected frameworks to code various examples of mathematical dialogue at differing levels of formality. A cursory discussion of music in Section 6.2.4 draws out some additional

---

[2] Dialogic is more general than *dialectic*, which aims to converge on a common ground (Sennett, 2012, pp. 18–20).

[3] Other discourses appeal, for example, not to reason, but to the emotions, or to arguments based on character (*viz.*, *logos*, *pathos*, *ethos*), per Burke and Zappen (2006).

[4] http://groups.inf.ed.ac.uk/maptask/

issues related to indeterminacy, non-verbal communication and problem selection, and further explain the role of context.

6.2.1 Core Theories

The primary ingredients we will use to build a formal theory of social creativity are *Information Flow* from Barwise and Seligman (1997), *Unified Concept Theory (UCT)* from Goguen (1999, 2006) (see Chapter 1), and the *Method of Proofs and Refutations* from Lakatos (1976). We review and contextualise these here, outlining some adaptations that are necessary for our project.

We briefly introduced the notions of infomorphisms and information channels above. The more formal definition of an information channel revolves around a *core*:

$$\mathscr{C} = (\text{tokens}(\mathscr{C}), \text{types}(\mathscr{C}), \models_{\mathscr{C}})$$

where $\models_{\mathscr{C}}$ is a binary relationship between tokens and types; $t \models_{\mathscr{C}} T$ stands for the statement "t is classified as being of type T in $\mathscr{C}$." The core is complemented by an indexed collection of classifications and maps

$$\{A_i = (\text{tokens}(A_i), \text{types}(A_i), \models_{A_i})\}_{i \in I}$$

$$\{f_i^{\vee} : \text{tokens}(\mathscr{C}) \to \text{tokens}(A_i), f_i^{\wedge} : \text{types}(A_i) \to \text{types}(\mathscr{C})\}_{i \in I}$$

with the property that

$$\forall i \in I, c \in \text{tokens}(\mathscr{C}), \alpha \in \text{types}(A_i): f_i^{\vee}(c) \models_{A_i} \alpha \text{ iff } c \models_{\mathscr{C}} f_i^{\wedge}(\alpha)$$

The elements $c \in \text{tokens}(\mathscr{C})$ are called *connections* between the various tokens $f_i^{\vee}(c)$. A good example would be English sentences (tokens) and their classification as dialogue moves (types – e.g., "attack", "conflict", "question", etc.), which are mapped into a graphical representation that shows the pattern of dialogical response together with the associated illocutionary points (e.g., assertions, inferences).[5] The result could be placed in correspondence with a computational model of the argument's logical structure.

Blends of various kinds can be easily spotted in the literature on mathematical conceptualisation and problem solving and in the informal logic of proof. However, the settings we are interested often require a dynamical and empirical approach to blending that is not present in straightforward *concept blending* in Unified Concept Theory (Goguen, 1999, 2006). The need for a somewhat more sophisticated blending approach was outlined in a discussion of dynamical systems and creativity in the context of music presented by Borgo and Goguen (2005). When thinking about music, Goguen (2004) diverges from his earlier work on concept blending "*because*

---

[5] See Reed et al. (2010) and Budzynska and Reed (2012) for an expanded discussion of this sort of example.

musical structure is inherently hierarchical, and hence cannot be adequately described using only atomic elements and relation instances among them." However, many aspects of the model were salvaged, as Borgo and Goguen turned to analogous *structural blending*, which draws upon the idea of semiotic systems with both level ordering and priority ordering: *"Levels express the whole-part hierarchy of complex signs, whereas priorities express the relative importance of constructors and their arguments."*

Andersen (2002) points out that semiotic structures can also express dynamics through the use of recursion, although Borgo and Goguen did not pursue this. We are interested in *dynamical blending* because of the importance of modelling not just hierarchical content, but evolving and emergent works-in-progress. Not only does discourse and its formal representation change over time, the very terms by which this representation is made may change as the context changes. Andersen (2002) writes that the basic metaphor for thinking is *travel*. But rather than considering a simple path that avoids obstacles, we might envisage a skier descending a slope covered with moguls. Through continued use, the landscape shifts, and the classifications of paths in terms of their homotopic features or their desirability may change. The *"relations between relations"* (Kockelman, 2011) that define semiotic systems can be hooked together and react back on themselves, as our representations, relations, and the world we live in evolve over time.

Lakatos's model of mathematical discourse provides an example of the need for dynamic approaches to meaning. A Lakatosian dialogue begins with a *conjecture* and an *example* and then – following structured rules, in a way that depends on the problem and the discussion to date – may yield a revised conjecture, or a revised example. These changes in meaning correspond to updates in a developing mathematical theory. It is through an informal and often hands-on process of arguing about conjectures and counterexamples that the underlying formal structure of a given mathematical domain is made clear.

In the work of Pólya (1981), there is another kind of constructive blend that develops in the course of decomposing a given problem into several interrelated *auxiliary problems*. The relationship between problems is described in terms of new variables, whose values are unknown. As the problem solution progresses, these unknowns are determined using the given data. Any given solution will traverse various intermediate states between the given data and the goal as it is worked out. There may be a degree of indeterminacy in the solution strategy (e.g., multiple possible paths to the goal). At another level, *problems* (and, indeed *solutions*) can be combined, like the differential operators in quantum mechanics. Deleuze (1968) considers related issues from a broad philosophical perspective,[6] drawing particularly on Albert Lautman's earlier discussion of dialectics in mathematics; see Larvor (2011) for a relevant survey.

Stahl (2006, 2010, 2013) has built an extensive research programme that studies mathematics in a social context, developing the theme of *"group cognition,"* and drawing on online interactions between students as a source of data. His notion of

---

[6] On auxiliary problems, see esp. (Deleuze, 1968, p. 239).

"*adjacency pairs*" is a broader category than "Lakatosian moves." Contemporary strategies from natural language processing, including the field of *argument mining* (Peldszus and Stede, 2013) which is gaining traction within the broader field of *discourse mining* (e.g., Stab and Gurevych (2014); Webber et al. (2012)), will ultimately be very relevant for tracing these logic-level "n-grams". In the current work we aim to sketch both argumentative and pre-argumentative structures: that is, we will consider the constructive features of *informal logic* (cf. Hitchcock (2006)).

6.2.2 Survey of Analytic Frameworks

In this section we will discuss a range of frameworks, under the headings "**I**", "**II**", and "**III**" depending on whether they have more to do with *dialogue*, *logic*, or *pragmatics*, respectively. These three classes parallel the three types of examples (dialogical, computational, and computer-mediated) and three fundamental strategies (discourse, formalisation, and modelling) that we introduced in connection with Figures 6.2 and 6.3. We apply the frameworks surveyed here to analyse concrete examples in Section 6.2.3.

6.2.2.1 (I) Dialogue

Walton (2003) considers the basic patterns in dialogue to be: **persuasion**, **negotiation**, **information seeking**, **deliberation**, and **quarrel**. In some earlier writings these were augmented with a sixth category *inquiry*, and with the subtype *pedagogy* and the mixed form *debate* (Walton, 1997). Aberdein (2007) indicates that "*Many other familiar argumentational contexts may be represented in terms of Walton's six basic types of dialogue by such hybridization and subdivision.*"

In a mathematics-specific context, Aberdein offers a discussion of proof dialogues instantiating Walton's dialogue types. Thus, we have *proof as inquiry, proof as persuasion, proof as information seeking, proof as deliberation, proof as negotiation, proof as eristic/debate*. Each of these is described in terms of an *initial situation*, the *main goal*, the *goal of the prover* and the *goal of the interlocutor*. Depending on which type of proof is under discussion, Aberdein indicates that the *main goals* are:

1. **Prove or disprove a conjecture** (inquiry),
2. **Resolve difference of opinion with rigour** (persuasion),
3. **Transfer of knowledge** (information seeking)
4. **Reach a provisional conclusion** (deliberation),
5. **Exchange resources for a provisional conclusion** (negotiation),
6. **Reveal deeper conflict** (eristic).

In general "*an utterance is appropriate if it furthers the goal of the dialogue in which it is made*" (Prakken, 2006). Prakken here is concerned especially with *persuasion dialogues*. He explains that in this context, some of the typical dialogue features are: **arguments**, **questions**, **claims**, **challenges**, **conceding**, and **retraction**.

In the context of informal mathematical discussions, Pease et al. (2014) recast persuasion in terms of *Lakatosian moves* relevant to conjectures and proof:

1. A **conjecture** is what is argued for.
2. **Surrender** consists of abandoning a conjecture in light of a counterexample.
3. **Piecemeal exclusion** defends a conjecture by dealing with exceptions through the exclusion of a class of counterexamples.
4. **Strategic withdrawal** uses positive examples of a conjecture and generalises from these to a class of object, then limiting the domain of the conjecture to this class.
5. **Monster barring** argues that a 'counterexample' can be ignored because it is not a counterexample, as it is not within the claimed concept definition. Using this method, the original conjecture is unchanged, but the meaning of the terms in it may change.
6. **Monster adjusting** is similar to monster barring: in the monster-adjusting case, an object that is proposed to be a counterexample is altered or reinterpreted so that it is no longer a counterexample. The object is still seen as belonging to the domain of the conjecture.
7. **Lemma incorporation** distinguishes between *global* and *local* counterexamples. The first would be counterexamples to the main conjecture, and the latter is a counterexample to one of the proof steps or lemmas.

The Speech-Act Annotated Corpus (SPAAC) presented by Leech and Weisser (2003) examines domain non-specific forms of discourse. Speech acts are conveniently organised into five superordinate categories: **expressive**, **interpersonal management**, **dialog control**, **mainly initiating**, **mainly responding** — plus several acts classified as "other" (**external to dialog goals**, **unspecified**).

6.2.2.2 (II) Logic

In the previous section, we made note of several frameworks for describing the flow of language at the (relatively high) level of discourse. One of these, the Lakatosian framework, can also be thought of as controlling the logical flow within a discussion. Specifically, the Lakatosian moves discussed above can be thought of as operators whose outcome depends on the way in which a new example is construed:

$$\text{conjecture} \oplus \text{counterexample} \mapsto \text{surrender this conjecture} \tag{6.1}$$

$$\text{conjecture} \oplus \text{exception} \mapsto \text{exclude a range of examples} \tag{6.2}$$

$$\text{conjecture} \oplus \text{examples} \mapsto \text{limit scope} \tag{6.3}$$

$$\text{conjecture} \oplus \text{monster} \mapsto \text{revised statement} \tag{6.4}$$

$$\text{conjecture} \oplus \text{monster} \mapsto \text{revised example} \tag{6.5}$$

$$\text{conjecture} \oplus \text{counterexample} \mapsto \text{revised approach} \tag{6.6}$$

In particular, the "revised approach" in 6.6 may be associated with changes to lemmas or to the conjecture itself. There is no reason why 6.1–6.6 should limit the range of possible "production rules". For example, one would expect there to be a set of discourse moves that take place at the "managerial" level and that move the discourse between conjectures in ways that are not explicitly connected with (counter)examples. There are various "computational" heuristics that underlie and motivate the discourse moves mentioned above.[7]

Bookkeeping that explicitly describes mathematical objects and the relationships between them is "logical" rather than merely "dialogical". For example, Pease and Martin (2012) introduced a typology of comments in mathematical discussions. Comments of these kinds move the conversation forward in a different way: *concepts*, *examples*, *conjectures*, *proof* (and *other*).

These Lakatos-inspired reflections remain abstract in the sense that they "tag" mathematical conjectures, examples, and lemmas as such, but do not consider other kinds of (often entirely mundane) mathematical objects. Corneli (2014) describes the following kinds of mathematical object types that are either supported explicitly in the PlanetMath.org mathematics website, or planned for some future version system: *article* [A], *link* [ℓ], *project* [$\mathbb{X}$], *post* [T], *solution* [S], *review* [R], *update* [$\natural$], *question* [Q], *correction* [C], *fork* [$\prime$], *outcome* [$\star$], *problem* [P], *collection* [L], *classification* [M], *conjecture* [$\mathbb{J}$], *group* [G], *user* [U], *request* [W], *heuristic* [H], and *ephemera* [$\mathbb{E}$]. In a system like PlanetMath, the underlying software logic depends on the specific implementation that describe how these elements connect and interact (Corneli, 2011). Object types are considered to exist within a "grammar" that constrains behaviours within the system (Corneli, 2014, pp. 74,160). This sort of explicit modelling may mirror the way such objects are discussed informally in text-based discussion threads, e.g., "the ideas underlying this question suggest the following broader conjecture ...".

Whether the development of a mathematical theory is construed as an evolving, dynamically-constructed tapestry of structure blends, or a growing network of inter-related terms and objects, we require a range of more or less mechanical operations to carry out the reasoning steps. One recent computational example has been developed by Ganesalingam and Gowers (2013), who describe an automatic problem solving program ROBOTONE which, they claim, works roughly in the same way that people do (in the limited domain of textbook problem solving). While this claim may be debated, as it stands the system offers a candidate mapping between "human operations" and "machine operations." In ROBOTONE, *"An individual move is an operation that transforms a specific problem state into another state in a sound fashion; thus individual moves correspond to application of tactics to a specific*

---

[7] For example, Minsky (2008–2009) mentions: *reasoning by analogy, dividing the problem into parts, changing the problem's description, focusing on a more specific example, making a simpler version, trying to identify what makes the problem hard, imagining what an expert would do, stopping what you're doing if you're stuck, retrieving the knowledge that tells you how to solve the problem,* and *asking for help.*

LCF-style prover state."[8] Ganesalingam and Gowers describe, in total, 27 different moves, in the broad categories **Deletion**, **Tidying**, **Applying**, **Suspension**, and **EqualitySubstitution**. The basic heuristic is to look at the problem state and apply the first possible move from an ordered list.[9]

6.2.2.3 (III) Pragmatics

The way people solve problems has been studied extensively, with the best-known work being that of Pólya (e.g., 1990a; 1990b; 2014; 1981). Empirical work continuing in this tradition has been developed by Alan Schoenfeld (e.g., 1985; 1987; 2010) and others. Pólya's high-level problem-solving heuristics follow a well-known outline:

1. *Understand the problem (unknown, data, condition),*
2. *Find the connection between the data and the unknown to obtain a plan of the solution,*
3. *Carry out the plan,*
4. *Examine the solution obtained.*

These can be broken down into further steps; in particular, via the famous heuristic: "If you can't solve a problem, then there is an easier problem you can solve: find it."

The empirical aspects of Schoenfeld's work on problem solving connect with earlier protocol-based methods for doing research in mathematics education, e.g., Lucas (1980), and Lucas et al. (1980), who built on earlier work in process coding by Kilpatrick (1967) as well as early research by Schoenfeld himself (1979). However, Schoenfeld found that the codings used by Lucas et al. (1980) were overly complex, even while they focused only on tactics rather than strategy. His primary coding is divided among stages that are clearly informed by Pólya: **Read**, **Analyze**, **Explore**, **Plan**, **Implement**, and **Verify**. These are supplemented by **New information and local assessments**, and **Transition**. In problem solving, Schoenfeld argues (1985, p. 4) *"it is what the person does rather than what the person produces"* that is important. Somewhat along these lines he insists that *omissions* (e.g., neglecting to plan) should be coded for, along with explicit behaviour.

One of Schoenfeld's central research strategies was to put people in small groups or pairs and have them talk through mathematical problems together. An alternative would have been to use speak-aloud protocols – but a dialogical format helped to alleviate situational pressure. "[W]*hen two students worked on the problem it was typical for one student to turn to the other and say something like, 'I have no idea what to do. Do you?'*"

---

[8] LCF stands for *Logic for Computable Functions* (cf. Milner (1972); Gordon et al. (1979); Gordon (2000)).

[9] Gordon (2000) explains why activities related to *deletion* are given particular priority: *"The steps of a proof would be performed but not recorded, like a mathematics lecturer using a small blackboard who rubs out earlier parts of proofs to make space for later ones."*

This not only produced more natural records of a thought process, but also helped to avoid answers that were formal for the sake of being formal (Schoenfeld, 1985, p. 279–281). Nevertheless, a social setting is not a guarantee of problem-solving success, as becomes clear from several dialogues that record attempts to solve this problem:

> *Three points are chosen on the circumference of a circle of radius R, and the triangle containing them is drawn. What choice of points results in the triangle with the largest possible area? Justify your answer as best you can.* (Schoenfeld, 1985, p. 319)[10]

In short: "*If one makes major strategic mistakes, then matters of tactics are of little importance*" (Schoenfeld, 1985, p. 289).[11] In connection with this observation, Pólya's (1981) expansion of the *planning* step is interesting. He writes that in order to form a plan, one should proceed in this way:

1. *Identify the goal* (what do you want?)
2. *Identify the conditions* (what do you have?)
3. *Decompose the problem* (introducing ancillary problems and new unknowns as needed)
4. *Connect the data to the problem*
5. *Determine any unknowns*

Schoenfeld (1985, p. 15) introduces a "macro-level" framework that supplements these increasingly detailed frameworks from Pólya. The macro framework characterises thinking in terms of four categories: *resources* ("genetic epistemology"), *heuristics* (per Pólya), *control* (comprising both "decision making" and "metacognition"), and *belief systems* (or "mathematical world view"). He points out that this framework is "*far from comprehensive*" and that it generally excludes both cognitive and social details (Schoenfeld, 1985, p. 16). *Mutatis mutandis*, if we consider a social framework then we must find a way to embed features like heuristics, control structures, and belief systems within it.

Pease et al. (2018) are working on *explanation* in mathematical texts. Explanations can be people-centred (paralleling Schoenfeld's macro-level framework) or domain-centred. Items from the following list can function either as an *explanandum*

---

[10] After a brief period of time spent *reading*, the first group of students spends the rest of the time *exploring* in a rather meandering fashion, even though they had a suitable conjecture within the first few moments of discussion (Schoenfeld, 1985, p. 294). Schoenfeld's commentary (1985, pp. 288–289) is as follows: (1) The students neglected to assess the potential utility of calculating the area of the equilateral triangle; (2) the discussants gave consideration to several interesting alternative problems that might have added insight, but did not pursue them vigorously; (3) progress was not monitored or assessed during the solution attempt. A second group described a "hunch" that the answer was an equilateral triangle, but spent most of the available time *implementing* a somewhat related demonstration to show the size of the largest inscribed right triangle. They had no satisfactory answer when asked by the investigator how what they found would relate back to the original problem.

[11] Given Schoenfeld's choice of words it is perhaps worth noting that "tactics-based proof systems" may or may not concern themselves with strategic matters; strategy does not appear to play a particularly significant role in the system described by Ganesalingam and Gowers (2013), for example.

or an *explanans*. For example, we might attempt to explain why we don't understand something, or we could point to the fact that we don't understand something *as* an explanation.

1. *abilities* (what can/can't we do, e.g., we can reduce the problem to P)
2. *knowledge* (what do/don't we know, e.g., X is wrong)
3. *understand* (what do/don't we understand, e.g., do you see why this is a contradiction?)
4. *value/goals* (what do/don't we want, e.g., X is a good idea)
5. *initial problem* (e.g., the initial problem P is harder than problem Q)
6. *proof* (e.g., A is not a useful approach)
7. *assertions* (e.g., M is subset of P)
8. *specific cases/instances* (e.g., there will always exist instance X that satisfies condition C_1)
9. *arguments* (e.g., let us suppose X. Then Y.)
10. *representation* (e.g., by reducing the problem to P)
11. *property* (e.g., we don't know if it has property P)

6.2.3 Pilot Study

In this section we present a novel application of the material surveyed above, namely an examination of the ways in which these concepts model real mathematical texts. This pilot study helps to clarify the salience and range of application of the concepts in our survey.

Referring to the foregoing material, we have extracted a large array of potential textual annotations at different levels of specificity. These are presented in overview in Table 6.1. There is clearly a degree of redundancy among the frameworks surveyed above, which we have attempted to express with a numbering scheme (*1a.*, *1b.*, etc.) that elides some of the redundancies present in the 13 frameworks mentioned above. Even with this compression, we arrive at a position that is at least as complex as that taken up in the process coding work of Lucas et al. (1980): indeed, our situation is bound to be somewhat more complex, since these authors considered only individual problem solvers working with a speak-aloud protocol, and not people working in groups. Nevertheless, in an initial survey it seems best to take a comprehensive view, rather than risk leaving something out for the sake of concision. We can now ask: Which components of this broad canvas of available frameworks are the most relevant? In order to address this question, we have intensively annotated several brief passages, drawing as needed from all of the above frameworks. In subsequent phases of research, we expect to be able to deal with longer passages (including informal dialogues leading to full proofs). In the current study, the authors sought direct consensus on which tags best apply to which portions of text. The texts, together with the added tags, are presented in Figures 6.4–6.8. The sources for these texts are described in Section 6.2.3.1.

0.	The general-purpose *SPAAC Classified List of Speech Acts*	("SA")
1a.	Walton's *patterns of dialogue*	("WD")
1b.	Aberdein's interpretation of these in the context of *proof dialogue*	("AD")
2.	Prakken's specialisation to *persuasion dialogues*	("PD")
3.	Pease et al.'s *Lakatosian moves*	("LD")
4.	Pease and Martin's *types of mathematical comments*	("MC")
5.	PlanetMath/Planetary's *types of mathematical objects*	("MO")
6a.	Pólya's *stages of problem solving from "How to Solve It"*	("PS")
6b.	Schoenfeld's refinements to this in the form of his *process coding*	("SS")
7.	Pólya's *stages of planning from "Mathematical Discovery"*	("PP")
8.	Schoenfeld's framework describing *factors in mathematical thinking*	("SF")
9.	Pease, Aberdein, and Martin's *components of explanation*	("CE")
10.	Ganesalingam and Gowers's *LCF-style tactics*	("RO")

Table 6.1: List of frameworks, with two-letter abbreviations

6.2.3.1 Data Sets

We are particularly interested in the MiniPolymath problems that were been posed, discussed, and solved online, on Terrence Tao's blog and the Polymath blog Tao et al. (2009, 2011). The problems – drawn from Mathematics Olympiads[12] – are interesting in that they are challenging enough to spur considerable discussion, but not so challenging as to go unsolved when people put their heads together.[13] There have been four such discussions to date – however, the experiment itself would be relatively easy to replicate. MiniPolymaths do not yet have the scope of the full "Polymath" projects, which dealt instead with research topics and in some cases resulted in published papers (cf. Barany (2010); Gowers and Nielsen (2009)). Nevertheless, unlike Lakatos's (1976) *Proofs and Refutations*, MiniPolymath data is "real" (and available online) – as opposed to "rationally reconstructed in fictional form."

We also consider brief excerpts from Schoenfeld's collected data set (several dialogues between students are presented in full in his book); an excerpt from a monologue presented in a public lecture by Timothy Gowers (2012); and a proof written by the ROBOTONE prototype system described by Ganesalingam and Gowers (2013), which operationalises the line of thinking from the lecture.[14] We emphasise that single author works addressed to an arbitrary audience *can* be coded using the frameworks we've described, although this is not the main intended application. Nevertheless, single author works provide a natural point of comparison, as we think about what the "social dimension" brings to mathematics.

---

[12] https://www.imo-official.org/

[13] Tao notes, regarding MiniPolymath 1: "*Of the 500-odd participants in the Olympiad, only a half-dozen or so managed to solve this problem completely.*"

[14] http://people.ds.cam.ac.uk/mg262/robotone.pdf

Figures 6.4–6.8 show the selected texts on the left, verbatim except for footnote-style anchors which cross-reference our consensus codings of text fragments. Details appear as marginal annotations to the right.

1 NATE: Well, my first thought is to see if the hy-
2 potheses seem reasonable.[ss3] The hypothesis that   [ss3]explore
3 $s = a_1 + \ldots + a_n$ not lie in M is certainly neces-
4 sary, as the last jump that the grasshopper takes
5 will land on s.[pp2] The grasshopper's other steps   [pp2]conditions
6 will land on a partial sums $a_{\sigma(1)} + \ldots + a_{\sigma(k)}$ for
7 some permutation σ, but we get to choose the
8 permutation. Thus it seems plausible that we can
9 avoid a given set of $n - 1$ points.[ss2]   [ss2]analyze
10 THOMAS: Quick observation.[sa2] The grasshopper   [sa2]inform
11 must make a first step.[sf2] This is always possi-   [sf2]heuristic (simplify)
12 ble, since the a_i are distinct and $|M| = n - 1$; that
13 is, there is always an a_i not in M.[pp2] However,   [pp2]conditions
14 let's say M matches all but one of the a_i. Then the
15 first step is uniquely determined. Still, according
16 to the claimed theorem, a second step must still
17 be possible.[pp3]   [pp3]decomposition

Fig. 6.4: Excerpt from MiniPolymath1

1 HAGGAI NUCHI: The first point and line P_0, l_0 can-
2 not be chosen[ce7] so that P_0 is on the boundary   [ce7]assertion
3 of the convex hull of S and l_0 picks out an ad-
4 jacent point on the convex hull.[mc2] Maybe the   [mc2]example (monster)
5 strategy should be to take out the convex hull of
6 S from consideration; follow it up by induction
7 on removing successive convex hulls.[ld7]   [ld7]lemma incorporation
8 HAGGAI NUCHI: More specifically, remove the sub-
9 set of S which forms the convex hull to get S_1;
10 remove the new convex hull to get S_2, and repeat
11 until S_n is convex. Maybe a point of S_n is a good
12 place to start.[ss5]   [ss5]implement
13 SRIVATSAN NARAYANAN: Can we just assume by in-
14 duction that we have proved the result for all the
15 "inner points" $S_2 \cup S_3 \cdot \cup S_n$.[ad5] The base case   [ad5]negotiation
16 would be that $S = S_1$, i.e., it forms a convex
17 polygon.[mc4]   [mc4]proof

Fig. 6.5: Excerpt from MiniPolymath3

6.2.3.2 Results

As illustrated above, several short texts have been marked up with codes corresponding to the frameworks introduced in Section 6.2.2. Figures 6.6–6.8, respectively, re-

1	DK: [reads the question][ss1]	[ss1]read
2	BM: Do we need calculus for this?[sf1] So we can	[sf1]resources
3	minimize, or rather maximize it.[mc1]	[mc1]concept
4	DK: My guess would be more like [indiscernable]	
5	my basic hunch would be that it would be –[ld1]	[ld1]conjecture
6	BM: An equilateral –[ld1]	[ld1]conjecture
7	DK: 60, 60, 60[mc1]	[mc1]concept
8	BM: Yeah.[sa2]	[sa2]ackn
9	DK: So what choice of points has to be where on	
10	the triangle[pp1] – these points are gonna be.[pp2]	[pp1]goal [pp2]conditions
11	BM: Try doing it with calculus – see if you can – just	
12	draw the circle[ss3] – see what we'll do is figure	[ss3]explore
13	out the right triangle –[ss8]	[ss8]transition
14	DK: Yeah, or why don't we find – or why don't	
15	we know the – some way to break this problem	
16	down into[sf2] – like, what would a triangle be for	[sf2]heuristic (decompose)
17	half the circle?[sf2]	[sf2]heuristic (symmetry)

Fig. 6.6: Excerpt from Schoenfeld [pp. 324–325]

1	GOWERS: What is the 500th digit of $(\sqrt{2}+\sqrt{3})^{2012}$?[ss1]	[ss1]read
2	Even this, eventually, a computer will be able	
3	to solve.[mc5]	[mc5]other (phatic)
4	For now, notice that total stuckness can make	
5	you do desperate things.[sf2] Furthermore, know-	[sf2]heuristic (total stuckness)
6	ing the origin of the problem suggests good things	
7	to try. The fact that it is set as a problem is a huge	
8	clue.[sf4]	[sf4]belief systems
9	Can we do this for $(x+y)$?[ss3] For e? Rationals	[ss3]explore
10	with small denominator?[sf2]	[sf2]heuristic (compute!)
11	And how about small perturbations of these?[sf3]	[sf3]control
12	Maybe it is close to a rational?[ld1]	[ld1]conjecture
13	m^{th} digit of $(\sqrt{2}+\sqrt{3})^n$?[sf2]	[sf2]heuristic (formal gen.)
14	$(\sqrt{2}+\sqrt{3})^2$?[sf2]	[sf2]heuristic (simplify)
15	$(2+2\sqrt{2}\sqrt{3}+3)$[mo2o]	[mo2o]ephemera
16	$(\sqrt{2}+\sqrt{3})^2+(\sqrt{3}-\sqrt{2})^2=10$[sf2]	[sf2]heuristic (compute!)
17	$(\sqrt{2}+\sqrt{3})^{2012}+(\sqrt{3}-\sqrt{2})^{2012}$ is an integer![ce11]	[ce11]property
18	And $(\sqrt{3}-\sqrt{2})^{2012}$ is a very small number.[ss7]	[ss7]local assessments
19	Maybe the final answer is "9"?[ld1]	[ld1]conjecture
20	We need to check whether it's small enough.[ss5]	[ss5]implement
21	$(\sqrt{3}-\sqrt{2})^{2012} < (\frac{1}{2})^{2012} = ((\frac{1}{2})^4)^{503} = (\frac{1}{16})^{503} <$	
22	$.1^{503}$, so we're in luck. . .[ss6]	[ss6]verify

Fig. 6.7: Partial transcript from Timothy Gowers's Maxwell Institute Lecture, November 2, 2012

produce our tagging of: a single-threaded discussion in Minipolymath 1, a portion of one of the threads in the multithreaded discussion in Minipolymath 3, a short passage from a student problem solving dialogue, the full solution to a challenge problem presented by mathematician Timothy Gowers, and a portion of a textbook-style problem solved by Ganesalingam and Gowers's program ROBOTONE.

The results of this exercise are summarised in Figure 6.9, which shows the total count of the tags used from each of the several tag sets available. For example, a grand total of two tags from tag set 0 ("SA") were used: "inform" was applied to

1 ROBOTONE: If A and B are open sets, then $A \cap B$ is

2   open.[ss1]   [ss1]read

3   Let x be an element of $A \cap B$.[mc2]   [mc2]example (arbitrary inst.)

4   Since $x \in A \cap B, x \in A$ and $x \in B$.[pp3]   [pp3]decomposition

5   Since A is open and $x \in A$, there exists $\eta > 0$

6   such that $u \in A$ whenever $d(x, u) < \eta$.[pp2]   [pp2]conditions

7   Since B is open and $x \in B$, there exists $\theta > 0$

8   such that $v \in B$ whenever $d(x, v) < \theta$.[pp2]   [pp2]conditions

9   We would like to find $\delta > 0$ s.t. $y \in A \cap B$

10   whenever $d(x, y) < \delta$.[pp1]   [pp1]goal

Fig. 6.8: Partial transcript of **ROBOTONE**'s proof that the intersection of two open sets in a metric space is open

code the short statement "Quick observation" in Figure 6.4, Line 10, and "ackn" is applied to code the one-word speech "Yeah" in Figure 6.6, Line 8.

In Figure 6.9, the tags attached to dialogical and monological texts have been distinguished, with contributions from single-author texts added as an "increment" above the tags used in dialogues.

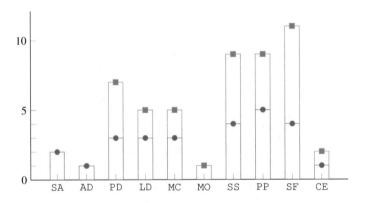

Fig. 6.9: Count of tags from the several schemes

6.2.3.3 Discussion

As noted above, the aim of this pilot study is to clarify the salience and range of application of the concepts in our survey. Given the small sample size, a limited number of applications for a specific tag set does not necessarily mean that it will be irrelevant in future studies: rather, even a few usages (as from the AD and MO tag sets) give an indication of the types of text where we would expect to see more replete usage of the corresponding tag sets.

Before discussing the findings, we will comment on some of the things that this pilot study did not attempt. Note that although they are available in Ganesalingam and Gowers (2013), we did not tally the explicit tactics used by **ROBOTONE** (RO). Rather than focusing on the LCF-style details, the coding used in Figure 6.8 gives an informal view of the processes involved in "expanding the definition." The study did not include Walton's patterns (WD) which in this context would be redundant with Aberdein's interpretation (AD); and similarly, we do not include tags denoting Pólya's stages of problem solving (PS), preferring Schoenfeld's slightly more detailed rendering (SS).

Table 6.2 presents a summary showing exactly which tags were selected. This table is ordered and divided into three segments to show whether the tag set is primarily associated with (I) dialogical, (II) logical, or (III) pragmatic discursive manoeuvres (this is according to the subdivisions of Section 6.2.2). The annotation "*" means that all of the tags in a given category were used, up to redundancy within the categories I, II, and II. Tags that have been used but that are redundant in this sense are enclosed in hard brackets (e.g., "conjecture" is part of LD, MC, and MO, but it is present in this only as a representative of LD). Similarly, we have tagged *examples*, including counterexamples, into MC. The annotation "∘" indicates that all but one of the tags was used: specifically, *plan* from the SS tag set is not used; note, however, that several specific tags related to *planning* from the PP tag set were applied.

SA	ackn, inform
AD	negotiation
PD	question
LD	[conjecture], lemma incorporation
MC*	concept, example (arbitrary inst.), example (monster), [proof], other (phatic)
MO	ephemera
SS∘	read, analyze, explore, implement, verify, local assessments, transition
PP	goal, conditions, decomposition
SF*	resources, heuristic (compute!), heuristic (decompose), heuristic (formal gen.), heuristic (simplify), heuristic (symmetry), heuristic (total stuckness), control, belief systems
CE	property, [assertion]

Table 6.2: Summary of tags used, by category

The most popular tag set was Schoenfeld's "macro-level" framework (SF), with 11 applications overall. Many of these deal with the application of specific heuristics, such as: *if you can compute something, do it!*; *it's a good idea to decompose a problem into sub problems*; and *try a simple case*. Note that a discussion about a heuristic, as in Lines 14–16 of Figure 6.6 – tagged "*heuristic (decompose)*" – is different from the application of a heuristic, as in Lines 10-17 of Figure 6.4 – tagged as *"decomposition"* from the Pólya planning (PP) tag set.

The "Pólya-Schoenfeld" tag set (SS) and Pólya planning tag set (PP) were both used frequently, with nine applications each, although not all of the tags were used. The Lakatos (LD) and comment-type (MC) tag sets were used with moderate frequency, with five applications each. We only used two tags from the SPAAC Classified List of Speech Acts (SA), despite this being a general-purpose lexicon, and having the largest set of available tags. (SPAAC-style general purpose conversational moves seem particularly likely to happen in in-person, real-time dialogues, which are not well represented in our data set.)

We included only one tag, *ephemera*, selected from our list of types of mathematical objects (MO). In the current data set, discussants typically referred to *concepts*, rather than to to concrete objects like *articles* where the definitions of these concepts could be found.

We also include only one tag, *negotiation*, from Aberdein's interpretation of proof dialogues (AD). Aberdein's discussion of the goals associated with proof includes "prove or disprove the conjecture" (corresponding to the tag *inquiry*) as one of six different intentional states. In the texts we examined, this was a goal that all of the participants shared: accordingly, using this tag would convey no information. We interpreted Lines 13-15 of Figure 6.5 to be (part of) a brief *negotiation* about the need for a "backward" operation in an induction proof.

Finally, we include one tag, *question*, from Prakken's framework (PD).[15] Lines 1-2 of Figure 6.5 – marked as *assertion* using a component of the explanation framework (CE) – might have, synonymously, been marked as a *claim*. The tag *"assertion"* is therefore recorded in hard brackets in Table 6.2. In addition to directly redundant tags, tagging these sample texts also makes more clear the relationships and interdependencies among the dimensions. For example, as noted above, PP supplies a dimension that expands on the idea of *planning* that is described abstractly in SS. MC includes examples, which are a necessary input for most of the elements of LD. The tag sets are also associated with different senses: not only "use versus mention", but also *use-to-explain* or *use-to-question*.

In terms of our earlier decomposition: SA, AD, PD, and LD were associated with *dialogical* features; MC and MO, together with an interpretation of LD, with *logical* features; and SS, PP, SF, and CE with *pragmatic* features.

Frameworks that are only used for one (AD, PD, and MO) or two (LD, CE) tags are nevertheless interesting and worthy of further attention and potential refinement. Other terms from these frameworks (for example, Prakken's *challenges*) are likely to appear in longer texts. Similarly, more instances of *negotiation* and *deliberation* about sub-problems and proof strategies would be likely to appear in more wide-ranging discussions (like the research-level Polymath projects). Note, as well, that a

---

[15] Note: for reasons of typographical convenience, the question tag is not explicitly recorded in Figures 6.4–6.8 – rather, we count each paragraph that includes at least one question mark as a question. We have also counted the question-like sentence on Lines 13-15 of Figure 6.5 – which is punctuated with a full stop – as a question.

framework that has proved to be a particularly popular source of tags may be calling out to be separated into several different "levels" (après Borgo and Goguen (2005)).

6.2.4 Direct Extensions

Many standard problem solving approaches can be implemented in a social way (Corneli, 2014, p. 193). Indeed, according to the Meadian hypothesis, the emergence of agency may be seen as social, as Martin and Gillespie (2010) explain.[16] Although the sample size in the pilot study presented above was too small to make strong conclusions, it nevertheless offers interesting clues about what "social thinking" brings to mathematics. In the first instance – as Tao noted – the MiniPolymath problems are not easy, and yet, working as a group, participants have been able to solve them at a (time-wise) competitive rate. Why might that be?

People in discussions are presumably more likely to *negotiate*. Indeed, the entire Lakatosian framework might be considered in terms of negotiation and an exchange of resources, rather than simply persuasion and the resolution of differences. Relatedly, discussants may be more likely to *plan*. They are, certainly, more likely to *discuss*, and as a result may possibly consider a wider range of *examples*. That said, at least in the texts we studied, single authors were more likely to ask *questions*, even if this was only to create a simulated conversation. A didactic text written by someone who knows what they are doing may be more likely than a meandering dialogue to simply get on with it and do *problem solving*. Single authors may tend to rely more on *heuristics* than on *negotiation* to overcome difficulties.

Compared with the 42 primary tags used by Lucas et al. (1980), the 27 tags that we used are less focused on problem solving *per se*, although there is a significant overlap in the terminology and sources used. The problem solving aspects may be addressable using our combined "pragmatic" tag set (that is, SS, PP, SF, and CE, the segment of our tag collection which bears the closest similarity to Lucas et al. (1980)) as the core of an information channel, and using these elements to map between "subjective" dialogical moves and "objective" state changes in a logical setting. To treat research-level discussions, this set of tags would need to be expanded in order to deal with problem identification, positing, and selection.

With ROBOTONE, we get the logical mapping for free, albeit in a monological rather than dialogical format; thus, *example (arbitrary inst.)* in Figure 6.8 corresponds to the moves – elided in that figure – expandPreUniversalTarget followed by peelBareUniversalTarget, and *decomposition* to the move expandPreExistentialHypothesis; etc. While ROBOTONE seems to be

---

[16] "[I]t *is only by acting toward ourselves as others do … that we recognize and understand ourselves as objects and authors of our own activity. As we learn to coordinate our acting with the acting of others, we differentiate and develop our selves and our abilities to self-determine. Eventually, we not only understand the perspectives (i.e., action orientations and possibilities) of numerous particular others, but also those perspectives explicit and implicit within the broader, more generalized social, cultural practices in which we are immersed."*

reasonably proficient at basic problem solving, it currently has no explicit social intelligence.

It would not be unreasonable use the moves described in the Lucas et al. (1980) tag set as a guide to problem solving behaviours – without yet requiring social intelligence. After all, this earlier tag set was designed to analyse single-author texts. Working from the other direction, systems like Singh's (2005) EM-ONE do possess at least rudimentary social intelligence. It would be natural to extend EM-ONE with a set of narratives related to the SA, AD, and PD (dialogical) tag sets. The biggest challenge for future work seems to be the development of the domain-specific pragmatic knowledge base related to MC, MO, and LD, and mappings between this register and the others.

Naturally, in different domains it will make sense to consider different types of annotations. There are different "relations between relations" to be considered, both within disparate fields of human endeavour, and in different situations within a given field. Music makes a useful initial point of comparison.

6.2.5 Additional Frameworks from Music Theorists

Our survey in Section 6.2.2 focused on mathematics, but included the domain-independent SPAAC tag set and the work of theorists Walton and Prakken which described arguments in some generality. A look at music can help broaden this perspective: many of the ideas in musical collaboration would apply in other forms of collaboration.

Cook (2001) proposes to think of a musical score as a "script," rather than as text that is complete in itself. In this way, the space between score and performance is understood as an open and non-linear one, and perhaps more easily conceivable as a continuous exchange between processes and products, comparable to our comments above on the relationship between discussion and proof. Bruce Ellis Benson's work on improvisation-as-dialogue identifies 11 types of performance situations that could cover virtually any type of music (Benson, 2003, pp. 26-30). Benson's typology ranges from fully notated works (types 1 to 3) to the deliberate subversion of expectations associated with a particular compositional or performative tradition, via real-time improvisation (type 11).

Types 7 to 11 in Benson's typology are well illustrated by examples in jazz and freer forms of improvisation, and are particularly useful in investigating open problem-solving spaces, where structure and meaning are formed and communicated in real time. On that front, Borgo and Goguen (2005) attempted a typology of real-time transitions in their joint work on free jazz, in an analysis of a recording by Sam Rivers.[17]

1. *sudden/unexpected segue* (an unprepared, immediate change with unexpected continuation)

---

[17] This work would match types 10 and 11 in Benson's categories.

2. *pseudo-cadential segue* (an implied cadence with sudden and unexpected continuation)
3. *climactic segue* (a peak moment that stimulates unexpected change and continuation)
4. *feature overlap* (one feature of the antecedent section is sustained and becomes part of the consequent section)
5. *feature change* (a gradual change of one feature that redirects the flow, usually subtly)
6. *fragmentation* (a gradual breaking up, or fragmenting, of the general texture and/or rhythm)
7. *internal cadence* (a prepared cadence followed by a short silence then continuation with new material)

In their experimental work with free improvisers, Canonne and Garnier (2012) relied on musicians' own subjective accounts of short improvised sessions in three-person teams, and found significant evidence of intersubjective structural patterns emerging in the interactions between participants. This led to a distinction between stable and oscillating behaviours, corresponding to coordinated musical sequences (representable as fixed points in phase space) and discoordinated sections (representable as spaces without fixed attractors). Canonne and Garnier identified four main strategies that improvisers used to convey intentions while playing: *Stabilization*, *"Wait and see"*, *"Playing along"*, and *Densification*. The decision to employ these strategies, as well as the end-result of each strategy employed, depends on the overall musical situation, understanding of other musicians' individual intentions and objectives, and on team preferences, based on, e.g., competence, range of instruments used, etc. As a result, "misrepresentations" and, by extension, "contrasting evaluations of a given situation" may occur. Improvisers therefore often resort to "meta-pragmatic" evaluations of their strategies while playing, e.g. repeating a strategy until intention is successfully conveyed, or re-evaluating a strategic goal in real time on the basis of new information gathered from another player's response (Canonne and Garnier, 2012, pp. 202–203). Similar issues, and more, would apply in any setting where people are not solving predetermined problems.

There is a range of further challenges for and limitations in the above annotation paradigms. Firstly, given the largely non-discursive, or at least non-verbal, nature of musical performance, any dialogic pattern reflecting decisions *vis-à-vis* structure or other parameters is usually represented post-hoc, and mostly through the aid of recordings. Other domains (including mathematics) have many non-verbal features that can limit the range of applicability of text-based or discursive methods. Secondly, musical situations that correspond to Benson's types 1-6 involve a high level of consensus as to what constitutes musical meaning, and what formal or structural prerequisites are necessary for its production. They are thus closer to what Hall (1992) describes as "low-context" (LC) situations – whereas types 8-11 involve highly subjective, "high-context" (HC) processes. The latter are prone to contrasting evaluations, and pose a range of challenges for modelling.

Contexts that change over time or that depend on the observer's perspective suggest the need to develop a theory of information flow that takes on emergent properties. At least among musicians, decisions reached verbally may be reconfigured and in some cases entirely reversed based on playing and listening sessions between discussions; analogous behavious may be found in mathematical settings. The frameworks introduced in this section suggest a range of domain independent ways of moderating group dynamics. Nevertheless, more work is necessary to arrive at a more conclusive representation of how individual aesthetic preferences and collective behaviour are negotiated within groups.

6.3 Related Work: Social Creativity on Computers

In this section, we give an overview of some of our efforts to go beyond the work surveyed above, following the plan laid out in Figure 6.1. Section 6.3.1 presents work that formalises the relationships between moves in the Lakatosian framework LD, described above. Section 6.3.2 describes more informal theorisation of peer learning and peer production, which is nevertheless able to express high-level topics in problem identification, positing, and selection. Section 6.3.3 describes an evolutionary computer system that is much more low-level, but which illustrates the potential of simulation studies for research in creativity. These three short sections are not closely related to one another; rather they provide a selection of approaches that will inform future work.

6.3.1 A Formal Representation of Lakatosian Creativity

Lakatos (1976) describes a notion of social creativity in mathematics which springs from the interaction of two conflicting theories, leading to the synthesis of a third theory that resolves inconsistencies. In Pease et al. (2017), we explore the connections along the pipeline running from philosophical theory to formal expression of mathematical arguments as dialogue games. This allows us to express linguistic structures of reasoning in terms of formal structured argumentation, abstract argumentation and argumentation semantics. Finally, coming full circle, we show that such implementations can provide value to mathematical communities. This work lays a foundation for a formally sound and linguistically coherent theorisation of collaborative intelligence and social creativity.

This interpretation of Lakatos through the lens of dialogue game theory (Hamblin, 1970) and, in particular, as a dialogue game ranging over structures of argumentation, allows us to keep track of the mutually consistent and mutually inconsistent portions of a mathematical dialogue. The practice of interaction between mathematicians is mediated by language, so our choice to rely on argumentation theory is, in the first instance, governed by the need to handle challenges presented by reasoning about linguistic expressions. On the other hand, in order to manipulate these structures computationally, there is a need for formal and ontological clarity.

We have adopted the Argument Interchange Format (AIF) (Chesñevar et al. (2006); Rahwan et al. (2007)) to handle the data. The understanding of Lakatos is refined and characterised as a set of update semantics on AIF structures. At a high level, the dialogue game is constrained to follow the flowchart in Figure 6.10.

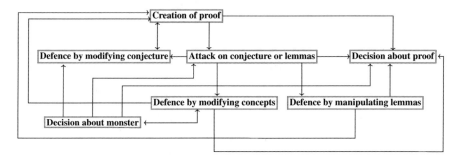

Fig. 6.10: Lakatos's informal logic of mathematical discovery represented as a flow chart

Whereas the Lakatosian moves in Section 6.2.2 were treated as a set of independent dimensions, in this formalism we see the constraints on their use. Previous work by Bex et al. (2013) has shown how AIF can be interpreted as a nonmonotonic system, with mappings built from AIF to the ASPIC+ structured argumentation formalism.[18] Prakken (2010) has shown how abstract argumentation systems in the style of Dung (1995) can be induced from ASPIC+, from where the argumentation semantics can be computed to provide labellings of the acceptability status of each argument. In our treatment, the abstract argumentation framework corresponds precisely to the theory that has been collaboratively created by the participants in a Lakatosian dialogue.

In addition, each of these formal steps is also available in implementation: details are described in Pease et al. (2017). Finally, an appendix to that paper shows how the model can also be retrospectively applied to examples of extant mathematical discussions from MiniPolymath (Tao et al., 2011). This demonstrates the depth of Lakatos' insight into mathematical creativity, and suggests that the formal characterisation is honest both to his original work and to the practical workflows used by mathematicians.

6.3.2 Patterns of Peeragogy

Corneli et al. (2015) use the descriptive language of *design patterns* to take stock of the common processes found in successful collaborations, a typical context for

---

[18] *ASPIC+* is follow-on work from the *Argumentation Service Platform with Integrated Components* (ASPIC) project: http://www.cossac.org/projects/aspic

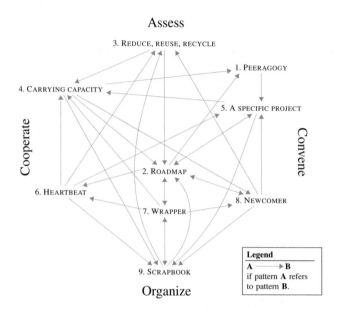

Fig. 6.11: Connections between the patterns of peeragogy

everyday social creativity. Their focus is on *peer produced peer learning* projects, in which the structure of the collaboration is not fixed in advance, and must be created alongside the project's other products. The central pattern describes the ways in which project participants collaborate to build a shared ROADMAP that gets them "from *here* to *there*" – possibly integrating multiple different "*heres* and *theres*." The eight additional design patterns describe additional "social glue," holding together and structuring work on the project (Figure 6.11). For example, the NEWCOMERS pattern describes interactions between experienced project members and beginners. The degree to which social glue and out-of-domain discourse is required varies according to a project's scale and scope. For example, in the Polymath project, discussants needed to determine a large-scale overall plan, including which problems to focus on, while in MiniPolymath a single problem is set in advance, and participants only needed to develop a suitable approach to solve it. Future work could formalise this material further, possibly by adopting the dialogue game treatment described above.

6.3.3 The Search for Computational Intelligence

Corneli and Maclean (2015) aim to present a minimal convincing computational simulation of social creativity that exhibits emergent results. Cellular automata are taken as an underlying domain, thought of as "multi-agent systems based on loc-ality with overlapping interaction structures" (Flache and Hegselmann, 2001). The novel approach that we described as a *search for computational intelligence* permits local adjustments to the behaviour of cells in the automaton. Change at this level is embedded in a higher-order evolutionary system called a *meta-cellular automata* or "MetaCA." That is, MetaCAs co-evolve rules for local behaviour based, in part, on the currently observed behaviour. From a philosophical perspective, this work is aligned with the notion from Mead (1932) of the social as emergent co-evolution: "an adjustment in the organism and a reconstitution of the environment." Our ini-tial simulations used a modified version of Goguen's Unified Concept Theory to carry out evolutionary steps that evolve local behaviours via concept blending over successive generations. However, we found that still-more sophisticated interactions between phenotype and genotype data (after Baldwin (1896)) were needed to pro-duce familiar "edge of chaos" (Mitchell et al., 1993) effects. Expanding on the semantically simple domain of cellular automata, future work could encode, e.g., mathematical problems in a cellular program (Sipper, 1997) and involve a group of agents in finding solutions to these problems as a society.

6.4 Summary

In this first part of this chapter, we developed a catalogue of different ways to the-orise mathematical conversations, and presented a brief pilot study that marked up several sample texts using this framework, in order to gain perspective on the salient dimensions. In the second part of the chapter, we surveyed recent work that explores several additional directions of analysis and design. Drawing on the frameworks and methods for theorising social creativity that we have described, we are in the process of synthesising a protocol which can both account for the behaviours observed in a mathematical text and dialogues, and also admit the possibility of computational support (Martin et al., 2017). In the move from the Lakatosian theory $\mathscr{LAK}$ to a "$\mathscr{LAK}++$" that brings in themes from social simulation and the design of social machines, we have the opportunity to be both more descriptive of everyday social reality in mathematics and other domains, and to explore more of what is comput-able.

6.5 Conclusion and Future Perspectives

One of the issues hinted at in our survey of frameworks was the 'black box' of mathematical content. By adding structured identifiers and suitable representations, we will be able to understand the substantive mathematical relationships, not just schematic relationships. For example, when performatives are attached to text frag-ments, a history of the evolution of core concepts in the discussion becomes available. Some segments may be tagged as explicitly Lakatosian; others might be seen as "peeragogical".

In developing "$\mathcal{LAK}++$", our strategy makes use of:

I. A (relatively) minimal set of performatives for the argumentation structure in the dialogue, such as *suggesting, asserting, retracting,* and *challenging.*

II. A set of relations between the mathematical structures under discussion, such as: *has_property, sub_conjecture, equivalent, stronger,* and *weaker.* This allows a model of *information flow* between structures, in the sense of Barwise and Seligman (1997).[19]

III. A set of meta-objects representing the conjectures to prove, and strategies to use to prove them, such as *goal, strategy* and *difficult.*

At an abstract level, a locution E that presents *an example of a concept* might map to a hypertextual representation that connects the example E to the concept C which it exemplifies, which could then be mapped in a formal model of the dialogue to the statement `example(C,E)`. The *Lightweight Social Calculus* described by Murray-Rust and Robertson (2014)[20] that was mentioned in Figure 6.3 is one suitable target language for this sort of relation.

Note that we do not require every conversation to happen within the same scope or the same formal model, since information channels can themselves be chained together and given multiple and emergent interpretations. In particular, we would like to build relationships between high-level features of discourse and the implicative and other structures that are carried by mathematical objects themselves.

Thus, for instance, we would summarise the utterance "*The following reformulation of the problem may be useful: Show that for any permutation s in S_n, the sum $a_s(1) + a_s(2) + a_s(j)$ is not in M for any $j =< n$*"[21] as

$$assert(equivalent(\text{main\_problem}, \text{any\_permutation})).$$

This statement might be flagged up (using a higher-level model) as an example (i.e., an example of a broader class of equivalent problem formulations).

The outline above reflects the view that much of an argument's structure is carried by relations between the mathematical objects under discussion. We do not want to have to represent the whole of mathematics in order to reason about individual proofs. Thinking in terms of the relationships between objects will offer a level of detail that allows us to represent most of the important structure of specific arguments.

Reflecting back over the work described in this chapter, some of the ways in which the methods outlined in I–III could develop are clear:

---

[19] These relationships go beyond those explicitly dealt with in the Lakatosian theory and show recursive (and other) relationships between theories. Cf. the comparison with intuitionistic logic in Restall (2005).

[20] Referred to in earlier work by Robertson (2005) as the *Lightweight Coordination Calculus.*

[21] Tao et al. (2009)

I′. As remarked in Section 6.3.2, in more complex domains, more kinds of moves are needed: for instance, *problem positing* as well as *problem solving*. We intend to progressively expand the approach outlined above to deal with more actively social problem scenarios, like Polymath.

II′. The ability to reason computationally about mathematical and musical structures was a core part of the COINVENT project. We have carried out preliminary experiments that integrate the agent-based model described in Section 6.3.3 with the simple structure annotations like those mentioned in II as CASL representations of mathematical and musical objects. Continuing to develop this work could lead to a convincing and useful simulation of social creativity in our target domains.

III′. In this work, we are not necessarily restricted to a Lakatosian or even an argumentation-based approach, although these continue to be relevant in many situations. For example, Confalonieri et al. (2015) explored an argumentation-based approach to evaluating the meaning, interest, and significance of concept blends, using a simplified version of the Lakatosian dialogue game from Pease et al. (2017). However, scenarios with "multiple right answers" (Corneli et al., 2015) require more elaborate coordination methods.

References

A. Aberdein. The informal logic of mathematical proof. In B. van Kerkhove and J. P. van Bendegem, editors, *Perspectives on Mathematical Practices: Bringing Together Philosophy of Mathematics, Sociology of Mathematics, and Mathematics Education*, pages 135–151. Springer. Logic, Epistemology, and the Unity of Science, Vol. 5, 2007. URL http://arxiv.org/pdf/math/0306298v1.

P. B. Andersen. Dynamic semiotics. *Semiotica*, 139(1/4):161–210, 2002.

J. M. Baldwin. A new factor in evolution. *The American Naturalist*, 30:441–451, 536–553, 1896.

M. Barany. '[B]ut this is blog maths and we're free to make up conventions as we go along': Polymath1 and the modalities of 'massively collaborative mathematics'. In *Proceedings of the 6th International Symposium on Wikis and Open Collaboration*. ACM, 2010.

J. Barwise. Heterogeneous reasoning. In *Conceptual graphs for knowledge representation*, pages 64–74. Springer, 1993.

J. Barwise and J. Seligman. *Information flow: The logic of distributed systems*. Cambridge University Press, 1997.

B. E. Benson. *The improvisation of musical dialogue: A phenomenology of music*. Cambridge University Press, 2003.

F. Bex, J. Lawrence, M. Snaith, and C. Reed. Implementing the argument web. *Communications of the ACM*, 56(10):66–73, 2013.

D. Borgo and J. Goguen. Rivers of consciousness: The nonlinear dynamics of free jazz. In *Jazz research proceedings yearbook*, volume 25, 2005.

K. Budzynska. Circularity in ethotic structures. *Synthese*, 190(15):3185–3207, 2013.

K. Budzynska and C. Reed. Speech acts of argumentation: Inference anchors and peripheral cues in dialogue. In F. Grasso, N. Green, and C. Reed, editors, *Computational Models of Natural Argument*, 2011. Papers from the 2011 AAAI Workshop.

K. Budzynska and C. Reed. The structure of ad hominem dialogues. In *COMMA*, pages 410–421, 2012.

A. Bundy. A science of reasoning: Extended Abstract. In *TABLEAUX '98 Proceedings of the International Conference on Automated Reasoning with Analytic Tableaux and Related Methods*, pages 10–17. Springer, 1998.

K. Burke and J. P. Zappen. On persuasion, identification, and dialectical symmetry. *Philosophy and Rhetoric*, 39(4):333–339, 2006.

C. Canonne and N. B. Garnier. Cognition and segmentation in collective free improvisation: An exploratory study. In E. Cambouropoulos, C. Tsougras, P. Mavromatis, and K. Pastiadis, editors, *Proceedings of the 12th International Conference for Music Perception and Cognition and 8th Conference of the European Society for the Cognitive Sciences of Music Joint Conference*, pages 197–204, 2012.

L. H. Carlson. *Dialogue games: An approach to discourse analysis.* Ph.D. thesis, Massachusetts Institute of Technology, 1982.

C. Chesñevar, J. McGinnis, S. Modgil, I. Rahwan, C. Reed, G. Simari, M. South, G. Vreeswijk, and S. Willmott. Towards an argument interchange format. *Knowledge Engineering Review*, 21(4):293–316, 2006.

R. Confalonieri, J. Corneli, A. Pease, E. Plaza, and M. Schorlemmer. Using argumentation to evaluate concept blends in combinatorial creativity. In S. Colton, H. Toivonen, M. Cook, and D. Ventura, editors, *Proceedings of the Sixth International Conference on Computational Creativity, ICCC 2015*. 2015. http://axon.cs.byu.edu/ICCC2015proceedings/7. 4Confalonieri.pdf.

N. Cook. Between process and product: Music and/as performance. *Music Theory Online*, 7(2):1–31, 2001.

J. Corneli. The planetmath encyclopedia. In C. Lange and J. Urban, editors, *The ITP 2011 Workshop on Mathematical Wikis (MathWikis-2011)*, 2011. URL http: //ceur-ws.org/Vol-767/paper-03.pdf.

J. Corneli. *Peer produced peer learning: A mathematics case study.* Ph.D. thesis, The Open University, 2014.

J. Corneli and E. Maclean. The search for computational intelligence. In Y. J. Erden, R. Giovagnoli, and G. Dodig-Crnkovic, editors, *Social Aspects of Cognition and Computing Symposium, Proc. Annual Convention of the Society for the Study of Artificial Intelligence and Simulation of Behaviour (SSAISB)*, University of Kent, Canterbury, UK, 20-22nd April 2015, 2015. http: //www.cs.kent.ac.uk/events/2015/AISB2015/proceedings/ socialComp/papers/SACCS-AISB2015_submission_6.pdf.

J. Corneli, C. J. Danoff, C. Pierce, P. Ricuarte, and L. Snow MacDonald. Patterns of peeragogy. In F. Correia, editor, *Pattern Languages of Programs Conference 2015*

(PLoP15), October 24-26, 2015, Pittsburgh, PA, USA, 2015. `http://www.hillside.net/plop/2015/papers/peopleeducation/19.pdf`.

G. Deleuze. *Difference and Repetition*. 1968. (trans. 2004, Paul Patton, London: Bloomsbury Academic).

P. Dung. On the acceptability of arguments and its fundamental role in nonmonotonic reasoning, logic programming and n-person games. *Artificial Intelligence*, 77(2):321–358, 1995.

A. Flache and R. Hegselmann. Do irregular grids make a difference? Relaxing the spatial regularity assumption in cellular models of social dynamics. *Journal of Artificial Societies and Social Simulation*, 4(4), 2001.

M. Ganesalingam. *The Language of Mathematics*. Springer, 2013.

M. Ganesalingam and W. Gowers. A fully automatic problem solver with human-style output. Technical report, 2013. arXiv:1309.4501v1.

J. Goguen. An introduction to algebraic semiotics, with application to user interface design. In *Computation for metaphors, analogy, and agents*, pages 242–291. Springer, 1999.

J. Goguen. Musical qualia, context, time and emotion. *Journal of consciousness studies*, 11(3-4):117–147, 2004.

J. Goguen. Mathematical models of cognitive space and time. In *Reasoning and Cognition: Proc. of the Interdisciplinary Conference on Reasoning and Cognition*, pages 125–128, 2006.

M. Gordon. From LCF to HOL: A short history. In *Proof, Language, and Interaction*, pages 169–186, 2000.

M. J. Gordon, R. Milner, and C. Wadsworth. *Edinburgh LCF: A mechanised logic of computation*, volume 78 of *Lecture Notes in Computer Science*. Springer, 1979.

W. Gowers and M. Ganesalingam. Modelling the mathematical discovery process, 2012. Maxwell Institute Lecture, Fri, November 2, 4pm – 5pm, James Clerk Maxwell Building, University of Edinburgh.

W. Gowers and M. Nielsen. Massively collaborative mathematics. *Nature*, 461 (7266):879–881, 2009.

E. T. Hall. Improvisation as an acquired, multilevel process. *Ethnomusicology*, pages 223–235, 1992.

C. Hamblin. *Fallacies*. Methuen, London, 1970.

G. Hirst. Context as a spurious concept. *arXiv preprint cmp-lg/9712003*, 1997.

D. Hitchcock. Informal logic and the concept of argument. *Philosophy of logic*, 5: 101–129, 2006.

J. Kilpatrick. *Analyzing the Solution of Word Problems in Mathematics: An Exploratory Study*. Ph.D. thesis, Stanford University, 1967.

P. Kockelman. Biosemiosis, technocognition, and sociogenesis: Selection and significance in a multiverse of sieving and serendipity. *Current Anthropology*, 52(5): 711–739, 2011.

I. Lakatos. *Proofs and Refutations: The Logic of Mathematical Discovery*. Cambridge University Press, 1976.

B. Larvor. Albert Lautman: Dialectics in Mathematics. *Foundations of the Formal Sciences VII*, 2011.

G. Leech and M. Weisser. Generic speech act annotation for task-oriented dialogues. In *Procs. of the 2003 Corpus Linguistics Conference*, pages 441–446. Citeseer, Centre for Computer Corpus Research on Language, Lancaster University, 2003. URL http://www.lancaster.ac.uk/fass/doc_library/linguistics/leechg/leech_and_weisser_2003.pdf.

M. M. Louwerse and S. A. Crossley. Dialog act classification using n-gram algorithms. In *FLAIRS Conference*, pages 758–763, 2006.

J. F. Lucas. An exploratory study of the diagnostic teaching of heuristic problem solving strategies in calculus. In J. G. Harvey and T. A. Romber, editors, *Problem-Solving Studies in Mathematics*, Wisconsin R&D Center Monograph Series. University of Wisconsin-Madison, School of Education, 1980. URL http://files.eric.ed.gov/fulltext/ED197962.pdf.

J. F. Lucas, N. Branca, M. Goldberg, M. G. Kantowski, H. Kellog, and J. P. Smith. A process-sequence coding system for behavioral analysis of mathematical problem solving. In G. Goldin and E. McClintock, editors, *Task Variables in Mathematical Problem Solving*. ERIC, 1980.

J. Martin and A. Gillespie. A neo-Meadian approach to human agency: Relating the social and the psychological in the ontogenesis of perspective-coordinating persons. *Integrative Psychological and Behavioral Science*, 44(3):252–272, 2010.

U. Martin, A. Pease, and J. Corneli. Bootstrapping the next generation of mathematical social machines. In *Off the Beaten Track Workshop at POPL 2017*, 21 January, 2017, Université Pierre et Marie Curie, Paris. 2017.

G. H. Mead. *The Philosophy of the Present*. Open Court, 1932.

R. Milner. Logic for computable functions description of a machine implementation. Technical report, DTIC Document, 1972.

M. Minsky. Essays on education (for OLPC). Technical report, Massachusetts Institute of Technology, 2008–2009. URL http://web.media.mit.edu/~minsky/OLPC-1.html. Available online.

M. Mitchell, P. Hraber, and J. P. Crutchfield. Revisiting the edge of chaos: Evolving cellular automata to perform computations. *Complex Systems*, 7:89–130, 1993.

D. Murray-Rust and D. Robertson. LSCitter: building social machines by augmenting existing social networks with interaction models. In *Proceedings of the companion publication of the 23rd international conference on World wide web companion*, pages 875–880. International World Wide Web Conferences Steering Committee, 2014.

A. Pease, J. Lawrence, K. Budzynska, J. Corneli, and C. Reed. Collaborative mathematics through dialectical, structured and abstract argumentation. *Artificial Intelligence* 246:181-219. Elsevier Science Publishers Ltd. Essex, UK, 2017.

A. Pease, A. Aberdein, U. Martin. The notion of 'simple proof'. Philosophical Transactions of the Royal Society A: Mathematical, Physical & Engineering Sciences, Royal Society, To Appear.

A. Pease, K. Budzynska, J. Lawrence, and C. Reed. Lakatos games for mathematical argument. In S. Parsons, N. Oren, and C. Reed, editors, *Fifth International Conference on Computational Models of Argument*, Frontiers in Artificial Intelligence and Applications. IOS Press, 2014.

A. Pease and U. Martin. Seventy four minutes of mathematics: An analysis of the third Mini-Polymath project. In *Proceedings of AISB/IACAP 2012, Symposium on Mathematical Practice and Cognition II*, 2012. URL http://homepages. inf.ed.ac.uk/apease/papers/seventy-four.pdf.

A. Peldszus and M. Stede. From argument diagrams to argumentation mining in texts: A survey. *International Journal of Cognitive Informatics and Natural Intelligence (IJCINI)*, 7(1):1–31, 2013.

G. Pólya. *Mathematical Discovery: On Understanding, Learning, and Teaching Problem Solving*. John Wiley & Sons, 1981.

G. Pólya. *Mathematics and Plausible Reasoning: Induction and Analogy in Mathematics*, volume 1. Princeton University Press, 1990a.

G. Pólya. *Mathematics and Plausible Reasoning: Patterns of plausible inference*, volume 2. Princeton University Press, 1990b.

G. Pólya. *How to Solve it: A New Aspect of Mathematical Method*. Princeton University Press, 2014.

H. Prakken. Formal systems for persuasion dialogue. *The Knowledge Engineering Review*, 21(02):163–188, 2006.

H. Prakken. An abstract framework for argumentation with structured arguments. *Argument and Computation*, 1, 2010.

I. Rahwan, F. Zablith, and C. Reed. Laying the foundations for a world wide argument web. *Artificial Intelligence*, 171:897–921, 2007.

C. Reed and K. Budzynska. How dialogues create arguments. In F. van Eemeren et al., editors, *Proceedings of the 7th Conference of the International Society for the Study of Argumentation (ISSA 2010)*. Sic Sat, 2011.

C. Reed, S. Wells, K. Budzynska, and J. Devereux. Building arguments with argumentation: the role of illocutionary force in computational models of argument. In *COMMA*, pages 415–426, 2010.

G. Restall. Logics, situations and channels. *Journal of Cognitive Science*, 6(2): 125–150, 2005.

D. Robertson. A lightweight coordination calculus for agent systems. In *Declarative agent languages and technologies II*, pages 183–197. Springer, 2005.

A. H. Schoenfeld. Can heuristics be taught? *Cognitive process instruction*, pages 315–338, 1979.

A. H. Schoenfeld. *Mathematical Problem Solving*. Academic Press, 1985.

A. H. Schoenfeld. What's all the fuss about metacognition. In A. H. Schoenfeld, editor, *Cognitive science and mathematics education*, pages 189–215. Lawrence Erlbaum Associates, 1987.

A. H. Schoenfeld. *How We Think: A theory of Goal-Oriented Decision Making and its Educational Applications*. Routledge, 2010.

R. Sennett. *Together: The Rituals, Pleasures and Politics of Cooperation*. Yale University Press, 2012.

P. Singh. *EM-ONE: an architecture for reflective commonsense thinking*. Ph.D. thesis, Massachusetts Institute of Technology, 2005.

M. Sipper. *Evolution of Parallel Cellular Machines*. Springer Heidelberg, 1997.

J. F. Sowa. Syntax, semantics, and pragmatics of contexts. In *Conceptual Structures: Applications, Implementation and Theory*, pages 1–15. Springer, 1995.

D. Sperber and D. Wilson. Pragmatics, modularity and mind-reading. *Mind & Language*, 17(1-2):3–23, 2002.

C. Stab and I. Gurevych. Identifying argumentative discourse structures in persuasive essays. In *Conference on Empirical Methods in Natural Language Processing (EMNLP 2014)*, pp. 46–56. Association for Computational Linguistics, Oct. 2014.

G. Stahl. *Group Cognition: Computer Support for Building Collaborative Knowledge*. MIT Press, Cambridge, MA, 2006.

G. Stahl. *Studying Virtual Math Teams*. Springer, 1st edition, Sep 2010. ISBN 1441956778. URL http://gerrystahl.net/vmt/book/studying.pdf.

G. Stahl. *Translating Euclid: Creating a Human-Centered Mathematics*. Morgan & Claypool, 2013. URL http://gerrystahl.net/pub/translating.pdf.

A. Stolcke, K. Ries, N. Coccaro, E. Shriberg, R. Bates, D. Jurafsky, P. Taylor, R. Martin, C. Van Ess-Dykema, and M. Meteer. Dialogue act modeling for automatic tagging and recognition of conversational speech. *Computational linguistics*, 26(3):339–373, 2000.

T. Tao et al. Minipolymath1 project. https://terrytao.wordpress.com/2009/07/20/imo-2009-q6-as-a-mini-polymath-project/, July 2009.

T. Tao et al. Minipolymath3 project. http://polymathprojects.org/2011/07/19/minipolymath3-project-2011-imo/, July 2011.

W. Thurston. On proof and progress in mathematics. *Bulletin (New Series) of the American Mathematical Society*, 30(2):161–177, 1994.

D. Walton. How can logic best be applied to arguments? *Logic Journal of IGPL*, 5 (4):603–614, 1997.

D. Walton. Is there a burden of questioning? *Artificial Intelligence and Law*, 11(1): 1–43, 2003.

B. Webber, M. Egg, and V. Kordoni. Discourse structure and language technology. *Natural Language Engineering*, 18(4):437–490, 2012.

M. Wolska and I. Kruijff-Korbayová. Analysis of mixed natural and symbolic language input in mathematical dialogs. In *Proceedings of the 42nd Annual Meeting on Association for Computational Linguistics*, page 25. Association for Computational Linguistics, 2004.

Part III
Concept Invention System and Applications

Chapter 7
Enabling Technologies for Concept Invention

Roberto Confalonieri, Tarek Besold, Mihai Codescu, and Manfred Eppe

Abstract The goal of the COINVENT project was not only to develop a novel, computationally feasible, formal model of conceptual blending that was sufficiently precise for capturing the fundamental insights of Fauconnier and Turner's theory, but also to implement a creative computational system based on this novel formal model. In this chapter, we overview COBBLE, the concept invention system prototype that we developed, and we describe its enabling technologies. The technologies we adopted and developed draw from interdisciplinary fields from ontologies, analogical reasoning, logic programming and formal methods.

7.1 Introduction

For humans conceptual blending is effortless. We are able to create new blends spontaneously and have no difficulty to understand new conceptual blends when we encounter them. This includes the identification of a relevant generic space, the identification of irrelevant features of the input spaces, the performance of the blend, and

Roberto Confalonieri
Free University of Bozen-Bolzano, Faculty of Computer Science, Dominikanerplatz 3, 39100, Bozen-Bolzano, Italy. e-mail: `Roberto.Confalonieri@unibz.it`

Tarek R. Besold
Digital Media Lab, Center for Computing and Communication Technologies (TZI), University of Bremen, Bibliothekstr. 5, D-28359 Bremen, Germany. e-mail: `tbesold@uni-bremen.de`

Mihai Codescu
Free University of Bozen-Bolzano, Faculty of Computer Science, Dominikanerplatz 3, 39100, Bozen-Bolzano, Italy. e-mail: `Mihai.Codescu@unibz.it`

Manfred Eppe
International Computer Science Institute, 1947 Center Street, Berkeley, CA-94704, USA. e-mail: `eppe@icsi.berkeley.edu`

© Springer Nature Switzerland AG 2018
R. Confalonieri et al. (eds.), *Concept Invention*, Computational Synthesis and Creative Systems, https://doi.org/10.1007/978-3-319-65602-1_7

the evaluation of the usefulness of the blend. In contrast, for an automated system each of these steps provides several challenges.

When implementing conceptual blending, even before facing the problem of identifying a relevant generic space, one needs to decide how to represent the input spaces. Rich, formal, but tractable representation languages are needed to model them. Algebraic specifications (Mosses, 2004), ontologies and formal logics (Mossakowski et al., 2015) are good candidates for this since they have clear semantics. Nevertheless, one has to find a tradeoff between expressiveness and computation, and focus on those languages for which efficient tools exist.

Then, when combining two input spaces, the shared semantic structure is of particular importance to steer possible combinations of blends. This shared semantic structure leads to the notion of generic space. Finding a generic space is a complex task since there may be different ways of looking for it. Elements within input spaces can be renamed before they are mapped one to another (Eppe et al., 2018, 2015), or they can be generalised by using refinement operators (Confalonieri et al., 2018; Troquard et al, 2018; Porello et al, 2018), or using some forms of anti-unification (Schwering et al., 2009), or they can be simply removed.

In general, the development of a computational framework for concept invention requires the implementation of a *workflow*, that enacts a concept invention process (see Chapters 2 and 3), and orchestrates different technologies and tools. Within the literature on conceptual blending, there exist only few attempts focusing on computational aspects, and infrastructures supporting computational creativity, and concept invention in particular, are scarce.

Notable approaches include (Goguen and Harrell, 2010; Pereira, 2007; Veale and Donoghue, 2000; Veale, 2012; Žnidaršič et al., 2016). Goguen and Harrell (2010) logically formalise conceptual blending in terms of algebraic theories, but the generic space is manually provided and optimality principles are not modelled. Pereira (2007) captures many elements of conceptual blending, but the notion of generic space is replaced by a generic domain that participates in all blend computations. The work by Veale and Donoghue (2000); Veale (2012) is a computational model of metaphor and analogy, which can be interpreted as blending, but its expressiveness is limited to the representation of simple graphs of concepts. ConCreTeFlows (Žnidaršič et al., 2016) is a Web- and cloud-based infrastructure that allows one to specify, execute and publish online workflows in order to implement computational creativity applications, also allowing one to specify a workflow for conceptual blending.

In the COINVENT project, we implemented the COBBLE system. COBBLE instantiates the amalgam-based concept invention model we developed (see Chapter 1), which is based on Goguen's proposal of a Unified Concept Theory (Goguen, 1999), and enacts the concept invention process described in Chapter 2. To this end, it represents input spaces as semiotic systems, it adopts and implements different solutions for computing a generic space, and it computes the blends as *colimits* of algebraic specifications. COBBLE implements a workflow for concept invention, and exposes its functionalities as RESTful APIs that can be used by other systems. In the following, we overview COBBLE and the technologies we used to implement it.

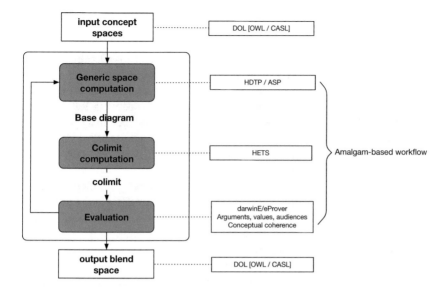

Fig. 7.1: COBBLE system architecture and enabling technologies

7.2 System Architecture and Enabling Technologies

The architecture of the COBBLE system is shown in Figure 7.1. It consists of several components, each of them responsible to carry out the following tasks:

- **Generic space computation module:** given two input concept spaces, this module finds their common structure or generic space. Finding the generic space is achieved in two ways: using HDTP (Schmidt et al., 2014) or using Answer Set Programming (Gelfond and Kahl, 2014). Both approaches find several candidate generic spaces. The main difference is that the ASP-based approach also finds all the generalised versions of the input spaces that lead to a generic space. The output of both modules is a base diagram that includes the generic space, the generalised input spaces and their morphisms.
- **Colimit computation module:** this module implements the colimit computation, which is the categorical operation used to compute a blend given two input spaces, a generic space, and the corresponding morphisms. The output of this module is a blending diagram.
- **Evaluation module:** this module evaluates the blends. The evaluation can be performed in different ways which usually depend on the application domain. Blends can be evaluated in terms of logical consistency, blending metrics such as optimality principles (Eppe et al., 2015), or by means of arguments and values, or conceptual coherence (Confalonieri et al., 2016b; Schorlemmer et al., 2016).

The modules of the COBBLE system were implemented using the following technologies and computational frameworks:

- **DOL:** The Distributed Ontology, Modeling and Specification Language (DOL)
  is an international ontology interoperability standard that provides a unified
  metalanguage for employing an open-ended number of formal logics (Mossakowski et al., 2015). In particular, DOL provides constructs for 'as-is' use
  of Ontologies, Models and Specifications (OMS) formulated in a specific ontology or specification language such as the Web Ontology Language (OWL) and
  CASL (Astesiano et al., 2002), and networks of OMS, including networks that
  specify blending diagrams.
- **ASP:** Answer Set Programming (ASP) is a declarative programming framework
  suitable to solve computational complex problems (Gelfond and Kahl, 2014).
  In COBBLE, the search for a generic space between two input spaces is implemented as a planning problem modeled in ASP, where actions are generalisation
  refinement operations over an input space, and the goal state is to make the two
  input spaces equivalent (Eppe et al., 2015; Confalonieri et al., 2018). ASP supports the specification of blends as amalgams (see Chapter 2, Section 2.3) and
  the implementation of an amalgam-based concept blending workflow according
  to which blends are generated by using different combinations of generalised
  input spaces.
- **HDTP:** The Heuristic Driven Theory Projection (HDTP) (Schmidt et al., 2014)
  is an analogy reasoner based on a restricted form of higher-order anti-unification
  that computes the structural commonalities between two input domains represented in a variant of first-order logic. In COBBLE, HDTP is used to find the
  generic space of two input space theories specified using a subset of the CASL
  specification language.
- **HETS:** the HEterogeneous Tool Set (HETS) system (Mossakowski et al.,
  2007) is a parsing, static analysis and proof management tool incorporating
  various provers and different specification languages, thus providing a tool for
  heterogeneous specifications. It supports the colimit computation of CASL and
  OWL theories and checks their logical consistency using theorem provers such
  as *Eprover* (Schulz, 2002) and *Darwin* (Baumgartner et al., 2004).
- **Arguments, values and audiences:** we specified an argumentation framework
  that makes use of values and audiences to generate arguments promoting and
  demoting a set of blends in order to decide which blends to keep or to reject
  (Confalonieri et al., 2016b).
- **Conceptual coherence:** we implemented a computational framework of conceptual coherence for description logic to decide which blends to accept or reject based on the coherence of the internal structure w.r.t. the input spaces and
  the generic space (Schorlemmer et al., 2016).

We consider the set of technologies and frameworks described above as *enabling
technologies* for concept invention. Each module was implemented as an independent component accessible by means of a RESTful API interface (Maclean and Winterstein, 2016). In this way, we were able to implement a system that is modular

and we have promoted the reusability of its functionalities. For instance, the generic space module API could be in principle re-used by other computational creativity infrastructures, such as ConCreTeFlows for instance, that need to find the generic space between two domain specifications.,

In the following sections, we overview some of these technologies. In particular, we describe how the generic space is computed in ASP and HDTP, and how a colimit is computed in the HETS system. The DOL language was already overviewed in Chapter 3, whereas a description of the argumentation and conceptual coherence frameworks can be found in Chapter 2, Sections 2.4 and 2.5 respectively.

7.3 Generalising Algebraic Specifications Using ASP

Answer Set Programming (ASP) is a declarative approach to solve NP-hard search problems (Gelfond and Kahl, 2014; Baral, 2003). ASP is often used for deliberation of autonomous systems (Eppe and Bhatt, 2013; Eppe et al., 2014) and other forms of logical reasoning, such as epistemic or abductive inference (Eppe and Bhatt, 2015), decision making under uncertainty (Confalonieri and Prade, 2014), and preference reasoning (Confalonieri and Nieves, 2011). In this work, we explore its use for computational creativity and logical theory generalisation.

An ASP program is similar to a Prolog program in that it follows a non-monotonic semantics, takes logic programming style Horn clauses as input, and uses negation-as-failure. However, instead of using Kowalski (1974)'s SLDNF resolution semantics as in Prolog, it employs Gelfond and Lifschitz (1988)'s *stable model semantics*, which makes it truly declarative. This means that the order in which ASP rules appear in a logic program does not affect the solution. Furthermore, the stable model semantics has the advantage that Answer Set Programs always terminate, while Prolog programs do not. For example, given a program $p \leftarrow not\ q.$ and $q \leftarrow not\ p.$, asking whether p holds results in an infinite loop for Prolog, while ASP returns two stable models as solution, namely the sets $\{p\}$ and $\{q\}$.

An ASP program consists of a set of rules, facts and constraints. Its solutions are called *stable models*. In this paper, we only consider so-called *normal* rules (Baral, 2003), which are written as:

$$a_0 \leftarrow a_1, \ldots, a_j, not\ a_{j+1}, \ldots, not\ a_n \tag{7.1}$$

in which $a_1, \ldots, a_n$ are atoms and *not* is negation-as-failure. When $n = 0$ the rule $a_0 \leftarrow$ is called a *fact* and the $\leftarrow$ is omitted. A constraint is a rule of the form $\leftarrow a_1, \ldots, a_j, not\ a_{j+1}, \ldots, not\ a_n$. Constraints are rules that are used to discard some models of a logic program.

The stable models of an ASP program are defined in terms of the so-called *Gelfond-Lifschitz reduction* (Gelfond and Lifschitz, 1988). Let $\mathscr{L}_P$ be the set of atoms in the language of a normal logic program P, then for any set $M \subseteq \mathscr{L}_P$, the

Gelfond-Lifschitz reduction P^M is the definite logic program obtained from P by deleting:

(i) each rule that has a formula *not a* in its body with $a \in M$, and
(ii) all formulæ of the form *not a* in the bodies of the remaining rules.

P^M does not contain *not* and M is called a *stable model* of P if and only if M is the minimal model of P^M. A stable model M of an ASP program P contains those atoms that satisfy all the rules in the program and, consequently, represents a solution of the problem that the program P represents.

ASP is interesting because it can capture complex knowledge representation problems, and also because efficient ASP implementations, such as *clingo* (Gebser et al., 2014), exist. The *clingo* solver offers a step-oriented, incremental approach that allows us to control and modify an ASP program at run-time, without the need of restarting the grounding of the solving process from scratch. To this end, a program is partitioned into a *base* part, describing the static knowledge independent of a step parameter t, a *cumulative* part, capturing knowledge accumulating with increasing t, and a *volatile* part specific for each value of t. The grounding and integration of these subprograms into the solving process is completely modular and controllable from a scripting language such as Python.

The ASP implementation we describe here follows this methodology of specifying and solving a problem incrementally. For further details about incremental solving, we refer to Gebser et al. (2015).

7.3.1 Modeling Input Spaces Using CASL

Goguen (1999) proposes to model the input concepts of blending as *semiotic systems*, which are essentially *algebraic specifications* described in a logical representation language. The main advantage of this approach is being able to provide a general enough, but computational feasible representation, while being able to resolve inconsistencies. We represent semiotic systems by using the Common Algebraic Specification Language (CASL) (Mosses, 2004).

Definition 7.1 (CASL specification). A CASL specification is a tuple $\mathfrak{s} = \langle \mathscr{S}\mathscr{T}, \underset{\sim}{\lesssim}, \mathscr{O}, \mathscr{P}, \mathscr{A} \rangle$ with:

- a set $\mathscr{S}\mathscr{T}$ of sorts, along with a preorder $\underset{\sim}{\lesssim}$ that defines a sub-sort relationship;
- a set $\mathscr{O}$ of operators $o : s_1 \times \cdots \times s_n \mapsto s_r$ that map zero or more objects of argument sorts $s_1, \cdots, s_n$ to a range sort s_r;
- a set $\mathscr{P}$ of predicates $p : s_1 \times \cdots \times s_n$ that map zero or more objects of argument sorts $s_1, \cdots, s_n$ to Boolean values;
- a set $\mathscr{A}$ of axioms;

We refer to the listed constituents of a CASL specification simply as the *elements*, denoted by e, and we say that two CASL specifications are *compatible* if all of their elements are equal.

spec HOUSE = BACKGROUND
then sorts *House* < *Thing*
           Person < *Thing*
    ops *house* : *House*;
       resident : *Resident*
    pred *liveIn* : *Resident* × *House*
    • *liveIn*(resident,house)
    • *on*(*house*) = *land*
    • ∀*h* : *House*, *r* : *Resident*
        • *liveIn*(*r*,*h*) ⇒ *inside*(*r*,*h*)
end

spec BOAT = BACKGROUND
then sorts *Boat* < *Thing*
           Passenger < *Thing*
    ops *boat* : *Boat*;
       passenger : *Passenger*
    pred *ride* : *Passenger* × *Boat*
    • *ride*(passenger,boat)
    • *on*(*boat*) = *water*
    • ∀*b* : *Boat*, *p* : *Passenger*
        • *ride*(*p*,*b*) ⇒ *inside*(*p*,*b*)
end

Fig. 7.2: The house and boat specifications in CASL

A classical concept blending example is the blend between the concepts house and boat (Goguen, 1999; Fauconnier and Turner, 2002). In Figure 7.2 we depict the axiomatisation of these concepts which is similar to how they are proposed by Goguen and Harrell (2006).

The CASL theories for HOUSE and BOAT introduce the sorts, operators and predicates that form the mental spaces *house* and *boat* by focusing on particular properties of these concepts necessary for understanding the basic meaning of the term, *house* and *boat*. A BACKGROUND CASL theory is used to define the sort THING, *land* and *water* as types of *medium*, the *on* operator, and *inside* as an anti-symmetric and transitive predicate. Given this background, in HOUSE, a 'house' is located on a plot of land and a person is a resident living in it. Similarly, in BOAT, a 'boat' is on water and a person is a passenger riding it.

7.3.2 Finding the Generic Space

Finding a generic space between two CASL specifications essentially means to determine which elements these specifications have in common, by considering their sorts, operators and axioms.

The problem of finding a generic space is computationally hard. We have employed ASP in order to model it as a planning problem through which we identify sequences of theory transitions that lead to a generic space. According to this approach, input spaces are generalised until they are equal and, therefore all possible generalisations of the input spaces are considered.

A theory transition can be either the removal of an element (generalisation) or the renaming of an element in a specification. Towards this, the input CASL specifications (s_1, s_2, from now on) are first translated into ASP facts, as described in Section 7.3.2.1. Second, elements in s_1, s_2 are renamed and generalised by sequences of theory transitions that are guided by an ASP solver until a generic space is found. Each transition is represented by a fact $exec(\gamma, s, t)$, where t is an iterator and γ is a transition operator that removes or renames elements in the input specifications (see Section 7.3.2.2). The execution of transition operators is repeated until the generalised versions of the input specifications are equivalent (Definition 7.1). We write $\mathfrak{s}(t)$ to denote the specification that results form the t-th transition of $\mathfrak{s}$. For example, after the first theory transition, the *house* concept might be the concept of a house that is not situated on any medium.

Once a set of transitions that leads to a generic space has been identified, blend candidates are generated by an amalgam-based process that combines generalised input specifications (see Chapter 2, Section 2.3). Each blend is calculated as a *colimit*, a category-theoretical operation that is implemented in the HETS system (Mossakowski et al., 2007). Theorem provers such as *Eprover* (Schulz, 2002) and *Darwin* (Baumgartner et al., 2004), which are embedded in HETS, are then queried in order to check for consistency.

For the sake of the house-boat example, a consistent house-boat blend is the combination of the generalised *boat* on the medium water, but without a passenger, and a generalised *house* with a resident, but without a medium, where 'passenger' in 'boat' is renamed to 'resident' in house.

Blend generation is not covered here and the way in which a colimit is computed in HETS can be found in Section 7.5. Also, note that different stable models, and therefore different generalisations and renamings, can be found by the ASP solver. Each combination leads to a different set of blends that needs to be evaluated. This can be done using certain metrics that are inspired by Fauconnier and Turner (2002)'s *optimality principles* of blending to assess the quality of the blend. This is not covered here and we refer the interested reader to Eppe et al. (2015, 2018).

7.3.2.1 Modelling Algebraic Specifications in ASP

In order to find the generic space and to avoid inconsistencies that arise from the naive combination of input specifications, CASL specifications are generalised using transition operators in a step-wise search process.

Firstly, renaming operators modify specifications by renaming their elements. Secondly, generalisation operators modify algebraic specifications by removing operators, sorts, predicates or axioms. In the following, we use t to denote a step-counter that represents the number of transitions that a specification has undergone. With this, we represent CASL specifications in ASP as follows:

▶ For each *sort* s in a specification $\mathfrak{s}$ with a parent sort s_p we state the facts:

$$sort(\mathfrak{s},s,t) \tag{7.2a}$$

$$hasParent(\mathfrak{s},s,s_p,t) \tag{7.2b}$$

A fact (7.2a) assigns a sort s to a specification $\mathfrak{s}$ at a step t, and (7.2b) assigns a parent sort.

▶ For each *operator* $o : s_1 \times \cdots \times s_n \mapsto s_r$ in a specification $\mathfrak{s}$ we have:

$$op(\mathfrak{s},o,t) \qquad (7.3a)$$

$$opHasSort(\mathfrak{s},o,s_1,1,t) \quad \cdots \quad opHasSort(\mathfrak{s},o,s_n,n,t) \qquad (7.3b)$$

$$opHasSort(\mathfrak{s},o,s_r,rng,t) \qquad (7.3c)$$

Facts (7.3b) and (7.3c) state the argument sorts and the range sorts of an operator. $1\ldots n$ determine the position of the argument sort and rng is simply a constant to denote that the sort is the range sort of the operator.

▶ Similarly, for each *predicate* $p : s_1 \times \cdots \times s_n$ in $\mathfrak{s}$ we generate the facts:

$$pred(\mathfrak{s},p,t) \qquad (7.4a)$$

$$predHasSort(\mathfrak{s},p,s_1,1,t) \cdots predHasSort(\mathfrak{s},p,s_n,n,t) \qquad (7.4b)$$

▶ For each *axiom a* we determine an equivalence class of that axiom, denoted eq^a, by passing the axiom to a respective Python function.[1] All logically equivalent axioms have the same equivalence class, e.g., $\neg a \vee b$ has the same equivalence class as $a \rightarrow b$. We also determine the elements, i.e, sorts, operators and predicates, that are involved in an axiom. This information is used in the preconditions of removal operators. For example, operator removal has the precondition that there exists no atom that involves the operator. Having computed the equivalence class eq^a and determined n_e elements that are involved in an axiom, we generate the following facts for each axiom a in a specification $\mathfrak{s}$.

$$ax(\mathfrak{s},a,t) \qquad (7.5a)$$

$$axInvolvesElem(\mathfrak{s},a,e_1,t) \quad \cdots \quad axInvolvesElem(\mathfrak{s},a,e_{n_e},t) \qquad (7.5b)$$

$$axHasEqClass(\mathfrak{s},a,eq^a,t) \qquad (7.5c)$$

Compatibility among two input specifications, as defined in Definition 7.1, is represented by atoms $incompatible(\mathfrak{s}_1,\mathfrak{s}_2,t)$, which are triggered by additional LP rules if, for $\mathfrak{s}_1$ and $\mathfrak{s}_2$, at step t, i) sorts or subsort relationships are not equal, or ii) operator or predicate names are not equal, or iii) argument and range sorts of operators and predicates are not equal, or iv) axioms are not equivalent.

Example 7.1. Let us consider the CASL theory of the HOUSE in Figure 7.2. Sorts, operators and axioms are translated to ASP facts as follows:[2]

---

[1] Ideally, one would check for logical equivalence of axioms. However, since FOL is generally undecidable we check for syntactic equivalence of normalized versions of axioms in the current version of our framework. Logical equivalence would be more difficult to solve due to the undecidability of FOL.

[2] Only some sorts, operators and axioms are shown.

spec HOUSE	$spec(sHouse)$.	
$House < Thing$	$hasSort(sHouse, House, 0)$. $hasParentSort(sHouse, House, Thing, 0)$.	By Eq. 7.2
op $house : House$	$hasOp(sHouse, opHouse, 0)$. $opHasSort(sHouse, opHouse, House, rng, 0)$. $hasNumArgs(sHouse, opHouse, 0)$.	By Eq. 7.3
pred $liveIn : Resident * House$	$hasPred(sHouse, opLivein, 0)$. $predHasSort(sHouse, opLivein, Resident, arg1, 0)$. $predHasSort(sHouse, opLivein, House, arg2, 0)$. $hasNumArgs(sHouse, opLivein, 2)$.	By Eq. 7.4
•$liveIn(resident, house)$	$hasAxiom(sHouse, 2, 0)$. $axHasEquivalenceClass(sHouse, 2, 2, 0)$. $axInvolvesPredOp(sHouse, 2, opLivein, 0)$. $axInvolvesPredOp(sHouse, 2, opInside, 0)$. $axInvolvesSort(sHouse, 2, Resident, 0)$. $axInvolvesSort(sHouse, 2, House, 0)$.	By Eq. 7.5

7.3.2.2 Formalising Transition Operators in ASP

We consider two kinds of transition operators for CASL specifications. The first kind involves the renaming of an element to the name of an element in another input specification. Since we consider syntactically equal elements to be conceptually equal in our implementation, this can be seen as identifying the commonalities among input spaces. The second kind is generalisation and involves the removal of an element in a specification. Generalisation operators are executed after all renaming actions have happened.

Each generalisation operator is defined via a precondition rule, an inertia rule, and, in case of renaming operations, an effect rule. Preconditions are modelled with a predicate *poss* that states when it is possible to execute a transition, and inertia is modelled with a predicate *noninertial* that states when an element of a specification stays as it is after a transition. Effect rules model how a transition operator changes an input specification. We represent the execution of a transition operator with atoms $exec(\gamma, \mathfrak{s}, t)$, to denote that a generalisation operator γ was applied to $\mathfrak{s}$ at a step t.

Removal operators. A fact $exec(rm(e), \mathfrak{s}, t)$ denotes the removal of an element e from a specification $\mathfrak{s}$ at a step t. It has different precondition rules for removing axioms (7.6a), operators (7.6b), predicates (7.6c) and sorts (7.6d):

$$poss(rm(e), s, t) \leftarrow ax(s, e, t), exOtherSpecWithoutEqivAx(s, e, t) \qquad (7.6a)$$

$$poss(rm(e), s, t) \leftarrow op(s, e, t), exOtherSpecWithoutElem(s, e, t), \qquad (7.6b)$$
$$0\{ax(s, A, t) : axInvolvesElem(s, A, e, t)\}0$$

$$poss(rm(e), s, t) \leftarrow pred(s, e, t), exOtherSpecWithoutElem(s, e, t), \qquad (7.6c)$$
$$0\{ax(s, A, t) : axInvolvesElem(s, A, e, t)\}0,$$

$$poss(rm(e), s, t) \leftarrow sort(s, e, t), exOtherSpecWithoutElem(s, e, t), \qquad (7.6d)$$
$$0\{ax(s, A, t) : axInvolvesElem(s, A, e, t)\}0$$
$$noOpUsesSort(s, e, t), noPredUsesSort(s, e, t),$$
$$isNotParentSort(s, e, t)$$

The precondition (7.6a) for removing an axiom from a specification is that an atom *exOtherSpecWithoutEqivAx(s,e,t)* holds. Such atoms are produced if there exists at least one other specification[3] that does not have an axiom of the same logical equivalence class. For the removal of other elements we have a similar precondition, i.e., *exOtherSpecWithoutElem(s,e,t)*, which denotes that an element can only be removed if it is not involved in another specification. Such preconditions are required to allow only generic spaces that are *least general* for all input specifications, in the sense that elements cannot be removed if they are contained in all specifications. We also require operators, predicates and sorts not to be involved in any axiom before they can be removed (denoted by $0\{ax(s, A, t) : axInvolvesElem(s, A, e, t)\}0$). Precondition (7.6d) for removing sorts has the additional requirement that no operator or predicate with an argument or range of the sort to be removed exists in the specification, which is implemented with *noOpUsesSort* and *noPredUsesSort* facts respectively. These are triggered by additional (simple) LP rules that we omit. Another condition for sort removal is that the sort is not the parent sort of another sort. Consequently, for sort removal, all axioms, operators and predicates that involve the sort must be removed first, and child sorts must also be removed first. The inertial rules for removing elements from a specification are quite simple:

$$noninertial(s, e, t) \leftarrow exec(rm(e), s, t) \qquad (7.7)$$

All *noninertial* atoms will cause an element e to remain in a specification (see rule (7.11)).

Renaming operators. A fact $exec(rename(e, e', s'), s, t)$ denotes the renaming of an element e of a specification s to an element e' in a specification s'. In contrast to removal, renaming can only be applied to predicates, operators and sorts. Axioms are automatically rewritten according to the renamings of the involved elements. Again, we have different preconditions for renaming operators (7.8a), predicates (7.8b) and sorts (7.8c):

---

[3] We focus on only two specifications here, but the approach can in general also be applied to more than two specifications.

$$poss(rename(e,e',\mathfrak{s}'),\mathfrak{s},t) \leftarrow op(\mathfrak{s},e,t), op(\mathfrak{s}',e',t), \tag{7.8a}$$
$$not\ opSortsNotEquivalent(\mathfrak{s},e,\mathfrak{s}',e',t),$$
$$not\ op(\mathfrak{s},e',t), not\ op(\mathfrak{s}',e,t), \mathfrak{s} \neq \mathfrak{s}'$$

$$poss(rename(e,e',\mathfrak{s}'),\mathfrak{s},t) \leftarrow pred(\mathfrak{s},e,t), pred(\mathfrak{s}',e',t), \tag{7.8b}$$
$$not\ predSortsNotEquivalent(\mathfrak{s},e,\mathfrak{s}',e',t),$$
$$not\ pred(\mathfrak{s},e',t), not\ pred(\mathfrak{s}',e,t), \mathfrak{s} \neq \mathfrak{s}'$$

$$poss(rename(e,e',\mathfrak{s}'),\mathfrak{s},t) \leftarrow sort(\mathfrak{s},e,t), sort(\mathfrak{s}',e',t), \tag{7.8c}$$
$$not\ sort(\mathfrak{s},e',t), not\ sort(\mathfrak{s}',e,t)$$

A common precondition for all three renaming operations is that the element e must exist in the specification $\mathfrak{s}$, and that e' must exist in $\mathfrak{s}'$. Furthermore, it must not be the case that e' is already part of $\mathfrak{s}$, and that e is part of $\mathfrak{s}'$. In case of renaming operators and predicates, the argument and range sorts of e and e' must also be equivalent for the renaming to become possible. For example, an operator $on : Thing \mapsto Medium$ cannot be mapped to an operator $liveIn : Thing \mapsto Person$, which has a different range sort. The inertia rules for renaming elements e in a specification are analogous to the inertial rule for removing elements:

$$noninertial(\mathfrak{s},e,t) \leftarrow exec(rename(e,e',\mathfrak{s}'),\mathfrak{s},t) \tag{7.9}$$

For renaming, we have the following set of effect rules that assign the new name for the respective element:

$$sort(\mathfrak{s},e',t+1) \leftarrow exec(rename(e,e',\mathfrak{s}'),\mathfrak{s},t), sort(\mathfrak{s},e,t) \tag{7.10a}$$

$$hasParent(\mathfrak{s},s',s_p,t+1) \leftarrow hasParent(\mathfrak{s},s,s_p,t), \tag{7.10b}$$
$$exec(rename(s,s',\mathfrak{s}'),\mathfrak{s},t)$$

$$hasParent(\mathfrak{s},s,s'_p,t+1) \leftarrow hasParent(\mathfrak{s},s,s_p,t), \tag{7.10c}$$
$$exec(rename(s_p,s'_p,\mathfrak{s}'),\mathfrak{s},t)$$

$$opHasSort(\mathfrak{s},o,s',n,t+1) \leftarrow opHasSort(\mathfrak{s},o,s,n,t), \tag{7.10d}$$
$$exec(rename(s,s',\mathfrak{s}'),\mathfrak{s},t)$$

$$predHasSort(\mathfrak{s},p,s',n,t+1) \leftarrow predHasSort(\mathfrak{s},p,s,n,t), \tag{7.10e}$$
$$exec(rename(s,s',\mathfrak{s}'),\mathfrak{s},t)$$

$$op(\mathfrak{s},o',t+1) \leftarrow exec(rename(o,o',\mathfrak{s}'),\mathfrak{s},t), op(\mathfrak{s},o,t) \tag{7.10f}$$

$$opHasSort(\mathfrak{s},o',s,n,t+1) \leftarrow opHasSort(\mathfrak{s},o,s,n,t), \tag{7.10g}$$
$$exec(rename(o,o',\mathfrak{s}'),\mathfrak{s},t)$$

$$pred(\mathfrak{s},p',t+1) \leftarrow exec(rename(p,p',\mathfrak{s}'),\mathfrak{s},t), pred(\mathfrak{s},p,t) \tag{7.10h}$$

$$predHasSort(\mathfrak{s},p',s,n,t+1) \leftarrow predHasSort(\mathfrak{s},p,s,n,t), \tag{7.10i}$$
$$exec(rename(p,p',\mathfrak{s}'),\mathfrak{s},t)$$

$$axInvolvesElem(\mathfrak{s},a,e',t+1) \leftarrow axInvolvesElem(\mathfrak{s},a,e,t), \tag{7.10j}$$
$$exec(rename(e,e',\mathfrak{s}'),\mathfrak{s},t)$$

In general, the rules state that a specification will contain an element e' at a step $t+1$ if an element e has been renamed to e' at step t. Rules (7.10a – 7.10e) state how renaming sorts affects the generalization. It also considers the effects on parent-child relations as well as predicate and operator arguments and range. Rules (7.10f, 7.10g) and (7.10h, 7.10i) describe the effects of renaming operators and predicates respectively. Rule (7.10j) states how the auxiliary predicate *axInvolvesElem* is affected by renaming.

Inertia. In order to use the inertia rules (Eq. 7.7 and Eq. 7.9), we need the following rules to state that elements e remain in a specification s if they are inertial:

$$sort(s,e,t+1) \leftarrow not\ noninertial(s,e,t), sort(s,e,t) \tag{7.11a}$$
$$op(s,e,t+1) \leftarrow not\ noninertial(s,e,t), op(s,e,t) \tag{7.11b}$$
$$pred(s,e,t+1) \leftarrow not\ noninertial(s,e,t), pred(s,e,t) \tag{7.11c}$$
$$ax(s,e,t+1) \leftarrow not\ noninertial(s,e,t), ax(s,e,t) \tag{7.11d}$$

Updating axiom equivalence. When operators, predicates or sorts that are involved in an axiom are renamed, then the axiom's equivalent class changes. Determining logical equivalence of FOL axioms is a well understood research domain on its own, and we make use of existing theorem proving tools here. Towards this, we use an external Python function *renElAndGetNewEqClass* in rule (7.12) during the ASP solving process, which updates the equivalence class by querying theorem proving tools that determine a new equivalence class for an axiom if elements are renamed. This happens by accessing an internal dictionary of axioms within Python, that is built dynamically during the ASP grounding process.

$$axHasEqClass(s,a,eq^a_{new},t+1) \leftarrow axHasEqClass(s,a,eq^a,t), \tag{7.12}$$
$$exec(rename(s,e_1,e_2,t),$$
$$axInvolvesElem(s,a,e_1,t), ax(s,a,t),$$
$$eq^a_{new} = @renElAndGetNewEqClass(eq^a,e_1,e_2)$$

Additional rules that update the *axInvolvesElem* atoms if elements are renamed are also part of our implementation.

7.3.2.3 Generic Space Search Process

The search process implemented in ASP finds a generic space by successively applying transition operators to the input specifications. To this end, we first apply only renaming operators to find the commonalities among input specifications. Then, we generalise elements that the input specifications do not have in common by applying removal operators. Note that a simple intersection operation (as in set theory) is not possible because of the preconditions that the transition operators have. These impose a strong restriction on the allowed order in which transition operators may occur and make the problem inherently non-monotonic.

A sequence of transition operators defines a *transition path*, which itself consists of a *commonalisation path* followed by a *removal path*.

Definition 7.2 (Transition path). Let $\mathscr{S} = \{\mathfrak{s}_1, \ldots, \mathfrak{s}_{|\mathscr{S}|}\}$ be input specifications to be blended. Let $\{\gamma_1, \ldots, \gamma_n\}$ be renaming operators and $\{\gamma_{n+1}, \ldots, \gamma_m\}$ be and removal operators where $t_1 < \cdots < t_n < t_{n+1} < \cdots < t_m$ are steps. Then, we define:

- The set of atoms $C = \{exec(\gamma_1, \mathfrak{s}_x, t_1), \cdots, exec(\gamma_n, \mathfrak{s}_y, t_n)\}$ as a commonalisation path of $\mathscr{S}$ (with $\mathfrak{s}_x, \mathfrak{s}_y \in \mathscr{S}$).
- The set of atoms $R = \{exec(\gamma_{n+1}, \mathfrak{s}_u, t_{n+1}), \cdots, exec(\gamma_m, \mathfrak{s}_v, t_m)\}$ as a removal path of $\mathscr{S}$ (with $\mathfrak{s}_u, \mathfrak{s}_v \in \mathscr{S}$).
- The set $C \cup R$ as a transition path of $\mathscr{S}$.

Since we have separated the commonalisation and removal process we need to decide when we switch from the one to the other. Hence, we define a predicate *crossSpaceMapPhaseEnded*(t) which determines the step t when the search for the cross space mapping is finished. This is used in the following choice rule for the commonalisation search process:

$$1\{exec(a, \mathfrak{s}, t) : renAct(a, \mathfrak{s}), poss(a, \mathfrak{s}, t)\}1 \leftarrow \text{not } crossSpaceMapPhaseEnded(t)$$
$$(7.13)$$

The *renAct* predicate denotes that a is a renaming operator. The removal and generic space search process is done using another choice rule as follows:

$$1\{exec(a, \mathfrak{s}, t) : removeAct(a, \mathfrak{s}), poss(a, \mathfrak{s}, t)\}1 \leftarrow notGenericReached(t), \quad (7.14\text{a})$$
$$crossSpaceMapPhaseEnded(t).$$

The predicate *notGenericReached* is triggered when the generic space has been reached, i.e., when the search terminates because the generalised versions of all input specifications are equal. This is the case when all axioms are logically equivalent, and all sorts, predicates and operators are syntactically equal. The *removeAct* predicate denotes that a is a removal operator.

Example 7.2. The generic space for the HOUSE and BOAT specifications depicted in Figure 7.2 is achieved by renaming the operators *ride* and *liveIn* to *ride_liveIn*, and sorts *Passenger* and *Resident* to *Passenger_Resident*, and by removing the *on(house) = land* and *on(boat) = water* axioms from the HOUSE and BOAT specifications respectively. The generic space and mappings are depicted in Figure 7.3.

spec GENERICSPACE = BACKGROUND
then sorts *Boat_House* < *Thing*
                Passenger_Resident < *Thing*
         pred *ride_livedIn* : *Passenger_Resident* ∗ *Boat_House*
end

HOUSE	⇐	GENERICSPACE	⇒	BOAT
House	⇐	Sort of the containing object	⇒	*Boat*
house	⇐	The containing object	⇒	*boat*
resident	⇐	The contained object	⇒	*passenger*
liveIn	⇐	Relation between contained and the containing object	⇒	*ride*

Fig. 7.3: The generic space for the *house-boat* blend

7.4 Finding Generalisations Between Logical Theories Using HDTP

The Heuristic-Driven Theory Projection (HDTP, Schmidt et al. (2014)) framework has originally been conceived as a mathematically sound theoretical framework and implemented engine for computational analogy-making.[4] More precisely, HDTP has been created for computing analogical relations and inferences for domains which are given in form of many-sorted first-order logic (FOL) representations: Source and target of the analogy-making process are defined in terms of axiomatisations, i.e., given by a finite set of formulae. From there, HDTP tries to align pairs of formulae from the two domains by means of anti-unification. Anti-unification, as introduced by Plotkin (1970) and Plotkin (1971), is the dual to the more prominent unification problem. Basically, anti-unification tries to solve the problem of generalising terms in a meaningful way, yielding for each term an anti-instance, in which distinct sub-terms have been replaced by variables (which in turn would allow for a retrieval of the original terms by a substitution of the variables by appropriate sub-terms).

The goal of anti-unification is to find a most specific anti-unifier, i.e., the least general generalisation of the involved terms (see Figure 7.4 for examples).[5] HDTP extends first-order anti-unification to a restricted form of higher-order anti-unification, as mere first-order structures must be considered as too weak for the purpose of analogy-making: Structural commonalities can be embedded in different contexts, and therefore would not be accessible by first-order anti-unification

---

[4] For details on analogy as cognitive faculty, computational models of analogy-making, and the corresponding relationship to conceptual blending see the dedicated account in Chapter 5.

[5] Plotkin (1970) has shown that for a proper definition of generalisation, for a given pair of terms there always is a first-order generalisation, and that there is exactly one least general first-order generalisation (up to renaming of variables).

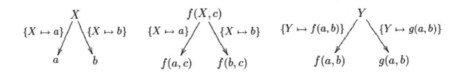

Fig. 7.4: Examples of first-order anti-unifications as given in (Schwering et al., 2009, p. 254): Minuscules represent instances, capitals represent variables, the terms in braces indicate substitutions

only. In Krumnack et al. (2007)'s conceptualisation of restricted higher-order anti-unification a new notion of substitution is introduced in order to restrain generalisations from becoming arbitrarily complex. Classical first-order terms are extended by the introduction of variables which may take arguments (where original first-order variables correspond to variables with arity 0), making a term either a first-order or a higher-order term. Subsequently, anti-unification can be applied analogously to the original first-order case, yielding a generalisation subsuming the specific terms.

As already indicated by the name, the class of substitutions which HDTP can apply during the generalisation step has been restricted to a certain set of operations (and compositions thereof). The following four types of substitutions are admissible: renamings, fixations, argument insertions, and permutations. Formally, these are defined as follows:

Definition 7.3 (Substitutions in Restricted Higher-Order Anti-Unification). Let $\mathcal{V} = \{x_1 : s_1, x_2 : s_2, \ldots\}$ be an infinite set of sorted variables, where the sorts are chosen from a set of sorts *Sort*. Associated with each variable $x_i : s_i$ is an arity, analogous to the standard arity of function symbols. For any $i \geq 0$, we let $\mathcal{V}_i$ be the variables of arity i.

1. A renaming $\rho(F, F')$ replaces a variable $F \in \mathcal{V}_n$ with another variable $F' \in \mathcal{V}_n$:
   $$F(t_1, \ldots, t_n) \xrightarrow{\rho(F,F')} F'(t_1, \ldots, t_n).$$
2. A fixation $\phi(F, f)$ replaces a variable $F \in \mathcal{V}_n$ with a function symbol $f \in \mathcal{C}_n$:
   $$F(t_1, \ldots, t_n) \xrightarrow{\phi(F,f)} f(t_1, \ldots, t_n).$$
3. An argument insertion $\iota(F, F', V, i)$ is defined as follows, where $F \in \mathcal{V}_n, F' \in \mathcal{V}_{n-k+1}, V \in \mathcal{V}_k, i \in [n]$:
   $$F(t_1, \ldots, t_n) \xrightarrow{\iota(F,F',V,i)} F'(t_1, \ldots, t_{i-1}, V(t_i, \ldots, t_{i+k-1}), t_{i+k}, \ldots, t_n).$$
   It "wraps" k of the subterms in a term using a k-ary variable, or can be used to insert a 0-ary variable.
4. A permutation $\pi(F, \tau)$ rearranges the arguments of a term, with $F \in \mathcal{V}_n$, $\tau : [n] \to [n]$ a bijection:
   $$F(t_1, \ldots, t_n) \xrightarrow{\pi(F,\tau)} F(t_{\tau(1)}, \ldots, t_{\tau(n)}).$$

A restricted substitution is a substitution which results from the composition of any sequence of unit substitutions.

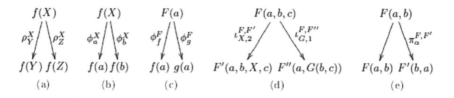

Fig. 7.5: Examples of higher-order anti-unifications reproduced from (Schwering et al., 2009, p. 255): As in Figure 7.4, minuscules represent instances, capitals represent variables, the terms in braces indicate substitutions

Krumnack et al. (2007) show that this new form of (higher-order) substitutions is a real extension of the first-order case, which has proven to be capable of detecting structural commonalities not accessible to first-order anti-unification—as already suggested by the examples of higher-order anti-unifications in Figure 7.5. Unfortunately, in the restricted higher-order case the least general generalisation loses its uniqueness as compared to the first-order case. Therefore, HDTP ranks generalizations according to a complexity order on the complexity of generalisation (based on a complexity measure for substitutions), and finally chooses the least complex generalisations as preferred ones.

From a practical point of view, it is necessary to anti-unify not only terms, but also formulae: HDTP extends the notion of generalisation also to formulae by basically treating formulae in clause form and terms alike (as positive literals are structurally equal to function expressions, and complex clauses in normal form may be treated component-wise). Furthermore, analogies in general not only rely on an isolated pair of formulae from source and target, but on two sets of formulae. Here, a heuristic is applied when iteratively selecting pairs of formulae to be generalised: Coherent mappings outmatch incoherent ones, i.e., mappings in which substitutions can be reused are preferred over isolated substitutions, as they are assumed to be better suited to induce the analogical relation. Once obtained, the generalised theory and the substitutions specify the analogical relation, and formulae of the source for which no correspondence in the target domain can be found may, by means of the already established substitutions, be transferred to the target, constituting a process of analogical transfer between the domains.

7.4.1 The Rutherford Analogy Between Atom and Solar System

Due to its quite accessible nature and general familiarity from physics or chemistry classes, Rutherford's analogy for deriving his model of the atom from a theory of the solar system, together with certain experimental observations and physical laws known by his time, has become a running example in the literature on computational analogy-making (see, for instance, Falkenhainer et al. (1989); Schwering et al. (2009)). For the sake of comparability with other approaches, we also follow this general pattern and use the Rutherford analogy to illustrate the generalisation and transfer steps HDTP.

Sorts:
  real, object, time
Entities:
  sun, planet, nucleus, electron : object
Shared functions of both theories:
  mass : object → real × {kg}   *dist : object × object × time → real × {m}*

Functions of the solar system theory:
  force : object × object × time → real × {N}   *gravity : object × object × time → real × {N}*
  centrifugal :object × object × time → real × {m}
Predicates of the solar system theory:
  revolves_around : object × object
Facts of the solar system theory:
  (α_1) *mass(sun) > mass(planet)* (α_2) *mass(planet) > 0* (α_3) *∀t : time : gravity(planet, sun, t) > 0*
  (α_4) *∀t : time : dist(planet, sun, t) > 0*
Laws of the solar system theory:
  (α_5) *∀t : time, o_1 : object, o_2 : object : dist(o_1,o_2,t) > 0 ∧ gravity(o_1,o_2,t) > 0 → centrifugal(o_1,o_2,t) =*
  −gravity(o_1,o_2,t)
  (α_6) *∀t : time, o_1 : object, o_2 : object : 0 < mass(o_1) < mass(o_2) ∧ dist(o_1,o_2,t) > 0 ∧ centrifugal(o_1,o_2,t) < 0*
  → revolves_around(o_1,o_2)

Functions of the atom model theory:
  coulomb : object × object × time → real × {N}
Facts of the atom model theory:
  (β_1) *mass(nucles) > mass(electron)* (β_2) *mass(electron) > 0* (β_3) *∀t : time : coulomb(electron, nucleus, t) > 0*
  (β_4) *∀t : time : dist(electron, nucleus, t) > 0*

Table 7.1: Domain formalisation of the solar system (S) and of Rutherford's atom model (T) as used by HDTP

Table 7.1 gives the initial domain formalisations, containing a governing theory of the solar system S and an account of Rutherford's alleged knowledge T about some aspects relating to the atom's structure. When provided with these inputs, HDTP computes a shared generalisation G between S and T, together with the corresponding sets of substitutions ϕ_S and ϕ_T for re-obtaining the covered domain parts $S_c \subseteq S$ and $T_c \subseteq T$.[6] Given ϕ_S, the set of anti-unifications inversely corresponding to the respective substitutions is used for obtaining the generalised source theory S' (given in Table 7.2), not only containing elements of the generalisation corresponding to axioms from S_c but also generalising axioms from $S \setminus S_c$. Also notice that for the given formalisations of S and T it holds that $T = T_c$, i.e., the target theory is entirely covered by the common generalisation G (which, when keeping in mind that formulae have been generalised via pair-wise matchings, also is an indication

---

[6] As already introduced in Chapter 5, we say that a formula is covered by the generalisation if it is in the image of the projection $\phi_S(G) = S_c$ or $\phi_T(G) = T_c$ respectively. Otherwise, the formula is called uncovered.

of the source theory S being the richer—i.e., better informed—theory as compared to T).

Sorts:
   real, object, time
Entities:
   X, Y : *object*
Functions:
   mass : *object* $\rightarrow$ *real* $\times \{kg\}$ *dist* : *object* $\times$ *object* $\times$ *time* $\rightarrow$ *real* $\times \{m\}$
   F : *object* $\times$ *object* $\times$ *time* $\rightarrow$ *real* $\times \{N\}$ *centrifugal* : *object* $\times$ *object* $\times$ *time* $\rightarrow$ *real* $\times \{m\}$
Predicates:
   revolves_around : *object* $\times$ *object*
Facts:
   (γ_1) *mass(X) > mass(Y)* (γ_2) *mass(Y) > 0* (γ_3) $\forall t$: *time* : *F(X, Y, t) > 0*
   (γ_4) $\forall t$: *time* : *dist(X, Y, t) > 0*
Laws:
   (γ_5*) $\forall t$: *time*, o_1 : *object*, o_2 : *object* : *dist(o_1,o_2,t) > 0 $\wedge$ F(o_1,o_2,t) > 0 $\rightarrow$ centrifugal(o_1,o_2,t) = $-$F(o_1,o_2,t)*
   (γ_6*) $\forall t$: *time*, o_1 : *object*, o_2 : *object* : *0 < mass(o_1) < mass(o_2) $\wedge$ dist(o_1,o_2,t) > 0 $\wedge$ centrifugal(o_1,o_2,t) < 0*
   $\rightarrow$ *revolves_around(o_1,o_2)*

Table 7.2: Generalised source theory S' based on the common generalisation between the solar system and the Rutherford atom (axioms not obtained from the covered subset S_c—i.e., not accounted for by the common generalisation G—are highlighted by *)

While this concludes the generalisation part, an additional transfer step adding information from the source to the target domain is performed when using HDTP for computational analogy-making. The generalised source theory S' (i.e., $S' = \phi_S^{-1}(S) = G \cup \phi_S^{-1}(S \setminus S_c)$) is used to transfer knowledge from the source theory S to the (originally smaller) target theory T: In the case of the Rutherford analogy, applying ϕ_T to S' re-instantiates T (as $T_c = \phi_T(G)$, and $T = T_c$), with the additional axioms originating from $\phi_T(\phi_S^{-1}(S \setminus S_c)) = \phi_t(\{\gamma_5, \gamma_6\})$ providing previously absent domain content, namely the governing laws describing the revolution of the electrons around the nucleus in the Rutherford-Bohr model of the atom.[7]

7.4.2 The Computational Complexity of HDTP

Given the expressive representation language and the powerful generalisation mechanism, HDTP can be expected to pose significant demands in terms of required computing resources. This intuition is confirmed when formally checking the complexity properties of the approach. Robere and Besold (2012) present a corresponding parameterised complexity analysis of HDTP, in which the focus is put exclusively on the generalisation mechanism (i.e., from the point of view of analogy-

---

[7] In cases for which $T_c \neq T$, when transferring knowledge from the source to the target domain, inconsistencies can arise, introducing the need for reasoning and repair capacities at the end of the analogy process.

making, the matching between input theories).[8] By defining three increasingly complex and expressive versions of higher-order anti-unification—successively admitting additional types of unit substitutions to be included in the anti-unification process—Robere and Besold (2012) obtain the following results for analogical matching using restricted higher-order anti-unification:

1. Anti-unification using only renamings and fixations is solvable in polynomial time.
2. Anti-unification using renamings, fixations and a bounded number of permutations is NP-complete and W[1]-hard with respect to the minimum number of higher arity variables (i.e., variables of arity at least 1) and the maximum number of permutations, and becomes fixed-parameter tractable only with respect to the maximum arity and the maximum number of subterms of the input terms, together with the maximum number of permutations.
3. Anti-unification using renamings, fixations, a bounded number of permutations, and argument insertions is NP-complete and W[1]-hard with respect to the minimum number of higher arity variables, the maximum number of permutations and the maximum number of argument insertions.

The parameterised analysis is complemented with an assessment of the approximation, theoretic complexity of the generalisation mechanism by Besold and Robere (2013). Using a measure of complexity for any composition of the substitutions allowed in restricted higher-order anti-unification introduced by Krumnack et al. (2007), and defining the optimisation problem as trying to find a generalisation which maximizes the complexity over all generalisations—i.e., a generalisation which maximises what Krumnack et al. (2007) call the "information load" over all chosen generalisations—it turns out that analogical matching using renamings, fixations, and a bounded number of permutations does not allow for constant-factor approximation algorithms.

7.5 Colimit Computation Using HETS

The HEterogeneous Tool Set (HETS) is a multi-formalism parsing, static analysis and proof management tool for heterogeneous specification (Mossakowski et al., 2007). The main idea behind HETS is to provide a tool for software specification, ontology development and modelling systems in different logics, each better suited for a certain goal or a certain aspect of the system being developed, using the abstract notion of institution to abstract the particularities of each formalism (Goguen and Burstall, 1992). Moreover, HETS provides support for translations between logics. In particular, one can obtain proof support for a logic with no dedicated provers by

---

[8] The analysis deliberately leaves out the re-representation of input theories by deduction in FOL. Although HDTP in its entirety encompasses both parts, from a complexity point of view re-representation can be identified fairly straightforwardly as undecidable due to the undecidability of FOL.

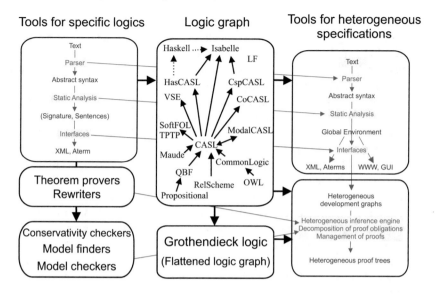

Fig. 7.6: Architecture of the Heterogeneous Tool Set

translating the proof goals along a logic translation (satisfying mild properties, that we do not discuss here; for further information see Mossakowski (2005)) and making the proof there, then translating back the result. The specification language supported by HETS is the Distributed Ontology, Modeling and Specification Language (DOL, discussed in detail in Chapter 3). HETS is complemented by Ontohub (Mossakowski et al., 2014), a repository engine for managing DOL files, providing version control as well as a Web interface for HETS.

The architecture of the HETS system is shown in Figure 7.6, which separates the logic-specific level, on the left, the logic-independent level, on the right, and the logic graph of HETS, placed in the middle and acting like a parameter for the entire tool. HETS uses Haskell (Peyton Jones, 2003) as implementation language; we present here only some relevant implementation details.

The left side of Figure 7.6 summarises how an individual logic is represented internally in HETS. First, we need to provide Haskell datatypes for the constituents of the logic, e.g., signatures, morphisms and sentences. This is done via instantiating various Haskell type classes, namely `Category` (for the signature category of the institution), `Sentences` (for the sentences), `Syntax` (for abstract syntax of basic specifications, and a parser transforming input text into this abstract syntax), and `StaticAnalysis` (for the static analysis, turning basic specifications into theories, where a theory is a signature and a set of sentences). All this is assembled in the type class `Logic`, which additionally provides logic-specific tools like provers and consistency checkers.

The logic-independent level has a similar architecture, but the specification language is now DOL. At the implementation level, the idea is that the heterogenous parser carries in its state the current logic, that can be altered explicitly or by translation to another logic. This determines which logic-specific parser and static analysis method will be invoked. As a result of the static analysis, HETS constructs heterogeneous *development graphs* (Mossakowski et al., 2006), that provide a formalism for proof management and theorem proving.

In the center of the HETS architecture we have the graph of supported logics and logic translations. It acts like a parameter for the entire tool, as modifications on the graph do not require reimplementation of the logic-independent part of the tool. HETS supports more than 25 logics, among them propositional logic, the CASL logic ((Mosses, 2004), multi-sorted first-order logic with subsorting, partiality and induction axioms), the higher-order logic of Isabelle (Nipkow et al., 2002) with its interactive theorem prover, OWL2 (OWL Working Group, 2009) and Common Logic (http://en.wikipedia.org/wiki/Common_logic). Proof support for first-order logic is obtained via a translation to a softly-typed variant of it, Soft-FOL (Lüttich and Mossakowski, 2007), similar to TPTP (Sutcliffe, 2010), which allows us to integrate automated theorem provers like SPASS (Weidenbach et al., 2002), Darwin (Baumgartner et al., 2004), Vampire (Riazanov and Voronkov, 2002) and Eprover (Schulz, 2002). For OWL2, the reasoners Pellet (Sirin et al., 2007) and Fact++ (Tsarkov and Horrocks, 2006) are integrated.

The core module for colimit computation in HETS is a method for computing the colimit in the category of sets and total functions. This is a well-known construction (Adámek et al., 1990). It performs a disjoint union of all the sets in a diagram, followed by a quotient to the equivalence generated by the relation that holds between two symbols in different nodes if there exists an edge between the two nodes such that the function labeling the edge maps one of the symbols to the other. This is followed by a selection step: we must choose a representative from each resulting equivalence class. The choice is important, as it determines the names of the symbols in the colimit. To be useful in practice, the choice should appear natural to the user. HETS currently implements a majority principle: the name that occurs most often in an equivalence class of the colimit is chosen as a representative whenever possible. A disambiguation method, which appends generated numbers to the names occurring more than once in the choices of representatives, is then applied. Mossakowski et al. (2017) discuss in detail the properties that the choice of names in the colimit should have and propose improvements on the current implementation of selection of names in HETS.

Colimit computation is then implemented in HETS in a specific way for each logic, when adding them to HETS as a new instance of the Logic class. For OWL ontologies, signatures are just tuples of sets of symbols of different kinds: classes, object properties, data properties and individuals. Signature morphisms map symbols to symbols while preserving their kind. Colimit computation for OWL signatures can thus be done by projecting the diagram that we compute the colimit of to each of the kinds, followed by computing the colimit in the category of sets for the resulting graph of sets and functions.

Example 7.3. We illustrate colimit computation in the category of sets using an example with OWL ontologies containing only concepts. In this case, computation of colimits of OWL signatures reduces to computing colimits of sets.

Let O_1 be an OWL ontology containing the concepts Woman, Person and Bank and O_2 another OWL ontology with the concepts Woman, HumanBeing and Bank. Let us assume to have a base ontology O that defines the concepts Woman and Person together with two theory interpretations.

```
interpretation I1 : O to O1   %% symbols are mapped identically
end

interpretation I2 : O to O2 = %% Woman is mapped identically
  Person |-> HumanBeing
end
```

In the colimit of the network of ontologies containing the interpretations I1 and I2 we have:

- a concept Woman, identifying the two concepts Woman in the two ontologies, as they have a common origin in O and the same name,
- a concept Person, identifying the concepts Person and HumanBeing, as they have a common origin in O, and the concept name Person is majoritary,
- two concepts Bank1 and Bank2, as the two Bank concepts do not have a common origin in O and therefore we must disambiguate their names.

For CASL ontologies, signatures have a set of sorts together with a subsorting relation on the set, total and partial function and predicate symbols with arities and result sorts. Signature morphisms map sorts to sorts such that subsorting relations are preserved and function/predicate symbols to function/predicate symbols such that the totality of function symbols is preserved: a partial function can be mapped to a total function, but not otherwise. Moreover, overloading relations must be preserved. Two operation symbols with the same name are in the overloading relation if their arities have component-wise a common subsort and their result sorts have a common supersort. Similarly, two predicate symbols with the same name are in the overloading relation if their arities have component-wise a common subsort. Preservation of overloadings means that whenever two symbols are in the overloading relation in the source signature of a morphism, their images through the morphism must be again in the overloading relation. The category of CASL signatures and morphisms has colimits (Mossakowski, 1998) and colimit computation for CASL signatures is implemented in HETS.

Example 7.4. We can now blend the concept House and Boat using the generic space and the theory interpretations from Example 7.2, that we assume to be written as two DOL interpretations named V1 and V2.

```
spec HouseBoat =
  combine V1, V2
end
```

The relevant fragments from the resulting theory, not coming from the background specification, can be found below. Note that no symbol name is majority, so arbitrary names for the symbols in the colimit are chosen.

```
sorts Boat_House, Medium, Passenger_Resident, Thing
sorts Boat_House, Passenger_Resident < Thing
op house : Boat_House
op land : Medium
op on : Thing -> Medium
op resident : Passenger_Resident
op water : Medium
pred inside : Thing * Thing
pred ride_liveIn : Passenger_Resident * Boat_House

. ride_liveIn(resident, house) %(Ax1)%
```

The user can decide to rename the constant house to houseboat:

```
spec HouseBoatRenamed =
 HouseBoat with house |-> houseboat
end
```

Finally, at the level of theories, we apply a known result of Goguen and Burstall (1992) that allows us to compute the colimit of a diagram of theories by first projecting it to a diagram of signatures, computing its colimit and then pairing the resulting colimit signature with the union of the set of sentences obtained by translating for each theory in the initial diagram its set of sentences along the sentence translation function induced by the structural morphism corresponding to the node of the theory in the colimit of signatures.

Example 7.5. In the boat-house example, adapted from (Goguen and Harrell, 2010), but using a richer axiomatisation of the concepts in OWL, assume we have an ontology with the concept House defined as follows:

```
Class: Artifact
    Class: Capability
    ObjectProperty: has_function
        Range: Capability

    ObjectProperty: is_located_on

    Class: Person
    Class: Plot
    ObjectProperty: is_inhabited_by
        Domain: House
        Range:  Person

    Class: ServeAsResidence
        SubClassOf: Capability

    Class: ArtifactThatHasResidenceFunction
```

```
        EquivalentTo: Artifact that has_function some
                                        ServeAsResidence
        SubClassOf: is_inhabited_by some Person

    Class: House
        SubClassOf: Artifact
            that is_located_on some Plot
            and has_function some ServeAsResidence
```

and another one with the concept Boat:

```
Class: Artifact
    Class: Capability
    ObjectProperty: has_function
        Range: Capability

    ObjectProperty: is_located_on
    ObjectProperty: contains

    Class: Person
    Class: BodyOfWater

    ObjectProperty: is_navigated_by
        Domain: Boat
        Range: Person

    Class: MeansOfTransportation
        SubClassOf: Capability

    Class: ArtifactThatHasTransportationFunction
        EquivalentTo: Artifact that has_function some
                                        MeansOfTransportation
        SubClassOf: contains some owl:Thing

    Class: Floating
        SubClassOf: Capability

    Class: ArtifactThatHasFloatingFunction
        EquivalentTo: Artifact that has_function some Floating
        SubClassOf: is_located_on some BodyOfWater

    Class: Boat
        SubClassOf: Artifact
            that has_function some MeansOfTransportation
            and has_function some Floating
            and is_navigated_by some Person
```

The base ontology extends the common part of the two ontologies with the abstract
concept Agent:

```
ontology base1 =
    Class: Artifact
    Class: Capability
    ObjectProperty: has_function
        Range: Capability
```

```
    ObjectProperty: is_located_on
    Class: Agent
end
```

The crucial part in this blend is to view a boat as a kind of "person" that lives in a house. We let a boat play the role of a person (that inhabits a house) by mapping the concept `Agent` to `Boat` and `Person`.

```
interpretation boat_personification : base1 to Boat =
    Agent |-> Boat

interpretation house_import : base1 to House =
    Agent |-> Person

ontology boat_house =
 combine boat_personification, house_import
 with Agent |-> Boat, House |-> BoatHouse
```

Note that since no name is majoritary, the implementation of colimit computation picks the name `Agent` for the equivalence class {`Agent`, `Boat`, `Person`} in the colimit. The user decides to rename it to `Boat`, and the concept `House` is renamed to `BoatHouse`. The relevant axioms of the `BoatHouse` concept in the colimit are

```
Class: BoatHouse
        SubClassOf: Artifact and is_located_on some Plot
                    and has_function some ServeAsResidence

Class: ArtifactThatHasResidenceFunction
        EquivalentTo: Artifact and has_function some
                                          ServeAsResidence
        SubClassOf: is_inhabited_by some Boat
```

Clearly, the possibilities for 'combining' the house and boat concepts do not stop here. For instance, a houseboat concept could be achieved as a colimit of the house and boat concepts by turning the boat into a habitat and moving the house from a plot of land to a body of water. This can be achieved by using a base ontology in which `Agent` is replaced by `Person` and by adding two additional classes, namely `Object` and `Site` (Kutz et al., 2014).

7.6 Conclusion and Future Perspectives

In this chapter, we overviewed COBBLE, a prototype of a concept invention system developed in the COINVENT project. We described the main enabling technologies that we adopted and developed for the development of COBBLE.

COBBLE implements a concept invention workflow that allows users to select input theories to be blended, to generalise them by choosing different techniques, and that computes blends as colimits of algebraic specifications.

In COBBLE, input spaces are modeled using DOL, an international ontology interoperability standard that provides a unified metalanguage for employing an open-ended number of formal logics (Mossakowski et al., 2015). In particular, DOL allows us to model blending diagrams, specified as algebraic specifications encoded in CASL or OWL.

The generic space of these specifications, an essential component of conceptual blending, can be either manually specified, or automatically computed. We described two different ways for computing the generic space.

On the one hand, we showed how the search of the generic space can be encoded as a planning problem in Answer Set Programming (Gelfond and Kahl, 2014), in which actions are renaming and removal operators, and states are transitioned specifications. The ASP encoding supports the computations of blends as amalgams and its implementation is available at `https://github.com/meppe/Amalgamation/tree/master`. Further information can be found in Eppe et al. (2015). On the other hand, the generic space can be computed by using HDTP (Schwering et al., 2009), an analogy reasoner based on a restricted form of higher-order anti-unification that computes the structural commonalities between two input domains represented in a variant of first-order logic.

We presented the HETS system, a parsing, static analysis and proof management tool incorporating various provers and different specification languages, thus providing a tool for heterogeneous specifications (Mossakowski et al., 2007). HETS implements the colimit categorical operation through which the blends are created.

COBBLE is a flexible and modular concept invention system prototype, in which the above functionalities are implemented and encapsulated as RESTful services. In this way, each functionality can be reused by other computational creativity systems by calling the corresponding API. Further technicalities are described in (Maclean and Winterstein, 2016).

COBBLE has been applied in two testbed scenarios, mathematical reasoning and melodic harmonisation, that we describe in the next two chapters.

There are a number of directions in which the system can be extended. First, we plan to build a better integration with the `Ontohub.org` platform, an ontology repository (Mossakowski et al., 2014). This would allow one to browse predefined ontologies and choose them for cross-domain blending. Second, we would like to extend the system with a rating mechanism that allows the user to specify which axioms of the input theories are more important than others, so that blend generation and evaluation can be interleaved. Finally, supporting the generalisation of theories in an interactive way, through argumentation for instance, is also another desirable characteristic for a system of this kind.

References

J. Adámek, H. Herrlich, and G. Strecker. *Abstract and Concrete Categories*. Wiley, New York, 1990.

E. Astesiano, M. Bidoit, B. Krieg-Brückner, P. D. Mosses, D. Sannella, and A. Tarlecki. CASL: The Common Algebraic Specification Language. *Theoretical Comput. Science*, 286(2):153–196, 2002.

C. Baral. *Knowledge Representation, Reasoning and Declarative Problem Solving*. Cambridge University Press, 2003.

P. Baumgartner, A. Fuchs, and C. Tinelli. Darwin: A theorem prover for the model evolution calculus. In S. Schulz, G. Sutcliffe, and T. Tammet, editors, *IJCAR Workshop on Empirically Successful First Order Reasoning (ESFOR (aka S4))*, Electronic Notes in Theoretical Computer Science, 2004.

T. R. Besold and R. Robere. When almost is not even close: Remarks on the approximability of HDTP. In K.-U. Kühnberger, S. Rudolph, and P. Wang, editors, *Artificial General Intelligence - 6th International Conference, AGI 2013, Proceedings*, volume 7999 of *Lecture Notes in Computer Science*, pages 11–20. Springer, 2013.

R. Confalonieri and J. C. Nieves. Nested preferences in Answer Set Programming. *Fundamenta Informaticae*, 113(1):19–39, 2011.

R. Confalonieri and H. Prade. Using possibilistic logic for modeling qualitative decision: Answer Set Programming algorithms. *International Journal of Approximate Reasoning*, 55(2):711 – 738, 2014.

R. Confalonieri, M. Eppe, M. Schorlemmer, O. Kutz, R. Peñaloza, and E. Plaza. Upward refinement operators for conceptual blending in $\mathcal{EL}^{++}$. *Annals of Mathematics and Artificial Intelligence*, 82(1–3):69–99, 2018. doi: 10.1007/s10472-016-9524-8.

R. Confalonieri, E. Plaza, and M. Schorlemmer. A process model for concept invention. In *Proceedings of the 7th International Conference on Computational Creativity, ICCC16*, pages 338–345, 2016b.

M. Eppe, E. Maclean, R. Confalonieri, O. Kutz, M. Schorlemmer, E. Plaza, and K-U. Kühnberger. A computational framework for conceptual blending. *Artificial Intelligence* 256:105–129, 2018.

M. Eppe and M. Bhatt. Narrative based postdictive reasoning for cognitive robotics. In *International Symposium on Logical Formalizations of Commonsense Reasoning (CR)*, 2013.

M. Eppe and M. Bhatt. Approximate postdictive reasoning with answer set programming. *Journal of Applied Logic*, 13(4):676–719, 2015.

M. Eppe, M. Bhatt, J. Suchan, and B. Tietzen. ExpCog: Experiments in commonsense cognitive robotics. In *International Workshop on Cognitive Robotics (CogRob)*, 2014.

M. Eppe, E. Maclean, R. Confalonieri, O. Kutz, W. M. Schorlemmer, and E. Plaza. ASP, amalgamation, and the conceptual blending workflow. In F. Calimeri, G. Ianni, and M. Truszczynski, editors, *Proceedings of the 13th International Conference on Logic Programming and Nonmonotonic Reasoning, LPNMR 2015*, Lexington, KY, USA, September 27-30, volume 9345 of *Lecture Notes in Computer Science*, pages 309–316. Springer, 2015.

B. Falkenhainer, K. Forbus, and D. Gentner. The structure-mapping engine: Algorithm and examples. *Artificial Intelligence*, 41(1):1 – 63, 1989.

G. Fauconnier and M. Turner. *The Way We Think: Conceptual Blending And The Mind's Hidden Complexities.* Basic Books, 2002.

M. Gebser, R. Kaminski, B. Kaufmann, and T. Schaub. Clingo = ASP + control: Preliminary report. *CoRR*, abs/1405.3694, 2014.

M. Gebser, R. Kaminski, B. Kaufmann, M. Lindauer, M. Ostrowski, J. Romero, T. Schaub, and S. Thiele. Potassco User Guide 2.0. Technical report, University of Potsdam, May 2015.

M. Gelfond and Y. Kahl. *Knowledge Representation, Reasoning, and the Design of Intelligent Agents: The Answer-Set Programming Approach.* Cambridge University Press, New York, NY, USA, 2014.

M. Gelfond and V. Lifschitz. The stable model semantics for logic programming. In *Proceedings of the Fifth International Conference on Logic Programming (ICLP)*, pages 1070–1080. The MIT Press, 1988.

J. Goguen. An introduction to algebraic semiotics, with application to user interface design. In C. L. Nehaniv, editor, *Computation for Metaphors, Analogy, and Agents*, volume 1562 of *Lecture Notes in Computer Science*, pages 242–291. 1999.

J. Goguen and D. F. Harrell. Style: A computational and conceptual blending-based approach. In S. Argamon, K. Burns, and S. Dubnov, editors, *The Structure of Style: Algorithmic Approaches to Understanding Manner and Meaning*, pages 291–316. Springer, 2010.

J. A. Goguen and R. M. Burstall. Institutions: Abstract model theory for specification and programming. *Journal of the Association for Computing Machinery*, 39: 95–146, 1992.

J. A. Goguen and D. F. Harrell. Foundations for active multimedia narrative: Semiotic spaces and structural blending. *Available at* `https://cseweb.ucsd.edu/~goguen/pps/narr.pdf`, Last accessed, June 2016.

R. Kowalski. Predicate logic as programming language. In *Proceedings of International Federation for Information Processing*, pages 569– 574, 1974.

U. Krumnack, A. Schwering, H. Gust, and K. Kühnberger. Restricted higher-order anti-unification for analogy making. In *Twentieth Australian Joint Conference on Artificial Intelligence*. Springer, 2007.

O. Kutz, J. Bateman, F. Neuhaus, T. Mossakowski, and M. Bhatt. E pluribus unum: Formalisation, use-cases, and computational support for conceptual blending. In T. R. Besold, M. Schorlemmer, and A. Smaill, editors, *Computational Creativity Research: Towards Creative Machines*, Thinking Machines. Atlantis/Springer, 2014.

K. Lüttich and T. Mossakowski. Reasoning support for CASL with automated theorem proving systems. In J. Fiadeiro, editor, *WADT 2006*, LNCS 4409, pages 74–91. Springer-Verlag, 2007.

E. Maclean and Winterstein. COINVENT system implementation and workflows, 2016. COINVENT Project Deliverable *Available at:* `http://www.coinvent-project.eu/fileadmin/publications/COINVENT_D8.5_v1.0.pdf`, Last accessed, July 2016

T. Mossakowski. Colimits of order-sorted specifications. In F. Parisi Presicce, editor, *Recent trends in algebraic development techniques. Proc. 12th International Workshop*, volume 1376 of *Lecture Notes in Computer Science*, pages 316–332. Springer Verlag, London, 1998.

T. Mossakowski. Heterogeneous specification and the heterogeneous tool set. Technical report, Universitaet Bremen, 2005. Habilitation thesis.

T. Mossakowski, S. Autexier, and D. Hutter. Development graphs—proof management for structured specifications. *Journal of Logic and Algebraic Programming*, 67(1–2):114–145, 2006.

T. Mossakowski, C. Maeder, and K. Lüttich. The Heterogeneous Tool Set. In O. Grumberg and M. Huth, editors, *TACAS 2007*, volume 4424 of *Lecture Notes in Computer Science*, pages 519–522. Springer, Heidelberg, 2007.

T. Mossakowski, O. Kutz, and M. Codescu. Ontohub: A semantic repository for heterogeneous ontologies. In *Proc. of the Theory Day in Computer Science (DACS-2014), satellite workshop of ICTAC-2014*, University of Bucharest, September 15-16, 2014.

T. Mossakowski, M. Codescu, F. Neuhaus, and O. Kutz. The Road to Universal Logic: Festschrift for the 50th Birthday of Jean-Yves Béziau, Volume II. chapter The Distributed Ontology, Modeling and Specification Language – DOL, pages 489–520. Springer International Publishing, Cham, 2015.

T. Mossakowski, F. Rabe, and M. Codescu. Canonical selection of colimits. In M. Roggenbach, editors, Recent Trends in Algebraic Development Techniques, *WADT 2016*, volume 10644 of *Lecture Notes in Computer Science*, pages 170–188, Springer, Cham, 2017

P. D. Mosses. *CASL reference manual: The complete documentation of the Common Algebraic Specification Language* Lecture Notes in Computer Science, Springer-Verlag, 2004.

T. Nipkow, L. C. Paulson, and M. Wenzel. *Isabelle/HOL — A proof assistant for higher-order logic*. Springer Verlag, 2002.

OWL Working Group. OWL 2 web ontology language: Document overview. W3C recommendation, World Wide Web Consortium (W3C), Oct. 2009. URL http://www.w3.org/TR/2009/REC-owl2-overview-20091027/.

F. C. Pereira. *Creativity and Artificial Intelligence: A Conceptual Blending Approach*. Mouton de Gruyter, 2007.

S. Peyton Jones. *Haskell 98 language and libraries: the Revised Report*. Cambridge University Press, 2003.

G. D. Plotkin. A note on inductive generalization. *Machine Intelligence*, 5:153–163, 1970.

G. D. Plotkin. A further note on inductive generalization. *Machine Intelligence*, 6: 101–124, 1971.

D. Porello, N. Troquard, R. Peñaloza, R. Confalonieri, P. Galliani, O. Kutz. Two approaches to ontology integration based on axiom weakening. *Proceedings of the Twenty-Seventh International Joint Conference on Artificial Intelligence, IJCAI-18*, 1942–1948, 2018. doi: 10.24963/ijcai.2018/268

A. Riazanov and A. Voronkov. The design and implementation of VAMPIRE. *AI Communications*, 15(2-3):91–110, 2002.

R. Robere and T. R. Besold. Complex analogies: remarks on the complexity of HDTP. In *Twenty-fifth Australasian Joint Conference on Artificial Intelligence*, volume 7691 of *Lecture Notes in Computer Science*, pages 530–542. Springer, 2012.

M. Schmidt, U. Krumnack, H. Gust, and K.-U. Kühnberger. Heuristic-driven theory projection: An overview. In H. Prade and G. Richard, editors, *Computational Approaches to Analogical Reasoning: Current Trends*, pages 163–194. Springer, 2014.

M. Schorlemmer, R. Confalonieri, and E. Plaza. Coherent concept invention. In T. R. Besold, O. Kutz, and C. Leon, editors, *Proceedings of the Workshop on Computational Creativity, Concept Invention, and General Intelligence (C3GI 2016)*, Bozen-Bolzano, Italy, August 20-22, 2016, volume 1767 of *CEUR Workshop Proceedings*. CEUR-WS.org, 2016.

S. Schulz. E – A brainiac theorem prover. *Journal of AI Communications*, 15(2/3): 111–126, 2002.

A. Schwering, U. Krumnack, K.-U. Kühnberger, and H. Gust. Syntactic principles of heuristic-driven theory projection. *Cognitive Systems Research*, 10(3):251–269, 2009.

E. Sirin, B. Parsia, B. C. Grau, A. Kalyanpur, and Y. Katz. Pellet: A practical OWL-DL reasoner. *Web Semant.*, 5(2):51–53, June 2007.

G. Sutcliffe. The TPTP world – infrastructure for automated reasoning. In E. M. Clarke and A. Voronkov, editors, *LPAR (Dakar)*, volume 6355 of *Lecture Notes in Computer Science*, pages 1–12. Springer, 2010.

N. Troquard, R. Confalonieri, P. Galliani, R. Peñaloza, D. Porello, O. Kutz. Repairing ontologies via axiom weakening. *Proceedings of the Thirty-Second AAAI Conference on Artificial Intelligence*, 1981–1988, 2018.

D. Tsarkov and I. Horrocks. Fact++ description logic reasoner: System description. In *Proceedings of the Third International Joint Conference on Automated Reasoning*, IJCAR'06, pages 292–297, Berlin, Heidelberg, 2006. Springer-Verlag.

T. Veale. From conceptual "mash-ups" to "bad-ass" blends: A robust computational model of conceptual blending. In M. L. Maher, K. Hammond, A. Pease, R. Pèrez, D. Ventura, and G. Wiggins, editors, *Proceedings of the Third International Conference on Computational Creativity*, ICCC 2012, pages 1–8, May 2012.

T. Veale and D. O. Donoghue. Computation and blending. *Cognitive Linguistics*, 11(3-4):253–282, 2000.

C. Weidenbach, U. Brahm, T. Hillenbrand, E. Keen, C. Theobalt, and D. Topic. SPASS version 2.0. In A. Voronkov, editor, *Automated Deduction – CADE-18*, LNCS 2392, pages 275–279. Springer-Verlag, 2002.

M. Žnidaršič, A. Cardoso, P. Gervás, P. Martins, R. Hervás, A. O. Alves, H. G. Oliveira, P. Xiao, S. Linkola, H. Toivonen, J. Kranjc, and N. Lavrac. Computational creativity infrastructure for online software composition: A conceptual blending use case. In *The Seventh International Conference on Computational Creativity (ICCC)*, Paris, France, 2016.

Chapter 8
Formal Conceptual Blending in the (Co-)Invention of (Pure) Mathematics[*]

Danny de Jesús Gómez-Ramírez and Alan Smaill

Abstract We claim that conceptual blending plays a key role in mathematical discovery and invention. We use a formalisation of blending in terms of colimits of many-sorted first-order logical specifications to illustrate the processes involved. In particular we present a development structured around notions from abstract areas of pure mathematics such as Commutative Algebra, Number Theory, Fields and Galois Theory. This development shows a new formal route which builds up the classical theory in the area, and also gives rise to new equivalences that characterise the notion of Dedekind Domain. We comment on the significance of this work for the computer support of abstract mathematical theory construction, as well as for (co-)inventing classic and new mathematical notions (i.e., inventing with the help of a computer program), and on the cognitive aspects involved.

8.1 Introduction

In the modern study of formal meta-models for general mathematics, i.e., meta-mathematics, it seems to be mandatory to start to develop computationally-feasible models for the most fundamental cognitive abilities required in the discovery of mathematical concepts and theories. For instance, the cognitive mechanism of conceptual blending has a seminal importance in this context, i.e., the mind's ability to process two concepts, identifying some commonalities between them, and sub-

Danny de Jesús Gómez-Ramírez
Vienna University of Technology, Wiedner Hauptstrasse 8-10, 1040 Vienna, Austria. e-mail: dagomez1982@gmail.com

Alan Smaill
Informatics Forum, 10 Crichton Street, Edinburgh, EH8 9AB, Scotland, UK. e-mail: A.Smaill@ed.ac.uk

[*] This chapter contains an expanded, combined and improved version based on some parts of (Bou et al., 2015) and (Gomez-Ramirez, 2015) as well as original material.

© Springer Nature Switzerland AG 2018
R. Confalonieri et al. (eds.), *Concept Invention*, Computational Synthesis and Creative Systems, https://doi.org/10.1007/978-3-319-65602-1_8

sequently integrating both in a new blended concept, which contains essential information of the input notions plus additional conceptual structures (Fauconnier and Turner, 2003).

So, formalisations of conceptual blending should be necessary, since this cognitive mechanism is nowadays recognised as one of the mind's most seminal abilities for creative reasoning, not only in a general context (Fauconnier and Turner, 2003), but also in highly abstract mathematical reasoning (Alexander, 2011).

So, in order to create such a theory, we need to present a specific formalisation of the notions of mathematical concept, formal morphisms among them, and conceptual blending of a pair of such concepts related by means of a generic space, which codifies formal analogical matches between them. Besides, in order to demonstrate a minimal meta-mathematical soundness, we need to show not only that it is possible to 'generate' classic mathematical concepts as formal blends of simpler ones, but also that it is possible to (co-)create new potentially valuable concepts from a mathematical perspective. Besides, in order to instantiate the 'universality' of this formalism it is highly desirable to present examples in several areas of (pure) mathematics.

Therefore, in the next sections we will fulfill the former requirements for a spectrum of examples coming from Commutative Algebra, Algebraic Number Theory, and Fields and Galois Theory. Specifically, we will show by using a formalisation of blending in terms of colimits of many-sorted first-order theories that the concept of prime ideal in a commutative ring with unity can be expressed as a formal blend of the notions of ideal over the same class of rings and the general notion of 'prime number' in a quasi-monoid with a divisibility relation. Besides, by computing this blend in the formalism of the Heterogeneous Tool Sets (HETS) (Mossakowski et al., 2007), within a CASL specification (Bidoit and Mosses, 2004), we will (co-)discover a new class of rings in Commutative Algebra, i.e., the *Containment-Division Rings* (CDR).[2] Furthermore, we will present a new theorem characterising one of the most fundamental notions in Algebraic Number Theory, namely, Dedekind Domains, as Noetherian CDR-s, as well as CDR-s satisfying a divisor chain condition.

In addition, we will show that it is possible to generate formally four of the most fundamental notions of Fields and Galois Theory by means of nine recursively generated blends, starting from five basic mathematical notions coming from several areas of mathematics such as Group Theory, Abstract Algebra and Topology.

8.2 Basic Terminology

We will describe our mathematical notions in many-sorted first-order logic (Meinke and Tucker, 1993). Here, a concept consists of the following parts: a signature $\Sigma = (S, F, R)$, where S is a set of sorts, F is a set of functional symbols, each of them

---

[2] An equivalent notion was independently found by Krull during the 20-s, but in a slightly more general context (see for instance Gilmer and Mott (1965)).

carrying a finite set of symbols of S specifying the n-tuple sort of the domain and the sort of the codomain (constants are functional symbols with empty domain), and R is a set of symbols for relations with the corresponding m-tuple sort.

In addition, a concept has a (finite) set of sentences A in many-sorted first-order logic, called the axioms of the concept.[3]

Finally, an interpretation M of a concept is just a collection of sets M_S, functions M_F and relations M_R, with elements indexed by the corresponding sets S, F and R, respectively, such that if M_g is an *interpretation* of $g : s_1 \times s_2 \times \cdots \times s_n \to s_m$, then $M_g : M_{s_1} \times M_{s_2} \cdots \times M_{s_n} \to M_{s_m}$.

Analogously, the corresponding property holds for the interpretations of the symbols in R.

For simplicity, we define the class of models of a concept as big as possible, i.e., given the signature Σ and the finite set of axioms A, we define the class of models of the concept defined by (Σ, A) as the class $\mathbb{M}$ of all interpretations M, such that the interpretation of any axiom of A is, in fact, true over M, i.e., $M \models_\Sigma A$. Here, we assume the standard definition of satisfaction in many-sorted first-order logic. Moreover, another way to express this is by saying that the class of models of a concept is just the dual of its set of axioms A in the class of all possible interpretations. This formalisation allows us to say, by definition, that two concepts C_1 and C_2 are equivalent if their corresponding classes of models coincide, i.e., if $\mathbb{M}_1 = \mathbb{M}_2$.

In conclusion, a concept for us consists of a triple $C = (\Sigma, A, \mathbb{M})$.

It is worth it to clarify at this point that for pragmatic reasons we avoid considering potentially infinite collections of axioms for defining concepts as in Formal Concept Analysis (Ganter and Wille (1997)). Effectively, the working mathematician uses normally concepts with finitely many axioms and the implementations for the conceptual operations can be done more straightforwardly in a 'finite' setting.

For the notion of morphism of concepts, we require the following condition: if $C_1 = (\Sigma_1, A_1, \mathbb{M}_1)$ and $C_2 = (\Sigma_2, A_2, \mathbb{M}_2)$ are concepts then a morphism $\phi : C_1 \to C_2$ is just a triple

$$\phi = (\phi_{\Sigma_1} : \Sigma_1 \to \Sigma_2, \phi_{F_1} : F_1 \to F_2, \phi_{R_1} : R_1 \to R_2),$$

such that the translation of the axioms of C_1 into C_2 induced by ϕ (i.e., $\phi(A)$) are deducible from the axioms A_2, that means $A_2 \vdash_{\Sigma_2} \phi(A_1)$.

It is a well-known fact that the collection of concepts with their morphisms forms a category $\mathbb{C}oncepts$. Moreover, in this category any V-shaped diagram, $\alpha : G \to C_1$ and $\beta : G \to C_2$, has a colimit (Mossakowski, 1997).

Now, for such a V-shaped diagram D, we will use a simplified version of the formalisation of Goguen (Goguen, 1999, 2001, 2005) for conceptual blending, i.e.,

---

[3] In general a concept can have infinitely many axioms. However, the daily concepts used by the working mathematician have in most of the cases a finite number of axioms.

we say that the colimit B of D is the *blending* of the concepts C_1 and C_2 with respect to (the identifications codified by) the concept G (through α and β).[4]

8.3 Specific Mathematical Concepts

In this section, we give explicit definitions of each of the structural concepts, which are used as basic conceptual blocks to generate classic and new mathematical notions. More precisely, some of them are explicitly very well-known concepts by the working mathematician, e.g., ideals over a commutative ring with unity, (meta-) prime number, (abelian) group, action of a group on a set and space of fixed points; whereas the others are often implicitly used in modern mathematics without receiving until now any kind of special name, e.g., bigroup, pointed (abelian) group and algebraic (bi)substructure. Moreover, for a more detailed description regarding mathematical properties of some of the explicitly well-known concepts presented in this section, the reader may consult (Lang, 2002).

Definition 8.1. A commutative ring with unity $(R, +. *, 0, 1)$ is a mathematical structure with two binary operations and two constants fulfilling the following axioms, i.e.,

1. $(\forall a \in R)(a + 0 = 0 + a = a)$
2. $(\forall a \in R)(\exists b \in R)(a + b = b + a = 0)$
3. $(\forall a, b, c \in R)((a + b) + c = a + (b + c)))$
4. $(\forall a, b \in R)(a + b = b + a)$
5. $(\forall a \in R)(a * 1 = 1 * a = a)$
6. $(\forall a, b, c \in R)((a * b) * c = a * (b * c)))$
7. $(\forall a, b \in R)(a * b = b * a)$
8. $(\forall a, b, c \in R)(a * (b + c) = a * b + a * c)$

The first three (four) properties mean that $(R, +)$ is an (abelian) group.

Moreover, R can be understood as the sort containing the elements of the corresponding commutative ring with unity. An ideal I is a subset of R satisfying the following axiom:

$$(\forall i, j \in I)(\forall s, r \in R)((s + j = 0 \rightarrow i + j \in I) \wedge r * i \in I).$$

We define a unary relation (predicate) *isideal* on the set (sort) of subsets of R corresponding to the former property. We also define

---

[4] This simplification emerges from the fact that, in this particular context, the trivial order given by equality and defined on each set of morphisms between concepts seems to be the most natural and simple to be considered. So, in this specific case the notions of $3/2-$colimit and colimit coincide (Goguen, 1999). Besides, due to this simplification, the weakening of theories should be done necessarily by hand, i.e., the elimination of some axioms of the concepts in order to obtain more coherent blendings.

$$\mathrm{Id}(R) = \{A \subseteq R : isideal(A)\}.$$

Ideals can be multiplied together using the following definition:

$$I \cdot_\iota J = \left\{ \sum_{k=1}^{n} i_k \cdot j_k : n \in \mathbb{N} \wedge i_1, \ldots, i_n \in I \wedge j_1, \ldots, j_n \in J \right\}.$$

On the other hand, we want to see the containment relation $\subseteq$ as a binary relation over the sort $\mathrm{Id}(R)$.

Summarising, this conceptual space (or concept) consists of sorts $R, \mathrm{Id}(R)$ and $P(R)$; operations $+, *, 0_R, 1_R, 1_\iota$ and $\cdot_\iota$; and the relations $\subseteq$ and *isideal*.

The former notions have a seminal importance in several branches of mathematics like commutative algebra, algebraic geometry and algebraic number theory. The canonical example is the set of the integer numbers $\mathbb{Z}$ with all the ideals given as the subsets containing multiples of a fixed integer (or prime) number n.

Definition 8.2. Let $(Z, *, 1, \|)$ be a the set with a binary operation $*$, such that 1 is the neutral element, i.e., for any $z \in Z$, $z * 1 = 1 * z = z$.

We also define an upside-down divisibility relation $\|$ defined as:

$$e \parallel g := g | e \Leftrightarrow (\exists f \in Z)(g = e * f)$$

Let us define a unary relation *isprime* on Z as follows: for all $p \in Z$, *isprime*(p) holds if $p \neq 1$,

and:

$$(\forall a, b \in Z)\,((ab \parallel p) \rightarrow (a \parallel p \vee b \parallel p))$$

Besides, we define the set (sort) of the prime numbers as:

$$Prime = \{p \in Z : isprime(p)\}$$

In the CASL language, we consider Z as a sort, $*$ as a binary operation, *prime* as a predicate symbol and $\|$ as a binary relation, all of them defined over the sort Z.

Definition 8.3. A pointed (abelian) group is a set B with an binary operation $*$ and a distinguished element $b \in B$ such that $(B \setminus \{b\}, *_{|B \setminus \{b\} \times B \setminus \{b\}})$ is an (abelian) group, and $b * c = c * b = b$ for all $c \in B$.

The canonical examples of pointed abelian groups are the familiar mathematical structures given by the integer, rational, real and complex numbers with the zero element and the product operation, respectively. Moreover, it can be shown that the axiom of choice has as special consequence the fact that any non-empty set with a distinguished element has at least one structure of pointed group (Horward and Rubin, 1998).

Definition 8.4. A distributive space consists of two sets D y K with two operations $\oplus : D \times D \rightarrow D$ and $\otimes : K \times D \rightarrow D$ such that

$$(\forall x \in K)(\forall y, z \in D)(x \otimes (y \oplus z) = (x \otimes y) \oplus (x \otimes z)).$$

Instances of distributive spaces are boolean algebras, the space of square matrices with entries over a field (e.g., the real or complex numbers) with the standard sum and product operations, as well as the elementary numerical systems mentioned before with both standard binary operations. In all these cases, $D = K$.

On the other hand, a vector space over a field K $(D, \oplus, \otimes)$ is also an example of a distributive space. Moreover, if $\dim D > 1$, then $D \neq K$, where $\dim D$ denotes the dimension of D as $K-$vector space.

Definition 8.5. An action of a group $(G, +, 0)$ on a set X is simply a function $* : G \times X \to X$ such that the following two conditions hold:

1. $(\forall a, b \in G)(\forall x \in X)((a + b) * x = a * (b * x))$.
2. $(\forall x \in X)(0 * x = x)$.

Definition 8.6. An algebraic substructure $\mathbb{S} = ((A, +_A, 0_A), (B, +_B, 0_B), i : A \to B)$ consists of two sets with binary operations defined over each of them and special constants, such that i fulfills the following properties:

1. i is an homomorphism: $i(0_A) = 0_B$ and $(\forall x, y \in A)(i(x +_A y) = i(x) +_B i(y))$.
2. i is injective: $(\forall x, y \in A)(i(x) = i(y) \Rightarrow x = y)$.
3. $(\forall x \in B)(\forall y \in A)((x +_B i(y) = 0_B) \Rightarrow \exists z \in A(i(z) = x))$.

The last condition can be rephrased as follows: the 'potential inverses' of elements of A, considered as elements in B, belong to A as well.

Usual examples of algebraic substructures are given by the natural injections $i_1 : \mathbb{Z} \to \mathbb{Q}$, $i_2 : \mathbb{Q} \to \mathbb{R}$ and $i_3 : \mathbb{R} \to \mathbb{C}$ (as well as the remaining meaningful combinations) with the addition operation and the zero element, respectively.

The main intuition with this definition is that when $(B, +_B, 0_B)$ has additionally an algebraic structure, as the one of a monoid, a semi-group or a group, then $(A, +_A, 0_A)$ would inherit automatically the same structure. This definition is a stronger notion than the one of embedding (i.e., an injective morphism) commonly used in the mathematical literature, since, in principle, the sets A and B have a very basic algebraic structure, e.g., we do not even require associativity for the corresponding operations. However, we impose the typical conditions for an embedding in 1) and 2) and additionally, we request condition 3) for including potential inverses of the smaller structure into itself. Now, if we restrict ourselves to the category of monoids, semi-group and groups, then these two notions coincide, because we can prove that, under these hypothesis, 3) would follow from 1) and 2).

Definition 8.7. Let X be a set and F a collection of functions from X to X. A subset Y of X is called the space of fixed points of F if

$$(\forall x \in X)(\forall f \in F)((f(x) = x) \leftrightarrow x \in Y)$$

Typical examples of spaces of fixed points appear in topology and in the setting of retractions between topological spaces (Munkres, 2000).

Apart of the former concepts, let us recall briefly the additional notions that will be reconstructed from some of the former ones through a process of formal conceptual blending.

Definition 8.8. Let R be a commutative ring with unity and $P \subseteq R$ an ideal. Then, P is a prime ideal if $R \neq P$, and for any $a, b \in R$, $a * b \in P$ implies that either $a \in P$ or $b \in P$. The collection of all prime ideals of R is called the (prime) spectrum of R.

Definition 8.9. A commutative ring with unity R is called containment-division ring if for any pair of ideals $I, J \in R$, $I \subseteq J$ if and only if J divides I as ideals, namely, there exists an ideal L such that $I = J \cdot_\iota L$.

Standard examples of CDR-s are Unique Factorisation Domains like the integer numbers.

Definition 8.10. A commutative ring with unity R is Noetherian if it satisfied the Ascending Chain Condition (ACC), i.e., any countable ascending collection of ideals $\{I_m\}_{m \in \mathbb{N}}$ stabilises, namely, there exists a m_1 such that $I_n = I_{m_1}$, for any $n \geq m_1$.

Definition 8.11. A Dedekind domain is a commutative ring with unity without zero-divisors such that any ideal can be written uniquely (up to the order (position) of the factors) as a product of finitely many prime ideals.

Dedekind domains are one of the central notions in Algebraic Number Theory (Janusz, 1996).

Definition 8.12. A field is a set $(F, +, 0, *, 1)$, such that $(F, +, 0)$ and $(F \setminus \{0\}, *, 1)$ are abelian groups and the $*$ distributes with respect to $+$, i.e.,

$$(\forall x, y, z)(x * (y + z) = x * y + x * z)$$

Definition 8.13. A field extension E/F consists of a pair of fields F and E, such that F is contained in E as a field, i.e., one can compute the binary operations in F by restricting the respective binary operations in E to the subset F.

Definition 8.14. The group of automorphisms of a field E, denoted by Aut$E$, is the collection of functions $\alpha : E \to E$, such that

1. α is a bijection.
2. α is compatible with the binary operations of E, i.e., for all $a, b \in E$, $\alpha(a \oslash b) = \alpha(a) \oslash \alpha(b)$, where $\oslash$ denotes $+$ or $*$.

Definition 8.15. The group of automorphisms of a field extension E/F fixing the base field F, denoted by Aut$_F(E)$, consists of the elements β of Aut$E$, i.e., automorphisms of E, such that for all $a \in F$, $\beta(a) = a$, it means that β is the identity function when it is restricted to the base field F.

This last concept is one of the most fundamental ones in Galois theory, since Aut$_F(E)$ is exactly the Galois Group of E/F, when this extension is Galois (Lang, 2002, Ch. 6,§1).

8.4 Defining the Blends

In this section we present a kind of 'conceptual factorisation' of some of the former concepts as formal blending ('conceptual product') of other concepts. Let us start with the notion of prime ideals over commutative rings with unity (or CDR-s). Specifically, we obtain the concept consisting of the collection of prime ideals over a CDR as a blend of the notions formed by 1) the concept described in Definition 1, denoted by $\mathbb{D}_1$, and 2) the concept defined by Definition 2, denoted by $\mathbb{D}_2$. So, let us define the generic space and the corresponding morphisms needed to form the desired V-diagram.

8.4.1 The Generic Space

The generic space $\mathbb{G}$ is formed by a set (sort) G with a binary operation $*_G$, a neutral element S and a binary relation $\leq_G$.

8.4.2 The 'Blending' Morphisms

The morphism to $\mathbb{D}_1$ is defined by the following:

$$\varphi(G) = \mathrm{Id}(R), \varphi(*_G) = *_\iota, \varphi(S) = 1_\iota \text{ and } \varphi(\leq_G) = \subseteq$$

Similarly, the morphism to $\mathbb{D}_2$ sends:

$$\delta(G) = \mathbb{Z}, \delta(*_G) = *, \delta(S) = 1 \text{ and } \delta(\leq_G) = \|$$

8.4.3 The Resulting Axiomatisation

From the axioms given in Definition 8.2 (kind of quasi-integers), we transfer into the blend only the fact that Z is a set with a binary operation $*$ having 1 as neutral element, and $\|$ is a binary relation, without integrating into the blend (at this stage) its formal definition.[5]

So, after using the same symbol for denoting the ring as a sort of element, or as the neutral element for the product of ideals $\cdot_G$, the blend has the form

$$(S, +, *, 0_S, 1_S, G = \mathrm{Id}(S), isprime, Prime, \cdot_G, \subseteq)$$

---

[5] So, this first blend emerges from a kind of weakening of the second concept involved. In the next sections we will see what kind of concepts are obtained when the corresponding axiom is included.

with all the corresponding axioms of the first conceptual space plus the translated version of the axiom defining the primality predicate. In particular, after doing the corresponding symbolic identifications, an element $P \in G$ (i.e., an ideal of S) satisfies the predicate *isprime* if and only if:

$$P \neq S \wedge (\forall X, Y \in G = \mathrm{Id}(S))(X \cdot_G Y \subseteq P \rightarrow (X \subseteq P \vee Y \subseteq P))$$

Now, it is an elementary exercise to see that this definition is equivalent to the fact that P is a prime ideal of S, i.e. to the condition

$$P \neq S \wedge (\forall a, b \in S)(a * b \in P \rightarrow (a \in P \vee b \in P))$$

Therefore, the predicate *isprime* turns out to be the predicate characterising the primality of ideals of S and the set (sort) *Prime* turns out to be the set of prime ideals of S.

In conclusion, the blended space consists of the axioms assuring that S is a commutative ring with unity, G is the set of ideals of S, *isprime* is the predicate specifying primality for ideals of S and *Prime* is the collection of all prime ideals of S.

On the other hand, let us include the axiom defining the upside-down divisibility relation:

$$(\forall a, b \in Z)(a \parallel b \leftrightarrow (\exists c \in Z)(a = c * b))$$

Furthermore, let us choose the same generic space and 'blend' morphisms as before.

Then, if we do the blend of the corresponding spaces, we obtain the former blended space (commutative ring with unity, its set of ideals and prime ideals and a predicate for the prime ideals) plus the translation of the corresponding version of the former axiom defining the relation $\parallel$, namely,

$$(\forall a, b \in G)(a \subseteq b \leftrightarrow (\exists c \in G)(a = c \cdot_\iota b))$$

where G denotes the set (sort) of ideals of R.

So, this is exactly the condition defining a CDR. In conclusion, we obtain as blend the composed notion of prime ideals over a CDR. In fact, this new notion was originally (co-)discovered by means of computing several kinds of formal blends of the former concepts with HETS.[6]

In addition, after doing a formal analysis of the containment-division condition, the concept of DCR is very closely related to the one defining a Dedekind domain, i.e., an integral domain such that every proper ideal can be written as a finite product of ideals (Coleman and Ribenboim, 1992, Theorem 37.1 and 37.8). Effectively, if we add the property of being Noetherian (Eisenbud, 1995), then both notions are equivalent. Moreover, we can replace the central notion defining being Noetherian,

---

[6] The concrete implementation in HETS of the former blend can be found in https://github.com/ewenmaclean/ICCC2015_hetsfiles/blob/master/ prime_ideals.dol

namely, the ascending chain condition (ACC); by a weaker version involving divisor chains of ideals, and still obtain an equivalent notion.

Specifically, let us say that a (commutative) ring satisfies the Divisor Chain Condition (DiCC) if for any chain of ideals $\{I_n\}_{n\in\mathbb{N}}$, where I_{m+1} is a divisor of I_m (i.e., $I_{m+1}|I_m$), there exists a n_1 such that $I_r = I_{n_1}$, for all $r \geq n_1$. So, the DiCC is obtained in a natural way by replacing the binary relation of containment by the upside-down divisibility relation (or 'upside-down dividend' relation) between ideals. More formally, the following theorem holds.

Theorem 8.1. *Let R be an integral domain, i.e., a commutative ring with unity without zero divisors. Then, the following conditions are equivalent:*

1. *R is a Dedekind domain.*
2. *R is a Noetherian CDR.*
3. *R is a CDR satisfying the DiCC.*

The core ideas of a proof of this fact can be found in (Gomez-Ramirez, 2015).

Besides, we can describe the concepts given in the last two conditions of Theorem 8.1 as a natural blend. For instance, the concept in the second condition can be expressed as a colimit of the notions of Noetherian commutative ring with unity (see Def. 10) and the notion of CDR (see Def. 9). So, we can represent the blended concepts of prime ideals (over CDR-s) (down part) as well as Theorem 8.1 (top part) in a diagrammatic way as shown in Figure 8.1. Note that in the middle of Figure 8.1 there are two ovals with names 'prime ideals' and 'Cont-Div. Rings' put together. They just denote the composed concept of the collection of prime ideals over a CDR. In fact, if we assume that the Noetherian condition can be re-written in a many-sorted first-order logic setting, then one can shown in a similar fashion as in the former case of prime ideals over a commutative ring with unity that the notion of Dedekind domain enriched with its prime spectrum can be decomposed as a formal blend of the notions of meta-primes and the notion of Noetherian domain with the collection of all its ideals.

8.5 Generation of Fundamental Notions of Fields and Galois Theory

In this section, we will sketch how to generate four fundamental concepts of Fields and Galois Theory by means of (our model of) formal conceptual blending starting by five of the concepts described above. It is worth it to mention that we could have chosen potentially any other formal mathematical theory (e.g. algebraic topology, algebraic geometry, number theory) to work with. There is no special property concerning Fields and Galois theory which allows us to express the corresponding concepts as a blend easier in comparison with other mathematical theories, except for the notion of finiteness, which can be explicitly avoided for the list of concepts presented here.

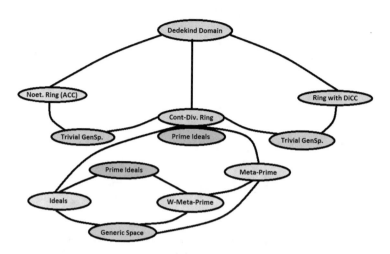

Fig. 8.1: The Notions of Prime Ideal (over CDR-s) and Dedekind Domains as Formal Conceptual Blends

So, the next graphics (Figures 8.2, 8.3 and 8.4) show a diagram with nine formal blends constructed in a recursive way, which shows how to generate the notions of field, field extension, group of homomorphisms of a field and $Aut(E/F)$ (e.g., the (Meta-)Galois Group of a (Galois) field extension) as a (recursive) blend of five (basic) concepts coming from several additional mathematical areas like group theory and topology. In this diagram the generic spaces are not shown as in the former graphic. Moreover, the concept where two lines meet upwards is the blending of the corresponding (down) concepts. For example, the concept of field is the formal blend of the concept of bigroup and the concept of distributive space.[7]

8.6 Summary

Let us summarise what we have shown here. We have modeled the notion of blend among two mathematical notions as a categorical colimit of theories defined in a many-sorted first-order logic setting.

Furthermore, by allowing weakened blends, i.e., blends using smaller axiomatisations of the input concepts, we fused the notion of an ideal of a commutative ring with unity (with the collection of all possible ideals of this ring) and the notion of a prime number (in a weakened version) of the integers, in order to express the

---

[7] The implementations, written with HETS in the common algebraic specification language CASL, can be found in the following link: https://github.com/dgomezramire/FieldsGaloisBlendingGeneration

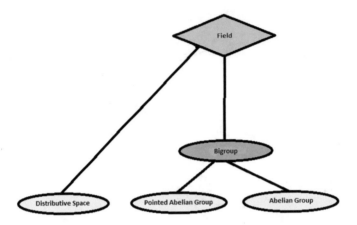

Fig. 8.2: Diagrammatic Representation for the generation of the concept of (mathematical) Fields through Formal Conceptual Blending

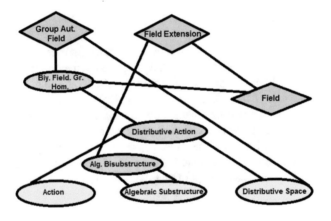

Fig. 8.3: Diagrammatic Representation for the generation of the concepts of Extensions of Fields and the Group of Automorphisms of a Field through Formal Conceptual Blending

collection of prime ideals of a commutative ring with unity as a formal blend. In addition, by choosing a very simple generic space identifying a minimal amount of sorts, we were able to co-discover a new class of commutative rings with unity, i.e., the 'containment-division rings' (CDR). These rings are essentially defined by the condition that containment and division among ideals are equivalent notions.

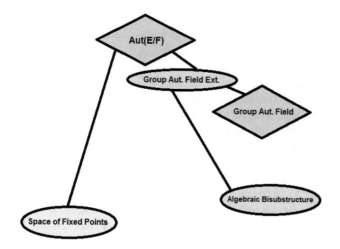

Fig. 8.4: Diagrammatic Representation for the generation of the concept of Group of Automorphisms of a Field Extension fixing the Base Field $Aut(E/F)$ through Formal Conceptual Blending

Now, with this terminology, the resulting blend was the concept of a prime ideal over a CDR (with the corresponding collection of all ideals of this ring). The concept of a prime ideal is a fundamental formal 'column' of the most successful modern approach to algebraic geometry given in terms of (affine) schemes (Grothendieck and Dieudonné, 1971). Furthermore, it is one of the key notions of commutative algebra and the corresponding dimension theory for commutative rings with unity (Eisenbud, 1995). So, the fact that we were able to generate mathematical seminal notions not only in the domain of complex analysis (e.g., the complex numbers (Fleuriot et al., 2014a)) and basic arithmetic (e.g., the integer (Bou et al., 2015)) but also in commutative algebra (e.g., prime ideals over a CDR) starts to show that formal conceptual blending can play a structural and 'omnipresent' role in mathematical creation, namely, it can be seen as a kind of 'meta-generator' of mathematical concepts.

Besides, it turns out that in a Noetherian setting (i.e., in a category where all the ideals are finitely generated) this new mathematical concept (CDR), being discovered with the help of this formal-cognitive tool (conceptual blending), is mathematically equivalent to a fundamental notion of algebraic number theory, e.g., Dedekind domains. Effectively, let us assume that we can re-express the condition of being Noetherian in a many-sorted first-order setting. Then, following an analogous route as the one described before, we can show that the composed notion of a prime ideal over a Dedekind domain jointed with its spectrum of ideals is obtained as a blend of the concepts of a Noetherian domain with its collection of ideals and meta-prime numbers over a weakened version of the integers.

Secondly, we started to work with the following five basic mathematical concepts, all of them supported by well-known examples and used very often implicitly and explicitly in modern mathematics: Abelian Group, Pointed Abelian Group, Distributive Space, Action of a group over a Set and Fixed Point Space. Furthermore, we continued by blending each of these concepts iteratively using very simple generic spaces inducing simultaneously the simplest kinds of analogical relation between the corresponding input spaces, namely, relations given by renaming sorts corresponding to sets, functions and relations. So, after doing nine times the operation of conceptual blending with a formalisation of colimits of theories in many-sorted first-order logic, we obtained four of the most fundamental concepts of Fields and Galois theory, i.e., the mathematical notions of Fields, Field Extension, Group of Automorphisms of a Field and Group of Automorphisms of a Field Extension fixing the base field. This last concept coincides with the notion of Galois Group when the corresponding extension is a Galois extension. We made and run explicitly all the related implementations in HETS.

The last collection of examples can be seen as foundational mathematical 'evidence' that formal conceptual blending plays a central role as a concrete 'meta-mathematical' operation allowing us to model more and more aspects of mathematical creativity. Now, we are not talking anymore about isolated mathematical concepts but about the conceptual production of entire theories with formal conceptual blending.

We can make a simple analogy with the Fundamental Theorem Arithmetic (i.e., the unique factorisation theorem in the integers) in order to understand better the idea behind generating these fundamental concepts of Fields and Galois theory. Let us consider for a while (mathematical) concepts as integer numbers, and formal conceptual blending as a product between numbers, i.e., if a concept B is the blend of the input concepts A and C, then C can be written as a formal product of A and C. So, one of the main claims here was to find an explicit prime factorisation of these particular four concepts of Fields and Galois theory.

The fact that it was possible to find such conceptual factorisation for notions in Fields and Galois theory, using prime concepts coming from other areas of mathematics like topology and group theory, implicitly suggests that if one modifies the order of the iterations and the sort identifications in the generic spaces, then it should be possible to find similar conceptual representations for mathematical concepts in other mathematical domains.

On the other hand, a very interesting question emerging in this context is the one of trying to determine when a mathematical concept can be seen as 'prime' concept in the sense that it cannot be decomposed as a non-trivial blending of two simpler concepts.

The main advantage of our procedure is that with the colimit formalisation of conceptual blending we have a quite concrete way of generating more efficiently (potential) creative definitions in comparison with approaches doing a rough combinatorial search. Besides, the manner in which we generate these basic concepts of Fields and Galois Theory offers a new formal route in comparison with the historic way in which these notions emerged, for example, by considering group of permutations of roots of specific polynomials (Edwards, 1984). Furthermore, as mentioned before the central principles of our way of generating concepts can be potentially applied to any area of (pure) mathematics.

8.7 Conclusion and Future Perspectives

We have seen that our particular formalisations of conceptual blending in pure mathematics not only have the conceptual 'power' for being considered as theoretical bricks for producing basic mathematical concepts, but also can be used to start to generate entire mathematical theories such as Fields and Galois Theory.

In conclusion, we have shown with ample examples that our formalisation of conceptual blending is a feasible conceptual tool for re-discovering and generating classical mathematical concepts, co-discovering new ones, starting to produce entire mathematical theories and originating concepts having pieces in different areas of pure mathematics. So, this work aims to serve also as strong formal support of the soundness of our approach towards a general formalisation of conceptual blending from both perspectives: a theoretical one, related with the relevance of this approach for pure mathematics; and a computational one, related with the appropriateness of our models for being successfully implemented.

Now, conceptual blending is just one of several fundamental cognitive mechanisms that the mind uses during mathematical research. So, it seems plausible to find a more general formal framework where one can identify, formalise and integrate a complete collection of such cognitive abilities, in order to be able to develop co-creative theorem assistants, which can help the researcher during his/her work at a higher qualitative level. More generally, our former work can be seen as an initial inspiration for solving the following more general question.

8.7.1 Artificial Mathematical Intelligence (AMI)

Modern mathematics are essentially founded and conceptually bounded on the Zermelo-Fraenkel set theory (ZFC), model, proof and recursion theory (Mendelson, 2010). That means that the solution of a solvable conjecture should be precisely described as a formal (logic) consequence of the axioms of ZFC, using a finite number of inference rules and initial premises. In other words, when a mathematician finally finds a correct solution of a conjecture, then the result of his/her research is simply a kind of computation of an ideal (and theoretically constructible) computer program, which starts to run all the possible proofs of provable theorems of ZFC, starting from a finite sub-collection of axioms and following precise (logical) mechanical deduction rules. Therefore, in comparison with the original goals of artificial intelligence (AI), it seems more plausible to be able to 'simulate' the way a mathematician 'thinks' about mathematical (solvable) conjectures, and to consider this as a more feasible sub-goal of modern AI. Let us call this problem *artificial mathematical intelligence* (AMI), i.e., the construction (implementation) of a computer program being able to solve essentially every human solvable mathematical conjecture (given to it explicitly in advance)[8] in less time than an average professional mathematician.

So, as mentioned before, a quite natural starting plan for solving AMI should begin with the identification, formalisation and integration of the most seminal cognitive processes used by the mathematician's mind on his/her research (e.g., thinking, doing sketches and writing the syntactic-mathematical formalities). This is in order to be able to 'simulate' his/her mind concretely in the special case of solving a mathematical postulate. Besides, the very nature of AMI as a concrete research question requires a strong interdisciplinary approach.

Furthermore, one can see the main results obtained in cognitive sciences during the last 30 years as a kind of implicit support for AMI. Effectively, canonical cognitive abilities have been identified, better understood and sometimes formalised as for example analogy making (Schwering et al., 2009), metaphor reasoning (G. Lakoff and R. Núñez, 2000) and conceptual integration (Fauconnier and Turner, 2003). Moreover, not only sophisticated computed programs have been required for verifying, and, strictly speaking, co-proving outstanding mathematical problems like the four-color theorem, the Feit-Thompson odd order theorem and the Kepler conjecture, but also there is a strong trend for integrating all of these software packages in order to generate a quite concrete form of Collaborative Theorem Proving (Fleuriot et al., 2014b). Additional works relevant in this context are presented in (Ganesalingam and Gowers, 2016) and (Buchberger et al., 2006).

Finally, this conceptual enterprise encompasses also a deep study into the (morphological-syntactic-semantic) foundations of mathematics, in order to obtain more precise and computationally-feasible re-formulations of seminal mathematical notions as, for instance, set, membership relation, formal (in)finiteness, mathematical proof, (un)solvable conjecture, (un)computable proof and (in)consistent theory, among others.

8.7.2 A Formal Vision

In the special case of mathematics, and due to the former reasons, it is plausible to find a complete (meta-)list of the additional cognitive formal processes that are used in a omnipresent manner by the working mathematician. Explicitly, the following list is an initial one and some of the cognitive tools described there are explicitly well-known, while others are more implicitly used, but equally important: inductive (recursive) reasoning, syntactic-semantic (s.s.) generalisation, particular-

---

[8] We assume that one can explicitly codify the conjecture into the program and additional formal evidence for it, e.g., specific cases where the conjecture holds. This would be the only input of this Universal Theorem Prover.

isation and simplification,[9] s.s. hypothesis' specialisation,[10] conceptual substratum/lining,[11] conceptual complement,[12] conceptual disjunction/conjunction,[13] and s.s. Reductio ab Absurdum.

So, inspired by the former considerations, we believe and hope that within a few years (e.g., a decade), there will be a cognitively-inspired software, which we can call now *the Universal Theorem Prover (UTP)*, that takes a solvable mathematical conjecture C as input, and after an amount of time less than that required by a professional mathematician, it solves C, namely, UTP gives an understandable mathematical proof or it offers a clear formal counter example.[14]

This vision comes, among others, from a global interdisciplinary view of mathematical research and also from a lot of outstanding progress in computational creativity, (interactive) theorem proving and cognitive sciences.

References

J. Alexander. Blending in mathematics. *Semiotica*, 187:1–48, 2011.

M. Bidoit and P. D. Mosses. *CASL User Manual*. Lecture Note in Computer Science 2900, Springer Verlag, Berlin Heidelberg New York, 2004.

F. Bou, J. Corneli, D. Gomez-Ramirez, E. Maclean, A. Peace, M. Schorlemmer, and A. Smaill. The role of blending in mathematical invention. In H. Toivonen at al., editors, *Proceedings of the Sixth International Conference on Computational Creativity (ICCC 2015)*. Brigham Young University, Provo, Utah, pages 55–62, 2015.

---

[9] These three processes encompass the heuristics used when a mathematician starts to vary the generality of the formal spaces where he/she needs to prove a particular conjecture, based (in the last case) on the explicit morphological representation of the elements of the corresponding class. For instance, if one needs to prove a conjecture C for all polynomials over the integers, then sometimes one starts with the simplest elements from a morphological perspective, e.g., monomials; then one continues with more elaborated expressions, e.g., binomials; until one gets the general argument for solving C.

[10] This is the process of modifying the hypothesis of C in several ways of generality in order to obtain a global idea of its solution.

[11] This formal ability abstracts the generic form of the elements of a mathematical structure described in a concept, and its dual operation.

[12] Suppose that a concept C contains all the mathematical structures satisfying the definition describing a second more specific concept C'. Then, the conceptual complement of C' (regarding C) is just the concept defined by all the structures satisfying C, but not C'.

[13] This is a natural extension to concepts of the corresponding set theoretical operations of disjuntion and conjunction.

[14] Here, it is important to clarify that we focus on 'solvable' conjectures, i.e., mathematical statements such that there exists a formal proof for them or for their negation. In particular, metastatements related with incompleteness and undecidability have in this context a second level of importance, because we aim to model the concrete meta-mathematical ability of the human mind which is involved just in the discovery/creation of formal mathematics.

B. Buchberger, A. Crăciun, T. Jebelean, L. Kovács, T. Kutsia, K. Nakagawa, F. Piroi, N. Popov, J. Robu, M. Rosenkranz, et al. Theorema: Towards computer-aided mathematical theory exploration. *Journal of Applied Logic*, 4(4):470–504, 2006.

E. A. J. Coleman and P. Ribenboim. *Multiplicative Ideal Theory*. Queen's Papers in Pure and Applied Mathematics, Ontario, Canada, 1992.

H.-M. Edwards. *Galois Theory*. Graduate Texts in Mathematics 101, Springer, 1993.

D. Eisenbud. *Commutative Algebra with a View Toward Algebraic Geometry*. Number 150 in Graduate Texts in Mathematics. Springer, New York, 1995.

G. Fauconnier and M. Turner. *The Way We Think*. Basic Books, 2003.

J. Fleuriot, E. Maclean, A. Smaill, and D. Winterstein. Reinventing the complex numbers. In T. R. Besold et al., editors, *Proceedings of the Workshop "Computational Creativity, Concept Invention, and General Intelligence"*, volume 1-2014 of *PICS*, Osnabrück, Germany, 2014a. Workshop at ECAI 2014, Prague.

J. Fleuriot, S. Obua, P. Scott, and D. Aspinall. ProofPeer: Collaborative theorem proving. *http://arxiv.org/abs/1404.6186*, 2014b. URL http://www.proofpeer.net/index.html.

G. Lakoff and R. Núñez. *Where Mathematics Comes From*. Basic Books, 2000.

M. Ganesalingam and W. Gowers. A fully automatic theorem prover with human-style output. *Journal of Automated Reasoning*, pages 1–39, 2016.

B. Ganter and R. Wille. *Formal Concept Analysis: Mathematical Foundations*. Springer, 1997.

R. W. Gilmer, and J. L. Mott. Multiplication rings as rings in which ideals with prime radical are primary. *Transactions of the American Mathematical Society*, 114.1, 40-52, 1965.

J. Goguen. An introduction to algebraic semiotic with application to user interface design. In *Computation for Methaphors, Analogy and Agents. C. L. Nehaniv, Ed. Vol. 1562*, pages 242–291, 1999.

J. Goguen. Towards a design theory for virtual worlds: Algebraic semiotics and scientific visualization as a case study. In C. Landauer and K. Bellman, editors, *Proceedings of the Virtual Worlds and Simulation Conference*. Society for Modelling and Simulation, pages 298–303, 2001.

J. Goguen. Steps towards a design theory for virtual worlds. In M.-I. Sánchez-Segura, editor, *Developing Future Interactive Systems*. Idea Group Publishing, pages 116–152, 2005.

D. Gomez-Ramirez. Conceptual blending as a creative meta-generator of mathematical concepts: Prime ideals and Dedekind domains as a blend. In T. R. Besold et al., editors, *Proceedings of the Workshop "Computational Creativity, Concept Invention, and General Intelligence" 2015*, volume 02-2015 of Publications of the Institute of Cognitive Sciences, University of Osnabrück, 2015.

A. Grothendieck and J. Dieudonné. *Eléments de Géométrie Algébrique I*. Springer, 1971.

P. Horward and J. E. Rubin. *Consequences of the Axiom of Choice*, volume 59. Mathematical surveys and monographs, American Mathematical Society, USA, 1998.

G. Janusz. Algebraic number theory (second edition). *American Mathematical Society*, 7, 1996.

S. Lang. *Algebra (revised third edition)*. Graduate Texts in Mathematics 211, Springer, 2002.

K. Meinke and J. V. Tucker. *Many-sorted Logic and its Applications*. John Wiley & Sons, Inc., New York, NY, USA, 1993.

E. Mendelson. *Introduction to Mathematical Logic. 5th edition.* Chapman & Hall//CRC, Boca Raton, USA, 2010.

T. Mossakowski. Colimits of order-sorted specifications. In F. P. Presicce, editor, *Recent Trends in Algebraic Development Techniques, 12th International Workshop, WADT'97, Tarquinia, Italy, June 1997, Selected Papers*, volume 1376 of Lecture Notes in Computer Sciences, pp. 316–332, Springer, 1997.

T. Mossakowski, C. Maeder, and K. Lüttich. The Heterogeneous Tool Set. In O. Grumberg and M. Huth, editors, *TACAS 2007*, volume 4424 of *Lecture Notes in Computer Science*, pages 519–522. Springer, 2007. URL http://www.informatik.uni-bremen.de/~till/papers/hets-tacas-toolpaper.pdf.

J. Munkres. *Topology. Second Edition.* Prentice Hall, Inc, 2000.

A. Schwering, U. Krumnack, K.-U. Kühnberger, and H. Gust. Syntactic principles of heuristic driven theory projection. *Cognitive Systems Research*, 10(3):251–269, 2009.

Chapter 9
Conceptual Blending in Melodic Harmonisation: Development and Empirical Evaluation in the Case of the CHAMELEON System

Maximos Kaliakatsos-Papakostas, Asterios Zacharakis, and Emilios Cambouropoulos

Abstract This chapter presents the CHAMELEON melodic harmonisation assistant that learns different aspects of harmony from expert-annotated data, blends learnt harmonies from different idioms using the COINVENT framework and harmonises user-given melodies. The learnt harmonic elements include chord types, chord transitions, cadences and bass voice leading, while blending is employed on the level of chord transitions. A methodology that integrates chord transition blending is utilised for constructing a compound chord transition probability matrix that combines information of two initial learnt harmonic idioms. This chapter also presents the key-findings of empirical studies on the perception of blends, focusing initially on results obtained from cadence blending and afterwards on the output of the CHAMELEON system. The empirical evaluation of the CHAMELEON system was performed through tests that were specifically designed for evaluating blending; results indicate that the COINVENT framework for conceptual blending is a promising tool for computational creativity in music.

9.1 Introduction

The conceptual blending theory by Fauconnier and Turner (2003) has proven to be a very useful tool for providing a musico-analytical perspective focusing on

Maximos Kaliakatsos-Papakostas
Department of Music Studies, Aristotle University of Thessaloniki, Greece. e-mail: `maxk@mus.auth.gr`

Asterios Zacharakis
Department of Music Studies, Aristotle University of Thessaloniki, Greece. e-mail: `aszachar@mus.auth.gr`

Emilios Cambouropoulos
Department of Music Studies, Aristotle University of Thessaloniki, Greece. e-mail: `emilios@mus.auth.gr`

© Springer Nature Switzerland AG 2018
R. Confalonieri et al. (eds.), *Concept Invention*, Computational Synthesis and Creative Systems, https://doi.org/10.1007/978-3-319-65602-1_9

cross-domain relations between musical and extra-musical domains such as text or image (e.g. see Tsougras and Stefanou (2015); Zbikowski (2002, 2008); Cook (2001); Moore (2013)). 'Intra-musical' blending, i.e. blending two musical spaces per se, is less straightforward (Spitzer, 2004; Antović, 2011) and has been recently approached methodologically in terms of structural blending (Goguen and Harrell, 2010), by integrating potentially conflicting structural elements, such as chords (Eppe et al., 2015), harmonic spaces (Kaliakatsos-Papakostas et al., 2017), or even melodic-harmonic material from different idioms (Cambouropoulos et al., 2015; Kaliakatsos-Papakostas et al., 2014; Ox, 2014). A more extended discussion and critical examination of conceptual blending processes in music is presented in Stefanou and Cambouropoulos (2015).

Within the context of the COINVENT project the applications and the extensions that conceptual blending has in music have been first studied under a theoretical point of view. In Tsougras and Stefanou (2015) a structural and hermeneutical analysis of 'Il vecchio castello' is given from Modest Mussorgsky's 'Pictures at an Exhibition', in an attempt to disclose both the intra-musical (combination of modal, tonal and coloristic harmonic spaces) and the extra-musical (contextual, symbolic and programmatic aspects) conceptual blending that the work incorporates. The proposed analysis showed how musical structure promotes meaning construction through cross-domain mapping. This research suggests that conceptual blending theory as an analytical tool can promote a richer structural interpretation and experience of Mussorgsky's work. The social aspect of social creativity, further discussed in Chapter 6 of this book, which is a crucial part of the COINVENT project, was examined in Stefanou (2015), where the theoretical and methodological developments in the study of social creativity in music were outlined, focusing on collaborative and improvised music-making. Particular reference was made to FolioHarmonies [1], a short qualitative study carried out as part of the COINVENT project, and documenting collaborative, open-ended problem-solving processes in the creation of original musical pieces. Finally, a critical investigation of the application of Fauconnier and Turner's conceptual blending theory in music was presented in Stefanou and Cambouropoulos (2015). This study aimed to expose a series of questions and aporias highlighted by current and recent theoretical work in the field, related to the common distinction between intra- and extra-musical blending as well as the usually retrospective and explicative application of conceptual blending. It was thereby argued that more emphasis could be given to bottom-up, contextual, creative and collaborative perspectives of conceptual blending in music.

The application of the COINVENT framework (Schorlemmer et al., 2014) has been used for generative conceptual blending of harmonic spaces, allowing the generation of new harmonic spaces that introduce blended and novel elements. Highly focussed examples of applying this framework for chord blending (Eppe et al., 2015) and cadence blending (Zacharakis et al., 2015a, 2017) have provided indications that computational conceptual blending is an efficient tool for computational creativity. An initial 'historical' evaluation of this argument was observed by obtaining the

---

[1] https://folioharmonies.wordpress.com – last accessed 15 March 2017.

tritone substitution cadence, which appears in jazz as a prominent chord progression, through blending two cadences belonging to earlier musical traditions, namely the perfect cadence in tonal music and the Renaissance Phrygian cadences (Eppe et al., 2015; Kaliakatsos-Papakostas et al., 2015; Zacharakis et al., 2017). This example, accompanied by empirical studies on the perception of blended cadences, is presented in further detail in Section 9.4.1.

The cadence blending methodology was modified to allow blending of chord transitions. In Kaliakatsos-Papakostas et al. (2016a) a system was presented that allows a music expert to specify arguments over given transition properties, in a process that makes the system capable of defining combinations of features in an idiom-blending process that is based on chord transition blending. A music expert could thereby assess whether the new harmonic idiom makes musicological sense and re-adjust the arguments (selection of features) to explore alternative blends that can potentially produce better harmonic spaces. The refined blending methodology that was developed in Kaliakatsos-Papakostas et al. (2016a) was combined with the learning methodology presented in Section 9.2 and expanded in blending Markov transition matrices as presented in Kaliakatsos-Papakostas et al. (2016c) and Kaliakatsos-Papakostas et al. (2017). The application of transition blending on chord transitions learned from data enabled the generation of compound harmonic idioms that comprise the chords and chord transitions of two initial idioms along with new connecting transitions and chords that are generated through transition blending. An algorithmic framework for learning elements from different levels of harmony has been developed in Kaliakatsos-Papakostas et al. (2016b), allowing idiom-independent learning of chord types through the General Chord Type (GCT) representation (Cambouropoulos et al., 2014; Cambouropoulos, 2015; Kaliakatsos-Papakostas et al., 2015), chord transitions (Kaliakatsos-Papakostas and Cambouropoulos, 2014), cadences and voice leading of the bass voice (Makris et al., 2015a,b). Transition blending was integrated in the idiom-independent learning and melodic harmonisation methodology, leading to the development of the CHAMELEON[2] (Creative HArmonisation of Melodies via LEarning and bLEnding ONtologies) melodic harmonisation assistant. The CHAMELEON system allows creative conceptual blending between two initial harmonic idioms, enabling various interesting music applications, ranging from problem solving, e.g. harmonising melodies that include key transpositions, to generative harmonic exploration, e.g., combining major-minor harmonic progressions or more extreme idiosyncratic harmonies. The CHAMELEON system is presented in Section 9.3.

Based on the interesting cadences that came out of the chord blending system, its ability to make fair predictions of the human-perceived dissimilarities between the blended cadences it produces was evaluated in Zacharakis et al. (2015a). Using the aforementioned behavioural data as a 'ground-truth' of human-based perceptual space of cadences, an evolutionary algorithm was employed in Kaliakatsos-Papakostas et al. (2016d) to adjust the salience of each cadence feature to provide a system-perceived space of cadences that optimally matched the ground-truth space.

---

[2] http://ccm.web.auth.gr/chameleonmain.html

This work was further expanded in Zacharakis et al. (2017), where a verbal attribute magnitude estimation method on six descriptive axes (preference, originality, tension, closure, expectancy and fit) is used to associate the dimensions of this space with descriptive qualities (closure and tension emerged as most prominent qualities). The novel cadences generated by the computational blending system were mainly perceived as one-sided blends (i.e. blends where one input space is dominant), since categorical perception seems to play a significant role (especially in relation to the upward leading note movement). The CHAMELEON system was shown to be able to express the harmonic character of diverse idioms in a creative manner, while the blended harmonies often extrapolated the two input idioms, creating novel harmonic concepts. The nature of the perceptual impact of the blended harmonisation products generated by the system was examined in Zacharakis et al. (2018), with experimental methodologies that were aimed at evaluating the creative output of a blending system. In the aforementioned work, the behavioural assessment of system-generated blended harmonisations revealed that the system succeeded in producing perceivable blends – across idioms, modes and types of chromaticism– that were equally preferred, compared to non-blends. Section 9.4 presents an overview of the most important findings from the above mentioned empirical studies.

9.2 Representing and Learning Harmonies for the Automated Harmonisation of Melodies

Melodic harmonisation tackles the problem of assigning harmony, i.e. chords, on a given melody. The first approaches to automated melodic harmonisation incorporated the encoding of human expert knowledge (e.g., Ebcioglu (1988)) in the form of rules that reflect certain musical styles explicitly (Pachet and Roy, 2001). Similarly, genetic algorithms (GA) have been used that relied on a set of rules for forming proper fitness functions; for an overview of such methods see Donnelly and Sheppard (2011) and Phon-Amnuaisuk and Wiggins (1999). Among the advantages of rule–based systems is that they allow human experts to describe the hierarchical structure of complex musical idioms with considerable accuracy by using grammar-related structures; applications of such methods have been presented for tonal or jazz music (Rohrmeier, 2011; Koops et al., 2013; Granroth-Wilding and Steedman, 2014).

In contrast to the rule-based methods, probabilistic techniques can be used for developing methods that learn from musical idioms, given a set of harmonically annotated pieces and proper harmonic representation. On the other hand probabilistic methodologies encompass the possibility to take 'unusual' and creative decisions. Many probabilistic methodologies have been proposed for tackling the four-voice harmonisation problem (Suzuki, 2013; Whorley et al., 2013) or the generation of chord sequences (Raczyński et al., 2013; Paiement et al., 2006). Probabilistic methodologies, however, especially hidden Markov models (HMMs), do not capture larger scale dependencies between remote harmonic parts (Pachet et al., 2011b), e.g., phrase endings. Additionally, there are important harmonic concepts, as the concept of cadences (Borrel-Jensen and Hjortgaard Danielsen, 2010), that can be considered separately in order to produce harmonisations that reflect coherency. The importance of the cadence is highlighted by the development of some probabilistic methodologies that focused on this concept. In Allan and Williams (2004) and Hanlon and Ledlie (2002) backwards propagation of the HMM was utilised, starting from the end (cadence part) and constructing the chord progression in a backwards fashion. In Yi and Goldsmith (2007) chord sequences that ended with a perfect cadence were rewarded, while in Yogev and Lerch (2008) the probable positions of cadences was estimated. An additional layer of probabilities for statistically learning the final chords explicitly of sequences was introduced in Simon et al. (2008), while a similar technique for fixing the ending or intermediate chords was presented in Kaliakatsos-Papakostas and Cambouropoulos (2014).

The melodic harmonisation methodologies that are integrated in the CHAMELE-ON melodic harmonisation assistant were presented in Kaliakatsos-Papakostas et al. (2016b) and incorporate modules for learning several harmonic aspects for radic-ally diverse idioms. This modular methodology allows the preservation of structural relations between remote harmonic parts, by learning and automatically employ-ing intermediate and final cadences. Specifically, this methodology allows learn-ing chord types through the idiom-independent General Chord Type (GCT) rep-resentation (Cambouropoulos et al., 2014; Cambouropoulos, 2015); cadence con-straints through capturing statistics on occurrences of the last pairs of chords in phrase endings; chord transition probabilities through the constraint hidden Markov model (cHMM) (Kaliakatsos-Papakostas and Cambouropoulos, 2014) that learns first-order GCT chord transitions and performs probabilistic harmonisation given the aforementioned cadence constraints as well as user-defined chord constraints; and bass voice leading through combinations of hidden Markov models (Makris et al., 2015a) and probabilistic modules that capture statistics about chord inver-sions and bass-to-melody distances (Makris et al., 2015b).

Expert annotations on a diverse collection of musical data from different historic eras and styles provide rich multi-level structural descriptions of harmony in differ-ent idioms, allowing the aforementioned modules to learn and create new music that accurately reflects the characteristics of these idioms. The expert annotations allow the extraction of structural harmonic features at various hierarchic levels, namely (a) harmonic reduction(s) of each musical work/excerpt (structural harmonic/non-harmonic notes are explicitly marked); (b) local scale/key changes (harmonic con-cepts relating to modulations can be learnt); and (c) grouping structure (cadential patterns at various hierarchic levels can be inferred).

The training dataset consists of over 430 manually annotated musicXML docu-ments in seven categories that reflect mainly genre categorisation, while there are various subcategories within genres that present notable differences in their har-monic structure. The seven main categories that comprise the training dataset are the following:[3]

---

[3] Categories 4, 5 and 6 may seem to overlap, but they are essentially different: category 4 includes harmonisations of initially monophonic folk melodies made by art music composers of European

1. Modal harmonisation in the Middle Ages (11th – 14th centuries): includes sub-categories of medieval pieces in the Organum and Fauxbourdon styles.
2. Modal harmonisation in the Renaissance (15th – 17th centuries): includes modal music from the 16th – 17th centuries along with modal chorales.
3. Tonal harmonisation (17th – 19th centuries): includes a set of the Bach Chorales, the Kostka-Payne corpus[4] and tonal harmonisation sets from the 18th – 19th centuries.
4. Harmonisation in National Schools (19th – 20th centuries): includes 19th – 20th century harmonisation of folk songs from Norway, Hungary and Greece.
5. Harmonisation in the 20th century: includes harmonisations of Debussy, Hindemith, Whitacre, Stravinsky and Schnittke among others.
6. Harmonisation in folk traditions: includes Tango (classical and nuevo styles), Epirus polyphonic songs and Rebetiko songs.
7. Harmonisation in 20th-century popular music and jazz: includes mainstream jazz, pieces from Bill Evans and a collections of songs from The Beatles.

This methodology allows the harmonisation of given melodic annotated files that comply with the 'input protocol', i.e., include the melody to be harmonised and information regarding some harmonic attributes that are not automatically inferred at this stage. The annotations of the input protocol include manual annotation of harmonic rhythm (the positions where chords should occur), harmonically important notes (important notes that should be considered with higher priority in the harmonisation process), key and phrase structure. Key structure is a higher level harmonic feature concerning the tonality or tonalities of the piece, while phrasing structure indicates the phrase grouping boundaries of the melody.

9.3 Blending Harmonic Spaces in the CHAMELEON System

The development of the CHAMELEON melodic harmonisation assistant is based on the statistical learning scheme described in the previous section, in combination with a mechanism that employs the core COINVENT conceptual blending model for blending chord transitions from two initial input idioms. The blended transitions are integrated into a compound matrix of transition probabilities that combines and extends the harmonic characteristics of the initial idioms. This methodology not only provides creative harmonic solutions to any given melodic harmonisation problem, but also addresses the problem of zero probability transitions in Markov models (Cleary and Teahan, 1995) by creating musically meaningful transitions that connect two 'non-connected' transition matrices; this problem has been addressed

---

National Schools, category 5 comprises 20th-century original compositions (not based on folk songs) and category 6 contains original harmonisations embedded in the folk idioms.

[4] This dataset consists of the 46 excerpts that are longer than eight measures from the workbook accompanying Kostka and Payne's theory textbook *Tonal Harmony*, 3rd edition (Kostka and Payne, 2004) and is available in machine readable format at http://theory.esm.rochester.edu/temperley/kp-stats/index.html.

with solutions that do not incorporate musical information, e.g., either by assigning arbitrary non-zero 'escape' probability values (Chordia et al., 2010) or by enforcing arc-consistency (Pachet et al., 2011a).

9.3.1 Blending and Rating Chord Transitions

Blending two initial harmonic idioms in CHAMELEON is based on blending input chord transitions from these idioms. The methodology for chord transition blending described in this chapter uses an algorithm that combines amalgam-based blending and completion, given that there is a dictionary of acceptable chord types, expressed as General Chord Types (GCTs) (Cambouropoulos et al., 2014). The proposed methodology is equivalent to the COINVENT framework, but is adjusted for the specific harmonic ontology (with the GCT representation), using a *dictionary* of chord types that are allowed in the emerging blends. This dictionary is built by gathering the chord types that are learned from the idioms that take part in the blending process and represent a part of the 'background knowledge' in the blending process. By assuming that specific chord types are allowed, the search space of possible chords that are allowed in blended transitions is not overwhelmingly large. Therefore, for the specific task of transition blending, the searching capabilities of the amalgam-based process are not necessary and can be omitted altogether.

The formal ontology of chord transitions that allows blending using the COINVENT framework is described as a set of properties that involve each chord independently and the chord transition as a whole (relations between the two chords forming the transition). Using the argument-based system presented in Kaliakatsos-Papakostas et al. (2016a), music experts were allowed to observe blending results obtained in various harmonic setups after enabling/disabling different sets of transition properties. After examination of several produced outcomes, a (non-conclusive) list of nine important properties was maintained:

1. *fromPCs*: the pitch classes included in the first chord,
2. *toPCs*: the pitch classes included in the second chord,
3. *DIChas0*: Boolean value indicating whether the Directed Interval Class (DIC) vector (Cambouropoulos, 2012; Cambouropoulos et al., 2013) of the transition has 0 (i.e. that both chords have at least one common pitch class),
4. *DIChas1*: as above but for DIC value 1 (i.e., at least one ascending semitone),
5. *DIChasMinus1*: as above but for DIC value -1 (i.e., at least one descending semitone),
6. *ascSemNextRoot*: Boolean value indicating whether the first chord has a pitch class with ascending semitone relation to the pitch class of the second chord's root,
7. *descSemNextRoot*: as above but with descending semitone,
8. *semNextRoot*: as above but with either ascending or descending semitone and

9. *5thRootRelation*: Boolean value indicating whether the first chord's root note is a fifth above the root of the second. Root notes of chords are computed with the General Chord Type (GCT) (Cambouropoulos et al., 2014) algorithm.

The notion of the generic space in the conceptual blending theory (Fauconnier and Turner, 2003) relates with the idea of induced schemas (Gick and Holyoak, 1983), which are abstract objects describing general attributes and relations in human perception and cognition. However, utilising image schemas for forming the generic space has recently been studied only on a theoretical level (Hedblom et al., 2016). In the COINVENT framework for conceptual blending, the role of the generic space is to reject possible blends that do not incorporate common elements of the input spaces, even if these elements are parts of the low-level description of the input spaces and not abstract concepts related to induced schemas. Indeed such low-level elements are required for representing conceptual spaces in the COINVENT framework, since blended spaces emerge by obtaining specific low-level elements from the inputs. After extensive experimentation during the development of the transition blending methodology and the cadence blending methodology discussed later (in Section 9.4.1.1), it became obvious that the inclusion of such elements in the generic space often deteriorated the creative capabilities of the system by imposing strict restrictions which in some cases did not allow the emergence of interesting blends. To this end, two types of properties were distinguished: the *necessary* and the *desired* properties of transition blending. *Necessary* properties are potentially incorporated in the generic space, while *desired* properties are not considered during the formulation of the generic space. Both necessary and desired properties are considered in rating and ranking the blends as described later. In Kaliakatsos-Papakostas et al. (2017), among the nine properties that describe transitions, only the *fromPCs* and *toPCs* properties were considered as *necessary*.

Regarding the blending process, generating amalgams is computationally expensive, since the generalisation paths that can be followed are many and the number of blends that can be created is in exponential relation with the number of properties and possible property values. Additionally, the blends produced by the amalgam-based process might incorporate chords that do not belong to desirable chord types, e.g. clusters of semitones or single note chords that are haphazardly rated as good blends. This fact requires the application of a subsequent filtering process that discards 'unacceptable' chords, based on which chords have types that do not belong to a predefined (potentially learned) dictionary of chords. The dictionary of acceptable chord types, denoted by $\mathcal{T}$, can be employed actively for the generation of all possible chords that have acceptable types, instead of filtering out blends that do not comply with type-related restrictions. Supposing a dictionary that consists of N chord types, all the possible chords that have to be examined are all 12 transpositions of each type, summing up to a total of $12\,N$ chords; *looping* through all acceptable chords, a total of $144\,N^2$ of possible chord transitions exists between them. For transition blending the generation of good blends is not a matter of constructing chords with complex types, but finding the chords that creatively satisfy transition attributes that come through blending the input transitions. Furthermore, given that the number of chord types in learned idioms (N) is not overwhelmingly

---

Algorithm 1 Computation of all possible blends

Input:(i) two input transition, I_1 and I_2, **(ii)** a dictionary of all acceptable chord types $\mathscr{T}$
Output: List of all possible blends ($\mathscr{B}$) of I_1 and I_2

$\mathscr{B} \leftarrow \emptyset$ ▷ % initialise and empty set of blends
$g \leftarrow$ getGenericSpace(I_1, I_2) ▷ % get the generic space of inputs
$\mathscr{C} \leftarrow \emptyset$ ▷ % initialise the set of all possible acceptable chords
                                                                                   ▷ % make the set of all possible acceptable chords

for $t \in \mathscr{T}$ **do**
   for $r \in \{0, 1, \ldots, 11\}$ **do**
      $c =$ makeChordWithRootAndType(r, t)
      $\mathscr{C} =$ append$(\mathscr{C}, c)$
   end for
end for

                                                                                   ▷ % for all chord pairs
for $c_1 \in \mathscr{C}$ **do**
   for $c_2 \in \mathscr{C}$ **do**
      $tr =$ formTransition(c_1, c_2) ▷ % form the transition from c_1 to c_2
                                                                                   ▷ % check if transition satisfies generic space
      if satisfies(tr, g) **then**
         $\mathscr{B} =$ append$(\mathscr{B}, tr)$
      end if
   end for
end for

Fig. 9.1: Algorithm for obtaining all possible transition blends of two input transitions, given a dictionary of acceptable chord types

large, looking for the best blend among the 144 N^2 possible pairs produced with the 'dictionary looping' process is more efficient than employing the amalgam-based process and subsequent dictionary filtering. The dictionary looping algorithm for producing blends is presented in Figure 9.1, while an illustration that compares the steps of the amalgam-based process and dictionary looping in given in Figure 9.2.

Rating and ranking the blends produced by the dictionary looping process (forming a set of blends denoted by $\mathscr{B}$) is an important step that allows *meaningful* blends to be distinguished and considered with higher priority for the next steps. Most *meaningful* blends are considered the ones that include a combination of all the *salient* features encompassed by the input transitions, as supported by studies on human creativity (Goel, 2014). In Kaliakatsos-Papakostas et al. (2017) a method has been proposed for automatically assigning salience values in each feature of transitions, which is based on statistics on the idiom that this transition belongs to. Through this method, the less common a feature is, among a set of given transitions within a harmonic context, the higher salience value it is assigned. Therefore, features that appear in fewer transitions are more characteristic of these transitions and have higher salience values, while features that appear in many transitions are not

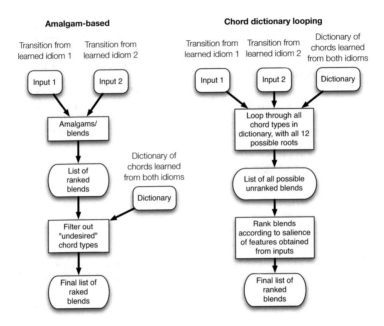

Fig. 9.2: Comparison of amalgams and dictionary looping for constructing the list of all ranked blends for a given pair of input transitions

salient for any of these transitions. The rating value of each blend in $\mathcal{B}$ is computed by summing all the saliences of features that this blend inherits from the input spaces. Therefore, better rated blends are the ones that incorporate a larger total of salience values inherited from the inputs (by inheriting a larger number of highly salient features), while lower ranked blends inherit either fewer or less-salient features.

9.3.2 Constructing a Compound Chord Transition Matrix of Two Idioms Using Blended Transitions

The chord transition blending methodology described above has been integrated into the melodic harmonisation assistant presented in Section 9.2 and in Kaliakatsos-Papakostas et al. (2016b). Specifically, chord transition blending is employed on the chord transitions learned from two harmonic idioms in the context of the cHMM algorithm, combining the independently learned chord transition matrices to generate a novel consistent composite harmonic space. Specifically, the 10 most common GCT chord transition tables learned from two *initial* idiom datasets are blended using the transition blending methodology, producing new blended transitions that connect and extend the transition possibilities of the initial idioms, generating a *compound* idiom. The produced compound idiom preserves some chord transition characteristics of the initial idioms. Before transition blending is applied, similar chords—in terms of GCT grouping (Kaliakatsos-Papakostas et al., 2015)—are identified and the most common-sense musical connections between the initial idioms are made, by enabling transitions that use such chords. Transition blending may produce transitions that incorporate chords that either belong to the initial learned idioms or not, i.e., new chords can potentially be invented. In the presented approach blends that incorporate at most one new chord in each transition are accepted, i.e., blended transitions between chords that do not belong to either initial idiom are rejected.

The final outcome of the presented methodology is a *musically meaningful* matrix of GCT chord transitions that extends the respective transition matrices of two initial idioms learned from data. The general form of a *compound* transition matrix is illustrated in Figure 9.3, which is built around the learned transition matrices of the initial idioms (I_1 and I_2). The transitions generated by blending pairs of transitions belonging to the two initial idioms are inserted into the compound matrix, enabling connections between the separate set of chords of each idiom. The sets of chords of each idiom are considered separate, even if some chords might have common attributes in both idioms, since they potentially have a different functional role in terms of the chords that come before or after in each dataset. As mentioned earlier, there is also a pre-blending algorithm that allows transitions between chords that are identical or similar.

The compound matrix of chord transition probabilities (as illustrated in Figure 9.3) incorporates a modified version of the transition matrices of the initial idioms I_1 and I_2. The probabilities therein are modified in comparison with the probabilities learned from data because of the insertion of other probabilities in other parts of the compound matrix and the required normalisation so that each row sums to 1. The A_{i-j} parts include transitions that have been created either from the pre-blending stage or through blending and lead directly from chords of I_i to chords of I_j. For example, a non-zero probability in A_{1-2} enables the transition from an I_1 chord to an I_2 chord. Parts B_{i-x} and B_{x-j} include blended transitions that lead from I_i to a new chord and from a new chord to I_j respectively. The described methodology does not populate the C part of the matrix, since in this methodology only transition blends that incorporate only one new chord (not belonging to I_i or I_j) are accepted – chords in C would include transitions between two new chords.

The presented methodology aims to interconnect and relate chords between I_i and I_j through inserting blended transitions that allow moving from chords in I_i to ones in I_j and vice-versa. Blended transitions that include new chords can be inserted in the compound matrix, but under the condition that every transition should have at least one new chord and depart from or lead to $I_i, i = 1, 2$. It is therefore assumed that blended transitions can include only one new 'pivot' chord for moving from I_i to I_j, discarding blends that include chords that are both new in both idioms. Additionally, it needs to be ensured that if a new chord is used, it should be preceded by a chord in I_i and be followed by a chord in I_j, in order to avoid the insertion

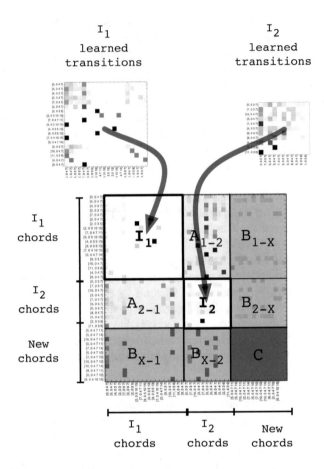

Fig. 9.3: Graphical description of a *compound* matrix that includes transition probabilities of both initial idioms and of several new transitions generated through
transition blending. These new transitions allow moving across the initial idioms,
creating a new compound idiom

of exclusively a terminal ('dead-end') or a beginning chord ('unreachable'). To this
end, transitions in B_{i-x}, which go from a chord of idiom i to a new (in both initial
idioms) chord created with transition blending, and transitions in B_{x-j}, which arrive
at chords in idiom j from new chords, are combined and form a 'chain' of two
transitions: $c_i \rightarrow c_x$ followed by a transition $c_x \rightarrow c_j$, where c_i is in idiom i and c_j is
in idiom j. Such chains of two consecutive transitions, connecting chords of i with
chords of j with an intermediate new chord, will be denoted as B_{i-x-j}.

Before blended transitions are inserted into the compound matrix, transitions that
are composed of identical or similar chords between the two initial spaces are inserted in the A_{1-2} and A_{2-1} parts of the matrix. These transitions use common or

similar chords to move between the two initial spaces. Specifically, in this step all the possible preceding and next chords of similar or common chords in one input idiom I_i are also considered as possible preceding or next chords of the ones in the other input idiom I_j, 'activating' the respective transitions in A_{1-2} and A_{2-1}. Two chords belonging to different initial idiom are considered similar if they belong to the same GCT group in the diatonic context of both idioms (as described in detail in Kaliakatsos-Papakostas et al. (2015)), i.e., if they (i) have the same root; (ii) have subset-related chord types; and (iii) both include pitch classes that are diatonic or not to the scale of both idioms.

By blending each of the 10 most common transitions of idiom 1 with the ones in idiom 2, 100 different applications of blending are possible. For keeping only applications of transition blending on pairs of transitions that do not incorporate harmonic characteristics that have already been examined in other pairs, blending is actually employed only on pairs of transition that incorporate a *maximal* subset of features from the generic spaces in regards to the *subsumption* relation. As explained in further detail in Kaliakatsos-Papakostas et al. (2017), the subsumption relation between generic spaces of different blending applications defines a partial order relation, i.e. the set of all possible generic spaces the subsumption relation satisfies the reflexivity, antisymmetry and transitivity relations. For instance, let us consider the generic space, $\mathcal{G}_{(x_1,x_2)}$, produced by blending the input transitions (x_1,x_2) and the set of all the generated blends in this blending application, $\mathcal{B}_{(x_1,x_2)}$. A generic space $\mathcal{G}_{(x_1,x_2)}$ *subsumes* another generic space $\mathcal{G}_{(y_1,y_2)}$, denoted as $\mathcal{G}_{(x_1,x_2)} \sqsubseteq \mathcal{G}_{(y_1,y_2)}$, if $\mathcal{G}_{(x_1,x_2)}$ is more general than or equal to $\mathcal{G}_{(y_1,y_2)}$. A more less general (or more specific) generic space includes more detailed harmonic descriptions about the requirements that the blends should incorporate, and therefore are considered as more descriptive and meaningful in the presented approach. Therefore, within the set of all 100 applications of blending that are available by two initial idioms, only the ones that incorporate generic spaces that are maximal subsets of the set of all generic spaces are considered. This filtering process reduces the number of required blending applications, while, at the same time, keeps only the applications of blending that incorporate the maximal overlapping of common harmonic information between the two initial spaces.

For each blending application that is finally performed, the topmost 100 blends are kept while the rest are discarded, forming a pool of best blends that are available for insertion it the compound matrix. The probability value that each blend receives for entering the compound transition matrix is calculated based on the probability values of the input transitions that produced these blends and the ranking placement of the blends in the blending quadruple; higher probability values of inputs leads to blends with higher probabilities, while the better the rate of the blend, the higher the probability (closer to the mean value of the input probabilities). Specifically, if the probability values (in the initial transition matrix of the idiom) of the inputs that produced a blend are p_{I_1} and p_{I_2}, then the *potential* of a blend, p_b, is computed as:

$$p_b = \frac{p_{I_1} + p_{I_2}}{2} \frac{\text{rate}(b)}{\text{rate}_{\max}}$$

where rate(b) is the rating value of the blend and rate$_{max}$ is the maximum rating value in the set of blends produced by the specific inputs.

Afterwards, blended transitions in the pool of best blends are categorised to the A_{i-j}, B_{i-x} or B_{x-i} categories and blends that belong to either B_{i-x} or B_{x-i} are matched in B_{i-x-j} chains/pairs for being considered as integrated elements. For inserting blends or chains of blends in the compound matrix, the user of the CHAMELEON system can select different intensities of blending through two parameters: the *rating-based selection* (RBS) and *probability intensity multiplier* (PIM), that define the number of blends to be embedded in the extended matrix and the relative values of probabilities of transitions outside the initial harmonic spaces (I_1 and I_2). For example a RBS value of 0.5 imports 50% of the most highly rated blends, while a value of 0 generates an extended matrix that includes only the initial spaces and the pre-blending common/similar connections. A PIM value of 0 reduces the probabilities of transitions in A_{i-j}, B_{i-x} and B_{x-i}, while larger PIM values increase the probabilities of transit outside the I_i and I_j parts, encouraging inter-idiom transitions.

9.4 Empirical Evaluation of Musical Creativity via Conceptual Blending

Even though creativity (human or computational) has been studied under several scientific aspects there is no commonly accepted definition, since many authors approach it from different perspectives (e.g., see Boden (2004) and Wiggins (2006); for a comprehensive discussion see Jordanous (2013) chapter 3). Especially evaluating creativity—either human or computational—is a non-trivial task since such processes involve the assessment of aesthetic quality of the creative products. Therefore, creativity is often evaluated via measuring partial constituent elements of the results of creative acts (e.g. novelty, value, surprise, problem solving ability, originality, divergence, etc.) (e.g. see Maher et al. (2013); Jordanous (2013)). In terms of evaluating a creative autonomous system, the two usual approaches are either to directly evaluate the product of the system or to evaluate the creative processes (Pearce and Wiggins, 2001). The former approach can be considered as a summative evaluation (see Jordanous (2013) chapter 1), whereby the overall creativity of a system is evaluated. The latter, which is discussed in detail in Chapter 10 of this book, is a formative evaluation process which provides evaluation feedback concerning the evolution of creative processes that the system performs during the development stage.

This section presents the summative approach (evaluation of the end products) of creative systems based on blending in harmony, while it takes into account the formative characteristics of the creative systems with a view to increasing their creative potential. The first system employs conceptual blending for inventing musical cadences. Specifically, the perfect and the Renaissance Phrygian cadences are used as input spaces and various cadential blends are produced based on musicological and blending optimality criteria. Empirical evaluation of the system based on a selection of generated cadences is presented, which allows a better understanding of perceptual relationships between cadences, by transforming pairwise dissimilarity ratings between cadences into a perceptual space. Additionally, a verbal attribute magnitude estimation method on six descriptive qualities (preference, originality, tension, closure, expectancy and fit) is described, which helped to associate the dimensions of this space with descriptive qualities (closure and tension emerged as the most prominent ones). Among the observations of this study was that the novel cadences generated by the computational blending system are mainly perceived as single-scope blends (i.e., blends where one input space is dominant), due to categorical perception induced by the upward leading note movement.

Evaluating the creativity of the CHAMELEON melodic harmonisation assistant was performed under the scope of conceptual blending and included a distinction into three components: value, novelty and blending rate perception of the product. The third component was employed in order to allow the identification of whether the generated hybrid or novel harmonic idioms (i.e., blends) were indeed perceived as such, i.e., whether listeners would classify harmonisations of (a) melodies in different styles from the learned harmonies (melody-idiom blends) and (b) harmonic blends between different harmonic idioms (cross-harmony blends) either as blends, indeed as completely novel harmonic idioms, or as belonging to either of the input idioms. An additional concern was the examination of potential influence induced by melody on this process, since the implied harmony of the harmonised melody potentially affects idiom perception. Two versions of a listening experiment were designed and conducted in order to address the above questions, as well as to evaluate the generated artefacts according to their perceptual novelty and value. These experiments incorporated melodies from different idioms harmonised by the system either with a single idiom (e.g., Bach's chorale style or Jazz) as melody-idiom blends or according to blended idioms. The general tasks of participants in both experiments included the idiom classification of harmonisations, along with attributions of preference and expectancy.

9.4.1 Empirical Evaluation of a Formal Model for Cadence Blending

Regarding the first set of experiments for the cadence blending system, the tonal perfect cadence and the modal Renaissance Phrygian cadence were blended (Figure 9.4). The perfect cadence is described as a functional dominant-to-tonic chord progression (Sears, 2015; Aldwell et al., 2010; Caplin, 1998), while the three- or four-voice Phrygian cadence is described as a contrapuntal progression (Barnett, 2002; Schubert, 1999; Collins, 2002) based on a two-voice linear movement and from a ♭vii6 chord leading to an I or i or Iomit3 chord with the tonic in the upper voice (see Figure 9.4), or, considering a C major or minor tonality, from a B♭ chord to a C or Cm or C^5. Within the context of the utilised cadence blending system,

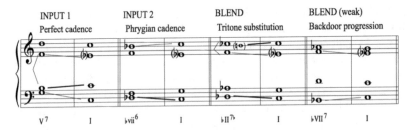

Fig. 9.4: Conceptual blending between the tonal perfect cadence and a Renaissance Phrygian cadence gives rise to the tritone substitution progression / cadence (the backdoor progression can also be derived as a blend). This figure is taken from Zacharakis et al. (2017)

the cadences are modelled as rich concepts that embody several properties with attached weights, based on functional properties that these properties convey, such as semitonal resolution of the leading note and type of harmonic progression expressed as distance between chordal roots, among others. The most prominent characteristics of the two cadences are assumed to be the upward leading note of the perfect and the downward leading note of the Phrygian cadence, while relatively prominent characteristics were considered to be the existence of the tritone (F and B notes) and the fifth/fourth motion of the roots in the perfect cadence. Even though the two input spaces (perfect and Phrygian) are represented as being equally important in the blending process, the perfect cadence can be assumed to be more prominent as a cadential schema in the mind of contemporary listeners, mainly due to the domination of characteristics of the classical tonal music over of the Renaissance modal music in today's music.

Blending optimality in the case of cadence blending is tackled through the assignment of a salience weight for each property that indicates the importance of a specific feature in a cadence. Specifically, three grades of salience were assumed, represented as numerical weight values 1, 2 and 3, where increasing values indicate increasing salience. The weight value of each feature was assigned by expert musicologists, while the scale from 1 to 3 indicates the existence of non-salient (value 1), relatively salient (value 2) and highly salient (value 3) features. Salience weights concern the input cadences (perfect and Phrygian), while relatively and importantly salient features are considered the ones that reflect important perceptual characteristics of the musical idioms. According to the previous paragraph, for the perfect cadence, the highly salient feature is the leading note to the tonic while the F-B tritone and fifth/fourth roots motion are relatively important. For the Phrygian cadence, the highly salient feature was the downward leading note. The basic assumption is that highly ranked blends should include as much of the most salient input features as possible, since this will promote the generation of blends that incorporate a stronger perceptual correlation with the characteristics that both inputs convey. Thus, the ranking of blends is based on the total salience, which is expressed as the sum of the feature weights a blend inherits from the inputs.

Among the most highly ranked cadences of the system is the tritone substitution progression (see Figure 9.4), as it incorporates most of the salient features of both cadences (it includes both the most salient upward and downward leading notes). It is worth noting that the computational system 'invents' this cadential type, which emerged in jazz, centuries after the main tonal/modal input cadences. The backdoor progression (also used in jazz) may also appear as a blend (depending on how blends are rated/selected), but much lower in the ranking. Many other blends are possible, seven of which were further examined empirically in the presented study, where the main research questions revolved around whether the generated blends were perceived as being single-scope blends (i.e., closer to one of the input cadences) or they are balanced double-scope blends (in between the perfect and Phrygian cadences). Additional inquiries included the examination of whether the new cadences were perceived by listeners as being between the input cadences (in case of double-scope blends) or as being interesting new versions of one of the input cadences (in case of single-scope blends), along with how listeners perceive the new cadences in terms of originality, expectancy, sense of closure and tension and which cadences they prefer.

Two subjective tests were conducted for evaluating the cadences produced by the system. The first one included a non-verbal evaluation listening test (following a preliminary study reported in Zacharakis et al. (2015a) based on the modelling of cadences presented in Eppe et al. (2015)) and a second verbal evaluation. In the first experiment, a pairwise dissimilarity rating listening test between the two input and seven blended cadences was conducted, while a Multidimensional Scaling (MDS) analysis on the acquired data produced a spatial configuration that was used as an indirect way to measure the relation of blends to the input cadences. The second experiment involved a descriptive type of subjective evaluation (Verbal Attribute Magnitude Estimation) for assessing qualities of the produced blends. In this experiment, the nine cadences were presented to listeners in two different harmonic contexts (tonal minor and Phrygian), resulting in 18 cadential stimuli. In this empirical experiment, listeners rated each cadence according to preference, degree of tension, closure effect, originality, expectedness and fit within the corresponding tonal/modal context.

9.4.1.1 Formal Description of Cadences

In this study, the formal description of cadences was similar to the description of transitions described in Section 9.3.1, but included more details about the penultimate chord of a cadence. Due to the fact that in cadences the final chord is considered fixed, the property concerning the pitch classes of the second chord (*toPCs*) was not included in the description. On the other hand, the properties of the root and the type of the first chord were considered as interesting to study in the context of cadences, introducing the properties *fcRoot* and *fcType* respectively. Similarly, the semitone difference between the roots of the first and the second chords was considered important, introducing the property *rootDiff*. Moreover, the existence of a tone movement to the root of the final chord (the tonic in the case of this study) was also considered important, since it is indicated to be relatively salient in terms of perception in the cadence blending example in Figure 9.4. The final list of properties describing a cadence was the following:

1. *fcRoot*: root of the penultimate chord (numeric value),
2. *fcType*: type of the penultimate chord (GCT type),
3. *fcPCs*: the pitch classes of the penultimate chord,
4. *rootDiff*: root difference of the cadence transition,
5. *DIChas0*: Boolean value indicating whether the Directed Interval Class (DIC) vector (Cambouropoulos, 2012; Cambouropoulos et al., 2013) of the transition has 0 (i.e. that both chords have at least one common pitch class),
6. *DIChas1*: as above but for DIC value 1 (i.e., at least one ascending semitone),
7. *DIChasMinus1*: as above but for DIC value −1 (i.e., at least one descending semitone),
8. *hasAscSemiToRoot*: Boolean value indicating whether the first chord has a pitch class with ascending semitone relation to the pitch class of the second chord's root,
9. *hasDescSemiToRoot*: as above but with descending semitone,
10. *hasSemiToRoot*: as above but with either ascending or descending semitone, and
11. *hasAscToneToRoot*: as *ascSemNextRoot*, but with tone.

Employing the COINVENT blending process on the aforementioned cadence description produced 84 blended cadences, all of which had some relation to both or either one of the inputs. For the perceptual tests that were performed, a subset of these cadences had to be used; the selection of cadences for this subset was made by expert musicologists and included blends from different levels of the ranking and diverse characteristics. As already stated previously, all cadences (that were assumed to be in C minor tonality/modality) consisted of two chords, the penultimate and the final/tonic. The final chord was a C minor, thus variation between the stimuli resulted from altering the penultimate chords. In order to preserve maximum uniformity in the formation of the chords, voice-leading was rendered by expert musicologists in four-voice harmony, with an effort to preserve minimal movement in the inner voices when possible.

9.4.1.2 Cadence Experiment 1: Investigating the Relative Perception of Input and Blends

In the first experiment, a pairwise dissimilarity listening test revealed the relative perception within the set of the generated cadences. In this test participants compared all pairs among the 9 selected cadences (two inputs and seven blends) using the free magnitude estimation method. Therefore, they rated the perceptual distances of 45 pairs (same pairs included) by freely typing in a number of their choice to represent dissimilarity of each pair (i.e., an unbounded scale) with 0 indicating a same pair (for a discussion of the advantages of this approach over a bounded magnitude estimation see Zacharakis et al. (2015b)). The dissimilarity matrices of cadence pairwise distances produced through this process allowed Multidimensional Scaling (MDS) analysis to generate geometric configurations that represent the relationships between all nine cadences. Through MDS the interpretation of salient perceptual dimensions was enabled.

Additionally, the spatial configuration obtained through MDS was interpreted through combining one sensory and one cognitive model in a similar manner to Bigand et al. (1996). The sensory model of auditory roughness of the penultimate chords was calculated by the use of the Vassilakis' algorithm (Vassilakis, 2001) as implemented by the MIR Toobox (Lartillot and Toiviainen, 2007) while the cognitive model was based on the difference between the chords within each pair, as calculated with the Tonal Pitch Space (TPS) model (Lerdahl, 2004).

During the experiment twenty listeners (students from the Department of Music Studies at the Aristotle University of Thessaloniki) initially became familiar with the range of cadences under study during an initial presentation of the stimulus set (random order). For the main part of the experiment participants were allowed to listen to each pair of cadences as many times as needed prior to submitting their dissimilarity rating. The pairs were presented in random order and participants were advised to retain a consistent rating strategy throughout the experiment. In total, the listening test sessions, including instructions and breaks, lasted around thirty minutes for most of the participants.

Figure 9.5 illustrates the spatial configuration derived from MDS and reveals some parameters that seem to have influenced the perception of the different cadences. The 1st dimension placement of cadences is defined by the existence of a leading note resolving to the tonic (upward semitone movement from B to C); cadences that do not include this leading note cluster at the negative side while the ones featuring an upward tone movement (Bb to C) cluster at the positive side. The plagal cadence (No. 6) that features a duplication of the tonic is positioned almost exactly in the middle of the 1st dimension. Therefore, the interpretation of the 1st dimension suggests a categorical perception dictated by the absence or presence of an upward leading note. While the interpretation of the 2nd dimension was not so straightforward, positioning of the cadences along it was attributed to a combination of the inherent dissonance of the penultimate chord (as reflected by its type and voicing layout) together with its distance from the final chord in the Tonal Pitch Space theoretical/cognitive model (Lerdahl, 2004). This notion resembles the decomposition of dissonance in two parts: static 'sensory dissonance' and dynamic 'tension dissonance', as suggested by Huron (Huron, 2006).

9.4.1.3 Cadence Experiment 2: Estimating the Magnitude of Specific Verbal Attributes of Inputs and Blends

Pairwise dissimilarity ratings in the first experiment provided a useful spatial representation of the perceptual space. Further interpretation of these relationships was

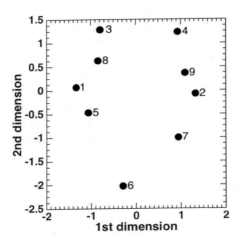

Fig. 9.5: The two-dimensional dissimilarity perceptual space of the nine cadences. The perfect and the Phrygian cadences (No. 1 and 2) are positioned far away from each other on the 1st dimension, which reflects the existence of an upward leading note to the tonic. The second dimension reflects at some extent the 'sensory dissonance' of the chords in the cadences. This figure is taken from Zacharakis et al. (2017)

achieved through a Verbal Attribute Magnitude Estimation (e.g., see Kendall and Carterette (1993a,b)) type of experiment whereby listeners rated the nine cadences on four descriptive scales, namely preference, originality, tension and closure effect. Originality is a key term for creativity evaluation (Jordanous, 2013; Hekkert et al., 2003) and relates to surprise and novelty (the opposite of expectancy), while these descriptive parameters are important for music perception and appreciation (Huron, 2006). Successions between tension and relaxation are regarded as important elements inducing musical emotions (Huron, 2006; Lerdahl and Krumhansl, 2007; Farbood, 2012; Lehne and Koelsch, 2015), while the closure effect is a specific characteristic of musical cadences (e.g., see Sears et al. (2014)) as they serve the purpose of concluding phrases, sections or pieces of music. Preference measures the extent to which participants may prefer some cadences over others. An extension of this experiment was additionally carried out, as the ratings on originality were not very consistent across participants, implying that there was a lack of a common understanding of this concept. To this end, the same experimental protocol was repeated with different participants and by requesting a rating on expectancy and fit, which are related to originality.

Among the research goals of this experimental process was to investigate the level of agreement between raters regarding judgements upon these descriptive scales and the examination of potential relationships between them. An additional concern was to examine the effect of different harmonic contexts on the perception of these particular cadences as expressed by the ratings. Finally the interpretation of these results in relation to the findings of experiment 1 was attempted. For this second experiment, each stimulus comprised a four-bar phrase, with a two-bar antecedent sub-phrase and a two-bar consequent sub-phrase. The first two-bar sub-phrase suggested the harmonic content with a four-chord progression and had two versions: the tonal version (stimuli 1-1 to 1-9) in C minor tonality and the modal version (stimuli 2-1 to 2-9) in C Phrygian mode. The second two-bar sub-phrase contained the two-chord cadential progression in slower harmonic rhythm to strengthen the effect of phrase closure, and has nine versions (the cadences of experiment 1). An attempt was made to maximise both voice-leading uniformity and harmonic idiom specification, while all stimuli lasted around 9 seconds. The set of participants of the first and second group (repetition group) comprised 26 and 25 students from the Department of Music Studies of the Aristotle University of Thessaloniki respectively. After a familiarisation process, the stimuli were presented in random order within the two different harmonic contexts.

In general, the effect of harmonic context (i.e., tonal vs. modal) was insignificant, except from expectancy, which was the only scale that featured a significant effect of harmonic context indicating an overall increase in modal context. Figure 9.6 shows the boxplot of all five rating scales aggregated for both harmonic contexts (keeping in mind that the overall expectancy exhibits an effect of harmonic context). This figure also reveals that cadences featuring an upward leading note (Nos. 1, 3, 5 and 8) received higher ratings for closure effect and tension, and lower ratings for preference regardless of harmonic context, a fact that supports the positioning of cadences along dimension 1 of the perceptual space (Figure 9.5). A strong trend was also revealed (using Page's trend test) for increasing closure effect from the positive to the negative side of the 1st MDS dimension, suggesting that this dimension reflects the perceived 'strength' of closure. According to a similar analysis, the overall tension was indicated to play a role in positioning along dimension 2.

As also depicted in Figure 9.6, preference was indicated to be strongly inversely correlated with closure effect, expectancy and fit (i.e., stronger closure/-expectancy/fit induces less preference than weak closure/expectancy/fit); the latter variables seem to have an almost similar effect. The variance of tension is independent from the variances of the other variables, since it showed medium correlations with closure effect, expectancy and fit. On the other hand, originality seemed to have been the least understood by the listeners since their ratings displayed the highest disagreement. Even though originality is a commonly agreed measure of creativity, this experiment indicated that the concept it conveys may not be clear within all contexts. In this experiment for instance, listeners might have understood the term 'originality' either as relating to 'novelty' and 'inventiveness' or to 'authenticity' and 'conventionality' (that relates to the root 'origin').

The ambiguity of the term 'originality' indicated by the disagreement of participants led to the design and implementation of an additional experiment that involved ratings on two additional scales: expectancy and fit. In this additional experiment there was high agreement between listeners for these two qualities, while expectancy was the only quality that exhibited an effect of harmonic context. In the

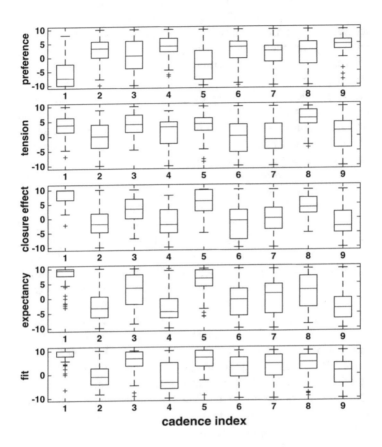

Fig. 9.6: Boxplots of the aggregated data for the nine cadences on the five descriptive scales

modal context, the expectancy of cadences that were unexpected in the tonal context was higher, indicating that the modal context is more 'flexible' concerning this variable.

The mean ratings on values of the main experiment, namely preference and closure effect, and of the additional one, namely expectancy and fit, were highly correlated. This indicates that participants preferred, in average, cadences that were less expected and also had a weaker closure effect. A generalisation of this comment should be avoided, however, since it might be the case that people prefer more expected/familiar cadences within a more unexpected harmonic background; more experimentation on this hypothesis is required to evaluate the aforementioned assumption. Furthermore, closure effect plays an important role in perceived similarity between two cadences and since closure is related to the existence of the upward leading note to the tonic, it reflects the previously discussed categorical perception of cadences. Tension is less related to the other qualities, however, tension is not completely independent from closure effect and expectancy, a comment that is along the lines of what Huron suggests (Huron, 2006). These results indicate that higher expectancy values, related to the presence of an upward leading note, are related to higher tension, but, according to the results of experiment 1, tension variations can be attributed to the inherent roughness (sensory dissonance) of the penultimate chord and the distance of the pair in the Tonal Pitch Space (tension dissonance). This is in accordance with other – complementary to Huron's – views with regard to musically induced tension in general (Lehne and Koelsch, 2015) and tonal tension in particular (Lerdahl and Krumhansl, 2007).

The perceived relationships in combination with qualitative characteristics obtained through these experiments are still valuable for enhancing the creativity of the system, despite the identified categorical perception for the examined cadences. Such information could be exploited by the cadence blending system during human interaction, by enabling refinement of the desired outcome based on the utilised descriptive qualities. This could be implemented by making the system capable of receiving user requests for returning blends with, e.g., more or less closure or tension, producing output that would be the result of conceptual blending, but at the same time would incorporate requested perceptual attributes.

9.4.2 Empirical Evaluation of the Output of the CHAMELEON System

For evaluating the CHAMELEON melodic harmonisation assistant, annotated melody files were used as inputs to this system for generating the stimuli that were used in the two experiments described below. The harmonic idioms that were mainly involved in these experiments were learned from sets of Bach chorales and Jazz pieces, while learned idioms based on sets for songs from The Beatles and pieces of Hindemith were also used. The Bach chorales and Jazz idioms were selected as the main idioms since they were assumed to be known and identifiable by students of the Music Department of the Aristotle University of Thessaloniki, who were the participants. This study included two experiments on different setups of blending harmonic spaces produced by the CHAMELEON system.

The first experiment was designed to provide indications about the effect of blending between the utilised idioms through perceptual tests on classifying the produced melodic harmonisations. Additionally, this experiment also addressed the effect of the implied harmony that the melody incorporates in the harmonisation process. To this end, tonal and jazz melodies were harmonised with the idioms of Bach chorales and Jazz, as well as with blended versions of these two, while additional harmonisations with the learned idioms of The Beatles and Hindemith or some of their blended versions were also used to produce material not pertaining to the Bach chorales and Jazz idioms.

For the second experiment, the learned Bach chorales harmonic idiom was transposed in several keys and blending between these transposed spaces created new idioms that introduced harmonic elements that extended the tonal idiom. The Bach chorales were chosen for this task since they are among the most characteristic paradigms of tonal music, making them perfectly suitable for examining whether the tonal character of this idiom can be drastically altered using blending-based techniques on transposed versions of this same tonal idiom. The extent of this alteration was assessed in this experiment by using harmonisations of a tonal traditional melody with the idiom of the Bach chorales, a 'wrong' harmonisation with a transposed version of the Bach chorales idiom in the wrong key, transposition-related blends and an extreme harmonic blend between the Hindemith and a transposed version of The Beatles idioms.

9.4.2.1 Experiment 1: Empirical Idiom Identification Applied on Blended Idioms

In the idiom blending experiment six sets of stimuli were presented, with each of the first five consisting of a different melody harmonised by the system according to the Bach Chorales idiom (tonal), the jazz idiom, some of their blends and by another idiom which came either as a blend (Beatles and Hindemith) or as another trained idiom (Hindemith). Two among these five harmonies featured tonal implied harmonies (the 'Ode to joy' and 'Ah vous dirai-je, maman' themes), two featured Jazz implied harmonies ('Summertime' and 'Someday my prince will come' themes) and a Greek folk song melody ('Tou Kitsou ē mana'). The sixth set comprised harmonisations both in major and minor modes as learned from a Bach chorale corpus and three of their blends. The harmonised melody in this set was composed specifically for this experiment that implies neither major nor minor characteristics (not including the third and sixth degrees).

The stimuli were presented simultaneously (Antović et al., 2016) to participants (40 students from the Department of Music Studies at the Aristotle University of Thessaloniki), who were provided with a questionnaire asking them to classify each stimulus in a five point Likert scale between Tonal and Jazz as well as a sixth option called 'Other'. Figure 9.7 illustrates the median and mean values of all participants' responses for all five categories provided for Likert scale classification, along with the percentage of classifications for the 'Other' category. Through statistics described thoroughly in Zacharakis et al. (2018), it was also observed that there was greater agreement between participants regarding classification when no blending at any level was involved, i.e. for melodies and harmonisations that come from the same idiom. Additionally, the preference ratings for all harmonisations was statistically insignificantly different for all melodies except for 'Ode to Joy' and the

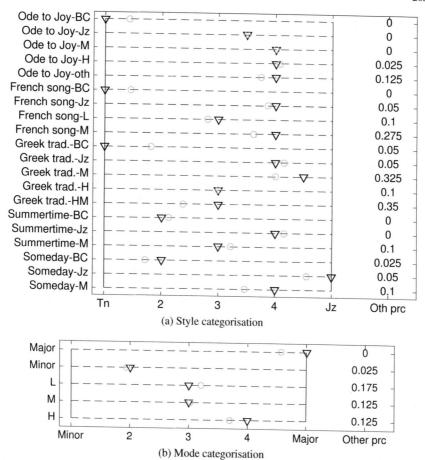

Fig. 9.7: Median (triangles) and mean (circles) value of the participants' responses regarding Likert scale classificaton and percentage of classifications to the 'Other' category for (a) style (Jazz-Bach) and (b) mode (major-minor) for all studied melodies and harmonisations. This figure is taken from Zacharakis et al. (2018)

major-minor melody, showing that the blended harmonisations are in most cases perceived as almost equally preferred as the non-blended ones.

Statistical analysis presented in Zacharakis et al. (2018) on classification attributions by the participants supports some facts that are illustrated in Figure 9.7. The harmonisations produced by the system for most melodies seemed to have generated distinguishable harmonic idioms, since participants attributed blends as belonging to intermediate categories of tonal-jazz, or other. An exception is observed for the 'Ode to Joy' melody, where the tonal harmonisation is perceived as different from the rest, which are perceived as close to jazz harmonisations. Furthermore, the implied harmony of the melody influences the classification of the harmonisations.

Specifically, the tonal harmonisations of the jazz melodies were classified as less tonal than the harmonisations of the tonal melodies. In the opposite direction, the jazz harmonisations of 'Some day my prince will come' were classified significantly as more jazz the tonal melodies – a fact that was not observed for the 'Summertime' melody.

9.4.2.2 Experiment 2: Empirical Classification of Type of Chromaticism

In this experiment, a total of 30 participants listened to the stimuli simultaneously (Antović et al., 2016) (in two sessions with 10 and 20 participants). A Scottish melody (Ye Banks and Braes) was used for the generation of all harmonisations, using the following harmonic idioms:

1. A tonal idiom as learned from a set of Bach chorales (indicated by 'Tn-1' and 'Tn-2' since it was presented twice).
2. A 'wrong' idiom obtained by transposing the Bach chorales idiom by three semitones ('BC_3').
3. A peculiar blend between the style of Hindemith and a transposition of The Beatles by three semitones ('BH').
4. Three blends between the 'correct' tonality of the Bach chorales idiom and its transposition by two, three and four semitones ('BL_2', 'BL_3' and 'BL_4' respectively).

The tonal harmonisation was presented twice to test consistency of the responses and therefore the final set of stimuli comprised seven harmonisations. Listeners were asked to classify each stimulus in one out of four categories: diatonic, chromatic, atonal and other. Additionally, the participants were asked to rate each stimulus according to preference and expectancy within a range from 1 to 5.

Figure 9.8 illustrates the histograms for the categorisation according to harmonic style, along with preference and expectancy ratings on the five-point scale. As illustrated by the graphs and supported by the statistical analysis provided in further detail in Zacharakis et al. (2018), different harmonisations were perceived as significantly different in terms of harmonic category, preference and expectancy. Specifically, the 'Tn-1' (first presentation of the Bach chorales harmonisation) was unanimously classified as diatonic, as highly agreed in the case of 'Tn-2' (second presentation), while these harmonisations were rated as the most expected ones. The less preferred and most unexpected ones were the 'wrong' and peculiar harmonisations ('BC_3' and 'BH' respectively), while these harmonisations were mostly classified as Atonal. The harmonisations with blends of Bach chorales in different tonalities ('BL_2', 'BL_3' and 'BL_4') were mostly rated as chromatic, while some participants also placed them in the tonal and 'other' categories (with 'BL_4' featuring the highest disagreement). Additionally, these blended harmonisations were slightly more preferred and significantly less expected than the clearly tonal ones, indicating that the system is able to produce less typical and unexpected alternatives that are equally or more preferred over typical ones.

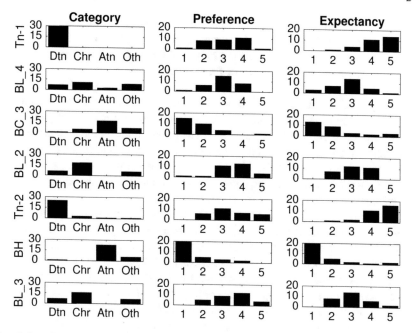

Fig. 9.8: Histograms of the responses regarding style classification (left), preference (middle) and expectancy (right) for the different harmonisations of Ye Banks and Braes. (1: Diatonic, 2: Chromatic, 3: Atonal, 4: Other). This figure is taken from Zacharakis et al. (2018)

9.5 Summary

This chapter presented an overview of the methodologies incorporated in the development of the CHAMELEON melodic harmonisation assistant and some of the empirical processes that were employed to evaluate harmonic blending and the output of this system. The CHAMELEON system learns several aspects of harmony from diverse musical data that are harmonically annotated by experts and creates harmonisations of user-given melodies that either reflect the harmonic characteristics of a learned idiom, or feature blended characteristics according to user choices. Several probabilistic modules allow the system to independently learn different aspects and levels of harmony, namely chord types, cadences, chord transitions and bass voice leading, from practically any musical idiom. The COINVENT framework for computational conceptual blending is employed for blending chord transitions belonging to two initial idioms, making a pool of blended transitions that are afterwards utilised to construct a compound harmonic idiom that extends the two initial idioms. This compound idiom incorporates direct connections between chords of the initial idioms as well as new chords and transitions, that creatively combine the harmonic elements of the initial idioms, allowing the generation of harmonisations that reflect either combined or novel harmonic characteristics in relation to the input idioms.

Before behaviourally evaluating the output of CHAMELEON, empirical experiments using the cadences produced by a cadence blending methodology indicated that the blending process, in some cases, may not produce output that is perceived as equally distant from the inputs. It was observed that the presence of a dominating 'boolean' feature, as the existence of a leading note to the tonic, in only one of the inputs introduced the effect of categorical perception; single-scope blends were generated that were perceived as belonging to the category of one of the inputs. Other perceived characteristics of the blends (e.g., tension, closure effect, expectancy), however, varied in relation to the inputs, indicating that this methodology produced new blended cadences with diverse characteristics.

The empirical evaluation of the CHAMELEON system indicated that the system is able to produce harmonisations that on one hand reflect the characteristics of the learned idioms (if no harmonic blending is involved), while on the other hand are perceived as either belonging to an 'intermediate' or to an 'other' idiom. Additionally, it was observed that blending different modulated versions of the same harmonic space can create new spaces that extrapolate to more adventurous but coherent spaces. For instance, the diatonic tonal idiom of the Bach chorales was extended to harmonic variations that featured increased chromaticism, while at the same time being rated as more unexpected and comparatively preferred in comparison with the harmonisations produced by using the initial spaces. Another interesting finding was that the implied harmony of the melody affected the perceptual classification of the harmonisations, introducing a melody-harmony level blending effect.

9.6 Conclusion

The application of conceptual blending theory in harmony and in melodic harmonisation through the CHAMELEON system revealed that this approach offers important possibilities for computational creativity. This was initially evident by the application of conceptual blending in musical cadences, which provided some kind of 'historical' evaluation of the effectiveness of this approach through the invention of the tritone substitution cadence from the perfect and Phrygian cadences. Extending the cadence blending methodology to a methodology that blends chord transitions and integrating it in a methodology that constructs a compound chord transition matrix for combining the chord transitions of two initial idioms, musically meaningful blends that feature characteristics from both initial idioms along with new harmonic elements were generated. This first integration of a blending process in a probabilistic system has shown that promising results can be achieved by using conceptual blending as a creative module in combination with other established techniques. A methodology for automatically assessing the salience of each feature based on a given dataset was employed, although not thoroughly evaluated.

Future work includes evaluating whether automatic assessment of saliences through data-driven statistics is perceptually relevant.

Empirical evaluation of the cadence blending output indicated that blends might not be perceptually 'balanced' between the inputs (in terms of distance from each input). Single-scope blends were mostly produced, since a dominating feature was involved. This study revealed that the notion of blending depends heavily on the selection of the input spaces and the extent at which they incorporate a highly salient feature. Evaluating the effects of blending proved not to be a trivial task and empirical evaluation methods had to be developed for assessing the characteristics of blending as implemented in the CHAMELEON system. Results indicate that the blended harmonisations featured blended or new harmonic characteristics (higher unexpectedness) with comparable preference with non-blended harmonisations, a fact that was interpreted as evidence of creative behaviour.

References

E. Aldwell, C. Schachter, and A. Cadwallader. *Harmony and Voice Leading*. Cengage Learning, 2010.

M. Allan and C. K. I. Williams. Harmonising chorales by probabilistic inference. In *Advances in Neural Information Processing Systems 17*, pages 25–32. MIT Press, 2004.

M. Antović. Musical metaphor revisited: Primitives, universals and conceptual blending. *Universals and Conceptual Blending (February 17, 2011)*, 2011.

M. Antović, D. Stamenković, and V. Figar. Association of meaning in program music: On denotation, inherence, and onomatopoeia. *Music perception: An Interdisciplinary Journal*, 34(2):243–248, 2016.

G. Barnett. Tonal organization in seventeenth-century music theory. In T. Christensen, editor, *The Cambridge History of Western Music Theory*, pages 407–455. Cambridge University Press, 2002.

E. Bigand, R. Parncutt, and F. Lerdahl. Perception of musical tension in short chord sequences: The influence of harmonic function, sensory dissonance, horizontal motion, and musical training. *Perception & Psychophysics*, 58(1):125–141, 1996.

M. A. Boden. *The Creative Mind: Myths and Mechanisms*. Psychology Press, 2004.

N. Borrel-Jensen and A. Hjortgaard Danielsen. Computer-assisted music composition – A database-backed algorithmic composition system. B.S. Thesis, Department of Computer Science, University of Copenhagen, Copenhagen, Denmark, 2010.

E. Cambouropoulos. A directional interval class representation of chord transitions. In *Proceedings of the Joint Conference ICMPC-ESCOM 2012 (12th International Conference for Music Perception and Cognition, & 8th Conference of the European Society for the Cognitive Sciences of Music)*, ICMPC-ESCOM 2012, July 2012.

E. Cambouropoulos. The harmonic musical surface and two novel chord representation Schemes. In D. Meredith, editor, *Computational Music Analysis*, pages
31–56. Springer, 2015.

E. Cambouropoulos, A. Katsiavalos, and C. Tsougras. Idiom-independent harmonic
pattern recognition based on a novel chord transition representation. In *Proceedings of the 3rd International Workshop on Folk Music Analysis (FMA2013)*, FMA
2013, June 2013.

E. Cambouropoulos, M. Kaliakatsos-Papakostas, and C. Tsougras. An idiom-
independent representation of chords for computational music analysis and generation. In *Proceeding of the joint 11th Sound and Music Computing Conference (SMC) and 40th International Computer Music Conference (ICMC)*, ICMC–
SMC 2014, 2014.

E. Cambouropoulos, M. Kaliakatsos-Papakostas, and C. Tsougras. Structural blend-
ing of harmonic spaces: A computational approach. In *Proceedings of the 9th
Triennial Conference of the European Society for the Cognitive Science of Music
(ESCOM)*, 2015.

W. E. Caplin. *Classical form: A theory of formal functions for the instrumental
music of Haydn, Mozart, and Beethoven*. Oxford University Press, 1998.

P. Chordia, A. Sastry, T. Mallikarjuna, and A. Albin. Multiple viewpoints modeling
of tabla sequences. In *ISMIR*, volume 2010, 2010.

J. G. Cleary and W. Teahan. Experiments on the zero frequency problem. In *Proc.
Data Compression Conference*, volume 480, 1995.

J. Collins. Renaissance modal theory: Theoretical, compositional and editorial perspectives. In T. Christensen, editor, *The Cambridge History of Western Music
Theory*, pages 364–406. Cambridge University Press, 2002.

N. Cook. Theorizing musical meaning. *Music Theory Spectrum*, 23(2):170–195,
2001.

P. Donnelly and J. Sheppard. Evolving four-part harmony using genetic algorithms.
In *Proceedings of the 2011 International Conference on Applications of Evolutionary Computation - Volume Part II*, EvoApplications'11, pages 273–282, Berlin, Heidelberg, 2011. Springer-Verlag.

K. Ebcioglu. An expert system for harmonizing four-part chorales. *Computer Music
Journal*, 12(3):43–51, 1988. ISSN 01489267.

M. Eppe, R. Confalonieri, E. Maclean, M. Kaliakatsos-Papakostas, E. Cambouropoulos, M. Schorlemmer, M. Codescu, and K.-U. Kühnberger. Computational
invention of cadences and chord progressions by conceptual chord-blending. In
International Joint Conference on Artificial Intelligence (IJCAI) 2015, 2015.

M. M. Farbood. A parametric, temporal model of musical tension. *Music Perception: An Interdisciplinary Journal*, 29(4):387–428, 2012.

G. Fauconnier and M. Turner. *The Way We Think: Conceptual Blending and the
Mind's Hidden Complexities*. Basic Books, New York, reprint edition, 2003.

M. L. Gick and K. J. Holyoak. Schema induction and analogical transfer. *Cognitive
psychology*, 15(1):1–38, 1983.

V. Goel. Creative brains: Designing in the real world?. *Frontiers in human neuroscience*, 8:241, 2014.

J. Goguen and D. F. Harrell. Style: A computational and conceptual blending-based approach. In S. Argamon and S. Dubnov, editors, *The Structure of Style: Algorithmic Approaches to Understanding Manner and Meaning*, pages 147–170. Springer, Berlin, 2010.

M. Granroth-Wilding and M. Steedman. A robust parser-interpreter for jazz chord sequences. *Journal of New Music Research*, 0(0):1–20, 2014.

M. Hanlon and T. Ledlie. CPU Bach: An automatic chorale harmonization system. 2002. URL http://www.timledlie.org/cs/CPUBach.pdf.

M. M. Hedblom, O. Kutz, and F. Neuhaus. Image schemas in computational conceptual blending. *Cognitive Systems Research*, 39:42–57, 2016.

P. Hekkert, D. Snelders, and P. C. Wieringen. 'Most advanced, yet acceptable': Typicality and novelty as joint predictors of aesthetic preference in industrial design. *British journal of psychology*, 94(1):111–124, 2003.

D. B. Huron. *Sweet Anticipation: Music and The Psychology of Expectation*. MIT Press, 2006.

A. K. Jordanous. *Evaluating computational creativity: A standardised procedure for evaluating creative systems and its application*. Ph.D. thesis, University of Sussex, 2013.

M. Kaliakatsos-Papakostas and E. Cambouropoulos. Probabilistic harmonisation with fixed intermediate chord constraints. In *Proceeding of the joint 11th Sound and Music Computing Conference (SMC) and 40th International Computer Music Conference (ICMC)*, ICMC–SMC 2014, 2014.

M. Kaliakatsos-Papakostas, E. Cambouropoulos, K.-U. Kühnberger, O. Kutz, and A. Smaill. Concept invention and music: Creating novel harmonies via conceptual blending. In *Proceedings of the 9th Conference on Interdisciplinary Musicology (CIM2014)*, CIM2014, December 2014.

M. Kaliakatsos-Papakostas, A. Zacharakis, C. Tsougras, and E. Cambouropoulos. Evaluating the General Chord Type representation in tonal music and organising GCT chord labels in functional chord categories. In *Proceedings of the 4th International Conference on Music Information Retrieval (ISMIR 2015)*, Malaga, Spain, 2015.

M. Kaliakatsos-Papakostas, R. Confalonieri, J. Corneli, A. Zacharakis, and E. Cambouropoulos. An argument-based creative assistant for harmonic blending. In *Proceedings of the 7th International Conference on Computational Creativity (ICCC)*, 2016a.

M. Kaliakatsos-Papakostas, D. Makris, C. Tsougras, and E. Cambouropoulos. Learning and creating novel harmonies in diverse musical idioms: An adaptive modular melodic harmonisation system. *Journal of Creative Music Systems*, 1 (1), 2016b.

M. Kaliakatsos-Papakostas, D. Makris, A. Zacharakis, C. Tsougras, and E. Cambouropoulos. Learning and blending harmonies in the context of a melodic harmonisation assistant. In *IFIP International Conference on Artificial Intelligence Applications and Innovations*, pages 520–527. Springer, 2016c.

M. Kaliakatsos-Papakostas, A. Zacharakis, C. Tsougras, and E. Cambouropoulos. Modelling cadence perception via musical parameter tuning to perceptual data.

In *IFIP International Conference on Artificial Intelligence Applications and Innovations*, pages 552–561. Springer, 2016d.

M. Kaliakatsos-Papakostas, M. Queiroz, C. Tsougras, and E. Cambouropoulos. Conceptual blending of harmonic spaces for creating melodic harmonisation. *Journal of New Music Research*, 46(4):305–328, 2017.

R. A. Kendall and E. C. Carterette. Verbal attributes of simultaneous wind instrument timbres: I. von Bismarck's adjectives. *Music Perception: An Interdisciplinary Journal*, 10(4):445–467, 1993a.

R. A. Kendall and E. C. Carterette. Verbal attributes of simultaneous wind instrument timbres: II. Adjectives induced from piston's "orchestration". *Music Perception: An Interdisciplinary Journal*, 10(4):469–501, 1993b.

H. V. Koops, J. P. Magalhães, and W. B. de Haas. A functional approach to automatic melody harmonisation. In *Proceedings of the First ACM SIGPLAN Workshop on Functional Art, Music, Modelling and Design*, FARM '13, pages 47–58, New York, NY, USA, 2013. ACM.

S. M. Kostka and D. Payne. *Instructor's Manual to Accompany Tonal Harmony, with an Introduction to Twentieth-century Music*. McGraw-Hill, 2004.

O. Lartillot and P. Toiviainen. A Matlab toolbox for musical feature extraction from audio. In *International Conference on Digital Audio Effects*, pages 237–244, 2007.

M. Lehne and S. Koelsch. Toward a general psychological model of tension and suspense. *Frontiers in psychology*, 6:79, 2015.

F. Lerdahl. *Tonal pitch space*. Oxford University Press, 2004.

F. Lerdahl and C. L. Krumhansl. Modeling tonal tension. *Music Perception: An Interdisciplinary Journal*, 24(4):329–366, 2007.

M. L. Maher, K. Brady, and D. H. Fisher. Computational models of surprise in evaluating creative design. In *Proceedings of the fourth international conference on computational creativity*, volume 147, 2013.

D. Makris, M. Kaliakatsos-Papakostas, and E. Cambouropoulos. A probabilistic approach to determining bass voice leading in melodic harmonisation. In *Mathematics and Computation in Music: Proceedings of the 5th International Conference, MCM 2015*, London, UK, June 2015a. Springer, Berlin.

D. Makris, M. A. Kaliakatsos-Papakostas, and E. Cambouropoulos. Probabilistic modular bass voice leading in melodic harmonisation. In *Proceedings of the 4th International Conference on Music Information Retrieval (ISMIR 2015)*, Malaga, Spain, 2015b.

A. F. Moore. *Song means: Analysing and interpreting recorded popular song*. Ashgate Publishing, Ltd., 2013.

J. Ox. Analogy and conceptual blending are part of a visualization toolkit for artists and scientists: Introducing the cognitive space transfer. *Methods*, 1:6, 2014.

F. Pachet and P. Roy. Musical harmonization with constraints: A survey. *Constraints*, 6(1):7–19, Jan. 2001. ISSN 1383-7133.

F. Pachet, P. Roy, and G. Barbieri. Finite-length Markov processes with constraints. *transition*, 6(1/3), 2011a.

F. Pachet, P. Roy, and G. Barbieri. Finite-length Markov processes with constraints. In *International Joint Conference on Artificial Intelligence (IJCAI) 2011*, pages 635–642, 2011b.

J.-F. Paiement, D. Eck, and S. Bengio. Probabilistic melodic harmonization. In *Proceedings of the 19th International Conference on Advances in Artificial Intelligence: Canadian Society for Computational Studies of Intelligence*, AI'06, pages 218–229, Berlin, Heidelberg, 2006. Springer-Verlag. ISBN 3-540-34628-7, 978-3-540-34628-9.

M. Pearce and G. Wiggins. Towards a framework for the evaluation of machine compositions. In *Proceedings of the AISB'01 Symposium on Artificial Intelligence and Creativity in the Arts and Sciences*, pages 22–32, 2001.

S. Phon-Amnuaisuk and G. A. Wiggins. The four-part harmonisation problem: A comparison between genetic algorithms and a rule-based system. In *Proceedings of the AISB'99 symposium on musical creativity*, pages 28–34. AISB, 1999.

S. A. Raczyński, S. Fukayama, and E. Vincent. Melody harmonization with interpolated probabilistic models. *Journal of New Music Research*, 42(3):223–235, 2013. DOI: 10.1080/09298215.2013.822000.

M. Rohrmeier. Towards a generative syntax of tonal harmony. *Journal of Mathematics and Music*, 5(1):35–53, Mar. 2011.

M. Schorlemmer, A. Smaill, K.-U. Kühnberger, O. Kutz, S. Colton, E. Cambouropoulos, and A. Pease. Coinvent: Towards a computational concept invention theory. In *5th International Conference on Computational Creativity (ICCC) 2014*, June 2014.

P. Schubert. *Modal Counterpoint, Renaissance Style*. Oxford University Press, 1999.

D. Sears. The Perception of Cadential Closure. In M. Neuwirth and P. Bergé, editors, *What is a Cadence?*, pages 253–286. Leuven University Press, 2015.

D. Sears, W. E. Caplin, and S. McAdams. Perceiving the classical cadence. *Music Perception: An Interdisciplinary Journal*, 31(5):397–417, 2014.

I. Simon, D. Morris, and S. Basu. Mysong: Automatic accompaniment generation for vocal melodies. In *Proceedings of the SIGCHI Conference on Human Factors in Computing Systems*, CHI '08, pages 725–734, New York, NY, USA, 2008. ACM.

M. Spitzer. *Metaphor and musical thought*. University of Chicago Press, 2004.

D. Stefanou. Investigating social creativity and concept invention in collaborative musical situations. In *Proceedings of the First International Conference on New Music Concepts*, Treviso, Italy, 2015.

D. Stefanou and E. Cambouropoulos. Enriching the blend: Creative extensions to conceptual blending in music. In *Proceedings of the 9th Triennial Conference of the European Society for the Cognitive Science of Music (ESCOM)*, 2015.

S. Suzuki. Four-part harmonization using probabilistic models: Comparison of models with and without chord nodes. In *Proceedings of the Sound and Music Computing Conference (SMC)*, pages 628–633, Stockholm, Sweden, 2013. Logos Verlag Berlin.

C. Tsougras and D. Stefanou. Conceptual blending and meaning xonstruction: A structural/hermeneutical analysis of the 'Old Castle' from Musorgsky's 'Pictures at an Exhibition'. In *Proceedings of the 9th Triennial Conference of the European Society for the Cognitive Science of Music (ESCOM)*, 2015.

P. N. Vassilakis. *Perceptual and physical properties of amplitude fluctuation and their musical significance*. Ph.D. thesis, University of California, Los Angeles, 2001.

R. P. Whorley, G. A. Wiggins, C. Rhodes, and M. T. Pearce. Multiple viewpoint systems: Time complexity and the construction of domains for complex musical viewpoints in the harmonisation problem. *Journal of New Music Research*, 42 (3):237–266, Sept. 2013.

G. A. Wiggins. A preliminary framework for description, analysis and comparison of creative systems. *Knowledge-Based Systems*, 19(7):449–458, 2006.

L. Yi and J. Goldsmith. Automatic generation of four-part harmony. In K. B. Laskey, S. M. Mahoney, and J. Goldsmith, editors, *BMA*, volume 268 of *CEUR Workshop Proceedings*. CEUR-WS.org, 2007.

N. Yogev and A. Lerch. A system for automatic audio harmonization. In *Proceedings of the 25-th VDT International Convention*, 2008.

A. Zacharakis, M. Kaliakatsos-Papakostas, and E. Cambouropoulos. Conceptual blending in music cadences: A formal model and subjective evaluation. In *Proceedings of the 4th International Conference on Music Information Retrieval (IS-MIR 2015)*, Malaga, Spain, 2015a.

A. Zacharakis, K. Pastiadis, and J. D. Reiss. An interlanguage unification of musical timbre. *Music Perception: An Interdisciplinary Journal*, 32(4):394–412, 2015b.

A. Zacharakis, M. Kaliakatsos-Papakostas, C. Tsougras, and E. Campouropoulos. Empirical methods for evaluating music structural blends: a case study on melodic harmonisation. *Musicae Scientiae*, 22(1):118–144, 2018.

A. Zacharakis, M. Kaliakatsos-Papakostas, C. Tsougras, and E. Campouropoulos. Creating musical cadences via conceptual blending: Empirical evaluation and enhancement of a formal model. *Music Perception: An Interdisciplinary Journal*, 35(2):211–234, 2017.

L. M. Zbikowski. *Conceptualizing Music: Cognitive Structure, Theory, and Analysis*. Oxford University Press, 2002.

L. M. Zbikowski. Metaphor and music. *The Cambridge handbook of metaphor and thought*, pages 502–524, 2008.

Part IV
Epilogue

Chapter 10
Evaluation of Creativity

Alison Pease and Joseph Corneli

Abstract This chapter develops a meta-evaluation of progress markers in Computational Creativity. We rely on an analysis of interview data with people who have applied several standard metrics. We use an existing meta-evaluation framework to distil findings in a format that will support comparison with future research on this topic.

10.1 Introduction

The goal of this chapter is to discuss the role of evaluation in computational creativity. Early writings on this area were developed by Ritchie (2001) and Pease et al. (2001). Pease et al. cast creativity in functional terms.[1] On this view, creativity is to be found amongst the "input, output and the process by which [the output] is achieved." Specifically, "Creativity may be seen as output minus input." With this understanding, creativity is fundamentally – but not merely – generative. It can be abstractly understood as happening in two phases or stages: "generation" and "evaluation." In effect, the generative stage generalises the input, and the evaluation stage assesses what is new and useful in this output. Ritchie (2001) calls the (salient aspects of the) input an *inspiring set*, and focuses on thinking about creativity within domains where there are known product-evaluation strategies: specifically, ways to

Alison Pease
Department of Computing, University of Dundee, Scotland, UK. e-mail: a.pease@dundee.ac.uk

Joseph Corneli
Goldsmiths College, University of London, UK. e-mail: j.corneli@gold.ac.uk

[1] This approach is reminiscent of Marr's (1982) description of *computational theories*: "a computational theory is commonly understood roughly speaking as at least a fairly precise characterization of inputs to the system, outputs of the system, and a spelled out hypothesis concerning the functional mapping between both ends."

© Springer Nature Switzerland AG 2018
R. Confalonieri et al. (eds.), *Concept Invention*, Computational Synthesis
and Creative Systems, https://doi.org/10.1007/978-3-319-65602-1_10

determine the *novelty* and *quality* of generated artefacts. Pease et al. (2001) follow Boden (2004) and embark on an explicit examination of "process" itself as potentially creative.[2]

The basic challenge, as outlined by Pease et al. (2001), is "to find a framework which is both practically useful and theoretically feasible." Theoretical feasibility means, at least in part, that an evaluation strategy should "reflect human evaluations of creativity" – in other words, that the framework should be "faithful" to everyday notions of creativity.

A decade after this challenge was framed, Jordanous (2011) examined the uptake and quality of various evaluation strategies that had been proposed in the intervening years. Drawing on the work of Pease et al. and other literature, Jordanous subsequently (2014) put forward a total of five "meta-evaluation" criteria: *Correctness*, *Usefulness*, *Faithfulness Usability*, and *Generality*. This high-level framework for meta-evaluation was complemented by preliminary empirical work that applied the framework to assess previous evaluation work. The core method used in the meta-level study was to involve third party experts, who audited evaluations that had been carried out by others.

In the present work, we make meta-evaluation more down to earth. Our primary source of empirical data is a series of interviews with people who have applied key evaluation strategies in computational creativity. Furthermore, these interview subjects were closely involved with the systems that were being evaluated, and their perspectives were, accordingly, largely practically-based. Importantly, the interviews did not focus on evaluation of the system or its outputs, but rather on meta-evaluation: that is, *evaluation of the evaluation strategies that were employed in the course of practical work on the project*. Since the interview subjects did not create the evaluation strategies they employed, we can largely avoid any potential for creator bias. We see practitioner perspectives as particularly relevant for process-oriented evaluation.

The outline of the chapter is as follows. Section 10.2 discusses the way evaluation has evolved since the early days of computational creativity research, in the context of broader progress in the field. Here we take the view that evaluation methods have evolved alongside the main systems. Section 10.3 describes several evaluation frameworks that are currently in use. Section 10.4 evaluates these frameworks, drawing on interviews with practitioners. We discuss our findings in terms of the meta-evaluation metrics proposed by Jordanous (2014), and develop a set of questions for further discussion by researchers in computational creativity who are concerned with evaluation and meta-evaluation. Section 10.5 presents a summary of the chapter.

---

[2] Boden's description of creativity in terms of processes that explore and enrich a conceptual space would later be presented in more explicit computational terms by Wiggins (2006).

10.2 A Short Historical Survey of Evaluation in Computational Creativity

The definition of the field of study that was originally adopted by the Association for Computational Creativity (and that remained current up until 2013) was spelled out as follows:[3]

> Computational Creativity is the study and simulation, by computational means, of behaviour, natural and artificial, which would, if observed in humans, be deemed creative.

The implied focus on human behaviour was subsequently dropped in an adapted definition proposed by Colton and Wiggins (2012). This version has been widely quoted in recent literature:[4]

> The philosophy, science and engineering of computational systems which, by taking on particular responsibilities, exhibit behaviours that unbiased observers would deem to be creative.

Nevertheless, in practice, researchers in computational creativity often work on domains that are typical of human creativity, particularly in the arts. This has had a strong effect on evaluation strategies. Computational models of artistic creativity are often connected with *artefact-centred evaluation* – where, at least in principle, it does not matter how the artefacts are created, or by whom. Ritchie's papers (2001; 2007) are foundational for this style of work.

Criticising the tendency to do "process-blind" evaluation, Colton (2008) observed that although artefact-centred evaluation seems to present a level playing field, in practice, it is not representative of the way we usually think about art. This is because everyday assessments of creative work by humans tends to take into account history-rich issues of process and identity.

Much more broadly, perceptions of creativity may be highly context-sensitive. Anna Jordanous (2013) surveyed the literature and found fourteen wide-ranging components of creativity that are frequently referred to by authors writing on this subject (Table 10.1). This work has subsequently been refined and validated via card-sorting studies and principal component analysis by van der Velde et al. (2015) who showed that, indeed, terms similar to the ones that Jordanous identified seem to be what people have in mind when they think about "creativity." Jordanous and Keller (2016) revisit and extend the original corpus-based research.

These concepts have been used by Jordanous and others to evaluate creativity in conjunction with the three-part assessment framework also proposed by Jordanous (2012): the so-named "standardised procedure for evaluating creative systems" (Method 10.1).

(In practice, the specific criteria used in Step 1 of Method 10.1 may be conveniently selected from Table 10.1.)

---

[3] Anna Jordanous, What is Computational Creativity? April 10, 2014 http://www.creativitypost.com/science/what_is_computational_creativity

[4] Jordanous and Keller (2016); Besold et al. (2015); Emmerson and Landy (2016); Green and Kaufman (2015); Toivonen and Gross (2015), among others.

C1. **Active Involvement and Persistence**	C8. **Originality**
C2. **Dealing with Uncertainly**	C9. **Progression and Development**
C3. **Domain Competence**	C10. **Social Interaction and Communication**
C4. **General Intellect**	C11. **Spontaneity/Subconscious Processing**
C5. **Generation of Results**	C12. **Thinking and Evaluation**
C6. **Independence and Freedom**	C13. **Value**
C7. **Intention and Emotional Involvement**	C14. **Variety, Divergence and Experimentation**

Table 10.1: Fourteen frequently-used criteria for creativity gathered from the literature in Jordanous's Ph.D. research

> Step 1. *Identify a definition of creativity that your system should satisfy to be considered creative.*
>
> Step 2. *Using Step 1, clearly state what standards you use to evaluate the creativity of your system.*
>
> Step 3. *Test your (potentially) creative system against the standards stated in Step 2 and report the results.*

Method 10.1: The Standardised Procedure for Evaluating Creative Systems (SPECS), from Jordanous (2012)

Although this work provides a thorough exploration of the "social construct" of creativity, Jordanous's survey does not attempt to state what creativity "is" in a way that is derived either empirically or from first principles. One may wonder whether creativity is anything other than a construct. Furthermore, there is nothing intrinsically tied to the concept of "creativity" in the structure of the three steps of Method 10.1, which could be straightforwardly adapted to assess any other qualitative feature of the system's behaviour.

The connection between computational creativity and artificial life has been taken up by some researchers (Saunders and Bown, 2015). This research trajectory is open to empirical criteria (e.g., viability, empowerment, complexity) – and tends to characterise "creativity" and "aesthetics" in these terms (Guckelsberger and Salge, 2016; Javaheri Javid et al., 2016).[5] The relationship between explicit, computable, metrics like these and the more subjective evaluation criteria outlined in Table 10.1 remains an open problem.

To be sure, Table 10.1 subsumes the key concepts in artefact-centred evaluation: C8 (Originality) and C13 (Value). Several of the criteria, such as C1, "Active Involvement and Persistence," focus on the context and workflow through which creativity happens. Other similar sets of criteria that can be found in the literature are:

- van der Velde et al. (2015)'s *originality, emotional value, innovation, intelligence, skill*;
- Colton's (2008) "tripod": *skill, appreciation* and *imagination*;

---

[5] Guckelsberger and Salge (2016) are particularly concerned with meanings that are created by agents, after Von Uexküll (1982).

- and Colton's more recent (2013) "spider": *skilful, appreciative, imaginative, intentional, adaptive, reflective, inventive, innovative.*

While criteria like "originality" continue to be largely *artefact-centred* and criteria like "intelligence" can be seen as *agent-centred*, the overall thrust is towards *process-centred* and *context-based* assessment of creativity.

Increased attention to context and process has had a noticeable effect on thinking in the field. For example, it has cast light on the importance of the prior (or ancillary) process whereby the system that is evaluated is itself created (Colton et al., 2014). Via a reflexive loop, the impetus to bracket software creation and software's creativity together has elicited increasing interest in software that writes software (Charnley et al., 2016). Thinking about automated program synthesis from a computational creativity point of view may require attention to the question: "how do people creatively write code?" (Colton, quoted in Moss (2015)). Software systems are themselves approached in increasingly contextual terms (Johnson, 2014; Jordanous, 2016); and creative contexts may themselves be analysed using software-like rules (Corneli, 2016). Within increasingly diverse and process-rich workflows, evaluation becomes correspondingly complex. Software is seen as requiring greater and greater levels of creativity and independence (Ventura, 2016). As part of the shift away from after-the-fact product-based evaluations, the locus of evaluation is increasingly embedded within the creative process itself (Bou et al., 2015).

10.2.1 Other Perspectives

The pragmatic approaches outlined above can be contrasted with other more philosophical points of view. Henri Bergson (1911) thought of "creativity" and "life" as nearly synonymous. Indeed, the connection between computational creativity and artificial life has been taken up by some researchers (Saunders and Bown, 2015). This research trajectory is open to empirical criteria (e.g., viability or complexity) and would tend to characterise creativity in these terms (Guckelsberger and Salge, 2016) (as opposed to using more abstract notions of 'fitness', as per, e.g., Gabora and Tseng (2014)). Related perspectives are developed in the anthropological work of James Leach (2004). Leach contrasts the "dominant Euro-American... 'appropriative mode'" (p. 152), in which creativity is "primarily intellectual" (p. 154), with the cultural views of creativity held by the Reite people of Papua New Guinea. Among the Reite, creativity is centred on the contingent "necessity of keeping the human world in existence" through action in accordance with traditional mythic knowledge (p. 165). The cultural background in the mainstream of computational creativity research seems to match the 'appropriative mode' described by Leach: the focus is on artefact creation and the mental processes involved therein, even when artefact quality is not the main concern. Nevertheless, as sketched above, some alternative perspectives are beginning to emerge in the field.

10.3 Evaluation Frameworks

The evaluation options listed in Table 10.2 are characteristic of the strategies that are available to, and used by, researchers for evaluation of computational creativity.

Measure	When to apply	Who applies	Outcome
Ritchie	*product-based*: apply when the system has produced a set of artefacts	≈ 100 novices or domain experts	A set of ratings that can be presented as 12 proportions
Jordanous	*process or product-based*: apply when the system can be used or its workflow clearly described	≈ 7 domain experts discuss process and product, using some subset of the 14 components listed in Table 10.1 or some other similar criteria	Interview data
Colton et al	*focus mostly on process*: apply at each development epoch	system developers	Diagrams describing the phases of system development

Table 10.2: Three evaluation methods characteristic of product-based, holistic, and developmental evaluation

The modus operandi of the evaluation strategy proposed by Ritchie (2007) (as an adaptation of Ritchie (2001)) is to establish whether the system can generate artefacts that are appropriate to a genre, while at the same time offering novelty within that genre. Human judgements of the artefacts are used, but evaluators are never asked "is the system creative?" – unlike some other product-based evaluations (Lamb et al., 2015). Derived measures provide a framework for further assessment (Method 10.2): however, again, Ritchie does not specify threshold values of these measures that are required for the system to be deemed "creative."

Step 1. *The system generates a pool of artefacts.*
Step 2. *These artefacts are rated according to their **typicality** and **novelty**.*
Step 3. *Derived metrics are computed from the ratings in Step 2.*

Method 10.2: The evaluation method used by Ritchie (2007)

As we saw in Section 10.2, the focus for Jordanous (2012) is to examine how the system is perceived. In effect, the question is whether users can project features like C1–C14 (or some subset of them) onto the system. Jordanous (2011) describes several example applications of Method 10.1 along these lines.

Lastly, Colton et al. (2014) take a high-level view that focuses on the system's evolution over time. In this framework, the features present in any given snapshot of the system are described using a schematic terminology advanced by Colton et al. (2011). The focus in this approach to evaluation (Method 10.3), however, is on establishing which entity is responsible for creating a new feature: namely, the developer, or the system itself?

Step 1. *The system's development history is divided into versions, and versions are divided into components.*

Step 2. *The logical workflow between components is diagrammed, and processes within components are characterised in terms of the **generative** and **administrative** acts which comprise them, following the typology proposed by Colton et al. (2011) (Framing, Aesthetic, Concept, and Example, at "ground," "process," and "meta" levels).*

Step 3. *Judgements are made about the system's autonomy and creativity based on the extent to which it takes responsibility for generative acts.*

Method 10.3: The evaluation method used by Colton et al. (2014)

10.4 Evaluating the Evaluation Frameworks

In the present work, we examine the three methods outlined in the previous sections in light of new and pre-existing criteria for "meta-evaluation." Our study draws on interview data with people who have had direct experience with the evaluation methods described above. In some cases these people have adapted, or abandoned, the existing strategies, in favour of other strategies that were deemed more suitable.

10.4.1 Methods

We arranged four hour-long interviews ($N = 4$). Participants were recruited via personal connections and via an open call at a recent Computational Creativity (CC) conference. The main inclusion criterion was that participants had applied some evaluation metrics to software in CC. All participants possessed doctorates in technical fields and were working as post-doctoral research assistants on multi-site projects in Computational Creativity. All participants were male. The interviews were semi-structured, following a protocol that was shared with participants. This followed the outline below:

1. Warm up: Academic background, familiarity with CC and evaluation.
2. Fact gathering: Which criteria were applied, why, and by whom? Who developed the software that the methods were applied to?
3. Ease of application: How much time and expertise was needed? Who was involved?

4. Usefulness of application: Did the results tell you anything useful?
5. Faithfulness to notion of creativity: What did the criteria measure?
6. Evaluation of the criteria: What properties should evaluation criteria in CC have? Are the current measures accurate? Do you have thoughts about improving the criteria or developing new ones?

These interviews were carried out face to face in a room with two interviewers and one interviewee. At the beginning of the interview participants were given an information sheet about the study, a consent form to sign, and were shown a copy of the interview guide so they could see the sorts of questions that they would be asked. All participants were offered a break partway through the interview. The interviews were audio-recorded.

After conducting the interviews, we transcribed them, and analysed the resulting text via a data-driven methodology based on grounded theory. Specifically, we iterated through the phases below:

I. We identified short textual 'codes' which describe key themes in the data and went through all of our data, identifying and revising our codes.
II. We grouped the data by collecting the codes of similar content into categories.
III. We grouped similar categories into concepts, which we used to formulate our resulting theory. We worked together by each independently reading a portion of the data and conducting analysis identifying factors related to evaluation.
IV. We compared these analyses and discussed any recurring differences, allowing us to align our results.

We used the Dedoose system – an online, computer-assisted, qualitative data analysis software tool – to perform our analysis.[6]

10.4.2 Findings

The four interviews were an average of 9,400 words each, and the overall transcript was 37,601 words long, in total. We identified a total of 38 codes, categories and concepts, across 355 excerpts. The codes were arranged hierarchically as shown in Figure 10.1.

10.4.3 Discussion

Participants mentioned that because they worked on a pre-defined project they did not always have the freedom to develop the software or their ideas about creativity and evaluation: thus, the resulting discussion should be read with that in mind.

---

[6] http://www.dedoose.com/

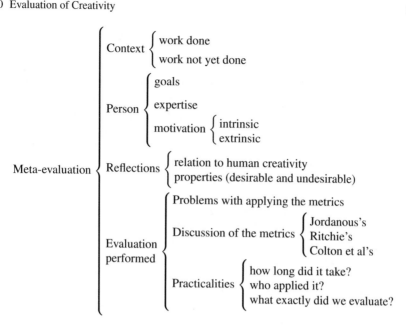

Fig. 10.1: A hierarchical view of our emergent theory

Participants commented on the difficulty of measuring progress in CC, describing the attempt to formulate and formalise evaluation criteria as a "great big meta problem" and a "strong, difficult problem." Perhaps given that they worked within relatively large consortia (of around 25 people) in which different tasks were carried out by different people, participants commented that one of the roles of an evaluation framework should be to provide a way of evaluating progress of the team, rather than just that of the system.

All three frameworks use words which are purposely left open to interpretation by the researcher, such as "novel," "valuable" (Ritchie, 2007); "domain competence" (Jordanous, 2013); and "framing," "aesthetic" (Colton et al., 2014). Participants pointed out that even given a domain-specific interpretation of these, the subjective nature of the terms can mean that interpretation is left open to participants in empirical work. In particular, if the empirical work is carried out in another language, further ambiguities and linguistic issues can arise, e.g., due to terminological collisions in translated texts given to study participants.

A meta-evaluation criterion for assessing evaluation frameworks was suggested: namely, to determine whether the evaluation measure can identify negative and positive instances of creative systems. Independent means of determining whether a system is creative are not available, in general, especially in a domain-independent sense. However, especially for systems that approach human-like creativity within a domain, there may be a workable consensus about approximately where the systems lies on the spectrum between "creative" and "not creative." It was suggested that frameworks which determine when a system is *less* creative than another might provide useful direction for research.

Some of the participants felt that the experiment-based frameworks (Ritchie, 2007; Jordanous, 2013) required more understanding of computational creativity than they possessed, and that the FACE model would be a better fit given their own background in computer science: "I felt the other two criteria, Jordanous and Ritchie, required a bit more understanding of computational creativity in general."

10.4.3.1 Experiment-based Frameworks

All participants had some prior familiarity with the ideas of both Ritchie (2007) and Jordanous (2013). They typically chose to apply the metrics in a very flexible way: picking and choosing aspects which suited them and omitting others. For example, a sub-selection of the 14 items in Table 10.1 might be seen by a given research team as both particularly relevant to their domain, and a concrete measure that they could ask participants to evaluate in experiments. In particular, there was a focus on novelty and value, which were identified by Ritchie and present as two of Jordanous's components (originality and value). Our respondents reported that other aspects of both frameworks, such as proportion calculations (Ritchie, 2007), ranking of the components by domain experts, and interviews based on system demonstrations (Jordanous, 2013) were not carried out.

Selection of components was partly based on pragmatic considerations: "we thought they were easy to evaluate – at least in terms of empirical evaluation – that's why we chose them." Components were broken down into smaller, more interpretable, domain-specific units, which were seen as easier and more objective for study participants to judge. Judgements were largely, though not always, made on output which had been generated by the system, rather than on a description of the system's process. In one case, in which one member of the research team was also an expert in the creative domain under consideration, that individual went through all of the 14 components and provided a rating based on knowledge of the system's processes as well as products.

The level at which output was evaluated was one interesting issue that shaped the selection of metrics: in particular, the creativity of a small part of a larger artefact might be difficult to assess. This was important for continuity of variable; a question could become meaningless or muddled if asked at the wrong level of output.

One participant selected originality and preference from Jordanous's 14 components model, since these were seen as relevant to the domain in which they were working. While these were closely connected to Ritchie's criteria, Ritchie's approach was not applied, since the system only generated one artefact per run (rather than a population) and thus the notion of proportions could not be established. In this case, the evaluation was done by an expert who was not involved in building the system, and followed system development over one and a half years. The dependence of Ritchie's criteria on a set of artefacts was seen as problematic, both in theory and in practice. The participant commented that we don't use the idea of proportions to evaluate human creativity: for instance, we don't know how many versions of a sonata Beethoven wrote before the final one, and nor is this especially relevant for our evaluation of his creativity. Furthermore, given that the system only produced one artefact per run (with a given set of initial conditions), there was no natural "set" of output artefacts to compare.

One participant liked the component-based approach because of its tactfully indirect way of approaching creativity. It was seen as more productive to ask participants questions concerning preferences, for example, rather than to ask whether they thought a particular artefact was "creative." In part, this was because of sociological factors in how the latter question is answered – participants in one study were students and it seemed likely that they would worry if they appeared to be judging the creativity of their professor, for example. Less value-laden questions about personal preference, or perception-based features, were seen as simpler and more likely to receive an honest answer. Additionally, questions concerning preferences were seen as more consistent. Translation problems arising in one study seemed to bias the results, requiring that study to be re-run.

Another participant felt that 14 components were too many for the purpose at hand, and that the whole set was tending towards an evaluation of general artificial intelligence. This contrasted with his own primary goal of building a tool for the purpose of aiding human experts in their creative work. For this, which he felt that five or six of the components would have been sufficient, commenting that "you get lost" with so many components.

It was felt that the components correlated well with human creativity, with one participant commenting that he "really liked" the components: "It was complete, it was sound," and another commenting on the importance of using them in combination: "It's not that these individual measures are measuring creativity, but maybe incrementally you're moving towards something that is creative." One participant particularly liked the emotional evocativeness of the components, commenting: "you get astonished, if you get moved, if you get a close personal experience with the work . . . I like it a lot."

10.4.3.2 System Development Framework

The FACE model was selected and applied only by system developers. Participants took from two days to a week to apply this model. By and large it was applied retroactively to describe work which had already been completed.

The FACE model was seen as rather complicated, and the diagrammatic notation was described as "difficult," "unintuitive," "a lot of subscripts and superscripts and parentheses." The concepts represented were seen as necessary, but the language as lacking clarity. One participant suggested using icons rather than algebraic notation: "I could imagine a version of it that has exactly the same information, but displayed with icons, for example, that have a different colour or shape, or where it fits together in an obvious way, because it does look like a big kind of algebraic mess." Participants did not all agree on this point, with others saying that "It was not so complicated," and it was "Easy – once you understood what the symbols mean." Along these lines, the question of how well it would scale arose, "I don't know how good it scales, on representing a very large system or – many phases of software development, like, ah, if the software evolves, ah, very much – these diagrams can be very very complicated or if the size of the system is very big, the boxes become very big."

Some participants questioned whether the FACE model actually measured progress in CC. One argued that it measures progress towards autonomous behaviour, rather than the creativity of the system, where progress could be made in the one but not in the other: "you identify the parts in which your software can be improved by making it more automatic. But it is not certain that replacing part of the system by a piece of code you make the system more creative." A further comment was that: "you're not measuring the creativity of the system: for me, you're trying to analyse, somehow, the steps that you put into your system and – in a critical way – that allows you, that helps you to analyse, in a critical way, what the system does and how you can improve it." One participant commented that while the model is a useful development tool, it doesn't help to decide whether the *output* is creative.

Broadly speaking the FACE model was seen as a useful tool for developers: "the FACE model measures or represents the steps that you follow to meet the specification of the system." The question of who should apply it arose: "the problem was, because it was myself that applied the model on something I developed"; and, "maybe by comparing the result of the model done by another person with what the system really does you can infer something interesting – maybe you can identify some creative results, or something that's missing there." Nevertheless, the complexity of the system was seen to weigh against its usefulness in practice, at least without sufficient training: "I can imagine a software engineer ... or professional software developer, having really troubles understanding the notations."

While all participants had done the evaluation at the end of the system development it was generally felt that it should be used in formative evaluation: "maybe it would have been good to develop a FACE model of the system early in the project, and use that as guidance," and "I really think the FACE model could be used kind of prescriptively." It was also suggested that the model could be useful for other members of the team, not just software developers.

10.4.3.3 Recommendations for Improving Evaluation Effectiveness in CC

Broadly there are two ways for project managers to improve the usefulness of evaluations. (1) Tailor your evaluation to the staff and expertise that you have; and (2) Tailor your staff to the sort of evaluation that you want to carry out. The second option might be a consideration when hiring new staff or for providing training to existing team members. One concrete suggestion would be to hold a tutorial in conducting experiments either within a given research consortium, or more broadly, e.g., in a conference like the International Conference on Computational Creativity

(ICCC). Such training might include qualitative and quantitative methods, ethics, and so on. Further issues to consider are as follows:

1. Consider wider roles that an evaluation framework may play:

   a. Providing a way of evaluating progress of a whole team, rather than just that of the system-developers.
   b. Evaluating progress in aspects that are not related to the system, such as philosophical advances.
   c. Considering the end-goal of a project or piece of work. For instance, if domain experts will interact with the system then there should be communication between developers and experts, and it may be useful to consider methodologies in Human-Computer Interaction, such as user-centred approaches.

2. Framework-specific recommendations:

   a. Process-based model. Provide more documentation, such as a user manual and further examples. Put on a training session. Provide domain-specific versions and examples. Develop the language further, with an emphasis on clarity of notation.
   b. Component-based model. Suggest concrete domain-specific suggestions of how each of the components can be measured, to combine qualitative with quantitative approaches.
   c. Proportion-based model. Suggest concrete domain-specific suggestions of how value and novelty can be measured.

10.4.3.4 Related Work

Jordanous (2011) noticed that, at least in the early days of the field, rigorous evaluations have not always been carried out. As evaluation became more prevalent, in a subsequent paper she outlined several dimensions for *meta-evaluation* (Jordanous, 2014, p. 4):

- **Correctness**: how accurately and comprehensively the evaluation findings reflect the system's creativity.
- **Usefulness**: how informative the evaluative findings are for understanding and potentially improving the creativity of the system.
- **Faithfulness**: how faithfully the evaluation methodology captures the creativity of a system (as opposed to other aspects of the system).
- **Usability**: the ease with which the evaluation methodology can be applied in practice, for evaluating the creativity of systems.
- **Generality**: how generally applicable this methodology is across various types of creative systems.

Jordanous (2014) used this framework to re-assess previous data on evaluation by engaging external (meta-)evaluators. In that study, the meta-evaluators had not applied the various evaluation methods themselves, but were shown results of several comparable system evaluations.

We can briefly consider the findings described above through the lens of Jordanous's meta-evaluation criteria.

Correctness — The important difference between building a system that is independently creative and one that supports a user's creative work was noted by several participants. What is understood by "creativity" in these two cases is likely to be different, or at least approached differently.

Usefulness — The difference between interrelated perceptions of usefulness, creativity, autonomy, and preference was noted. For instance, evaluation metrics that were useful for meeting an initial product specification might have little direct connection with those geared towards building a creative system. The degree to which goals have been specified in advance contributed to the salience usefulness (or not) of the measures.

Faithfulness — One participant suggested that several of Jordanous's components could "expand on what's between the spaces of being useful and being creative." The subjective nature of direct creativity evaluations was noted, and participants tended to prefer objective measures (whether of small-scale perceptual data, or intersubjectively verifiable holistic outcomes).

Usability — Evaluation metrics were generally selected that were feasible to apply, given the background of the people applying them and resources available. Adaptations were often made that simplified the original methods. In this respect we can point to one interesting negative finding, which is that none of the participants opted to combine the several methods into one coherent analysis.

Generality — The level of output (e.g., small components of larger work) as well as the scale of the system (e.g., one involving many complicated interconnected modules) both appear to present challenges for evaluation. Another related issue is the level of analysis: if an evaluation metric is applied by a larger team, the demands placed on it will be different from a metric that can be applied in an ad hoc fashion by one individual. Similarly (see "Correctness" above), co-creativity and autonomous creativity may be evaluated differently.

10.5 Summary

We have carried out a meta-evaluation of progress markers in Computational Creativity. We began with an historical survey of evaluation in this field, focusing on three evaluation metrics: component, process, and proportion-based models. We carried out interviews with people who had applied these metrics, and built an emergent framework for analysis, using a method based on grounded theory. We provided an extended discussion of our findings, supported by quotes from research subjects. Based on this material, we provided recommendations for improving evaluation effectiveness in CC. We then connected our findings to a pre-existing meta-evaluation framework in order to provide a summary that findings in future studies can be compared to.

---

1. **Perspective of the evaluator.** Personality and background are relevant to metric development and application. For example, research questions like "What is a joke?" lead naturally to evaluation questions like "Is X joke-like?" and "Is X a good joke?" Experiment-based methods tend to be selected by people with a social science background. FACE is designed to be carried out by system developers.

---

2. **Increasing the user friendliness of evaluation methods.** How might we provide guidance to (potential) users of the metrics; e.g.:

- domain-specific guidance, fleshing out what value/novelty/framing and so on mean in specific domains?
- guidance relative to the level of the artefact that will be evaluated: holistic or smaller chunks; relative to what context?

---

3. **Ways to develop or improve existing measures.** How did you come up with your metrics? Do you have suggestions for ways to:

- "Focus on the negative," i.e., identify ways in which the system fails to be creative (e.g., not working at all, or producing the "wrong" thing, etc.).
- Use metrics that focus on something other than creativity (for instance, preference) and then draw inferences about creativity.

---

4. **Non-system-centred criteria.** All evaluation criteria currently centre on the system and/or its output. What about other ways of assessing progress in CC (e.g., progress at the level of philosophical theories)? Keep in mind that ICCC has several different kinds of papers apart from "system" papers.

---

5. **Additional questions for discussion.**

- What are your motivations for using the evaluation method you developed, and what do you think the motivations of others who use them are?
- Machine learning has really taken off in recent years. What would be the conditions that would make the study of "machine creativity" similarly relevant?

Table 10.3: Questions for future research

10.6 Conclusion and Future Perspectives

Our meta-evaluation of the FACE, Jordanous, and Ritchie models is more than just a side-by-side comparison. It also gives a holistic perspective on the way evaluation has been applied in computational creativity. Since specific methods are applied inconsistently, a higher level of analysis may be useful.

In future work, we plan a second round of interviews with the researchers who devised the main evaluation criteria discussed above. Our questions are inspired by the analysis of the first set of interviews (Table 10.3). We plan to analyse the new dataset using the same meta-evaluation criteria we applied in Section 10.4.3.4, which will allow us to compare the findings. As a brief meta-meta-evaluation, we can comment that the criteria proposed by Jordanous (2014) seem useful for this purpose.

References

H. Bergson. *Creative evolution*. Henry Holt and Company, [1907] 1911.

T. R. Besold, M. Schorlemmer, and A. Smaill, editors. *Computational Creativity Research: Towards Creative Machines*. Springer, 2015.

M. A. Boden. *The creative mind: Myths and mechanisms*. Psychology Press, 2004.

F. Bou, J. Corneli, D. Gómez-Ramírez, E. Maclean, A. Smaill, and A. Pease. The role of blending in mathematical invention. In S. Colton, H. Toivonen, M. Cook, and D. Ventura, editors, *Proceedings of the Sixth International Conference on Computational Creativity, ICCC 2015*. Association for Computational Creativity, 2015. URL http://axon.cs.byu.edu/ICCC2015proceedings/3.2Bou.pdf.

J. Charnley, S. Colton, M. T. Llano, and J. Corneli. The FloWr online platform: Automated programming and computational creativity as a service. In A. Cardoso, F. Pachet, V. Corruble, and F. Ghedini, editors, *Proceedings of the Seventh International Conference on Computational Creativity, ICCC 2016*, 2016. URL http://www.computationalcreativity.net/iccc2016/wp-content/uploads/2016/01/74_The-FloWr-Online-Platform-Automated-Programming.pdf.

S. Colton. Creativity versus the perception of creativity in computational systems. In *AAAI Spring Symposium: creative intelligent systems*, pages 14–20, 2008.

S. Colton. Some guiding principles, December 2013. URL https://www.cs.helsinki.fi/group/discover/ascc2013/ColtonGuidingPrinciples.pdf. Lecture at Computational Creativity Autumn School II, Porvoo, Finland, 2013.

S. Colton and G. A. Wiggins. Computational creativity: The final frontier? In *Proceedings of the 20th European conference on artificial intelligence*, pages 21–26. IOS Press, 2012.

S. Colton, A. Pease, and J. Charnley. Computational creativity theory: The FACE and IDEA descriptive models. In *Proceedings of the Second International Conference on Computational Creativity*, 2011.

S. Colton, A. Pease, J. Corneli, M. Cook, and T. Llano. Assessing progress in building autonomously creative systems. In D. Ventura, S. Colton, N. Lavrac, and M. Cook, editors, *Proceedings of the Fifth International Conference on Computational Creativity*, 2014. URL `http://computationalcreativity.net/iccc2014/wp-content/uploads/2014/06//8.4_Colton.pdf`.

J. Corneli. An institutional approach to computational social creativity. In A. Cardoso, F. Pachet, V. Corruble, and F. Ghedini, editors, *Proceedings of the Seventh International Conference on Computational Creativity, ICCC 2016*, 2016. URL `http://www.computationalcreativity.net/iccc2016/wp-content/uploads/2016/06/paper_9.pdf`.

S. Emmerson and L. Landy. *Expanding the Horizon of Electroacoustic Music Analysis*. Cambridge University Press, 2016.

L. Gabora and S. Tseng. The social impact of self-regulated creativity on the evolution of simple versus complex creative ideas. In *Proceedings of the Fifth International Conference on Computational Creativity*, pages 8–15, 2014.

G. Green and J. C. Kaufman. *Video Games and Creativity*. Academic Press, 2015.

C. Guckelsberger and C. Salge. Does empowerment maximisation allow for enactive artificial agents? In *Proc. 15th International Conference on the Synthesis and Simulation of Living Systems (ALIFE16)*, pages 704–711. MIT Press, 2016.

M. A. Javaheri Javid, T. Blackwell, R. Zimmer, and M. Majid al Rifaie. Analysis of information gain and Kolmogorov complexity for structural evaluation of cellular automata configurations. *Connection Science*, 28(2):155–170, 2016.

C. G. Johnson. Is it time for computational creativity to grow up and start being irresponsible? In *Proceedings of the Fifth International Conference on Computational Creativity, Ljubljana, Slovenia, June 10-13*. 2014.

A. Jordanous. Evaluating evaluation: Assessing progress in computational creativity research. In *Proceedings of the second international conference on computational creativity (ICCC-11). Mexico City, Mexico*, pages 102–107, 2011.

A. Jordanous. A standardised procedure for evaluating creative systems: Computational creativity evaluation based on what it is to be creative. *Cognitive Computation*, 4(3):246–279, 2012.

A. Jordanous. *Evaluating Computational Creativity: A Standardised Procedure for Evaluating Creative Systems and its Application*. Ph.D. thesis, University of Sussex, 2013.

A. Jordanous. Stepping back to progress forwards: Setting standards for meta-evaluation of computational creativity. In *Proceedings of the Fifth International Conference on Computational Creativity*, pages 129–136, 2014.

A. Jordanous. Four PPPPerspectives on Computational Creativity in theory and in practice. *Connection Science*, 28:194–216, 2016.

A. Jordanous and B. Keller. Modelling creativity: Identifying key components through a corpus-based approach. *PloS one*, 11(10):e0162959, 2016.

C. Lamb, D. G. Brown, and C. Clarke. Human competence in creativity evaluation. In *Proceedings of the Sixth International Conference on Computational Creativity June*, volume 102, 2015.

J. Leach. *Modes of Creativity*. Berghahn Books, 2004.

D. Marr. *Vision: A Computational Investigation into the Human Representation and Processing of Visual Information*. Henry Holt and Co, Inc., 1982.

R. Moss. Creative AI: Software writing software and the broader challenges of computational creativity, March 2015. URL http://bit.ly/2tRiIgV.

A. Pease, D. Winterstein, and S. Colton. Evaluating machine creativity. In *Workshop on creative systems, Fourth International Conference on Case Based Reasoning*, pages 129–137, 2001.

G. Ritchie. Assessing creativity. In *Proceedings of the AISB'01 Symposium on Artificial Intelligence and Creativity in Arts and Science*, pages 3–11. SSAISB, 2001.

G. D. Ritchie. Some empirical criteria for attributing creativity to a computer program. *Minds and Machines*, 17:67–99, 2007.

R. Saunders and O. Bown. Computational social creativity. *Artificial Life*, 21(3): 366–378, 2015.

H. Toivonen and O. Gross. Data mining and machine learning in computational creativity. *Wiley Interdisciplinary Reviews: Data Mining and Knowledge Discovery*, 5(6):265–275, 2015.

F. van der Velde, R. A. Wolf, M. Schmettow, and D. S. Nazareth. A semantic map for evaluating creativity. In *The Sixth International Conference on Computational Creativity (ICCC 2016)*. Association for Computational Creativity, 2015.

D. Ventura. Mere Generation: Essential barometer or dated concept? In A. Cardoso, F. Pachet, V. Corruble, and F. Ghedini, editors, *Proceedings of the Seventh International Conference on Computational Creativity, ICCC 2016*. 2016.

J. Von Uexküll. The theory of meaning. *Semiotica*, 42(1):25–79, [1940] 1982.

G. A. Wiggins. A preliminary framework for description, analysis and comparison of creative systems. *Knowledge-Based Systems*, 19(7):449–458, 2006.

Printed in the United States
By Bookmasters